The Birth
of the
New Testament

The Birth

⤍ *of the* ⤎

New Testament

*The Origin and Development
of the First Christian
Generation*

RAYMOND F. COLLINS

CROSSROAD • NEW YORK

1993

The Crossroad Publishing Company
370 Lexington Avenue, New York, NY 10017

Copyright © 1993 by Raymond F. Collins

Printed in the United States of America

Library of Congress Cataloging-in-Publication Data

Collins, Raymond F. 1935–
    The birth of the New Testament : the origin and development of the first Christian generation / by Raymond F. Collins.
        p.   cm.
    Includes bibliographical references and index.
    ISBN 0-8245-1276-6
    1. Bible. N.T. Thessalonians, 1st—Criticism, interpretation, etc.   2. Christianity—Origin.   I. Title.
BS2725.2.C65   1993
227'.8106—dc20   93-16647
                                                      CIP

Contents

Abbreviations

Versions of the Bible

GNT[3]	K. Aland, M. Black, C. M. Martini, B. M. Metzger, A. Wikgren, eds., *The Greek New Testament* (3d ed.)
KJV	King James Version (Authorized Version)
N-A[26]	K. Aland, ed., *Novum Testamentum Graece* (26th ed.)
NIV	New International Version
NJB	New Jerusalem Bible
NRSV	New Revised Standard Version
REB	Revised English Bible
RNAB	Revised New American Bible (New Testament only)
RSV	Revised Standard Version

Periodicals, Reference Works, and Serials

AB	Anchor Bible
ABD	*Anchor Bible Dictionary*
ABR	*Australian Biblical Review*
AGJU	Arbeiten zur Geschichte des antiken Judentums und des Urchristentums
AnBib	Analecta biblica
Ang	*Angelicum*
ANRW	*Aufstieg und Niedergang der römischen Welt*
ANTF	Arbeiten zur neutestamentlichen Textforschung
APOT	R. H. Charles, ed., *Apocrypha and Pseudepigrapha of the Old Testament*
ATR	*Anglican Theological Review*
BAGD	W. Bauer, W. F. Arndt, F. W. Gingrich, and F. W. Danker, *Greek-English Lexicon of the NT*
BASOR	Bulletin of the American Schools of Oriental Research
BeO	*Bibbia e oriente*

BETL	Bibliotheca ephemeridum theologicarum lovaniensium
BEvT	Beiträge zur evangelischen Theologie
Bib	*Biblica*
BibLeb	*Bibel und Leben*
BibT	*The Bible Today*
BLit	*Bibel und Liturgie*
BNTC	Black's New Testament Commentaries
BSac	*Bibliotheca Sacra*
BT	*The Bible Translator*
BTB	*Biblical Theology Bulletin*
BU	Biblische Untersuchungen
BWANT	Beiträge zur Wissenschaft vom Alten und Neuen Testament
BZ	*Biblische Zeitschrift*
BZNW	Beihefte zur *ZNW*
CBQ	*Catholic Biblical Quarterly*
CEB	Commentaire évangélique de la Bible
CNT	Commentaire du Nouveau Testament
ConBNT	Coniectanea biblica, New Testament
CP	*Classical Philology*
CurTM	*Currents in Theology and Mission*
DS	Denzinger-Schönmetzer, eds., *Enchiridion symbolorum*
Ebib	Etudes bibliques
EDNT	H. Balz and G. Schneider, eds., *Exegetical Dictionary of the New Testament*
EKKNT	Evangelisch-katholischer Kommentar zum Neuen Testament
ETL	*Ephemerides theologicae lovanienses*
ETS	Erfurter theologische Studien
ExpTim	*Expository Times*
FilolNT	*Filologia Neotestamentaria*
FRLANT	Forschungen zur Religion und Literatur des Alten und Neuen Testaments
GBS	Guides to Biblical Scholarship
GNS	Good News Studies
GTA	Göttinger theologische Arbeiten
GTJ	*Grace Theological Journal*
HBT	*Horizons in Biblical Theology*
HNTC	Harper's New Testament Commentaries
HTKNT	Herders theologischer Kommentar zum Neuen Testament
HTR	*Harvard Theological Review*
Int	*Interpretation*

IDB	G. A. Buttrick, ed., *Interpreter's Dictionary of the Bible*
JBC	R. E. Brown, et al., eds., *Jerome Biblical Commentary*
JBL	*Journal of Biblical Literature*
JETS	*Journal of the Evangelical Theological Society*
JSNT	*Journal for the Study of the New Testament*
JSNTSup	JSNT – Supplement Series
KEK	Kritisch-exegetischer Kommentar über das Neue Testament
LCL	Loeb Classical Library
LD	Lectio Divina
LS	*Louvain Studies*
LSJ	Liddell-Scott-Jones, *Greek-English Lexicon*
LTP	*Laval théologique et philosophique*
LTPM	Louvain Theological and Pastoral Monographs
MTZ	*Münchener theologische Zeitschrift*
NedTTs	*Nederlands theologisch tijdschrift*
NICNT	New International Commentary on the New Testament
NIGTC	The New International Greek Testament Commentary
NJBC	R. E. Brown, et al., eds., *The New Jerome Biblical Commentary*
NovT	*Novum Testamentum*
NovTSup	Novum Testamentum, Supplements
NTAbh	Neutestamentliche Abhandlungen
NTD	Das Neue Testament Deutsch
NTOA	Novum Testamentum et Orbis Antiquus
NTS	*New Testament Studies*
NTTS	New Testament Tools and Studies
OBO	Orbis biblicus et orientalis
PG	J. Migne, ed., *Patrologia graeca*
PL	J. Migne, ed., *Patrologia latina*
RB	*Revue biblique*
ResQ	*Restoration Quarterly*
RevistB	*Revista bíblica*
RevThom	*Revue thomiste*
RivB	*Rivista biblica*
RNT	Regensburger Neues Testament
SANT	Studien zum Alten und Neuen Testament
SBFA	Studii biblici franciscani Analecta
SBLDS	SBL Dissertation Series
SBLSBS	SBL Sources for Biblical Study
SBLSS	SBL Semeia Studies
SBS	Stuttgarter Bibelstudien
SBT	Studies in Biblical Theology
ScEccl	*Sciences ecclésiastiques*

SCHNT	Studia ad corpus hellenisticum novi testamenti
SD	Studies and Documents
SNTSMS	Society for New Testament Studies Monograph Series
SPap	*Studia papyrologica*
ST	*Studia theologica*
STK	*Svensk teologisk kvartalskrift*
TD	*Theology Digest*
TDNT	G. Kittel and G. Friedrich, eds., *Theological Dictionary of the New Testament*
TPINTC	Trinity Press International NT Commentaries
TQ	*Theologische Quartalschrift*
TTZ	*Trierer theologische Zeitschrift*
TZ	*Theologische Zeitschrift*
WBC	Word Biblical Commentary
WUNT	Wissenschaftliche Untersuchungen zum Neuen Testament
ZGB	Maximilian Zerwick, *Graecitas biblica*
ZNW	*Zeitschrift für die neutestamentliche Wissenschaft*
ZST	*Zeitschrift für systematische Theologie*
ZTK	*Zeitschrift für Theologie und Kirche*

Introduction

In some respects the history of the New Testament begins in 1930–31. At that time A. Chester Beatty had acquired ten leaves of what could only be described as a quite imperfect codex of the Pauline epistles, the so-called Chester Beatty Papyrus II, now preserved in the Chester Beatty Museum in Dublin. The eight leaves in fairly good condition contain large sections of Romans, Philippians, and Colossians. The ninth and tenth leaves, of which Beatty had acquired only small fragments, contain small bits of text from 1 Thessalonians.

While Beatty was acquiring his ten leaves of the ancient codex, the University of Michigan was in the process of obtaining six additional leaves of the same codex. In the winter of 1932–33 the university acquired still another twenty-four papyrus leaves belonging to the same codex. Some two years later Beatty himself obtained forty-six leaves more of the codex.

According to the usual system of identifying biblical manuscripts, the newly found codex was given the identifying siglum P^{46}. Since many of its eighty-six leaves were numbered, specialists were able to determine that the codex once contained 104 leaves. Its text consisted of Romans, Hebrews, 1-2 Corinthians, Ephesians, Galatians, Philippians, Colossians, and 1 Thessalonians. Since the manuscript can be reasonably dated to about 200 C.E., P^{46} ranks as the oldest of the ancient manuscripts containing a collection of Paul's letters.[1]

The Oldest Manuscript of the Oldest New Testament Text

The ninth and tenth leaves of Beatty's original acquisition were so fragmented that they had lost any sign of their enumeration. His ninth "leaf" contained only two small fragments, a larger fragment of 3½ x 1¼ inches and a smaller fragment of 1¾ x ¾ inches, but only a single fragment of the tenth leaf remained. It measured 3⅛ x 1⅝

1

inches. Once all eighty-six extant leaves of the codex had been compared with one another, scholars could determine that the ninth and tenth "leaves" of Beatty's first collection[2] were, in fact, parts of the ninety-fourth and ninety-seventh leaves of the original codex.

The recto side of the ninety-fourth leaf contains, on its two fragments, part of the title of Paul's first letter to the Thessalonians and a bit of the text of 1 Thess 1:1. The verso side contains part of 1 Thess 1:9–2:3. On the recto side of leaf ninety-seven, there is some text from 1 Thess 5:5–9, while a portion of 1 Thess 5:23–28 appears on the verso side. Since the remaining eighteen leaves of P[46] have yet to be discovered, these three small papyrus fragments are all that we have as a witness to the text of 1 Thessalonians in this ancient codex.

Together, the fragments contain part of the title of the letter and parts of four sections of text. The manuscript, in other words, has portions of sixteen lines of text, but it has only twenty-seven complete words. Five of these "complete words" have been transcribed in abbreviated form, according to traditional scribal practice. These are the words "God" in 1 Thess 1:9 and 2:2 (twice) and "Son" and "Jesus" in 1:10.

Despite the relatively small portion of the text of 1 Thessalonians that it contains, P[46] is important for the study of the letter. It is the oldest manuscript witness to a text that scholars generally consider to be not only the first of Paul's extant epistles but also the oldest written text in the New Testament.[3] The manuscript predates the Sinaiticus and Vaticanus codices, the oldest manuscripts with a complete text of 1 Thessalonians, by more than a century. Since it is as old as it is, P[46] serves as a quality control factor for the later manuscript tradition of 1 Thessalonians.

While the number of complete words of 1 Thessalonians that P[46] contains is relatively small, those who read the letter with a specifically theological interest are undoubtedly pleased to find in P[46] not only the abbreviated divine names, but also "living" (1:9) as a description of God and a recognizable portion of the confessional formula of 1:10. The rhetorician is happy to find in the extant fragments not only one instance of Paul's characteristic "you know" (2:2), but also complete pronouns in the first- and second-person plural. Its (fragmentary) verb endings and abundant pronouns reflect the dialogical rhetoric of the letter.

The historian is pleased to find in the fragmented remnants of 1 Thessalonians mention of the apostle's "welcome" (2:1) as well as clearly recognizable portions both of his name and that of the Thessalonians (1:1), not to mention the appearance of the fragmented title, so significant for the history of the New Testament canon. Students of epistolary literature are glad to find portions of the letter's farewell remarks with its striking "I adjure" (5:27), a mention of the "letter" itself (5:27), and a reference to "grace" (5:28).

Other Papyri Manuscripts of 1 Thessalonians

Although the Beatty papyrus is the oldest and, if only for that reason, the most important ancient papyrus witness to Paul's first letter to the Thessalonians, it is not the only ancient witness to the text. Oxyrynchus Papyrus 1598, known to biblical scholars as P[30], is also older than our oldest complete manuscript of the letter. P[30] comes from the late third century. It consists of two badly mutilated leaves, containing some portions of 1 Thess 4:12-13, 16-17; 5:3, 8-10, 12-18, 25-28, along with some bits of 2 Thess 1:1-2.[4] These leaves are presently to be found in the library of the State University of Ghent (Belgium). At present no other portion of the codex to which P[30] belongs seems to be in existence.

As was the case with P[46], the fragments of 1 Thessalonians that have been preserved in P[30] attest to the fidelity with which the ancient scribes copied the oldest of Paul's letters. Nonetheless a few words appear in P[30] that are not found in many of the later and complete copies of the letter, namely, an "all" in the credal formula of 5:10 ("who died for us *all*") and an "among you" in the exhortation of 5:10 ("help the weak *among you*"). It would seem that the papyrus also has a shorter form of the Greek adverb translated as "most highly" in 1 Thess 5:13 (NRSV), but the words of the papyrus are difficult to read at this point. Although one should not draw major conclusions from such tiny pieces of evidence, these three variants coalesce to suggest a reading of 1 Thessalonians 5 in P[30] that demonstrates a rhetorical posture different from that which emerges from the perusal of the chapter in a modern edition or in any one of the other ancient manuscripts.

The third ancient papyrus witness to the text of Paul's first letter is the third-century papyrus, P[65]. Its single badly mutilated leaf, 6¼ x 1⅞ inches, is presently located in the Vitelli Papyrus Institute of the University of Florence (Italy). About sixty scattered words of 1 Thess 1:3-2:1, and 2:6-13 can be found on the extant portions of its thirty lines of text.[5] For the most part these "words" are only word fragments. These fragments and the twenty-six complete words in the papyrus, most of which are particles,[6] generally concur with the reading of 1 Thessalonians found in the later manuscript tradition.

For completeness' sake a fourth papyrus needs to be mentioned. This is P[61], presently found in New York's Pierpont Morgan Library under the rubric "P. Colt 5." P[61] is among the most recent of the biblical papyri. It was transcribed about 700 C.E., that is, more than three full centuries after the great uncial manuscripts of 1 Thessalonians. Since this papyrus contains only bits of seven words in 1 Thess 1:2-3 — some twenty-one letters altogether[7] — and is of such recent vintage, its existence is not of great importance for understanding the birth of the New Testament.

Such is not the case, however, for the early parchment manuscripts of the New Testament, whose text has been transcribed in the majuscule style. Among these manuscripts, some of the most important are the fourth-century Sinaiticus (ℵ) and Vaticanus (B) codices, the fifth-century Alexandrinus (A) and Ephraemi rescriptus (C) codices, and the sixth-century Codex Claromontanus (D). Despite the existence of some textual variations among these various manuscripts and despite the omission of 1 Thess 1:2-2:8 from the extant pages of the Ephraemi rescriptus, these uncials provide the reader with a remarkably similar Greek-language text of what is presumably the most ancient writing in the New Testament, the so-called First Letter to the Thessalonians.

∞ 1 ∞

A Visit to Thessalonica

Among the expressions that are clearly discernable in the Chester Beatty Papyrus (P^{46}) is the word "visit" (*eisodon*). Appearing on the verso side of the ninety-fourth leaf, it comes from 1 Thess 2:1. On the recto side of that same fragment are incomplete words whose preserved letters come from "Paul and Silvanus" and "Thessalonians" in 1 Thess 1:1. Thus, the oldest fragment of what may well have been Paul's oldest letter attests to the visit of Paul and a companion named Silvanus to a group of people living in the city of Thessalonica.

The City

Thessalonica, modern Salonika, was located at the head of a bay (the so-called Gulf of Salonika) on the Thermaic Gulf, the best natural harbor on the Aegean. Cassander, one of Alexander the Great's generals, established the city in 315 B.C.E., on the site of a previous settlement, perhaps the ancient city of Therme.[1] Inhabitants for the new city were gathered from among twenty-six different villages located on the shores of the Gulf.[2] The way this new settlement was populated was in keeping with the political and self-aggrandizing purposes typical of Alexander's era. Cassander named the new city after his wife, Thessalonica, who was none other than the half-sister of Alexander.

Enhanced by its location on the axis between Asia Minor and the Adriatic, the city of Thessalonica soon became the chief port of Macedonia. During the Macedonian era, it enjoyed considerable prosperity. Twice it received a visit from Philip V. In the second century B.C.E. Thessalonica played an important role in the Macedonian resistance to Roman intrusion, but it finally succumbed in the battle of Pydna (168 B.C.E.). Roman victory brought Macedonian independence to an end. Pursuing a divide-and-conquer policy, the Romans carved the

5

Macedonian kingdom up into four regions. Thessalonica became the capital city of the region whose territory lay between Strymon and Axios.

The Roman conquest did not, however, completely eradicate Macedonian resistance. In 149 B.C.E. an uprising occurred under the leadership of Andriscus, pretender to the Macedonian throne (Pseudo Philip VI). Thessalonica initially resisted Andriscus, but, under his leadership, the First Roman Legion was defeated (the fourth Macedonian war). The Macedonian revolt was finally quelled in 148, when the forces of Andriscus were defeated by those of Quintus Caecilius Metellus, who then ruled over the region until 146.

Metellus was called a "Savior" (*Sōter*),[3] the oldest indication of Roman benefaction to Thessalonica yet to be found. The epithet might well have evoked the memory of Metellus's victory over Andriscus. For the citizens of Thessalonica, immunity from tribute came with Metellus's victory in 148.[4] Since the settlement of 167 the citizenry of Thessalonica had been recognized as free, but it had not been exempt from taxation. As of 148 they enjoyed a tax-exempt status. In 148 B.C.E. Macedonia became a Roman province, the first of the Roman provinces in the East. Thessalonica was selected as the capital city of the reunified territory.

During its Roman period, Thessalonica increased in importance. Its geographical location on the Via Egnatia, the crossroad between east and west, and the access to the Mediterranean provided by its port on the Aegean ensured the political, commercial, and military[5] importance of the city. The Via Egnatia ran through the very heart of the city on an east-west axis. It led to the Adriatic port of Dyrrachium. Across the Adriatic from Dyrrachium (Durazzo in modern Albania) was the port of Brindisium (Brindisi in modern Italy). From there the Via Appia led to Rome.

A few years after Andriscus's defeat in 148 B.C.E., Roman forces under the leadership of L. Tremelus Scrofa had to put down yet another Macedonian revolt. During the second half of the second century B.C.E., Roman military forces were not as successful in their skirmishes with the Scordisci as they had been in quelling uprisings led by the various pretenders to the Macedonian throne. It may be that the Thessalonians' occasional exemption from levies of monies and men led to the citation of some Romans as benefactors of the city of Thessalonica.[6]

Snippets of a story of Roman military activity and occasional political mismanagement in the province of Macedonia during the first half of the first century have been told by Cicero, Livy, Appian, Plutarch, and other ancient authors. During this period it is hardly likely that Thessalonica was immune from the costs of Roman military efforts and the greed of some governors, but specific reference to the city of Thessalonica in the literary evidence is quite spotty.[7]

By 49 B.C.E., Thessalonica had become part of Pompey's Eastern realm. At this time the city was virtually a second Rome. Authority was vested – at least theoretically – in its senate and people. Pompey's stay in Thessalonica, however, lasted hardly a year. In Thessalonica Pompey gathered troops for his battle against Caesar's forces. Pompey was to be defeated at Pharsalus. The conflict between Pompey and Caesar's forces certainly took its toll on the city of Thessalonica and its inhabitants. Later, when the armies of Brutus and Cassius advanced on Macedonia in 42 B.C.E., Thessalonica sided with the cause of Antony and Octavian. Following the Triumvir's victory at Philippi and in gratitude for the support of the Thessalonians, Roman benefaction was showered upon the city.

This benefaction might even have included (official) Roman ratification of the city's free status and a grant of immunity from taxation.[8] Thessalonica's status as a free city ensured some form of self-governance and allowed the city to mint coinage, both its own coinage and the coinage of the realm. Numismatic evidence celebrates the city's freedom and identifies Antony and Octavian as autocrats.[9] A new era had begun. Games, perhaps dedicated to the goddess Eleutheria,[10] were inaugurated to celebrate the coming of these new times.[11] They were times of peace and concord.

Under the autocrats Thessalonica enjoyed a certain amount of local autonomy. The city did not fall under the jurisdiction of the *Ius Italicum*. Local political power was vested in the popular assembly (*dēmos*), the council (*boulē*), local magistrates (*politarchai*), the city treasurer, and some other civic officials, including the directors of the public games (*gymnasiarchon* and *agōnothetē*), youth leaders (*ephebarchon*), the superintendent of works, and architects.[12] This form of local political organization probably did not begin under the autocrats. It is more likely that the system of politarchs was a traditional form of governance that the Romans fostered for their own purposes.[13]

Names of several Thessalonians with positions of civic leadership appear on a variety of extant artifacts. Among them are Diogenes, Kleon, Sopas, Eulandros, and Protogenes. These individuals are cited as politarchs on a stele that cites a civic decree. It had been apparently designed for a temple of Caesar. The names of the politarchs Asklepiodoros, Sosipatros, Zoilos, Athenogenes, and the son of Dionysius appear on an inscription that comes from the early second century.[14] The politarchs, apparently the highest city officials, may have been the indigenous agents of Roman rule.[15]

Since Thessalonica was not a Roman colony, it was not required to absorb large numbers of furloughed Roman soldiers, as were some

other cities in the province. The Roman civil wars of the years 44–
31 B.C.E. took their toll on Thessalonica, as they did on other cities
and towns of Macedonia. With the victory of Octavian over the forces
of Marc Antony and Cleopatra at Actium in 31 B.C.E., a peace and
prosperity came upon Thessalonica such as it had not apparently previously experienced. The emperor, cited as the son of a god, was
repeatedly honored as a benefactor of the city. Before the turn of the
century, the Thessalonian poet Antipater could sing of his city as "the
mother of all Macedonia."[16] Shortly thereafter Strabo, the Greek geog-
rapher, proclaimed Thessalonica as "the mother city of contemporary
Macedonia."[17]

To this day a systematic excavation of Thessalonica has not yet been
carried out.[18] The ancient city will probably never be fully excavated
since the ruins of old Thessalonica lie under the second most important city in modern Greece. What artifacts as have been found are
generally the results of accidental discoveries, the results of the de-
molition of old city walls, street construction, and the remodeling or
razing of old buildings.

Among the chance finds are a temple to Serapis,[19] some sculp-
ture belonging to an Egyptian cult, a black stone sphinx, fragments
of a statue of Augustus, numerous inscriptions,[20] and various coins.
The troves come from Thessalonica's Roman period. A fragmentary
inscription on a marble plaque, perhaps coming from a Samaritan
synagogue, has also been discovered, but this dates from the later
Byzantine period (fourth–sixth century C.E.).[21] Only two of ancient
Thessalonica's sites have been adequately excavated. These are the
second-century C.E. Roman Forum and various Roman constructions
in the southeastern part of the old city – the Octagon and Palace of Galerius, the Arch of Galerius, and the Rotunda – all dating from about
300 C.E.

Although the artifacts that have been discovered are few and the
specific literary evidence rather limited, it is clear that the Thessalonica that Paul and his companions visited was a thriving city,
quite conscious of its ties with Rome, but enjoying a fair amount of
self-governance.

Paul mentions that he and his companions had suffered and been
shamefully treated at Philippi prior to their arrival in Thessalonica
(2:2).[22] It is quite likely that he and his co-workers traveled from
Philippi to Thessalonica along the Egnatian Way. The distance between Philippi and Thessalonica was just over one hundred miles and
the Via Egnatia was the principal route that joined one city to the other.
Paul does not make mention of any stops along the route, nor does he
say how long it took for his band to go from one city to the other.[23]
From the way he writes about the difficult times in Philippi, one gath-

ers that his difficulties must have taken place very shortly before his arrival in Thessalonica.

About a century before Paul's arrival in Thessalonica Julius Caesar had written about barbarian raids that imperiled those who traveled the Via Egnatia,[24] but that danger was so much past history by the time that Paul and his companions went to Thessalonica. Roman military victories and the *Pax Augustiana* made travel along the route relatively safe and sure. Paul and his companions were men on a mission. Paul describes them as "apostles of Christ" (*Christou apostoloi*, 2:7). A Roman peace and Roman roads enabled them to pursue that mission.

A Working Visit

When he wrote to the Thessalonians Paul reminisced at length about his visit. In recalling his prayer of thanksgiving, he first described what happened to the Thessalonians as a result of his visit (1:2-10).[25] Then, having specifically introduced the visit (*eisodon*) as a topic of communication (1:9), Paul begins to reflect upon what he and his companions had done in Thessalonica (2:1-12). Since he had already mentioned the impact of the visit upon the Thessalonians and taken note of its impact upon others (1:7-8), it is almost as if he wants to "unpack" for his hearers what the visit meant for him and his companions:

> [1]You yourselves know, brothers and sisters, that our coming to you was not in vain, [2]but though we had already suffered and been shamefully mistreated at Philippi, as you know, we had courage in our God to declare to you the gospel of God in spite of great opposition.
>
> [3]For our appeal does not spring from deceit or impure motives or trickery, [4]but just as we have been approved by God to be entrusted with the message of the gospel, even so we speak, not to please mortals, but to please God who tests our hearts.
>
> [5]As you know and as God is our witness, we never came with words of flattery or with a pretext for greed; [6]nor did we seek praise from mortals, whether from you or from others, [7]though we might have made demands as apostles of Christ. But we were gentle among you, like a nurse tenderly caring for her own children. [8]So deeply do we care for you that we are determined to share with you not only the gospel of God but also our own selves, because you have been very dear to us.
>
> [9]You remember our labor and toil, brothers and sisters; we worked night and day, so that we might not burden any of you while we proclaimed to you the gospel of God. [10]You are wit-

nesses, and God also, how pure, upright, and blameless our conduct was toward you believers. [11]As you know, we dealt with each one of you like a father with his children, [12]urging and encouraging you and pleading that you lead a life worthy of God, who calls you into his own kingdom and glory.

The modern translations of this passage generally indicate that these are the first twelve verses of chapter two of Paul's first letter to the Thessalonians. The New Revised Standard Version begins a new paragraph at verse 9. Such divisions were not part of Paul's original text. The division of the New Testament into chapters, to which we have been long accustomed, was introduced by Stephen Langton, a thirteenth-century archbishop of Canterbury, who died in 1228. The division into verses comes from a sixteenth-century editor of the New Testament, Robert Estienne (1503-59) who inaugurated the practice in his 1551 edition of the New Testament. The paragraph division at verse 9 is the result of a decision by the editors and translators of the NRSV. Different editors and translators prefer to divide the material otherwise.[26]

In Paul's Greek text other kinds of devices would have been used to indicate the breaks in his thought. His choice of words, his *lexis*, to use the language of Greek rhetoric, would have indicated that some thoughts flow from one another. This is not always apparent in modern translations, where editors and translators must try to produce a readable text and provide their readers with the kind of sense units to which they are accustomed, notably shorter in English than in German, for example.

A Reflection

Paul's reflection on his visit proceeds in a pattern of thought whose various components are linked together in mosaic-like fashion by means of the conjunction *gar* (literally, "for"), one of the most common particles in the Greek language.[27] Thus, 2:1-12 can be divided into four sense units, verses 1-2, 3-4, 5-8, 9-12,[28] each of which is introduced by a *gar* in Paul's Greek text (but the particle's appearance in verses 1, 5, and 9 is not explicitly reflected in the NRSV translation).[29] Paul's reflection on his visit seems to be a companion piece to 1:2-10, where several of the same themes had already been touched upon.

Paul's first recital of events led to a mention of his visit, his *eisodos* ("welcome"; 1:9), a topic picked up again in 2:1, where *eisodos* is translated as "coming" in the NRSV. Nonetheless, there is a significant difference between the respective points of view of the two accounts. In 1:2-10, Paul narrates what he and his companions know about the

Thessalonians ("For we know," *eidotes,* 1:4); in 2:1-12, he narrates what the Thessalonians know about Paul and his companions ("You yourselves know," *autoi gar oidate,* 2:1). The topic of the earlier narrative was what happened among the Thessalonians as a result of the visit; the topic of the second narrative is what happened to the visitors.

The extended discussion is the longest description of Paul's missionary activity to appear in any of his letters. Writing about his mission, he tells about the activity that consumed his time and energy. "We worked night and day," he wrote. His efforts were so memorable that the Thessalonians could remember his "labor and toil" (2:9). This is the only feature of Paul's visit that the Thessalonians are explicitly stated to have "remembered."[30] Elsewhere in 1 Thessalonians, the verb *mnēmoneuō,* "to remember," occurs only in 1:3, where Paul writes about what he and his companions remembered when they prayed.

Although the use of the verb *mnēmoneuō* in 2:9 is singularly striking, it is part of what might be called the "recall motif,"[31] so characteristic of the first letter to the Thessalonians. What Nils Dahl calls various "superfluous rehearsals and reminders"[32] are sprinkled throughout the letter. They recall the dynamic interaction between Paul and the Thessalonians. The use of such formulas is particularly concentrated in 2:1-12, where we read: "you yourselves know" (*autoi gar oidate,* 2:1), "as you know" (*kathōs oidate,* 2:2), "as you know" (*kathōs oidate,* 2:5), "you remember" (*mnēmoneuete,* 2:9), "you are witnesses" (*hymeis martures... egenēthēmen,* 2:10), "as you know" (*kathaper oidate,* 2:11).[33]

The presence of these reminders and the extensive reminiscence about his visit – a reminiscence that takes up a quarter of the letter – make it all but certain that the letter was written relatively soon after Paul's visit to Thessalonica.[34] In any event, 1 Thessalonians was certainly written before the so-called Second Letter[35] to the Thessalonians. The latter letter was, in any event, probably not written by the Apostle himself,[36] yet it seems to make reference (2 Thess 2:2) to the "first letter to the Thessalonians," the only extant letter from the Apostle himself to the Thessalonians.

Working Night and Day

The Thessalonians were aware of the kind of persons that Paul and his companions were (1:5).[37] It is said that the Thessalonians remembered their "labor and toil." Paul says that he and his companions "worked night and day." The expressions give some hint of the time and energy spent at work. The hendiadys "labor and toil" (*ton kopon hēmōn kai ton mochthon*) suggests fatigue and weariness, hardship and distress.[38] Paul will use the expression again in a later letter, when he rehearses the variety of adverse circumstances that he encountered as an apostle of Christ (2 Cor 11:27).[39]

He and his companions worked "night and day."[40] Typically those who had a job worked "from sunrise to sunset,"[41] but Paul and his companions began their work before sunrise and continued to work throughout the day. We don't know just how long they worked. Most probably they worked until sundown. Paul's language does not suggest that he stopped working in order to proclaim the gospel. He proclaimed the gospel as he worked. The workers put in a long day. While they did so, they proclaimed the gospel of God.

Paul and his companions worked hard and long, but in his letter to the Thessalonians Paul does not tell us specifically what they did. The usual connotation of the term used by Paul ("*ergazomai* – to work") suggests some form of manual labor.[42] In other letters Paul will be rather specific in affirming that he really did manual labor;[43] he will add the qualifying phrase "with one's hands," to the verb "to work." In his letter to the Thessalonians Paul will exhort his correspondents to "work with your hands" (4:11). Paul's urging the Thessalonians to be involved in manual labor should be interpreted – at least to some extent – in the light of the paraenetic motif of the imitation of Paul (cf. 1:6).[44] In an autobiographical passage of a later letter, Paul wrote "we grow weary from the work of our own hands" (*kopiomen ergazomenoi tais idiais chersin*, 1 Cor 4:12). This passage from a letter to the Corinthians is striking insofar as it links the notions of manual labor and growing weary in a fashion that recalls Paul's linking of work and fatigue in 1 Thess 2:9.

Tradition has identified Paul's trade as that of a "tentmaker" (*skēnopoios*).[45] Scholars have typically suggested that Paul learned the weaver's trade[46] in his native Cilicia,[47] a region of modern Turkey, well-known in ancient times for its goats whose hair (*cilicium*) provided the raw material from which was made a fabric used for a variety of things, including, at least on occasion, tents. Weaving was, however, a trade despised by the rabbis. Thus, weaving material for tents would have been an unlikely trade for Paul to have exercised.

A number of modern scholars, following up on reflections by some Church Fathers and paying due attention to some ancient translations of Luke's Acts,[48] have suggested that Paul was most likely a leather-worker, an artisan who cut and sewed together pieces of leather in order to make tents. The shop on the agora in which he worked would have been designated by the tentmaker's shield,[49] but the trade would have involved Paul in more than mere tentmaking. Karl Don-fried has suggested that Paul's work might even have involved him in the production of parchment codices.[50] A home-made codex, a kind of parchment notebook, would have been useful for a florilegium of biblical texts and bits of Christian tradition. Indeed, Paul could have used such a codex for the writing of his letters.

Working Rabbis

Rabbinic tradition extolled the value of manual labor, even for a rabbi. "Rabban Gamaliel the son of R. Judah the Patriarch said: 'Excellent is study of the Law together with worldly occupation, for toil in them both puts sin out of mind. But all study of the Law without labor comes to naught at the last and brings sin in its train.' "[51] "R. Ishmael...said: 'He that learns in order to teach is granted the means to learn and to teach; but he that learns in order to perform is granted the means to learn and to teach, to observe and to perform.' "[52] Commentators on the *Mishnah* emphasized the father's responsibility in this regard. Thus, "a man is obliged to teach his son a trade; whoever does not teach his son a trade teaches him to become a thief,"[53] a saying attributed to R. Judah upon which the Talmud comments "it is as though he taught him brigandage."[54]

By his own account, Paul worked at Thessalonica so as not to burden any of the Thessalonians (2:9).[55] He seems to have desired his independence. He did not want to be dependent upon a patron. Paul was not, however, totally self-sufficient during his Thessalonian stay. His letter to the community of Christians at Philippi thanks them for providing him with means for his sustenance on at least two occasions (Phil 4:16).[56] The generous support afforded by the Philippians does not mean that they were affluent. The contrary seems rather to have been the case.[57] Paul's acceptance of financial support from a group of Christians seems to have been, in any case, rather unusual practice.[58] Only the Philippians came to Paul's assistance and he was, as he mentions in his note of thanks to them (Phil 4:10–20, v. 15), in needy straits.

Although Paul wanted to enjoy economic self-sufficiency, it is not at all clear that he looked upon his tiresome efforts as truly ennobling. Rather he appears to have regarded his manual labor as a burden to be borne for the sake of the gospel.[59] In this regard Paul was not altogether unlike some philosophers, contemporary with himself, who thought that the exercise of a trade was the best way to maintain a livelihood and support oneself.

Working Philosophers

Philosophers had other ways of assuring their livelihood,[60] for example, charging fees, enjoying the hospitality of a benefactor, and begging.[61] Some philosophers, especially Sophists, did charge fees.

Other philosophers were critical of the practice, as Socrates had been some centuries earlier. The philosophers who did not charge for their services criticized those who did. They themselves did not want to appear greedy. They were also anxious not to compromise their own freedom. In a later but clearly self-conscious reflection Paul explains that he took a similar tack. He rejected the idea of taking a fee (*misthos*)[62] for preaching the gospel (1 Cor 9:17–18).

Other philosophers chose to enter into the households of the rich and powerful, teaching the children of their patrons and traveling about with them. Cynics contemporary with Paul rejected this as a truly viable option for the philosopher. It was judged to be not only demeaning but also an ill-advised compromise with hedonism. In his letter to the Thessalonians Paul rejects this option as the way to go (2:9).[63] As for the possibility of begging, Paul's extant letters do not provide us with even the slightest suggestion that Paul might have gone begging in order that his needs might be met. As a matter of fact, he seemed to have been very reluctant to accept the support of even already committed Christians.[64] On the other hand, Paul was not adverse to asking for money. He was quite willing to sponsor a collection for the saints in Jerusalem,[65] but that was another matter.

The result of all this was that Paul, like some of the Cynic philosophers of his time, albeit the minority,[66] worked in order to make a living. Dio Chrysostom (ca. 40–ca. 112 C.E.) worked as a gardener, Demetrius of Sunium (first century C.E.) as a porter, and the cynicizing Musonius Rufus (25–80 C.E.) worked on a farm, a choice of employment that Musonius considered to be ideal for a philosopher: "pupils would seem to me benefitted by seeing him [the philosopher] at work in the fields, demonstrating by his own labor the lessons which philosophy inculcates – that one should endure hardships, and suffer the pains of labor with his own body, rather than depend upon another for sustenance."[67]

Greek philosophical tradition had it that Socrates had conducted philosophical discourse in the shoeshop of a man named Simon,[68] whom the Cynics considered to be also a philosopher. The Cynics portrayed Crates as reading in Philiscus's shoemaking shop and Antisthenes as having frequented Simon's shop. Moreover, Lucian associates the philosopher Cyniscus with Micyllus, a shoemaker. Thus, from a Cynic standpoint, the leatherworker's shop would appear to be almost an ideal place for philosophical discourse.

Speaking and Working

Paul cut and sewed as he spoke. He says that he preached the gospel while he worked.[69] If, as is likely, Paul worked in a shop on the agora, he would have had ample opportunity to voice the good news about God. Working at his trade would not only insure Paul's freedom to preach the gospel, it would also provide him with people with whom he could speak, an audience for the gospel.[70] There Paul would have met other artisans and laborers, those who came to buy (and/or for repairs?) – including, perhaps, some soldiers in need of a tent – and passersby. In this fashion, the leatherworker's shop served as a useful and perhaps privileged locale for Paul's initial proclamation of the gospel in Thessalonica.[71] The workshop would have also provided an appropriate locale for the individual exhortation about which Paul reminisces in 2:11, "we exhorted each one of you" (*hena hekaston hymōn...parakalountes*).

Can one be more specific and suggest that the shop in which Paul worked was, in fact, a workshop within someone's household? Abraham Malherbe has offered this suggestion.[72] He has argued that the household was the primary locale for Paul's missionary activity in Thessalonica. He claims that the house in which Paul resided while in Thessalonica was not a *domus,* the kind of manor owned by the rich, but an *insula,* with shops on the ground floor facing the street and living quarters above or behind the shops.

The Acts of the Apostles tells of Paul's staying in Corinth with Aquila and Priscilla, with whom he shared a common trade (Acts 18:1-3). Acts also says that Paul stayed in Jason's house while he was in Thessalonica (Acts 17:7). So it is not unreasonable to assume, Malherbe asserts, that Jason too was a leatherworker and that Paul made use of Jason's shop while he was preaching the gospel.

While this is a possible scenario, it is not very probable. Aquila and Priscilla had already become Christian before Paul met up with them in Corinth, but Jason – to whose house Paul makes no specific reference in his letter – was probably one of Paul's first converts in Thessalonica.[73] It is, moreover, hardly likely that every householder who provided hospitality for Paul was a leatherworker. Was Gaius (Rom 16:23), for example, also a leatherworker? Paul gives no real hint that leatherworking was that man's trade. In any case it is certain that Lydia, with whom Paul stayed during his sojourn in Philippi, was not a leatherworker. She was, as Luke indicates, a seller of purple cloth (Acts 16:14-15).[74]

Thinking Back

Exercising his trade while he preached, Paul appears to manifest a work ethic remarkably similar to that of various Cynic philosophers who were his contemporaries. His attitude toward his work is like that

of many of those same philosophers. Paul's reflection on his visit to
Thessalonica (2:1-2) is remarkably similar, for example, to a reflection
on the ideal philosopher[75] written by Dio Chrysostom, one of Paul's
younger contemporaries:

> But to find a man who with purity [*katharōs*] and without guile
> [*kai adolōs*] speaks with a philosopher's boldness [*parrēsia-*
> *zomenon*], not for the sake of glory [*mēte doxēs charin*], nor
> making false pretensions for the sake of gain [*met' 'ep agryriō*],
> but [*all'*] who stands ready out of good will and concern for his
> fellowman, if need be, to submit to ridicule and the uproar of
> the mob – to find such a man is not easy but rather the good
> fortune of a very lucky city, so great is the dearth of noble, inde-
> pendent souls, and such the abundance of flatterers [*kolakōn*],
> charlatans and sophists. In my own case I feel that I have chosen
> that role, not of my own volition, but by [*ouk; ap'... all'hypo*]
> the will of some deity. For when divine providence is at work for
> men, the gods provide, not only good counsellors who need no
> urging, but also words that are appropriate and profitable to the
> listener.[76]

The language and style of Dio's reflections, the *lexis* and *syn-*
taxis of his discourse, are quite like the language and style used by
Paul to describe his visit to the Thessalonians in 2:1-12. As for their
respective choice of vocabulary, we can compare Dio's "with purity" (*katharōs*) with Paul's "not from... impure motives" (*oude ex*
akatharsias, v. 3), his "without guile" (*kai adolōs*) with Paul's "not
from trickery" (*oude en dolō*, v. 3), his "speaks with a philosopher's
boldness" (*parrēsiazomenon*) with Paul's "we had courage" (*epar-*
rēsiasametha, v. 2), his "for the sake of glory (*mēte doxēs charin*)
with Paul's "nor did we seek praise" (*oute zētountes... doxan*, v. 6),
and his "flatterers" (*kolakōn*) with Paul's "words of flattery" (*logō ko-*
lakeias, v. 5). The similarity of vocabulary is all the more striking in
that two of the Pauline terms in this short list (*dolos* and *kolakia*) do
not occur elsewhere in his letter and one of them (*kolakia*) is hapax
in the entire Pauline corpus.

In terms of style, one cannot help but notice the contrasts that run
throughout Paul's reflections on his activity among the Thessalonians.
It might even be said that the use of *contradictio,* a classical figure
of speech, is the dominant characteristic of the entire composition.
"Not this, but that" runs throughout the verses, almost as a refrain:
"our coming was not in vain, but... we had courage" (vv. 1-2); "our
appeal does not spring from deceit... but... we speak" (vv. 3-4); "we
never came with words of flattery... but we were gentle among you"
(vv. 5-8). A similar antithetical style is to be found in the passage from

Dio Chrysostom, who writes of the man who "speaks... not for the sake of glory... but... who stands ready out of good will and concern." This is the same Dio Chrysostom who says of himself that he had been chosen "not of my own volition, but by the will of some deity."

The "not only... but also" construction brings the discourse of each author to a point of climax. Dio wrote about the gods providing "not only good counsellors... but also appropriate words." Paul describes his group as having shared "not only the gospel of God but also our own selves" (v. 8). The use of this antithetical style adds verve and emphasis to the discourse of both Paul and Dio Chrysostom. Closely related to the use of contrast is the respective authors' use of comparison. Again, emphasis is the goal of the rhetorical device.

The similarities between the two passages does not stop at their language and style. At bottom, there is a similarity of content that prompts further comparison between the two passages. One can note the use of the first person, as both authors issue forth in an autobiographical confession, Dio Chrysostom using the first-person singular and Paul the first-person plural. Strikingly, each of the authors reflects on the fact that they have been chosen by the deity and given a specific message to announce. Dio writes: "I have been chosen by the will of some deity" and continues by announcing that "the gods provide... words that are appropriate and profitable to the listener." Similarly, Paul writes: "we have been approved by God" and continues with the announcement that we have been "entrusted with the message of the gospel."

In each of the authorial commendations, a triangular relationship significantly serves as a focus of the author's reflection. Dio writes about himself, the deity/the gods, and men/the listener. Dio concludes his reflection on the ideal philosopher with a pertinent, albeit brief, codicil in which he makes the description apply to himself. By means of the philosopher words have come from the gods for the benefit of people. Paul writes about himself and his companions, God, and "you," his readers/listeners.[77] The message of the gospel comes from God for the benefit of those whom God calls into his own kingdom and glory through those to whom he has entrusted the message.[78]

Despite the very real similarities between Paul's words to the Thessalonians and Dio Chrysostom's description of the ideal philosopher there are significant differences between the two communications. Some of the major differences can be summed up under the rubrics of the personal, theological, ambassadorial, and familial qualities of Paul's language.

Personal Involvement

The personal tone of Paul's discourse is readily apparent. We have already noted Paul's use of the recall motif. He appeals to the Thessalonians' knowledge (vv. 1, 2, 5, 11), their memory (v. 9), and their witness (v. 10). He uses pronouns deftly and allows for rhetorical interplay among them.[79]

Twelve times he uses the pronoun "you," most often in the oblique cases of the Greek language – four times in the genitive (vv. 6, 7, 8, 9), twice in the dative (vv. 8, 10), and five times in the accusative (vv. 1, 2, 9, 12 [2x]). Since the subject of the verb is indicated by the form of the verb in the Greek language, Paul has no need to use the pronoun "you" in the nominative case (*hymeis*).[80] Nonetheless, Paul underscores the implicit subject of the verb "to know" in verse 1 by the insertion of an emphatic "yourselves" (*autoi*), a pronoun that serves to contrast the experience of the Thessalonians themselves with that of those who have only heard about the Thessalonians' experience (1:9). Moreover, he carefully distinguishes the "you" to whom he is writing from all "others" (*allōn*, v. 6).

The pronoun "we" is used six times in this section of the letter, four times in the genitive (vv. 1, 2, 3, 4) and twice in dative (vv. 8, 9). Particularly striking in this regard is the appearance of the phrase "us to you" (*hēmōn pros hymas*), which is repeated at the beginning of the exposition (vv. 1, 2). In the first instance the juxtaposition of the two pronouns is highlighted by means of the article. Were one to translate Paul's "our coming to you" a bit more literally, it might be rendered "our coming, the one to you." There could be no doubt that Paul was emphasizing the fact that he and his companions had gone to the Thessalonians. Indeed their personal presence among the Thessalonians was further underscored by Paul's use of the phrase "among you," literally, "in your midst" (*en mesō hymōn*) in verse 7.

The interrelationship between the Thessalonians and the Pauline party is further highlighted by the use of the reflexive pronoun (*heautos*). The pronoun occurs twice in each of the last two units of Paul's description of the visit (vv. 7, 8, 11, 12),[81] that is, in those very passages where Paul uses warm language to describe the intensity of affect that bound him and his companions to the Thessalonians: "But we were gentle among you, like a nurse tenderly caring for her own [*heautēs*] children. So deeply do we care for you that we are determined to share with you not only the gospel of God but also our very own selves [*tas heautōn psychas*], because you have become very dear to us.... we dealt with each one of you like a father with his [*heautou*, literally, "his own"] children, urging and encouraging you..." (2:7–8, 11).

In translation, verse 8 seems to express one of the main purposes of Paul's letter: "so deeply do we care for you that we are determined to share with you not only the gospel of God but also our very own selves, because you have become very dear to us" (NRSV). In this translation the verse adequately captures the intensity of Paul's description of the relationship between his party and the Thessalonians, but it does raise a few questions for the interpreter.

First of all, the translation seems to suggest that Paul was describing a relationship that existed at the time that he was writing. The main verb (*eudokoumen,* "we are determined") is, however, in the imperfect, a tense that normally indicates some action in the past.[82] As a result, most recent translations of 2:8 render the verse in such a way as to imply that it describes Paul's affect at the time of his original visit. The REB, for example, translates the verse: "our affection was so deep that we were determined to share with you not only the gospel of God but our very own selves."[83]

Secondly, the NRSV translates *omeiromenoi hymōn* as "deeply we care for you." Most translations and commentaries on the passage similarly render the verb *omeiromomai* as if it describes the affection that existed between Paul's group and the Thessalonians.[84] Paul does not otherwise use the verb. It is not even found elsewhere in the New Testament[85] — it's a real *hapax!* Editors opt for a translation like that of the NRSV because the verb suggests longing with intense desire when it is used in Job 3:21, and this is the only other place in the entire Bible where the word appears.[86]

Norbert Baumert, however, has suggested that this rare verb really connotes separation, so he translates Paul's words as "having been separated from you."[87] From Baumert's point of view, although the entire sentence speaks of Paul's affection for the Thessalonians, the phrase *omeiromenoi hymōn* does not specifically do so. If the phrase really does suggest Paul's separation from the Thessalonians, as Baumert contends, verse 8 speaks of Paul's disposition as he was writing to the Thessalonians[88] rather than his affection at the time when he was with them:[89] "having been separated from you, we were determined to share with you not only the gospel of God but also our very own selves." Such a translation would not change one's overall view of the relationship between Paul and the Thessalonians; it would, however, modify somewhat one's impression of the situation at the time of Paul's visit and would put Paul's writing of his letter into a very clear perspective.

Paul's use of pronouns and his rehearsal of the bonds that linked him and his companions to the Thessalonians is due, in large measure, to the fact that his is an epistolary communication. His description of the visit to the Thessalonians is incorporated into a letter, the very nature of which is that it focuses on presence and friend-ship.

In the interplay of pronouns that punctuates Paul's reflection on his visit to the Thessalonians, all six pronouns in the first person[90] are in the plural number. The eight verbs in the first person are likewise in the first-person plural.[91] Five of these verbs are qualified by particip-ial constructions, in the plural number.[92] While security may have prompted the ordinary traveler in Paul's time to travel with others,[93] Paul not only traveled with Silvanus and Timothy, he also worked with them and preached with them. Theirs was a cooperative effort. They declared the gospel of God. They were approved by God. They spoke in order to please God. They did not come with words of flattery; they were gentle. They were determined to share the gospel and their very own selves. They worked day and night, presumably in the leather-worker's shop, as they proclaimed the gospel of God. They acted purely, uprightly, and blamelessly among the Thessalonians. They sent greetings and the thoughts expressed in the letter are those of all three senders.

Only three times in this letter does Paul depart from his use of the first-person plural.[94] Not once does he do so in the autobiographical confession (2:1–12), where the "we" resounds as if it had been struck with tympany. As a group, the three men could be called "apostles of Christ" (2:7). It was *their* visit to the Thessalonians that Paul was recapitulating as he wrote 2:1–12.

A Theological Context

When the words of Paul are compared with those of Dio Chrysos-tom, it is not only Paul's use of pronouns that stands out, it is also Paul's theological language that is striking.[95] Whereas Dio wrote about "some deity" and "the gods," Paul wrote about only one God. The God about whom he spoke and about whom he wrote was *ho theos* ("the God"). It appears that there is but one God for Paul.[96] "God" can serve as his name. Indeed, in 1 Thessalonians, Paul's God is called by no name other than "*ho theos* – God."

That Paul and his companions acknowledged but one God is read-ily apparent when he first mentions God as he reflects back on what he and his companions had done when they visited the Thessalonians. Having juxtaposed those who had visited with those who were visited in 2:1, Paul says that it was the visitors' own God who had provided them with the courage that they needed for the task at hand: "we had courage in our God to declare to you the gospel of God" (2:2). Paul writes about "our God," "the[97] god of us" (*tō theō hēmōn*). The turn of phrase is striking. Just a few verses earlier Paul had described the result of his visit to the Thessalonians: they had turned from idols to serve a living and true God (1:9). Paul's apologetic tone makes it clear that Paul had disdain for those other "gods" who would not have been living and true.[98] The Thessalonians had only recently turned toward that God. Paul, then, was clearly making a point when he noted in 2:2 that it was their own God who had emboldened Paul and his companions to speak among the Thessalonians.[99]

The way in which Paul continues to describe God in his autobiographical reflection makes it clear to one familiar with the Jewish tradition that Paul's God was the God of Jewish tradition. When he writes about his having received the word of God, he describes God as one "who tests our hearts" (2:4). The language is very Jewish. It evokes Semitic anthropology, in which the heart represents the human person to the very depths of its being.[100] The idea that God tests the human heart seems to be a reminiscence of Jer 11:20,[101] a passage in which the prophet speaks of God as one who tries the heart and the mind. Similar phrases are to be found in the Greek Bible at Jer 12:3; 17:10; Ps 138:3; and Prov 17:3. The phrase evokes an image of God as a divine tester. Its appearance in the autobiographical confession is consistent with the mild oath that twice punctuates Paul's description of his visit ("as God is witness," 2:5, 10)[102] and thereby guarantees the truthfulness of Paul's assertions.

Beyond its specificity as a reminiscence of biblical language and as a warrant for the truth of Paul's affirmations, the description of God as one "who tests our hearts" evokes the image of a God who intervenes in the lives of human beings, a God who is interested in them and who has expectations of them. That characterization of God is fleshed out as Paul writes of the God who approved himself and his companions and entrusted the gospel to them. This is the God whom they strove to please.[103] This pattern of divine initiative and human response is taken up again at the end of Paul's description of his visit when he writes about the Thessalonians' having been called into God's kingdom and glory and Paul's urging that they lead a life worthy of the God who calls them. That they have been called ("who calls," a present participle)[104] indicates that those to whom this letter is addressed have also been caught up into an ongoing relationship with God. Their relationship with the one God was, in fact, the focus of the first part of Paul's epistolary diptych (1:2-10). In this passage Paul had summed up the highlights of what he and his companions had learned about the Thessalonians' situation (1:2-10).

The fact that Paul can write about God who calls "into his own kingdom and glory" suggests another important dimension of Paul's characterization of God. Paul rarely writes about the "kingdom of God."[105] He does so here (2:12). Paul's language shows that he views

God from the perspective of apocalyptic theocentrism.[106] The kingdom is the final and ultimate reality, the act of God, when the one God
will reign as king. By means of a hendiadys, Paul describes that reign
as a glorious reign. The coming of his kingdom is the final manifestation of his glory.[107] Paul's categories of thought are not only those of
the Jewish biblical tradition; they are also those of Jewish apocalyptic
expectation.

Paul's *weltanschauung* is patently distinct from that of Dio Chrysostom. Although Paul and his companions were similar to the ideal
philosopher in many respects, they are different from the philosopher,
precisely because of that worldview.[108]

Ambassadors, Qualified and Sent on a Mission

One important feature that distinguishes Paul from Dio and that is
developed as a distinctive trait in the autobiographical glimpse of
Paul contained in 1 Thess 2:1–12 is the ambassadorial role that Paul
attributes to himself and his companions. Whereas Dio Chrysostom
wrote about the gods providing the philosopher with words that are
appropriate and profitable to the listener, Paul states: "we have been
approved by God to be entrusted with the message of the gospel"
(2:4). The choice of vocabulary is typical of Paul, but the way in which
the vocabulary is used is quite unusual.[109] Paul's phraseology is so unusual that it suggests that he has something in mind that does not
usually occupy the focus of his thought.

In the New Testament, the use of the *"dokim* – approval" word
group is typically Pauline.[110] Paul uses the verb *dokimazō,* which generally means "to test and approve,"[111] some fifteen times in his various
letters.[112] With the exception of 1 Thess 2:4, Paul always uses the verb
in the active voice, with a human person or group of persons as its subject. Sometimes the use of the verb suggests self-examination (1 Cor
11:28 and 2 Cor 13:5; cf. Gal 6:4); at other times it refers to another's
examination and approval (1 Cor 16:3; 2 Cor 8:22).

In 1 Thess 2:4 God is the real subject of "to test and approve"
in both instances.[113] Paul's choice of this exceptional verb can be
explained by the fact that the verb was used in political circles to describe the process whereby a potential magistrate or a citizen destined
for some other significant political post was scrutinized and then officially approved for his functions.[114] Should the process prove to be
favorable to the candidate, he was said to be *dokimos,* that is, qualified
and approved.[115] Paul and his companions were not, however, scrutinized by mere human authorities; they were scrutinized and found
qualified by God himself.

Among the extant documents from the Hellenistic chancery attesting to this process, the verb "*dokimazō* – to scrutinize" was frequently followed by an infinitive clause specifying the precise function for which the candidate had been "scrutinized and approved." Paul uses such an infinitive clause as he writes that he and his companions were approved by God "to be entrusted with the message of the gospel." No other New Testament author uses the verb "*pisteuō* – to believe" as often as does Paul. He constantly uses the verb and its cognates to speak of the belief of the communities that he had evangelized.[116] Only in 2:4 does Paul use the verb in the passive voice.[117] He and his companions have been entrusted (*pisteuthēnai*) with the message of the gospel (*to euaggelion*).

That the editors of the NRSV have chosen to translate *to euaggelion* as "the message of the gospel" indicates that "gospel," a Pauline commonplace, bears an unusual connotation in 2:4. The editors generally translate *euaggelion* simply as "gospel."[118] Paul writes of "our gospel" (1:5), the "gospel of God" (2:2, 8, 9), or the "gospel of Christ" (3:2). 1 Thess 2:4 is the only place in Paul's letter when *to euaggelion* is used without further qualification. As Paul explains his situation in 2:4, it is obvious that he wants to underscore the fact that God has confided a particular message to himself and his companions.[119] It is this point that is accentuated in the NRSV's translation of the phrase. Thus 2:4 states – and quite plainly for Hellenistic ears – that Paul and his companions are God's duly approved spokespersons and the message that they carry comes from God himself.

When Paul adds that the God who has judged himself and his companions to be qualified and has entrusted them with a mission is the same God "who tests our hearts," he seems to suggest that their role is, from his own point of view at least, akin to that of the prophets of old, the *pro-phētai*, those who spoke (*phēmi*) on behalf (*pro*) of God in a pre-eminent and critical fashion.[120] Paul's speaking about his commission to proclaim the gospel is his way of describing his own "conversion experience," which is really a prophetic call. Typically Paul makes reference to his call in terms that recall the call of Jeremiah, to whom allusion is made in the phrase "who tests our hearts" (Jer 11:20).[121]

The term "prophet" is not, however, formally used when Paul reflects on his visit to Thessalonica in 2:1-12. He has chosen rather to speak of himself and his companions as "apostles of Christ" (*Christou apostoloi*, 2:7[122]). The way in which Paul introduces this terminology is such that it serves to establish a legitimate claim upon the Thessalonians. Since Paul and his companions were apostles of Christ, they might have made demands upon the Thessalonians. They, however, chose to forgo the exercise of their rights.[123]

Readers who are familiar with Paul's later letters might be sur-

prised that this is the first time that the word "apostle" appears in
1 Thessalonians and that the term is in the plural. In his later correspondence, specifically in the prescript of his letters to the Romans,
the Corinthians, and the Galatians,[124] Paul will use the term "apostle"
in the singular, but he does not do so in the protocol of the present
text, where his name stands alongside those of Silvanus and Timothy without further qualification. Paul's use of the term "apostle" in
the plural to describe Silvanus, Timothy, and himself highlights the
solidarity-in-mission that characterized Paul's visit to Thessalonica.

A cognate of the verb *apostellō,* meaning to "send away" or "send
off," "apostle" suggests that those to whom it applies have been sent.
In fact, the New Testament usage of the Greek word, where it applies
to persons, is relatively new. In some ways it recalls the Jewish institution of the *shaliah,* the emissary sent on a specific mission by one
congregation to another. Thus an "apostle" is essentially an agent or
accredited representative.[125] As Paul describes himself and his companions as those who have been sent, he does not identify them as
having been sent by some Christian congregation or some ordinary
individual. He identifies them as "apostles of Christ,"[126] with "Christ"
in the emphatic first position. The absolute use of "Christ" is striking,
recurring elsewhere in this letter only in 3:2 and 4:16.[127]

Properly speaking, the term is an adjective derived from the Greek
verb *chriō,* meaning to "rub or smear with oil or a scented unguent."
The words were used of rubbing oils and anointed objects or persons.
Among Greek-speaking Jews and in the Greek Bible (LXX) the adjective was used of anointed priests and patriarchs, but it was especially
used in reference to the anointed kings of Israel. Apart from Dan 9:26
and Sir 46:19,[128] the unqualified use of *christos* as an adjectival noun,
"the anointed one" – let alone as a proper noun – does not appear
in the Greek Bible. Paul appears to be breaking literary ground as he
writes of himself and his companions as "envoys of the anointed one."
The language would be mysterious indeed if the Thessalonians had not
heard from Paul about someone called the "Anointed One."

In 2:7, Paul states that he and his companions were envoys of this
"Anointed One." That Paul writes of the "Anointed One" in the genitive
case implies not only that they have received a particular commission
from the Anointed One, but also that they somehow belonged to this
Anointed One.[129] It is apparent, in other words, that Paul attributed
some real authority to the one whom he called the "Anointed One."
The authority somehow extended even to the Thessalonian Christians since it was in their capacity as envoys of the "Anointed One"
that Paul and his companions could have made demands upon the
Thessalonians.

One other indication of the ambassadorial quality of Paul's language can be discerned in the way in which he recalls the exhortation that he addressed to various Thessalonian Christians at the time of his visit. The visitors had urged and encouraged the Thessalonians, pleading with them to lead a life worthy of God (2:12). The verbs employed by Paul are words typically employed in Hellenistic paraenesis, where they suggested some sort of moral authority. In their present context, however, they are part of a letter. This is not without significance since the verb *parakaleō*, "to urge,"[130] serves a conventional function in ancient letters, particularly in the authoritative communications of delegated officials.[131] It was an expression of diplomatic tact, subtly communicating not only what was to be done but also the real authority that lay behind the communication. Paul's authority to urge the Thessalonians to follow appropriate patterns of conduct was an alien authority. He and his companions exhorted the Thessalonians in the name of someone else. Later in the letter, he would spell out the authority under whose aegis he and his companions exhorted the Thessalonians: "we . . . urge you," he writes, "in the Lord Jesus." One who is Lord demands obedience.

A Family at Home

Paul compared the authority that he and his companions enjoyed with that of a father in 2:11–12: "we dealt with each one of you," he writes, "like a father with his [own] children, urging and encouraging you and pleading that you lead a life worthy of God."

Mothers

This brings us to the familial or domestic quality of the language that Paul employs in 2:1–12.[132] In this autobiographical confession, Paul uses language that properly belongs to the family circle. He speaks of his "brothers and sisters" (*adelphoi,* 2:1, 9). He uses maternal and paternal imagery (vv. 7 and 8), the language of mother, father, and children. The familial language that Paul employs in 2:1–12 is used to express some quality of the relationship that existed between Paul's group and the Thessalonian Christians. Interestingly enough, the passage is devoid of any reference to God as Father, even though Paul has employed that very terminology earlier in his letter (1:1, 3).[133]

Paul's maternal language stands in apposition to the identification of himself and his companions as envoys of the Anointed One. Paul's reflection begins with a "but," which sharply contrasts the demands that Paul and his fellow travelers, in their authoritative capacity as the designated envoys of the Anointed One, might have made upon the Thessalonians with the fashion in which they actually exercised their authority: "But we were gentle among you, like a nurse tenderly caring for her own children. So deeply do we care for you that we are determined to share with you not only the gospel of God but also our own selves, because you have become very dear to us" (2:7b-8). As envoys, they delivered the message, "the gospel of God," but they also expended their own lives' energies, their *psychai*.[134] They poured themselves out for the benefit of the Thessalonians.

They were "like a nurse tenderly caring for her own children." The language of Paul's formal simile[135] is a bit unusual. "Nurse" (*trophos*) is not otherwise used in the New Testament. The word evokes one who feeds or nourishes, effectively, a wet-nurse. The expression was often used for a mother who nursed her children. It is only in 2:7 that Paul uses the verb, "to care tenderly" (*thalpē*).[136] The expression suggests warmth and heat. It was commonly used in a metaphorical sense with the meaning of to cherish or comfort. An emphatic "her own" (*heautēs*) intensifies the image still further. If a nurse cares for those confided to her care ever so warmly, how much more does a mother care for the child at her breast! With this kind of affection did Paul and his companions minister among the Thessalonians ("among you," v. 7a). Paul's simile breathes the pathos of his appeal.

Although unusual for Paul, this poignant metaphor was not without analogy in ancient times, as a variety of sources attest.[137] Plutarch, the philosophical moralist and biographer contemporary with Dio Chrysostom, cited the good example of nurses as he urged moralists to seize the opportune moment in which to speak out: "When children fall down, the nurses do not rush up to berate them, but they take them, wash them, and straighten their clothes, and, after all this is done, then rebuke them and punish them." In similar fashion Dio recalls that "nurses, after giving the children a whipping, tell them a story to comfort and please them."[138] In the Dead Sea Scrolls, the Teacher of Righteousness is presented in the guise of a nursing father: "Thou hast made me a father unto sons of kindness and a nursing father to men of wonder and they have opened their mouths as suck[lings of the breasts of his mother and] as the play of a child in the bosom of his nursing fathers" (1QH 7:20-22).[139]

In Qumran's collection of Thanksgiving Hymns, similar imagery is used of God: "Over them as (a mother) who hath compassion upon her babe and as a nursing-father in the bosom, Thou nourishest all Thy works" (1QH 9:36).[140] Plutarch describes Tethys, consort of the god Okeanos, as "the kindly nurse and provider of all things."[141] Since the cult of this divine pair was celebrated on the island of Samothrace, an island to which visitors from Thessalonica traveled at the time of Paul, Karl Donfried has suggested that the image of the nurse might have been familiar to Paul's correspondents who had previously been idol worshipers (1:9).

It is, moreover, known that a Dionysiac cult was celebrated at Thessalonica from at least 187 B.C.E. In the Dionysiac mysteries, the female attendants representing divine women were called "nurses."[142] In sum, it is quite likely that Paul's unusual metaphor would have struck a familiar cord in the hearts of those to whom he was writing when he wrote to them about his maternal affection.

Children

Like a mother,[143] Paul and his companions gave their lives for the benefit of the Thessalonian Christians, and they were "gentle" among them (2:7b). The terminology is consistent with the image of the nurse tenderly caring for her children and it is consistent with the moralist's description of the ideal philosopher with which Paul's autobiographical confession in 2:1-12 has so many similarities.[144] The phrase "gentle among you" makes full sense, but is that what Paul really wrote? This question has been debated by New Testament textual critics throughout the generations.

"Gentle – ēpioi"[145] is the reading of verse 7b in the vast majority of the medieval Greek copies of Paul's letter, but the most ancient manuscripts,[146] including the third-century P[65], the fourth-century Sinaiticus and Vaticanus codices, the fifth-century Codex Ephraemi Rescriptus, and the sixth-century Codex Claromontanus, read "nēpioi – children." Since nēpioi – children is the more difficult reading, contemporary textual critics[147] are inclined to think that it is the more primitive of the two possibilities and that "ēpioi – gentle" represents a correction that was deliberately made by various scribes in order to make better sense of Paul's words.[148]

Does "nēpioi – children" make any sense? Although the expression might be taken as a vocative form of direct address,[149] it seems to be an example of Paul mixing his metaphors. He clearly shifts his images in Gal 4:29 and does so in 2:7b-12, where he writes of himself and his companions as mother, brothers, and father. Why not as children as well? Such a rapid change of imagery is a bit perplexing to the reader, whether modern or medieval. Yet, if Paul passes as quickly from one metaphor to another as he is wont to do, one cannot exclude the possibility of his having mixed his metaphors in 2:7. He has juxtaposed the images of children and a mother, in order to describe his presence among the Thessalonians.[150] The two metaphors related to one another within the same semantic field. Paul's rapidly shifting figures touch upon various aspects of his apostolic presence among the Thessalonians.[151]

Father

Paul has certainly mixed his metaphors by the time that he comes to the final and climactic section of his reflection on his visit to Thessalonica (2:9–12). Three times he appeals to the Thessalonians to recall his presence and activity among them: "You remember... you are witnesses... as you know." The last expression recalls the appeal to the Thessalonians' knowledge in 2:2 and 5. In verse 11, Paul uses the strongest possible comparative conjunction[152] to introduce his appeal to the Thessalonians' experience of his visit: "As [*kathaper*] you know, we dealt with each one of you like a father with his children, urging and encouraging you and pleading that you lead a life worthy of God, who calls you into his own kingdom and glory."

Here Paul's construction is a bit unusual. The comparative clause lacks a principal verb,[153] a deficiency for which the NRSV's editors have compensated by adding an interpretive "we dealt": "we dealt with each one of you like a father with his children." The way in which Paul uses the paternal metaphor[154] is quite similar to the way in which he had introduced the maternal metaphor in verse 8. The two images are expressed in remarkably similar fashion.[155] Both come at the end of a clearly delineated subsection of the reflection. In each case Paul's linguistic expression consists of:

1. an introduction of the metaphor by a clause containing the verb "are" (*egenēthēmen*), a qualifying phrase and the pronoun "you": "but we were children among you" (v. 7) – "how pure, upright, and blameless our conduct was[156] toward you believers" (v. 10).

2. the simile containing a parental image and an emphatic reference to one's own children: "like a nurse tenderly caring for her own children" (v. 7) – "like a father with his own children" (v. 11).

3. an explanation of the image: "so deeply do we care for you that we are determined to share with you not only the gospel of God but also our own selves" (v. 8) – "urging and encouraging you and pleading that you lead a life worthy of God" (v. 12).

A father is not only one who sires children; he is one who also takes it as his life's work to provide for the socialization of his children. A rabbinic adage summed up the Jewish tradition in this regard: "The father is bound in respect of his son, to circumcise, redeem, teach him Torah, take a wife for him, and teach him a craft."[157] Indeed the biblical tradition[158] shared with the wisdom oracles of the East the idea that it is a father's responsibility to pass on to his children moral instruction, human experience, and social and religious tradition. The passing on of traditional lore from one generation to the next, thereby allowing for the socialization of the new generation, was a paternal activity. Hence Paul likens the activities of the evangelist to those of a father toward his own children.[159]

Brothers and Sisters

Paul's use of maternal and paternal images allows the reader to grasp something of the intensity and character of the relationship that bound him and his companions to the Thessalonians, their very own children, their *tekna*,[160] a term used in reference to the Thessalonians only in 2:7 and 2:12. As he reflects on his visit to Thessalonica, Paul uses another kinship term to refer to the Christians whom he had evangelized. He calls them his "brothers and sisters" (*adelphoi*, literally, "brothers,"[161] 2:2, 9).

This turn of phrase is characteristic of Paul. In his seven extant letters,[162] he uses the term *adelphos* some 113 times. In more than half of those instances, 63 times in all, the expression serves as a formula of direct address.[163] In none of his later letters, however, does the term *adelphos* appear with the density that it does in 1 Thessalonians.[164] In this letter Paul uses the expression "brothers and sisters" (*adelphoi*) as a formula of direct address 14 times.[165] The vocative *adelphoi* is the only formula of direct address employed by Paul in our text.

What does it mean for Paul to describe the Christians of Thessalonica as his "brothers and sisters"[166] with such frequency? Commentators generally note that in classical and Hellenistic Greek the expression was metaphorically used by those who belonged to the same religious group, for example, those who participated in the cults of various Egyptian mystery religions.[167] Pharisaic groups were known as brotherhoods and Josephus reports that the Essenes were "like brothers."[168] Indeed Hans von Soden opines that "*adelphos* is one of the religious titles of the people of Israel taken over by the Christian community."[169]

Paul's use of "brothers and sisters" to describe the Thessalonians may serve to situate the community to which he was writing within the perspectives of the history of religions, but it might also prove useful to inquire whether the expression might be read from a sociological perspective. Certainly the frequency of the expression in 1 Thessalonians would seem to be an expression of the intensity of the bond that linked Paul and his companions to the Thessalonians.[170] Upon further reflection it would seem that the natural locale for such familial language is the home. It is in the home that families are at home. Kinship language is the language of the home.

Paul does not explicitly refer to a home in 1 Thessalonians, but from his later letters it is apparent that Christian groups normally gathered in homes.[171] The home group was the basic unit of the church, just as it was the basic unit of society.[172] The fact that Paul has made such extensive use of kinship language in 1 Thessalonians, a letter in which he warmly recalls his visit to the Thessalonians and the bonds that continue to link himself to them, makes it more than likely that Paul was writing to a community that had gathered in a home and that Paul had participated in such home gatherings when he and his companions were present in Thessalonica. It was not only in the leatherworker's shop that Paul proclaimed the gospel of God; he also did so in Christian homes, where he and his companions acted as mother and father toward the Thessalonian Christians.

From Paul's description of his visit to the Thessalonians, one gathers the impression that he and his companions were warmly received by the Thessalonians, indeed, that they were received into a Thessalonian home where they were treated like brothers and could act like mothers and fathers. This situation contrasts rather sharply with the reception that Paul and his companions had received in nearby Philippi just a short while previous to the Thessalonian visit. There Paul and his companions had suffered and been shamefully mistreated (2:2). In Thessalonica he found a home where his brothers and sisters gathered.

Another's Reflection

Was Paul's visit really so copacetic? In a later account of the visit of Paul and his companions to Thessalonica, Luke seems to suggest otherwise:

[1]After Paul and Silas had passed through Amphipolis and Apollonia, they came to Thessalonica, where there was a synagogue of the Jews. [2]And Paul went in, as was his custom, and on three sabbath days argued with them from the scriptures, [3]explaining and proving that it was necessary for the Messiah to suffer and to rise from the dead, and saying, "This is the Messiah, Jesus whom I am proclaiming to you." [4]Some of them were persuaded and joined Paul and Silas, as did a great many of the devout Greeks and not a few of the leading women. [5]But the Jews became jealous, and with the help of some ruffians in the marketplaces they formed a mob and set the city in an uproar. While they were searching for Paul and Silas to bring them out to the assembly, they attacked Jason's house. [6]When they could not find them, they dragged Jason and some believers before the city authorities, shouting,

"These people who have been turning the world upside down have come here also, ⁷and Jason has entertained them as guests. They are all acting contrary to the decrees of the emperor, saying that there is another king named Jesus." ⁸The people and the city officials were disturbed when they heard this, ⁹and after they had taken bail from Jason and the others, they let them go. ¹⁰That very night the believers sent Paul and Silas off to Beroea. (Acts 17:1–10a)

Scholars today are hesitant to use this Lukan account as a primary source of information about Paul's stay in Thessalonica.[173] They point to its stereotypical character[174] as an indication that Luke has thoroughly reworked the material at his disposition in such a way as to create a narrative of his own cloth. His own literary techniques and theological perspectives are readily apparent. Luke has recourse to a fixed narrative schema in his description of the events in Thessalonica: Paul preaches in the synagogue, some Gentiles are converted, the Jews become hostile.[175] In the words of Dieter Lührmann, Luke "modeled the story after what he thought Paul usually did."[176]

In his magistral commentary on the Acts of the Apostles, Ernst Haenchen notes that the author has made free with tradition.[177] Thus Luke has simplified his account of Paul's visit to Thessalonica in order to sustain the central focus of his overall narrative. Richard Pervo suggests that the way in which Luke deals with Paul's adventures in Acts – and Acts 17:1–10a is an adventure story! – bears remarkable similarity with the adventure stories found in Greco-Roman novels.[178] On the other hand, one cannot afford to be hypercritical.[179] Luke has not written his account of Paul's visit to Thessalonica as a simple figment of his imagination.

From this perspective – and without denying that priority must be accorded to Paul's first-hand account of the events[180] – we should take at least a brief look at Acts 17:1–10a to see what it says about Paul's visit. The account can readily be divided into four subunits:[181]

- Verses 1–3: The Proclamation of the Gospel

- Verse 4: Its Positive Result

- Verses 5–7: Rejection by the Jews

- Verses 8–10a: Vindication and Salvation

Verses 1–3: The Proclamation of the Gospel

¹After Paul and Silas had passed through Amphipolis and Apollonia, they came to Thessalonica, where there was a synagogue

of the Jews. [2]And Paul went in, as was his custom, and on three sabbath days argued with them from the scriptures, [3]explaining and proving that it was necessary for the Messiah to suffer and to rise from the dead, and saying, "This is the Messiah, Jesus whom I am proclaiming to you."

Although Luke's account focuses[182] upon the travels of Paul, his hero, and Silas, a representative of the Antiochene Christian community (Acts 15:22) and the designated successor of Barnabas in the Pauline entourage (Acts 15:40), Luke has already indicated to his readers that the party that traveled along the Egnatian Way to Thessalonica did not consist solely of these two men. Paul wanted Timothy – at least – to go with him. Timothy did accompany Paul and Silas as they went on their way visiting different cities (Acts 16:3-4). Thus Timothy was with Paul and Silas as they traveled from one Macedonian city to the other.

During the course of the hundred-mile journey between Philippi and Thessalonica Paul and Silas must have stopped somewhere. Perhaps they stopped in Amphipolis or Apollonia.[183] Yet they seem not to have tarried in either of these cities, perhaps because neither of these two cities had a Jewish community large enough to sponsor a synagogue.[184] When the travelers arrived in Thessalonica, Paul, the hero of the narrative whom Luke portrays as the compleat Jew,[185] entered the synagogue as was his custom. On three sabbaths,[186] he discussed the meaning of the scriptures. The burden of his message was the heart of the early Christian kerygma, namely, that Jesus was the Messiah, that the Messiah was to suffer and be raised from the dead, and that the scriptures testified to this.[187] Luke's Paul followed the patterns of Hellenistic rhetoric. Beginning with the premise that the Messiah must suffer and be raised, Paul argued that Jesus was the Messiah.[188]

Verse 4: A Positive Result

[4]Some of them were persuaded and joined Paul and Silas, as did a great many of the devout Greeks and not a few of the leading women.

Luke tells his readers that Paul had limited success in preaching to the Jews. Only some of them (*tines*) were convinced by the argument,[189] in which Paul explained and attempted to prove that Jesus was the Messiah. By way of contrast Luke mentions that Paul made inroads among the pagans, notably among the God-fearing Greeks of whom a great many (*plēthos polu*) were won over by his message, not a few (*ouk oligai*) leading women among them. The letter to the Thessalonians gives no mention of this small group of Jewish-Christian believers. Rather it gives the impression that the Thessalonian Christians had formerly been pagans (1:9).

Luke's not so subtle notation that the preaching of the gospel made inroads among the Gentiles and was attractive to the upper classes is fully in keeping with his own theological and narrative agenda.[190] Not only does Luke develop a "Jew first, then Gentile" motif throughout his account, he also narrates the entire story in such a way as to show that one can be a Christian and still have social aspirations.[191]

Verses 5–7: Opposition

> [5]But the Jews became jealous, and with the help of some ruffians in the marketplaces they formed a mob and set the city in an uproar. While they were searching for Paul and Silas to bring them out to the assembly, they attacked Jason's house. [6]When they could not find them, they dragged Jason and some believers before the city authorities, shouting, "These people who have been turning the world upside down have come here also, [7]and Jason has entertained them as guests. They are all acting contrary to the decrees of the emperor, saying that there is another king named Jesus."

Luke's narrative continues as he introduces to the scene a paired set of contrasting characters. Opposite a great many of the devout Greeks and not a few of the leading women are the Jews and some ruffians. Jews are compared with Gentiles and ruffians with its leading female citizens. There is no mistaking where Luke's narrative sympathies lie. Allied with the Jews are some "evil characters from the marketplace" (*ton agaraion andras tinas ponērous*). Chris Manus describes these people as "a good-for-nothing set of street thugs."[192] They cause a riot in town.

The sequence of events is not unlike the ten other mob scenes that Luke describes in his adventure story.[193] Acts 17:5 is the only place in his writings that Luke uses the verb "to form a mob." Perhaps he has coined the expression himself in order to describe the confusion that he wanted to evoke.[194] By inciting a mob, the Jews[195] were able to throw the entire city into confusion.[196]

The Jews, with their bullies, attacked Jason's house, apparently believing either that Paul and Silas were lodging there[197] or that they had at least taken refuge there. Jason[198] was probably a Christian[199] — at least by the time that Luke wrote his account — but Luke does not explicitly mention this as a fact. For the rest, Luke does not tell us much about him, not even whether he was a Greek or a Jew.[200] He only says that Jason offered hospitality to Paul and Silas and that, as a result, he had incurred the wrath of the crowd, the violation of his house, and judicial incrimination. Indeed the stated purpose of the attack upon Jason's house was to bring Paul and Silas before the assembly, the *dēmos,* a responsible political body.[201]

Since the unruly mob was unable to find Paul and his companion, they set upon Jason and some other Christians. They dragged them before the local magistrates, the politarchs, who acted in place of the Roman authority. Luke calls these who had been arrested "brothers" (*adelphoi*), a term that suggests their status as Christians.[202] The NRSV and REB translations – unlike the NIV, RNAB, and NJB – elucidate Luke's terminology by calling these Christians "believers" and "members of the congregation."

Luke does not, however, indicate whether the Christians who were hauled before the politarchs were neophyte Christians from Thessalonica or whether they were members of Paul's entourage. Commentators generally assume that they were new Christians, but the fact of the matter is that Luke does not tell his readers that they were.[203] Presumably – but again this is not stated[204] – these Christians were found in Jason's house. If so, Jason's home[205] served as a venue for Christian gatherings. Whether or not these Christians actually gathered in Jason's home and were to be found in Jason's home when they were trapped by the mob, the fact that the members of the congregation were called "brothers (and sisters)" indicates once again that some Thessalonian home served as the locale for gatherings of Christians.

Having hauled Jason and his fellow Christians before the magistrates, the Jews formulate the charge: "These people who have been turning the world upside down have come here also, and Jason has entertained them as guests. They are all acting contrary to the decrees of the emperor, saying that there is another king named Jesus" (Acts 17:6b-7).[206] Order has not yet been restored to the courtroom since the charge has been shouted out (*boōntes*). What does the charge against Jason and the others really mean?

First of all, it would appear that the Jews accuse the Christians of fomenting public disorder, thereby exculpating themselves from the mob scene that Luke has described. It was not Jason, but the newcomers who were turning the world upside down. Jason's crime was to have offered them hospitality,[207] that is, aiding and abetting those who were fomenting political unrest. Luke's language is a bit ambiguous, but it seems preferable to construe his reference to the agitators as a reference to Paul and his entourage rather than as a reference to those who were dragged before the magistrates along with Jason. It was claimed that Paul's group was "turning the world upside down."[208] The mention of the "world"[209] in the charge betrays Luke's perspective. He was convinced that Paul's proclamation of the gospel, even at Thessalonica, had implications for the entire world.[210]

The visitors are said to have acted contrary to the decrees of the emperor by saying that there is another king, one named Jesus. Ultimately, the accusation is not that the visitors had committed treason, but that they were urging the citizenry of Thessalonica to violate their oaths of loyalty to the emperor.[211] Apparently there was something in Paul's preaching that the mob – maliciously – or Luke – inadvertently – took to mean that Paul and his companions were advocating a change of political loyalties.

Oaths of allegiance to the emperor – "I swear . . . that I will support Caesar Augustus, his children and descendants, throughout my life, in word, deed and thought . . . "[212] – were employed during Roman rule. Such oaths might be considered "decrees of the emperor." Responsibility for administering them fell to local officials, in this case, the politarchs of Thessalonica. Hence it was before the politarchs that Jason and his companions were forced to make their appearance, charged with supporting a pretender king, Jesus, and urging people to violate their allegiance to the emperor who ruled the "world."[213]

Verses 8–10a: Vindication and Salvation

[8]The people and the city officials were disturbed when they heard this, [9]and after they had taken bail from Jason and the others, they let them go. [10]That very night the believers sent Paul and Silas off to Beroea.

Luke's narrative interest continues to focus on Paul. As he had previously done in his story, Luke once again describes Paul escaping the clutches of plotting Jews with the assistance of loyal disciples.[214] "That very night" adds a note of dramatic urgency to the narrative. The believers[215] take advantage of the first opportunity to get Paul out of town and on his way to Beroea, some fifty miles distant. There a repeat scenario will take place (Acts 17:10–15). Jason and the other companions who had been dragged before the politarchs[216] posted bail and were released. The local officials had no interest in retaining them. Luke's narrative interest is on Paul, not on Jason and the believers at Thessalonica.

Luke mentions that the charges brought against them surprised the people (*ton ochlon,* literally, "the crowd") and the politarchs. Does that mean that the mob (*ochlopoiēsantes,* v. 5) didn't know what it was getting into? That the charges laid against the Pauline party and those laid against Jason and his companions came as news to them? If so, Luke has accentuated the idea that it was "the Jews" who alone were truly responsible for the situation. Or should the "crowd" of verse 8 (the NRSV's "people") be identified with the "assembly" (*dēmos*) of verse 5? The linguistic ambiguity results from the terseness of Luke's narrative.[217] The narrator is relatively disinterested in the lot of the secondary characters in his story.

In reality, the bail posted by Jason and the others might have had to be forfeited had they been found to harbor[218] those against whom the real charge was being brought, namely, Paul and his companions. If so, they would have had every interest in seeing Paul's group get on their way as soon as possible. In any case, the messengers of the gospel were sent on their way to continue their task of preaching the gospel to the world (the *oikoumenē*), and that is the main interest of Luke's narrative.

Summing Up

Upon review, the Lukan account of Paul's visit to Thessalonica is not only succinct. It is also an account whose language and episodic presentation are characteristic of Luke. His narrative focus leads him to focus more on the adventures of Paul, his hero, than to give a detailed description of what actually happened in Thessalonica. He is more interested in the conversion of some Gentiles and the Jews' growing hostility to the gospel than he is in the real situation of the church at Thessalonica.

Thus it is that Acts 17:1–10a presents a picture of Paul's visit to Thessalonica different from that reflected by the apostle himself, not only in 1 Thess 2:1–12, but also elsewhere in the letter.[219] The epistle breathes not a whisper of the existence of a Jewish minority within the Christian community of Thessalonica, nor does it evoke the memory of a Pauline visit to a Thessalonian synagogue.[220] It does not recall, let alone give thanks for, the hospitality tendered by Jason. Its christology does not focus on Jesus as a royal figure,[221] nor does it give evidence of the rhetorical argument from scripture in its christological exposition. It hardly attests to the unruly opposition of a Jew-baited mob, nor does it tell about Paul's hasty retreat from the Macedonian capital.

On the other hand, Paul's letter reminds us that Paul had visited Thessalonica in the company of Silas and Timothy.[222] It does reflect the existence of a Gentile Christian community at Thessalonica,[223] and intimates, through its abundant use of kinship language, that this community met in someone's home. It bears witness to the fact that this community existed under some duress,[224] and that Paul's visit was not long enough to respond to all their faith needs.[225] Above all it proclaims that the heart of the Christian kerygma was the death and resurrection of Jesus. It is to that proclamation that we must now turn.

∽ 2 ∝

The Gospel of God

In his reflections on the visit to Thessalonica, Paul often refers to the gospel of God (*to euaggelion tou theou*): "We had courage in our God to declare to you the gospel of God in spite of great opposition" (2:2). "We are determined to share with you not only the gospel of God but also our own selves" (2:8). "We worked day and night ... while we proclaimed to you the gospel of God" (2:9). The proclamation of the gospel of God was not only the focus of Paul's activity while he was in Thessalonica; it was also an activity that arose from the very depths of his being.

Within his letter, Paul explicitly mentions "the gospel of God" only in these three passages.[1] The formula would, nonetheless, soon become one of Paul's favorite expressions. Later in his life he would write about "the gospel of God" in letters to Christians at Rome and in Corinth.[2] As a matter of fact, among New Testament authors, it is Paul who most often writes about "the gospel." Of the seventy-six times that the word "*euaggelizomai* – gospel" occurs in the New Testament, forty-eight occurrences – 63 percent of the total – are to be found in the seven letters that Paul wrote.[3] The related verb, "*euagelizomai* – to bring the good news," occurs some nineteen times in his extant correspondence, including 1 Thess 3:6.[4]

Our Message of the Gospel

The "message" is obviously something very important for Paul,[5] something in which he and his companions had a personal stake and vested interest. They have received the message from God and it somehow touches them in the very depths of their being. With regard to the personal character of this message, today's reader should take note of its prominence in 2:1–12, a passage whose literary form is that of the

37

"autobiographical confession."[6] Within this relatively short pericope the term "gospel" appears four times (2:2, 4, 8, 9). This concentration of usage is without parallel in the New Testament, that is, apart from the similarly autobiographical reflection in 1 Cor 9:12b-23. One could say that the gospel is the leitmotif or major theme of Paul's autobiographical confession. Indeed, Willi Marxsen considers 2:1-12 to be "an apology for Paul's gospel."[7] In extraordinary fashion Paul describes the gospel as his very own message.[8] It is "*our* message of the gospel"[9] (1:5). The formula is so striking that it was taken over by the deutero-Paulines,[10] thereby entering into the later tradition about Paul.

The message was entrusted to Paul and his companions by God "who tests our hearts" (2:4). This is not an offhand remark. The allusion to Jer 11:20[11] points to some self-conscious similarity between Jeremiah and the evangelists. Since the heart is the very core of one's personal being,[12] Paul is really suggesting that he and his companions had been examined by God himself to the very depths of their being, where God alone can scrutinize. For them to have been entrusted with the message does not result in some superficial kind of activity; being entrusted with the message is something that affects the messenger to the very depths of his being.

The intense personal involvement of Paul and his companions with the message is highlighted whenever Paul writes about their "message."[13] When he first introduces the topic in his letter, he calls it "our message," the personal message of himself and his companions to the Thessalonians. Personal pronouns interface one another when he writes, "our [*hēmōn*] message of the gospel came to you [*hymin*]" (1:5). How much the imparting of that message meant to Paul and his companions is indicated when he wrote, "we are determined to share with you not only the gospel of God but also our own selves" (2:8) and again that "we worked day and night ... while we proclaimed to you the gospel of God" (2:9). His pouring out of the gospel is akin to his pouring out his vital forces, his very life.[14] Indeed, Paul and his companions worked day and night so that the gospel might be proclaimed.

Paul's Boldness

Although the need to proclaim the gospel of God rose from the very depths of their being and consumed their lives' strength, the proclamation of the gospel was not an easy task for Paul and his companions. They needed to be strengthened for the task at hand. That they were. They were inspired and emboldened by God himself to do what they had to do: "we had courage in our God to declare to you the gospel of God in spite of great opposition" (2:2).

The impact of Paul's rhetoric deserves further reflection. Paul is describing a contrast experience. He compares the Thessalonians' acceptance of his message[15] with the suffering and mistreatment that he and his companions had received at the hands of the Philippians.

At Thessalonica, Paul and his companions declared the gospel of God in spite of great opposition *(en pollō agōni)*.[16] They were emboldened to do so by God himself. Paul's use of the ingressive aorist indicates that the source of the initiative is none other than God,[17] but what does he mean by "having courage" *(eparrēsiasametha)*? W. C. van Unnik has suggested that this verb, *"parrēsiazomai* – to be made courageous," was part of the kerygmatic language of the early church.[18] It belonged to the semantic register of materials that early Christians used to describe the missionary activity of the first evangelists. The terminology that they chose evokes memories of the boldness with which the Jewish prophets of old had spoken.[19] It conjures up the memory of Jeremiah, who, in so many ways, is Paul's prophetic model.[20]

While Paul may well have had a prophetic consciousness as he spoke,[21] mention of his boldness might have had another impact upon his Hellenistic audience. Hellenistic moralists were wont to talk about the "boldness – *parrēsia"* with which they spoke. Boldness suggests that freemen have a right to speak. The term evokes an openness to the truth and a willingness to speak despite any obstacles that might be present.[22] When Paul wrote about the boldness with which he and his companions spoke, he was proclaiming their openness to the full truth of the gospel and the frankness with which they spoke.[23] They experienced a profound freedom to speak despite any difficulties that they might have encountered.

As a rhetorical term "having courage" belongs to the same semantic domain as "great opposition." While the term may evoke the notion of internal anxiety or that of physical suffering, the athletic metaphor suggests Paul's struggle on behalf of the gospel,[24] a struggle that was not without parallel with the struggle in which the Hellenistic moralists were engaged.[25]

Paul's Power

Paul certainly believed that God had scrutinized and approved the apostles for their mission of proclaiming the gospel (2:4). As clearly as Paul claims divine approval, he affirms that God had entrusted himself and his companions with the message and had empowered them to proclaim it (2:2). Paul had made a similar point earlier on in the letter when he wrote about the power of the gospel. In the reminiscence of his prayer of thanksgiving (1:2–10), Paul wrote: "our message came to you not in word only, but also in power and in the Holy Spirit and with full conviction" (1:5). He emphatically underscores the idea that, although the message had come from him and his companions, the power with which the message was proclaimed came from God.

Paul uses the rhetorical devices of *contradictio* ("not . . . but") and *repetitio* ("in power and in the Holy Spirit and with full conviction") to emphasize the point. Contradiction[26] and repetition[27] are devices that Paul often uses to get his point across. In the contrast[28] and redundancy we catch an echo of the oratorical style of Paul who proclaimed the gospel to the Thessalonians, but we cannot overlook the fact that Paul's written letter was intended to be read aloud to the Thessalonians (5:27).

There is some parallelism between 2:2b, "we had courage in our God to declare to you the gospel of God in spite of great opposition," and 1:5a, "our message of the gospel came to you not in word only, but also in power and in the Holy Spirit and with full conviction." In both instances Paul is writing about the proclamation of the gospel and in both case he makes use of a construction with *en* ("in") to describe the speaking out of the gospel by himself and his companions: "we had courage in our God to declare to you the gospel"; and "our message of the gospel came to you . . . *in* power and *in* the Holy Spirit and *with*[29] full conviction." Because Paul employs the rhetorical device of repetition for emphasis' sake, there is really no need to distinguish among the three terms in the latter expression.[30] Virtual synonymity is a characteristic feature of *repetitio.* Taken together, therefore, "power," "Holy Spirit," and "full conviction" generally describe the power inherent in Paul's proclamation of the gospel.

Each member of the triadic expression in 1:5a deserves, nonetheless, some brief commentary. Among New Testament authors, "power – *dynamis*" generally denotes a "mighty work," that is, a "miracle." Paul will use the term in this sense in his first letter to the Corinthians, where he cites the miracles that he has worked as an authenticating sign of his apostolate (1 Cor 12:12).[31] In 1 Thess 1:5, however, "power" is used in the singular and must be taken in its root sense, that is, precisely as "power."[32] Paul considers that the power of God, made manifest in the mighty works of his various emissaries, is at work in the proclamation of the gospel.[33] The proclamation of the gospel is a manifestation of God's power.

Occasionally Paul juxtaposes "power" and "spirit." He does so in the hendiadys of 1 Cor 2:4–5, where "the spirit and power" clearly means the "power of God."[34] He uses the phrase the "power of the spirit" (Rom 15:13 and 19) to speak about divine power. When Paul writes about the power of God active in his proclamation of the gospel in terms of the spirit, one must not think that he had a trinitarian understanding of God.[35] Paul was a first-century Christian who stood within the parameters of the Jewish biblical tradition. For him "the holy spirit" is another way of speaking about God's power. The power of God that was active in creation[36] was active in the proclamation of the gospel. Paul and his companions were inspired speakers who proclaimed the gospel of God.[37]

The third member of the triadic expression, "with full conviction," is somewhat difficult to interpret. The translation of *en plērophoria pollē* by "full conviction" appears in the NRSV and many modern English-language translations of the passage. The translation raises an immediate question. Who is fully convinced? Were Paul and his companions fully convinced of what they had to say or did they speak in such a way that their hearers were fully convinced? F. F. Bruce believes that it is the Thessalonians who were convinced,[38] but other commentators focus on the conviction of Paul and his companions.[39]

It is not at all certain, however, that *plērophoria* means "conviction." *Plērophoria* is a rare word. It does not occur in the extant classical literature, and appears just once in a papyrus text and four times elsewhere in the New Testament. Juxtaposed with "power" and the "holy spirit," *plērophoria* characterizes Paul's manner of preaching the gospel.[40] Béda Rigaux has suggested that the intensified (by the adjective *pollē*) expression implies superabundance.[41] It may well be that the sense of the expression is best captured by the New Jerusalem Bible's "full effect" or my own "full force."[42] According to Helmut Koester, the boldness with which Paul and his companions spoke (2:2), their joy and strength in adversity (1:6), were expressions of that "full force."

The idea that the merely human words of Paul and his companions must be distinguished from the power of God and that it is truly the power of God that is at work in the proclamation of the gospel, stated with such rhetorical verve in 1:5, is echoed in 2:13 as Paul again reminisces about his prayer of thanksgiving. He and his companions gave thanks to God: "for this, that when you received the word of God that you heard from us, you accepted it not as a human word but as what it really is, God's word, which is also at work in you believers." The thought of 2:13 recalls that of 1:5. That Paul expresses the conviction that the power of the gospel is God's power at work on more than one occasion and in different literary contexts only serves to show just how deeply it was that he held this conviction.[43]

In both instances, 1:5 and 2:13, there is a none too subtle interplay between "us" and "you," with a striking emphasis on "us": "*our* gospel" in 1:5; "heard from *us*" in 2:13. In both cases Paul has used the rhetorical device of contradiction to contrast the human words of himself and his companions with the power of God. In both cases the ultimate emphasis lies on what God has done. The perspective of 2:13 is, however, quite different from that of 1:5.

Hearing the Message

In 1:5 Paul recalls how the gospel of God came to the Thessalonians. The emphasis lies upon those who have proclaimed the gospel, and Paul highlights the fact that in their proclamation of the gospel the power of God was at work. In 2:13, the emphasis lies upon the reception of the gospel by the Thessalonians. It is a gospel that they have heard (*logon akouēs*), a gospel that they have heard from Paul and his companions (*par'hēmōn*).

The language of 2:13 is a bit complex and somewhat convoluted. It is almost as if Paul wants to say two things at once, namely, that the word that the Thessalonians have heard is a word that they have heard from Paul and his companions *and* that it is the word of God, which is energetically at work among the Thessalonian believers.[44] The result is that Paul has created a strange expression in which two genitival phrases[45] modify the single noun *logon* ("word"): "*logon akoēs par'hēmōn* – that you heard from us" (literally, "of the hearing from us") and "*tou theou* – of God." He has created a grammarian's nightmare, the run-on clause.

Paul's run-on clause results from the fact that he wants to hold in some sort of creative tension the three parties to the proclamation of the gospel: those who proclaim it, those who receive it, and God whose word it is. His social world can be described in terms of that triangular relationship that includes himself and his companions, God, and those among whom he works.

The Messengers

As far as those who proclaim it are concerned, Paul has characterized his activity in the Thessalonian workshop as proclaiming the gospel: "We proclaimed to you the gospel of God" (2:9). The turn of Paul's phrase brings together the "we," the "you," and "God" around a single focus, "the gospel." At this point Paul's jargon echoes the characteristic vocabulary of the early church, its kerygmatic language. In early Christian circles "*kēryssō* – to proclaim" was an in-word, jargon used to succinctly describe what the early missionaries were doing when they announced the gospel to those who were not yet Christian.[46] They were heralds of good news.

In 1 Thessalonians Paul resorts to this "technical language" with relative infrequency. For clarity's sake, he prefers the language of "speaking" (*laleō*) and "the word" (*logos*).[47] By the use of such terms he explains, for the benefit of the Thessalonians, what he meant by "proclaiming the gospel." He and his companions had spoken to the Thessalonians. By so doing, they had declared the gospel (*lalein to euaggelion*, 2:2).[48] Indeed, Paul seems to suggest that it was their mission in life to speak to Gentiles (2:16).[49] The essential function of those commissioned as apostles is to speak.[50]

Paul and his companions spoke as apostles of Christ. They spoke so as to please God (2:4); God was displeased when they were unable to speak (2:16). To please is, primarily, "to desire to please," "to live in order to please."[51] By their speaking, Paul and his companions sought to please God. That was their goal, as the purpose clause of 2:4 emphatically states: "we speak, not to please mortals, but to please God." With the help of rhetorical contradiction, the clause highlights the purpose of Paul and his fellow preachers. The following paragraph (2:5-8) offers an explanation of what Paul meant when he stated that he and his companions were not out to "please mortals."[52]

"We never came," Paul wrote, "with words of flattery" (2:5). Flattery was well known in Paul's world, where it was generally despised. Among orators it compared unfavorably with the frankness implied by *parrēsia*,[53] a quality that Paul had claimed for his own speech (2:2). That Paul did not intend to please his Thessalonian audience – and deliberately avoided words of flattery in any such pursuit – does not mean that the speakers' mien was inconsequential for the message that they were proclaiming.

Long before Marshall MacLuhan had written "the medium is the message,"[54] Paul had stated, "you know what kind of persons we proved to be among you for your sake" (1:5). Rather than miracles, it was the conduct of the preachers that authenticated their message. Their character was proof of the veracity of their words. Not only were they joyful in the face of adversity and bold when confronted by possible opposition,[55] they were also like children, and mothers, and fathers among the Thessalonians.[56] They toiled hard, so as not to burden any of the Thessalonians to whom they were speaking. Eschewing words of flattery, they strove to please God.

In his thank-filled reminiscence of his visit to Thessalonica, Paul said "you know what kind of persons we proved to be among you." In the autobiographical confession that follows, Paul wrote: "you are witnesses and God also how holy and righteous and blameless was our behavior towards you" (*hymeis martyres... hōs hosiōs kai dikaiōs kai amemptōs hymin egenēthēmen*, 2:10). A mild oath and the rhetorical device of repetition provide emphasis for what Paul says. Whereas Paul had previously distinguished what the Thessalonians could know from that to which only God could bear witness (2:5), he now calls upon the community of Thessalonians and God himself as witnesses to the kind of conduct that he and his companions exhibited among the Thessalonians: it was "pure, upright, and blameless."

Since virtual synonymity for emphasis' sake is the hallmark of *repetitio,* it is hardly necessary to distinguish among the adverbs[57] chosen by Paul to describe his behavior among the Thessalonians. The global impression is that the missionaries' conduct was beyond reproach in every respect. Some exegetes try, nonetheless, to capture the precise nuance in each term chosen by Paul in his emphatic affirmation of the exemplary lifestyle of himself and his companions.

"Pure" (*hosiōs*) is a term that is not otherwise found in Paul's extant writings. It is, however, found in the Greek Bible,[58] where it connotes an interior attitude that goes beyond mere external observance. It suggests a profound religious attitude that moves a pious person to adopt a way of life consistent with his or her piety.[59]

"Upright" (*dikaiōs,* from the root *dikai-,* elsewhere rendered as "righteous" or "just") is a Pauline term. At the time that Paul was writing to the Thessalonians, the term had not yet acquired the precise and characteristic Pauline nuance that it will affect as a result of the controversy with the "Judaizers," to which Romans and Galatians bear witness. The affirmation that the apostles' conduct was "upright" simply suggests that it was in conformity with correct standards of behavior.[60]

When one pays due respect to the quality of Paul's rhetoric, one ought not distinguish "pure" from "upright" as if the first suggested interior motivation and the second external behavior or the first faithful observance of the divine law and the second faithful obedience to human law. Not only has Paul used both terms in a single repetitive construction, he was also a Jew whose understanding of the human person, his anthropology, did not easily admit of adequate distinctions between internal motivation and external conduct.[61]

"Blameless" (*amemptōs*) is likewise a Pauline term – at least insofar as New Testament usage is concerned. Because Paul has used this term exclusively in his correspondence with the Thessalonians and the Philippians who supported his Thessalonian endeavors,[62] Rigaux has remarked that the term is reserved for the Macedonian churches.[63] Suggesting freedom from any fault with respect to a given norm, "blameless" reiterates the notion evoked by "upright," yet in a negative fashion.[64] Paul prayed that the Thessalonians would live like him, blamelessly. He sent Timothy as his delegate to ensure that they did so (3:2). As for himself, he could only say that he and his companions conducted themselves according to accepted standards of behavior; they were free from fault insofar as those standards were concerned.[65] In a word, or three, the conduct of Paul and his companions among the Thessalonian Christians was simply unimpeachable.

The personal integrity of Paul and his companions was evident in the manner in which they proclaimed the gospel, the preeminent forum in which they encountered the Thessalonians. That they spoke so as to please God, who scrutinized their very hearts, has its counterpart in the affirmation that their words did not spring "from deceit[66] or impure motives[67] or trickery" (2:3). The repetition provides a complement to the avowal of their desire to speak so as to please God (2:4).

The rhetoric of Paul's denial, using language taken from the catalogues of vices and the Hellenistic moralists,[68] shows that the personal integrity of himself and his companions extended to their very words. They were different from the charlatans and mountebanks known to the Thessalonians. Not only did Paul and his companions not speak so as to deceive, they also avoided self-serving and self-aggrandizing. Their speech was not a pretext for greed (2:5)[69]; neither did they seek praise from other human beings (2:6).

The integrity of the personal conduct of Paul and his companions with regard to – and on behalf of – the Thessalonians,[70] along with the quality of their speech, was the sign that authenticated their word. The "message of the gospel" (euaggelion)[71] was indeed a spoken "word" (logos),[72] but it was also an appeal (paraklēsis, 2:3). Their spoken word was not only an announcement of good news, it was also an exhortation. Indeed, Paul reminded the Thessalonians how he and his companions had urged (parakalountes) and encouraged and pleaded with the Thessalonians to lead a life worthy of God (2:10). The integrity of their personal conduct provided legitimating grounds for their exhortation. Theirs was an *ethos* appeal.

Ways of Speaking

We can return to the content of this appeal as we try to determine what it was that Paul and his companions said to the Thessalonians. For the moment, let us only note that Paul used a variety of verbs to describe the fashion in which he spoke to the Thessalonians: "to declare" or "speak" (laleō, 2:2, 4),[73] "to share the gospel" (metadidōmi to euaggelion, 2:8),[74] "to proclaim the gospel" (kēryssō to euaggelion, 2:9), "to urge" (parakaleō, 2:12),[75] "to encourage" (paramytheomai, 2:12),[76] "to plead" (martyromai, 2:12), "to tell beforehand" (prolegō, 3:4),[77] "to give instructions" (paraggelias didōmi, 4:2), "to tell beforehand" (proeipon, 4:6), "to direct" (paraggelleō, 4:11).[78]

One of the remarkable features of Paul's linguistic usage – apart, that is, from the variety of verbal expressions used to describe his proclamation of the gospel among the Thessalonians – is that all of these verbs are used in the plural, whether in the affirmative or participial form.[79] As he wrote to the Christians at Thessalonica, Paul was well aware that the proclamation of the gospel was an endeavor in which he and his companions were cooperatively engaged.

A Chain of Communication

Paul highlights the idea that "good news" had been proclaimed in oral fashion by stating emphatically that the Thessalonians had heard the message. What he and his companions had communicated was the word of God "that you heard from us" (akoēs par'hēmōn, 2:13). Paul's turn of phrase puts the hearing (akoē) of the word in the spotlight. This is the only time in the letter that Paul actually states that the Thessalonians heard what his group of travelers had to say.[80]

In the light of what he will later write to other congregations,[81] Paul's choice of vocabulary is rather significant. A comment by James D. G. Dunn is apropos. Dunn writes: "The reference to hearing is not simply a logical link in the chain between believing and preaching; it also reflects Paul's self-consciousness as a preacher, as one who thought in terms of communication by the spoken word and whose success depended on winning the sort of attentive hearing which so often resulted in commitment among his hearers. Paul was well aware of how critical that transaction was between speaker and hearer – when, mysteriously, not merely words are conveyed, but an understanding, a conviction, a life-changing commitment."[82]

In the letter to the Romans, Paul will take a reflective look at the importance of hearing the word when he writes:

> But how are they to call on one in whom they have not believed [episteusan]? And how are they to believe [pisteusōsin] in one of whom they have never heard [ēkousan]? And how are they to hear [akousōsin] without someone to proclaim [kēryssontos] him? And how are they to proclaim him [kēryxōsin] unless they are sent [apostalōsin]? As it is written, 'How beautiful are the feet of those who bring [euaggelizomenōn] good news!' But not all have obeyed the good news [tō euaggeliō]; for Isaiah says, 'Lord, who has believed [episteusen] our message [tē akoē hēmōn]?' So faith [pistis] comes from what is heard [ex akoēs], and what is heard [akoē] comes from the word of Christ. (Rom 10:14-18)

The key terms of this self-conscious reflection are all to be found in the autobiographical confession of 1 Thess 2:1-12. In the letter to the

Romans Paul's reflection on the gospel was prompted by the realization that the Jews had not accepted the gospel. He found a scriptural
warrant for the Jews' failure to receive it in a passage from the trito-
Isaiah, Isa 53:1, "Who has believed what we have heard?" Recourse
to Isaiah allowed Paul to further flesh out his reflection on the gospel
with a citation from Isa 52:7, "How beautiful upon the mountains are
the feet of the messenger who announces peace [*hōs euaggelizomenou akoēn eirēnēs*], who brings good news [*hōs euaggelizomenou
agatha*], who announces salvation."

The apologetic note is of primary concern in Romans. For our
purposes it is more important to note that Paul has constructed a
chain of being sent – proclaiming – hearing – believing – being
called (*apostellō – kēryssō/euaggelizesthai – akouō – pisteuō –
epikaleō*).[83] This is the chain of salvation.[84] The key link in the chain
is "hearing."[85] Those who have been sent have been duly authorized
and commissioned,[86] as Paul states in 1 Thess 2:1-12 (esp. vv. 4,
7). Preaching leads to belief, as Paul affirms in 1 Thess 2:13.[87] The
entire process has, moreover – at least so it seems from what Paul
has to say in his letter to Rome – eschatological significance.[88] The
moment was no less critical when Paul proclaimed the gospel to
the Thessalonians than it was when he wrote to the Romans. The
preaching of his message was characterized by an eschatological
urgency.

When Paul writes about the word "which you heard from us"
(2:13), he emphasizes that the word of God that he preached was
an oral proclamation. It was a proclamation that he and his companions were particularly qualified to make. The Thessalonians heard with
their own ears what the apostles had to say.[89] There is, however, more
to their having heard the gospel than the mere physical hearing of the
words spoken by Paul and his companions.

Paul reiterates the fact that they "accepted" (*dechesthai*, 1:6; 2:13)
the word.[90] The Thessalonians' acceptance suggests that they received
the message avidly.[91] Paul's choice of language is consistent with his
intimation of the warm welcome that he and his companions had
received from the Thessalonians (1:9). The verb ("*dechesthai* – receive") which Paul twice (1:6; 2:13) – and characteristically – uses
to describe the Thessalonians' reception of the gospel was typically
employed in the kerygmatic vocabulary of the early church to describe the hospitable reception of Christian missionaries, with the
implication that those who receive them are open to their message.[92]

The "acceptance" of the message by the Thessalonians implies that
they have become believers.[93] Paul is quick to affirm that it is through
the power of God that they became believers. God's word is "at work
in you believers" (2:13). Just as the power of God was at work among

those who proclaimed the gospel, God is operative among those who receive the message.[94]

They have become "believers." Paul uses this expression[95] almost as if "the believers" was the proper name for Christians. The term was destined to become a technical term in early Christianity. Paul himself would use the term in a way similar to that in which later generations would speak of "Christians." In Paul's Greek "the believers" is a present participle, suggesting that faith is not a one-time event but an ongoing way of life.[96] What belonging to a group of believers implies remains to be analyzed, but it most certainly implies that "the believers" at Thessalonica are in a situation similar to that of other Macedonian and Achaian believers (1:7). Indeed their situation is similar to that of Paul and his companions themselves (1:6; 4:14). Along with the missionaries they believed "that Jesus died and rose again" (4:14). Because of their reception of the word, the Thessalonian believers had become part of a community of faith.

While calling the Thessalonians "believers" allows Paul to write enthusiastically about their new situation, he adds a nuance by reminding the Thessalonians (and us) that they had truly "received" (*paralabontes*, 2:13) the word of God. They had received and accepted it.[97] "The reception of the word" implies as much about the way in which Paul proclaimed the gospel as it does about the way the Thessalonians received the message.[98]

Paul returns to the topic of what the Thessalonians received from him and his companions in 4:1, where it is clear that what the Thessalonians had received included some elements of the Jewish ethical tradition: "you learned from us how you ought to live and so please God." "*Parelabete* – you learned" seems to echo the Hebrew *qibbel,* a technical term used in rabbinic circles to connote the faithful reception of traditional material that had been passed along from a teacher to one of his disciples.[99]

In Paul's subsequent letters, Paul always uses the verb "*paralambanō* – to learn" to describe a faithful acceptance of what has been taught by another human being. There is an intimation of tradition in Paul's use of the word.[100] Thus, when Paul writes about the Thessalonians' receiving "the word of God that you heard from us," he is implying that they had received the word just as he had passed it along to them.

God is the third "party" in the proclamation of the gospel. Whether one considers things from the standpoint of those who proclaimed the message or from the standpoint of those who have received it seems to make little difference. God is always present in the process. He is present with his power. Paul and his companions have been scrutinized and commissioned by God (2:4). By God were they entrusted with the message (2:4). They declared the gospel[101] in order to please God (2:2). Under God's power, the message of the gospel came to the Thessalonians (1:5; 2:2) and was accepted by them (2:13). Although the Thessalonians heard the words of human beings (*logon tōn an-thrōpōn*, 2:13), they accepted them as the word of God. The words were those of Paul and his companions. The power inherent in those words was not that of the human messengers; it was God's (1:5).

Thus, although it is surprising that a second "thanksgiving period" appears in a single Hellenistic letter, it is not really so surprising that Paul and his companions gave thanks to God for the warm reception of the gospel by the Thessalonians. Nor is it surprising that Paul calls *his* message[102] "the gospel of God"[103] or "the word of God."[104] In a change of pace, Paul also speaks of "the word of the Lord" (1:8)[105] and "the gospel of Christ."[106] Do all these expressions have the same meaning?

God's Co-worker

This is a question that needs to be answered. Before attempting to do so, it might be good to look at a passage in 1 Thessalonians that should provoke some surprise. It is a passage that has perplexed many scribes throughout the ages and one that continues to puzzle interpreters to-day. The passage is one in which Paul describes Timothy, one of his fellow apostles, as "our brother and co-worker for God in proclaiming the gospel of Christ" (*ton adelphon hēmōn kai synergon tou theou en tō euaggeliō tou Christou*, 3:2).

The problem with this description of Timothy is that the Greek manuscript tradition offers eight different readings of Paul's words.[107] The problematic verse does not appear in any one of the three ancient papyrus manuscripts of 1 Thessalonians.[108] As a result evidence of the existence of the problem is relatively late. Nonetheless, the oldest extant majuscules offer different readings of Paul's text. These two witnesses, the fourth-century Codex Sinaiticus (ℵ) and the fourth-century Codex Vaticanus (B), are generally considered to be the best of the ancient witnesses to the Greek text of the New Testament.

The Sinaiticus reads 3:2 as *kai diakonon tou theou en tō euaggeliō tou Christou*, that is, "and God's servant in the gospel of Christ," while the Vaticanus (B) reads *kai synergon en tō euaggeliō tou Christou*, that is, "and co-worker in the gospel of Christ." A comparison of just these two witnesses reveals that the first major difference between the two readings is whether, having called Timothy "our brother" (*ton adelphon hēmōn*) — thus defining Timothy's relationship with Paul and Silvanus, and presumably with the Thessalonians as well[109] — Paul calls Timothy a "co-worker — *synergos*" or a "servant — *diakonos*." The second significant difference between the two readings has to do with whether the qualifying expression "of God – *tou theou*" is present in that definition or not. If "of God" was present in Paul's text, he would be continuing to reflect the same triangular model of structuring social relationships as we have hitherto seen him do.

Text critics are of the opinion that "co-worker for God – *synergon tou theou*"[110] offers the strongest claim among the various readings. This reading seems to lie at the origin of all the others. If accepted, as it should be, this reading makes a bold claim in Timothy's regard, a claim that was apparently so bold as to be found objectionable by many of the ancient copyists.

Many of these scribes – a notable exception was the copyist who transcribed the sixth-century Codex Claromontanus (D)[111] – modified the text so as to portray Timothy as someone with a more modest role. He was either "Paul's brother and co-worker,"[112] or "Paul's brother and God's servant" in proclaiming the gospel of Christ." Either of these descriptions would have been fine. They would have startled no one, but Paul's "our brother and God's co-worker" was just a bit too much. Hence, the scribal corrections of the text.[113]

Many of the scribal corrections are reflected in various English-language translations of 1 Thessalonians. The KJV has "our brother, and minister of God, and our fellow labourer" and the RSV has "our brother and God's servant."[114] Among the newer versions, the New Translation has a unique rendering of the problematic phrase. In the form of an independent sentence, the translation states: "He is God's servant in the work of the good news about Christ."

In the light of our analysis of Paul's presentation of three parties to the proclamation of the gospel, there is no real difficulty in accepting the judgment of modern text critics and rendering the phrase, as does the NRSV, "our brother and co-worker for God in proclaiming the gospel of Christ."[115] Timothy is one of the band of three that have been scrutinized by God and commissioned to proclaim the gospel. He was one of those in whom God's power was at work when the word of God was brought to the Thessalonians. He was one through whom God worked, one who was God's co-worker.

The Gospel of God

What was the "gospel of Christ" whose proclamation made Timothy God's co-worker? What was the "gospel" entrusted to Paul and his companions? What was the "gospel of God" that they proclaimed as they worked at the leatherworker's trade? That it was "good news" is implied by the very etymology of the word *euaggelion* – gospel.[116]

It was obviously good news from God (*euaggelion tou theou*) for

God had entrusted the good news to Paul and his companions (2:4). It was also good news about God, God-talk,[117] for Paul's gospel was the gospel of God. It told of who God was, what he had done, what he was doing, and what he was going to do. Paul and his companions had been sent by the Anointed One (2:7). He had some good news to announce about the Anointed One, for his was the gospel of Christ (3:2). His word was from the Lord and about the Lord.[118]

Is it possible to be more specific and identify the contents of this good news? Thomas Söding has summed up its basic elements under the rubrics of (1) its future-eschatological perspective; (2) the gospel of God; (3) the gospel of Christ; (4) soteriology; and (5) the universality of the gospel and the call of the Gentiles.[119]

What, in fact, is the content of the message that had come from God? What was Paul's message? What was it that he and his companions said to the Thessalonians? What did they actually teach them? We are fortunate that Paul's letter gives a good number of indications about what Paul and his companions said to the Thessalonians. Sometimes he explicitly recalls what he said to them (2:11–12; 3:4; 4:6); at other times the tenor of his language provides significant clues.

The Resurrection of Jesus

Those who received the apostles' word were believers (2:13). When Paul wrote his response to the problem that was troubling the Thessalonians, apparently addressing himself to something that was lacking in their faith (3:10), he said: "we believe that Jesus died and rose again" (*Iēsous apethanen kai anestē,* 4:10). The introductory formula, "we believe – *pisteuomen,*" shows that this short creed was an expression of the common faith of Paul and the Thessalonians. The first-person plural reaches out to express a common bond between Paul and his companions, on the one hand, and the believing Thessalonians, on the other.

Paul offers this succinct formulation of their common faith as a premise for his argumentation[120] and support for his plea that the Thessalonians should not grieve as people without hope. Paul appeals to the faith assent that they had given to Jesus' resurrection in order to convince them that they should not grieve. In addition, Paul uses this expression of faith as a point of departure for his future reflection as he attempts to come directly to grips with the problem that was troubling the believers at Thessalonica. The credal formula serves as a premise for a kind of logical appeal. Basing himself on the common credo, Paul argues that, "through Jesus, God will bring with him those who have fallen asleep."

Paul's manner of speaking clearly suggests that it is God who raised

Jesus from the dead. In similar fashion,[121] he says, God will bring with Jesus those who have died. While the future resurrection of the dead, which Paul apparently believed would take place during his own lifetime,[122] is part of the supplementary instruction that Paul is sending to the Thessalonians in this letter, the fact that Jesus had died and that God had raised him from the dead was part of the faith shared by the apostles and the Thessalonians.

That Jesus had died and had been raised was the very heart of the good news that the traveling missionaries had announced to the Thessalonians. Before Paul wrote to the Thessalonians he had received a report from people in Macedonia and Achaia that the Thessalonians were waiting for the Son of God, Jesus whom God had raised from the dead (1:10). In the opinion of D. E. H. Whiteley, this is "one of the most important verses in the New Testament. It was written some twenty years after the Resurrection and it expresses in a few words much of the essence of Christianity."[123]

The report closely linked the apostles' visit with the conversion of the Thessalonians and their expectation that Jesus who had been raised from the dead as God's Son would rescue them from the wrath to come: "The people of those regions report about us what kind of welcome we had among you, and how you turned to God from idols, to serve a living and true God, and to wait for his Son from heaven, whom he raised from the dead – Jesus, who rescues us from the wrath that is coming" (1:9-10).

Paul uses this report to illustrate what he had just said, namely, that everyone was talking about the faith of the Thessalonians. The modern reader of 1 Thessalonians recognizes more than a little enthusiasm in Paul's words, as he wrote: "the word of the Lord has sounded forth from you not only in Macedonia and Achaia, but in every place [*en panti topō*] your faith in God has become known, so that we have no need to speak about it" (1:8). Paul's graphic preterition not only emphasizes the faith of the Thessalonians, as a kind of *captatio benevolentiae* for their benefit, but also tells us that the faith of the Thessalonian Christians was well known by the Christians living in Macedonia and Achaia.

The Situation

Verses 9 and 10, with their introductory "*gar* – for," explain the apostles' enthusiasm. They clarify the reasons why people were talking about the faith of the Thessalonians and why the apostles were so enthusiastic. The clarification focuses on the conversion, service, and expectation of the Thessalonians. These three elements flesh out what Paul had succinctly described as "your faith in God" (1:8). The expression is loaded. One cannot help but notice that, although the English-language translation of the words contains not a single definite article, the article is used three times (*hē, hē, ton*) in Paul's Greek phrase (*hē pistis hymōn hē pros ton theon*). It is, once again,[124] almost as if Paul wants to say two things at once, namely, that he was writing about their faith and that this faith was in God. That faith "in God" was "theirs" is really surprising, for they had been idol-worshiping Gentiles. Their faith in God entailed, as Paul would shortly explain, their turning away from those idols.

In Greek, an "idol" (*eidōlon*) meant simply "an image." The "image" could be a graphic representation or the product of one's thought. Of itself, the term evoked no negative connotation. Among Hellenistic Jews, however, the term *"eidōlon* – idol" had acquired a precise nuance, one with negative connotations. These Greek-speaking Jews used the term "idol" to refer to representations of gods, which were in fact non-gods,[125] representations prohibited by the decalogue itself.[126]

Idols abounded in a Hellenistic town like Thessalonica. The head of Zeus figured prominently on the city's coinage at the time of the apostles' visit.[127] Another series of coins featured the head of Janus laureate on one side of the coin and the twins Castor and Pollux on the other, perhaps in respect of the Cabiros cult celebrated in Thessalonica at the time.[128] Still other coins offered a representation of the goddess Nike[129] and Julius Caesar *Theos*.[130] A statue represented a divinized Augustus.[131] Sometime previously (ca. 143 B.C.E.), a statue had been dedicated to Zeus Olympus. A modern trove contains an inscription (39–38 B.C.E.), with a dedication "to Osiris and all the other gods and goddesses in the precinct."[132]

Syncretism was the religious hallmark of first-century Thessalonica. In addition to the civic cult, the cults of the Egyptian gods, particularly Isis[133] and Serapis, were celebrated in Thessalonica, as was the cult of Dionysius.[134] The poet Antipater had written often about Zeus, the most important of the gods, and the offspring of Zeus. That native of Thessalonica had something to say about the images of Athena, Aphrodite, Alcides, and Ares painted on the ceiling of the Roman home of Gaius Julius Caesar, the adopted son of Augustus.[135] More than a century after the apostles' visit, the perduring religious syncretism of Thessalonica, likely involving the Cabiros, Osiris, and the local *neoi* and *epheboi*, received remarkable expression in the apotheosis of Fulvus, the four-year-old son of Marcus Aurelius, who died in 165 C.E.[136]

In the middle of a city whose religious life was characterized by such diversity and syncretism, where religious celebration and civic cult were inextricably intertwined, Paul and his companions declared the *euaggelion tou theou,* God's good news. Throughout his letter Paul writes of "God" in the singular. All thirty-six instances of his use of the word *theos* are in the singular.[137] It would appear, then, that the God of whom he and his companions spoke when they proclaimed the gospel to the Thessalonians was unique. Turning to God entailed a turning away from idols, who were non-gods. The service of the living God and the service of idols were incompatible with one another.[138] To serve the living and true God is to turn radically and completely away from the cult of the various local deities.[139] The turning from and to,[140] about which Paul writes in 1:9, is a transparent metaphor for a religious conversion. The symbol suggests a real change from one directional orientation to another. It implies a reordering of one's life and a new vision of life.

In Paul's view, humanity was neatly divided into two camps: "those who knew God" and those who did not.[141] He and his companions clearly counted themselves among those who knew God. Hence they could talk about "our God," particularly when they were evoking their experience of God, as they did in 2:2 and 3:9. The experience of God would seem to be implicit in the idea of "knowing God." To know God was not simply to know about God; it was somehow to have experienced God. The Thessalonians had experienced God's love, of which their election was a very real manifestation (1:4). In any event, the God about whom Paul spoke was a God whom he and his companions had experienced. They had experienced the power of God in the very proclamation of the good news. Having spoken about God, they saw the Thessalonians turn from their idols and turn toward God. They left the camp of those who did not know God to join the camp of those who did. News of this turn of events was spreading throughout Macedonia and Achaia – indeed in every place thereof, as Paul enthusiastically proclaims in 1:8 – along with the news of the welcome that Paul had received among the Thessalonians. The conversion of the Thessalonians was a source of joy for Paul and his companions, the joy that one experiences in the presence of God (2:19–20).

The Living and True God

The God to whom the Thessalonians turned was a God who was "living and true." Paul's description of God in these terms vividly contrasts the God whom the Thessalonians had come to know through his preaching from the statues of inert deities that graced their city and the figures of lifeless gods that adorned their coins. The God of Paul and the Thessalonians was a God who was "alive." The descriptive epithet identifies God by means of his original trait.[142] It distinguishes him from all other beings and most especially from the static representations of gods with whom the Thessalonians were so familiar. This kind of language was employed in the Jewish missionary sermon,[143] but it seems to have had particular rhetorical effect on the Thessalonians since it led them to change their basic allegiance and fundamental lifestyle.

The contrast implied by Paul's choice of the word "living" to describe God is further drawn out as Paul identifies the God to whom the Thessalonians have turned as a God who is "true." The implication is that the idols from whom they turned are false,[144] but Paul has no need to spell out that implication in a letter whose primary purpose seems to be one of encouragement. By its very nature, however, a letter presupposes more than it actually expresses.[145] Since Paul does not further exploit God's truth – it does not contribute to his argumentation in 1 Thessalonians![146] – and since it is found in a passage in which Paul is reminiscing on what he has heard about the Thessalonians' faith, one can only infer that Paul had spoken to the Thessalonians about God in such a way that they knew what he meant when he called the living God a true God. The truth of God is a presupposition of Paul's letter and harks back to his earlier discourse with the Thessalonians.

The manner in which Paul describes the living God suggests yet another contrast, that between the living God and those who have died. That such a connotation belongs to the Pauline description of God as a living God is obvious from the way in which Paul develops his thought in 1:9-10. Within the context of an enthusiastic thanksgiving report, Paul identifies the Thessalonians who have turned to the living and true God as a group of people who are waiting for the Son of God whom God has raised from the dead. Paul's words identify the living God as one who has raised Jesus from among those who have died. That the resurrection of Jesus, as an act of the living God, was a focal point of Paul's proclamation to the Thessalonians is again suggested later in the letter when Paul appeals to the Thessalonians' belief that Jesus has been raised as a major premise in his plea that they should not lose hope just because some members of their community had died (4:13-18).[147] In retrospect, his description of God as "living and true" prepares the way for his response to the problem that was troubling the Thessalonians, who were beloved by Paul and by God.

The name of the one whom God had raised from the dead was Jesus. This is the theophoric name of a human being who had lived in Palestine at an earlier point in time, but Paul does not indicate in his letter to the Thessalonians that he had told the Thessalonians much about this Jesus except the fact that he had died and been raised from the dead. The death of Jesus is explicitly attested in 4:14 and 5:9, but it is fully suggested by the affirmation that God had raised Jesus from among the dead.[148]

That Jesus is affirmed to have been among the dead implies that his human life had run its full course. That "the dead" is in the plural suggests that, having lived a complete span of life, Jesus is in solidarity with other human beings whose lives have ended in death. The Jesus about whom Paul spoke to the Thessalonians did not die a natural death. Rather, he was killed by "the Jews" (2:14-15). Paul's letter does not, however, indicate that Paul specifically spoke about the crucifixion of Jesus nor that imperial authorities were in collusion with "the Jews" when Jesus was put to death. Indeed the tenor of Paul's correspondence is such that it is not altogether certain that Paul had spoken with the Thessalonians about the Jews' responsibility for the death of Jesus.[149]

God's Son

Paul calls the one whom God had raised from the dead "the Son of God" ("his Son – *ton huion autou*") in 1:10. It was the Son of God for whom the converted Thessalonian Christians were now waiting.[150] They were an expectant group. Their future expectation of the Son of God indicates that their turning to the living and true God implied a shift in what Paul Ricoeur would call their monumental time. Their vision of time had changed because they were now waiting for the Son of God from heaven.

The vocabulary that Paul uses to describe the situation of the Thessalonians in 1:9-10 is rather unusual for him. His turn of phrase is different from the typical expressions that a modern reader recognizes in the later and longer letters. It is even different from the language that runs throughout the rest of the present letter. In this regard, Béda Rigaux writes about the pre-Pauline and archaic character of the vocabulary in 1:9-10.[151] The quality of Paul's language reflects Paul's personal interaction with early Christian preaching. Since, however, the language is atypical of Paul, it must reflect the kind of language with which Paul and his companions had spoken to the Thessalonians. Otherwise, his message would have bordered on the incomprehensible.

God's Kingdom

Another unusual turn of phrase in Paul's letter is his reference to the kingdom of God in 2:12. There, as he was bringing his reflection on the visit to the Thessalonians to a close, Paul wrote about God "who calls you into his own kingdom and glory." Paul does not often write about the kingdom of God (*hē basilea tou theou*). The expression appears five times in the relatively long first letter to the Corinthians (4:20; 6:9, 10; 15:24, 50), just once in the letter to the Romans (14:17) and the letter to the Galatians (5:21), and in no other place of Paul's extant writings except for 1 Thess 2:12.[152]

The expression was an intrusion into the thought patterns of Hellenized Christians, as were the Thessalonians. In the Greek that they spoke the meaning of the term "*basileia* – kingdom" alternated between a functional sense, royal dignity, and a geopolitical sense, a territory ruled by a king.[153] First-century Macedonians would not have spoken about a kingdom of a god, let alone the kingdom of God. The expression "kingdom of God" is a Semitism.[154] It might well symbolize the coherent center of Paul's own thought.[155] The expression would, however, have been so much nonsense in Paul's letter had he previously spoken to the Thessalonians about the kingdom of God.

The expression that Paul uses in 2:12 is, in fact, a hendiadys, "his own kingdom and glory." The pair of nouns suggests that God reigns as a glorious king. Within Judaism the notion of the glorious reign of God is an apocalyptic concept. It bespeaks the dramatic revelation of God as king, a manifestation that will bring the present order of things to closure. For Hellenists like those to whom Paul wrote his letter to the Thessalonians, this was a brave new world, and the concept was one that would have been unthinkable had Paul and his companions not spoken to them about it.[156]

Having proclaimed the kingdom to the Thessalonians, Paul could write to them about their expectation of Jesus as God's "Son." Within the range of Paul's extant letters, this too is unusual language. "*Christos* – Christ" and "*Kyrios* – Lord" are Paul's favorite christological expressions.[157] The identification of Jesus as "*Huios* – Son" correlates with another title used by Paul, namely, that of "Father," an epithet that Paul attributes to God in 1:1, 3 and 3:11, 13. That the Thessalonians were expecting Jesus in his capacity as Son implies that it was as Son that Jesus was raised from the dead. It also implies that the paternity of God was revealed in the resurrection. These elements were part and parcel of Paul's proclamation to the Thessalonians. Indeed the expectation of the imminent presence of Jesus as Lord was, arguably, the core of Paul's proclamation of the gospel.[158]

God's Wrath

The Son of God was expected by the Thessalonian Christians as one who would deliver them from the wrath that is coming. The age in which the Thessalonians were living was an age that existed under the threat of divine wrath. God's wrath is an expression of the negative side of God. It is an eschatological notion that forms, as it were, the obverse side of the coming of God as king. The Thessalonians to whom Paul wrote were not only awaiting the kingdom of God, to which they were called, but they were also expecting the arrival of Jesus, God's Son, as the one who was to deliver them from the wrath to come.

Impending Reality

The Thessalonian Christians existed in a state of expectation of Jesus' arrival as Son. The tone of Paul's language is such that we are led to believe that the Thessalonian Christians expected that God's wrath would soon be manifest and that Jesus-Son would appear as deliverer in the proximate future. To appropriate the language of later theology, the Thessalonians expected an imminent parousia.

Their present and future deliverance was a factor that affected the quality of their lives. They were an expectant group. They awaited Jesus as Son and deliverer and they expected that the awaited one would soon appear. In 4:17 Paul intimates that he and the Thessalonians could expect the parousia during their lifetimes.[159] Undoubtedly it was the fact that some of their number had died before the awaited event, which contributed to the situation that prompted Paul to write this letter and to write it as he did. More needs to be said about this at a later moment in this study, but it is apparent from 1:10 that the Thessalonians were an expectant people. They lived in expectation of God's wrath and their deliverance from it. Paul had, in other words, introduced them to a *weltanschauung* that had not previously been theirs.

That God-Father raised Jesus-Son from the dead is one aspect of the dynamic activity of God implicit in the Pauline proclamation of God as the living God. That God had scrutinized the hearts of Paul and his companions and entrusted the message to them is yet another expression of God's active vitality. There are still other manifestations of this vitality, some of which directly affected the Thessalonians themselves. God's vital power was at work in Paul's proclamation of the gospel to them. Through the coming of the gospel God chose the Thessalonians to be among his own people.

The idea of election, of people like the Thessalonians being classed among the chosen, is fraught with implications for a Jew like Paul. Election and ethnicity are no longer coterminous. If God, through the activity of Paul and his companions, in which his own power was at work, chose the Thessalonians, the God of whom Paul writes is neither inactive nor a figure from the past. He was a living God who had a way to choose the Thessalonians as his own and has effectively done so.

That God chose the Thessalonians is closely related to his love for them. Israel's deuteronomic history shows the close link between the election and God's love for his people. The use of the perfect tense in 1:4, when Paul describes the Thessalonians as "beloved" by God, indicates that God has loved the Thessalonians in the past and that he continues to love them in the present time of Paul's writing to them.[160] In Paul's biblical tradition the love of God is closely related to the election of the chosen people and the covenant that God has made with them.

Moral Exhortation

If Paul's letter does not explicitly affirm that Paul had spoken to the Thessalonians about God being a God who "called" them, it is nonetheless quite likely that Paul did speak to them about the God who had called and was calling them. Along with "living" (1:9) and "giving" the Holy Spirit (4:8), "calling" (2:12; 5:24) is one of three present participles used by Paul to characterize the God who is true.[161] The similarity of grammatical form leads one to believe that Paul, who had spoken to the Thessalonians about the living God, likewise spoke to them about the calling God. This is all the more likely when we consider that in 2:12, Paul writes about the God who calls the Thessalonians into "his own kingdom and glory," the topical focus of Paul's proclamation of the gospel.

God's call is a specification of the Thessalonians' election by God.[162] It suggests an ethical dimension and points to the way of life to be followed by those whom God has chosen. It implies a new relationship with the God who calls them.[163] For God to call the Thessalonians is for him to lay claim to the service of those whom he has chosen. And those to whom Paul is writing have indeed changed their lives in response to Paul's proclamation in such a way that they could be recognized as those who serve[164] the living and true God (1:9).

What God calls the Thessalonians to is "to lead a life worthy" of himself.[165] Their comportment is to be in keeping with their acknowledgment of the God whom they recognize as living and true. Having been called implies that they are to live in a manner that befits those who have been chosen by God. While God's call is different from his election, God's calling the Thessalonians to lead a life worthy of himself is a consequence of his having chosen them. It is, in fact, a covenantal motif. Since Paul had urged and encouraged and pleaded with the Thessalonians to lead a life worthy of God while he was with them (2:12), it is quite likely that the Thessalonians were aware that God had *called* them to lead precisely this kind of life.

From this final remark in Paul's autobiographical confession one should conclude that Paul had exhorted the Thessalonians to live as God's own people. The inference is substantiated later in the letter when Paul introduces his first moral exhortation (4:1-12) with this reminder: "Finally, brothers and sisters, we ask and urge you in the Lord Jesus that, as you learned from us how you ought to live and please God (as, in fact, you are doing), you should do so more and more. For you know what instructions we gave you through the Lord Jesus" (4:1-2).

The passage is striking because of its use of the language of tradition.[166] Paul employs the verb *"paralambanō* – learn," corresponding to the Hebrew *qibbel,* "receive," even though he does not use the correlative verb *"paradidōmi* – proclaim,"[167] corresponding to the Hebrew *masar,* "give," in this particular context. Paul's reminder harks back to 2:12, where Paul, reflecting on his own experience, recalls that he had urged (*parakalountes*) the Thessalonians to lead a life (*peripatein*) worthy of God (*axiōs tou theou*). Now, he asks and urges (*parakaloumen*) the Thessalonians to live (*peripatein*) so as to please God (*areskein theō*).

Paul takes care to remind his listeners that he had already taught them how to live, and he commends them because they had responded positively to his exhortation. So, in 4:1-2, he simply encourages the Thessalonians to continue to respond as they have previously done. What are they responding to? "Instructions" that Paul had already given them. The expressions *"parelabete* – learned" and *"edōkamen* – gave," both of which are in the aorist indicative, indicate a specific event in past time. That time was the time of Paul's having instructed those whom he had evangelized.

In other words, moral exhortation accompanied Paul's proclamation of the gospel. He spoke about God reigning as king, he spoke about God having loved and chosen the Thessalonians, but he also spoke about what it meant for them to be God's people. Paul's exhortation can be appropriately summed up under the rubric of God's call. The purpose of God's call, his will, is that the Thessalonians live as those who truly belong to him.

Paul describes this way of a life as "serving a living and true God" (1:9), "a life worthy of God" (2:12), and "living so as to please God" (4:2). In 4:3 he states succinctly: "This is the will of God: your sanctification." Sanctification, writes Horst Balz, "refers to the total orientation to God which includes being totally claimed by God."[168] Paul's theological terminology sums up in a single word what God's call has meant for the Thessalonians. It is a matter of their belonging totally to God and manifesting such belonging in their conduct, in short, their sanctification.

Sanctification

Sanctification or holiness is the unifying theme of the paraenetic unit contained in 4:3-8.[169] It is not only that sanctification is announced as the theme of the pericope in verse 3. The *hagia-* root ("holy") appears repeatedly in the pericope. Moreover, the triple emphasis on God, you, and sanctification functions in such a fashion as to hold the topos together as a single unit. The three key terms of 4:3a, "this is the will of God [*tou theou*], your [*hymōn*] sanctification [*hagiasmos*]," correspond to three similar terms in 4:8, "God [*ton theon*], who also gives his Holy [*to hagion*] Spirit to you [*eis hymas*]." By means of the *inclusio* the pericope is set off as an easily identifiable unit of material.

Since Paul introduces the unit with a repeated reference to the instructions that he had given to the Thessalonians (4:1, 2) and since he will recall the sanction about which he had already told the Thessalonians (4:6), there can be little doubt that at least the substance of the exhortation had previously been imparted to the Thessalonians. The comprehensive demonstrative of 4:6b, "the Lord is an avenger in all these things [*peri pantōn toutōn*], just as we have already told you and solemnly warned you," is an indication that Paul had already spoken about the things that he is now touching upon in his letter.

Instructions

That Paul is able to write about the instructions (*tinas paraggelias*) "which we gave you through the Lord Jesus" indicates that the earlier oral paraenesis had the force of a command.[170] "*Paraggelia* – instruction" is cognate with the verb "*paraggelō* – direct," which appears in 4:11.[171] By means of this catchword the two principal subsections of Paul's paraenesis (4:1-12) are linked together. The connotation of both noun and verb is that of the command. As a result of his preaching, Paul's authority had been recognized. His exhortation was then considered to be something more than merely sage advice.

The directives that Paul had previously given (4:2) bore upon what it would mean for the Thessalonians to live as God's own people. Earlier in his letter Paul had succinctly reminded the Thessalonians of the burden of his oral exhortation: "urging and encouraging you and pleading that you lead a life worthy of God [*eis to peripatein hymas axiōs*[172] *tou theou*], who calls you into his own kingdom and glory" (2:12). The purpose of Paul's exhortation was that the Thessalonians lead a life worthy of God. What that implied is recalled in 4:1-12, as Paul reminds the Thessalonians that he and his companions had taught them how "to live and please God" (*peripatein kai areskein theō*).

For Paul, pleasing God is a matter of having a proper attitude toward life.[173] Pleasing God is a matter of being discriminating in one's life. Pleasing God is a matter of options, making choices. At the conclusion of the paraenetic unit in 4:3–8 Paul writes, "whoever rejects this rejects not human authority but God" (4:8). One can serve God or not. One can live so as to please God or not. One can reject God; one does so by not living according to the instructions that Paul had given.

The purpose of Paul's exhortation to the Thessalonians was that they lead a life (*peripatein,* literally "to walk") that was worthy of God and appropriate to their calling, that would please God and would show that they did not disregard God. He exhorted them to live as God's own people, his holy ones. Their way of life was to be in accordance with their calling because they, the Thessalonians to whom Paul was writing, had enjoyed an experience of God. Their experience was different from that of the Gentiles who had not known God (4:5). God had called them to live a life worthy of himself: he had called them in holiness (4:7).

God's Call

God had called the Thessalonians to live as his people. For the Thessalonians, God's call was not merely a memory of the past. Even as Paul wrote, God was calling the Thessalonians to live as his people. Twice Paul uses the present participle "calling – *kalōn*" as a descriptive epithet for God – once in his reminder of the paraenetic element of his proclamation (2:12), once again toward the end of his letter when he writes "The one who calls you is faithful, and he will do it" (5:24).[174] The God who has called the Thessalonians and continues to call them is not a God who has abandoned them to their own power. God's fidelity involves his providing for those whom he has chosen.

What this means comes to still fuller expression in 4:8, where, immediately after having written about the call of God in holiness (4:7), Paul writes about God "who also gives his Holy Spirit to you." The "also" (*kai*) is emphatic,[175] perhaps even epexegetical.[176] The living God whom Paul has made known to the Thessalonians is one who is constantly giving his Spirit. The giving of the Spirit is a manifestation of divine vitality. The Spirit that God is giving to the Thessalonians is the Holy Spirit. The structure of Paul's phraseology is such as to emphasize that the Spirit that is given is the *holy* Spirit *for the Thessalonians.*[177] They are called in holiness and continue to be given the Holy Spirit, the enabling gift of God that empowers them to live as God's own people. Whoever rejects the call and the gift of God rejects God himself.

That God plays an active role in the sanctification of the Thessalonians comes to further expression in Paul's wish prayers, "And may he so strengthen your hearts in holiness that you may be blameless before our God and Father at the coming of our Lord Jesus with all his saints" (3:13) and "May the God of peace himself sanctify you entirely; and may your spirit and soul and body be kept sound and blameless at the coming of our Lord Jesus Christ" (5:23).[178] These wish prayers show that God is the power behind the Thessalonians' ability to live in a way that is fitting for God's people. The horizon of Paul's prayer is the eschatological future. He prays that God be active in assuring the holiness (*en hagiasmō*, 2:13; *hagiasthai*, 5:23) and blamelessness (*amemptous*, 3:13; *amemptōs*, 5:23) of the Thessalonians until that future.

This reading of some of the paraenetic motifs recalled by Paul in his letter to the Thessalonians unpacks, somewhat, Paul's terse description of the God whom he had proclaimed to the Thessalonians as a "living and true God." God's vitality was manifest not only in his entrusting of the message of the gospel to Paul and his companions (2:4), but also in his activity on behalf of the Thessalonians. The God whom Paul had proclaimed was a God who had called and was calling the Thessalonians to live in a manner worthy of himself. God was also a God who gave his sanctifying Spirit to the Thessalonians. By so enabling the Thessalonians to respond to the call to lead a life in holiness God manifests that he is indeed a faithful God, a God who is true.[179] God's fidelity is as dynamic as is his vitality.

Taught by God

In 4:9, in the introduction to his topos on the bonds of familial love that ought to bind the Thessalonian Christians to one another, Paul writes that they are those who have been "taught by God" to love one another. The Thessalonians are "God-taught." The expression sounds strange to contemporary ears, but it was no less strange to the ears of Paul's Thessalonian hearers. The expression "*theodidaktoi* – God-taught*,*" does not appear in any other Hellenistic writing known to us. The term is apparently of Paul's own coinage, built on the analogy of the Homeric and Hellenistic expression "*autodidaktos –* self-taught."[180]

The new word was deliberately provocative. Some scholars are of the opinion that Paul coined the term to serve as a corrective to the self-reliance urged by Epicureans.[181] Calvin Roetzel[182] claims, however, that. Paul's neologism made explicit what was implicit in the term "*autodidaktos* – self-taught," as it was used in Hellenistic Jewish circles. Philo of Alexandria, for instance, used "*autodidaktos –* self-taught" to describe people who have received wisdom and knowledge from God, presumably without the benefit of human teachers. With his new term, Paul has reworked the Jewish notion of "self-taught" in such a way as to emphasize the social responsibilities of the "God-taught" and to restore a future dimension to the eschatological perspective of the Thessalonians.

What the Thessalonians have been taught by God is to "love one another," that is, to love the brothers and sisters. The introduction of kinship language into the pair of exhortatory verses found in 4:10-11 is striking. Paul has clearly identified *"philadelphia* – love of the brothers and sisters"[183] as the topic under discussion: "Now concerning love of the brothers and sisters." He then reminds the Thessalonians that they have been God-taught in that regard. So there is no need to write. The *preteritio* only serves to emphasize the importance of the topic. He commends them because they already love the brothers and sisters throughout Macedonia. Having appealed to their goodwill by his pastoral commendation, Paul urges them to continue in their sibling love, and to do so more and more.[184] He appeals to them as *"adelphoi* – brothers and sisters," using language that is both striking and typical.[185]

Closely associated with the admonition to love one another is the exhortation "to aspire to live quietly, to mind your own affairs, and to work with your own hands...so that you may behave properly towards outsiders and be dependent on no one" (4:11-12). Since Paul interrupts his exhortation with the parenthetical *"kathōs hymin pareggeilamen* – just as we directed you," it would seem that the substance of this exhortation was part and parcel of the exhortation that Paul and his companions had addressed to the Thessalonians while they were in Thessalonica. The verb *"pareggeilamen* – directed," which Paul has chosen to punctuate his exhortation, is forceful. Indicating a real command, not otherwise used in Paul's letter,[186] it evokes the force and authority of Paul's moral exhortation.

In sharp contrast with this reminder of how authoritatively and forcefully he had addressed the Thessalonians, Paul's epistolary reminder adopts another tone: "we urge you, brothers and sisters"[187] (4:10). The choice of the verb *"parakaleō* – urge" demonstrates tact and sensitivity, all the while suggesting that the ultimate authority on the basis of which the exhortation is being made is an authority other than the personal authority of the sender of the letter.[188] It would seem that the implied authority is that of "God the Father," since the Thessalonians are, in Paul's words, really "God-taught."

Kinship language pervades the exhortatory unit in 4:9-12. The bonds of kinship that link the Thessalonians to one another, and to all believers, set them apart from others. There are insiders and outsiders *(tous exō,* 4:12). Those bound by ties of kinship are clearly insiders, while the outsiders are those who are not so bound. From this perspective, the paraenesis of 4:9-12 is really an exhortation on socialization within the kinship community. In some respects it parallels the immediately preceding exhortation, 3:3-8, which is likewise concerned with the issue of what it means to be a member of the kinship community.

Before proceeding to further analysis of that exhortation, it might prove useful to reflect on the singularity of the expressions "*hēgapē-menoi hypo tou theou* – beloved by God" in 1:4 and "*theodidaktoi* – God-taught" in 4:9. Each of these expressions occurs but once in Paul's first letter; each of them is unique in the extant Pauline corpus. Each of them highlights a singular aspect of the relationship that exists between the God whom Paul had preached and to whom the Thessalonians have turned and the Thessalonians themselves. They have been loved by God in the past and they continue to be loved by him.[189] They have been loved by God, and they have been taught by God.

The juxtaposition of these two ideas might remind the reader of Paul's letter of the folktale that has been incorporated into the fourth gospel.[190] The father who truly loves the child assures the child's socialization by teaching it a trade. Within Paul's social world teaching was essentially a paternal responsibility.[191] In his letter Paul uses a paternal metaphor to describe his own interaction with the Thessalonians, that is, he and his companions were present among them, "urging and encouraging you and pleading that you lead a life worthy of God, who calls you into his own kingdom and glory" (2:12).

"To urge – *parakaleō*" is the very verb with which Paul introduces his paraenesis in 4:10b. Here he urges the Thessalonians "to aspire to live quietly," an oxymoronic expression whose focus is the exhortation "to live quietly – *hēsychazō*." Taking his cue from Philo,[192] Roetzel shows that "to live quietly – *hēsychazō*" connotes an eschatological attitude. In no way does "to live quietly – *hēsychazō*" imply a political or social quietism. Rather, "to live quietly – *hēsychazō*" is "a form of listening or faithful watching appropriate to the arriving eschatological Kingdom. The waiting is active, and its sphere is social."[193] That the Thessalonians should aspire (*philotimeisthai*)[194] to have this attitude serves to underscore its intensity.

There is, in sum, no little similarity between the paraenesis that Paul recalls in 2:11-12 and the exhortation that he addresses to the Thessalonians in 4:9-12, albeit not without a reminder (4:11) about what he had told them while he and his companions were among them. If one can describe 2:11-12 as a reminder of a paternal exhortation, then it does not seem unwarranted to similarly describe the paraenesis of 4:10b-12 as a bit of fatherly advice. It is, however,

clearly associated[195] with a paraenetic *preteritio* in which the name
of God appears, a God whom Paul characterizes as one who exercises
a paternal function.

In other words, the fashion in which Paul recalls his oral exhortation in 1 Thessalonians not only seems to suggest that his appeal had an
eschatological and social thrust but also that the image of God-Father
was associated with his paraenesis. In any event, the way in which
Paul refers to the resurrection of Jesus in 1:10 indicates that the resurrection was an action by which God revealed Jesus to be His Son,
thereby implicitly revealing Himself as Father. The paternity of God
about which Paul writes in 1 Thessalonians has an eschatological quality. It is associated with the coming of the kingdom. The Father-God
who raised Jesus from the dead has loved and taught the Thessalonians. In so doing, he manifested that the Father of Jesus was Father
to the Thessalonians. Appropriately, then, Paul could write about "our
God and Father," perhaps more appropriately rendered as "God, our
Father" (1:3; 3:11,13).[196]

A Note

Perhaps the reader should take note, at this point, of the slippage in
Paul's imagery. Although Paul has described God as Father in 1:3, he
uses the paternal metaphor to describe himself and his companions
in 2:12, a reflection whose paternal image points to the particular
relationship between the apostles and each of the Thessalonians. The
paternal similitude is implicit in 4:9–10a, with God as the referent, and
in 4:10b-12, with Paul and his companions as the referent. The latter
similitude is appropriate insofar as Paul and his companions deliver
to the Thessalonians the message that God has entrusted to them. By
delivering the message, with all that it implies, the apostles exercise a
paternal function. They are like fathers to the Thessalonians.

On the other hand, insofar as the situation of Paul and his fellow
travelers and present greeters is similar to that of the Thessalonians,
they legitimately consider the Thessalonians as their brothers and sisters, with God as their common Father. This slippage in Paul's use of
kinship imagery may go a long way in helping to explain how Paul
can refer to himself and his companions as "infants," all the while
maintaining that their role is comparable to that of parents (2:7).[197]

The Eschatological Future

Eschatological urgency characterized Paul's moral exhortation, both
in its written form and in its oral expression. In his reminder of the

exhortation that he had addressed to his beloved Thessalonians, Paul wrote that "we dealt with each one of you like a father with his children, urging and encouraging you and pleading that you lead a life worthy of God, who calls you into his own kingdom and glory" (2:11-12). Paul's "*eis* – into" expresses the dynamic orientation of his beloved Thessalonians toward God's kingdom and glory. The Thessalonians to whom Paul is writing were, in fact, dynamically oriented toward the future.

On the negative side, they were waiting for the wrath that is coming, a wrath from which they were being rescued. On the positive side, they were waiting for the presence of Jesus as Lord. The alternatives were succinctly stated later in the letter. Paul wrote: "God has destined us not for wrath, but for obtaining salvation through our Lord Jesus Christ" (5:9). Wrath and salvation are the alternatives that lie on the eschatological horizon.

Paul and his companions had obviously spoken to the Thessalonians about the manifestation of God's wrath. Since their visit, the Thessalonians had been waiting for Jesus "who delivers us from the wrath that is to come" (1:10).[198] This wrath was, in the language of later theological jargon, the eschatological wrath of God.[199] It is the negative aspect of the coming of God's kingdom, when the present order of things will be brought to closure.

The Thessalonians apparently expected that the wrath of God would soon be made manifest. 1 Thess 4:17 indicates that Paul expected that he and his companions, along with many of the Thessalonians, would be alive at the time of Jesus' coming as Lord. Theirs was an expectation of an imminent parousia,[200] the coming of Jesus as Lord in the relatively near future.

Jesus as Lord

The expected proximity of Jesus' coming provides the context for the wish prayers that Paul has incorporated into his letter at 3:14, "may he so strengthen your hearts in holiness that you may be blameless before our God and Father at the coming of our Lord Jesus with all his saints," and 5:23, "may your spirit and soul and body be kept sound and blameless at the coming of our Lord Jesus Christ." The expectation of the imminent parousia provided Paul with the excitement out of which he could proclaim: "For what is our hope or joy or crown of boasting before our Lord Jesus at his coming? Is it not you? Yes, you are our glory and joy!" (2:19-20).

These four passages (2:19; 3:14; 4:15; 5:23) are the only places in this letter in which Paul uses the quasi-technical term *parousia* to describe the coming of Jesus as Lord. All four of them convey the impression that the coming of Jesus was eagerly awaited and that Jesus would come soon. In each of the four passages, when Paul talks about the coming of Jesus, he designates Jesus as "*Kyrios* – Lord." One can only infer that Paul and his companions had spoken to the Thessalonians about the coming of Jesus as Lord and that they had conveyed the impression that Jesus would appear as Lord in the relatively near future.

Because the Thessalonians had come to know Jesus as Lord through the preaching of Paul and his companions, Paul was able to invoke Jesus-Lord as an authority figure not only when he wrote his letter to them, but also when he and his companions were among the Thessalonians urging them to live in a way that was consistent with God's activity among them. Paul began the paraenesis of 4:1-12 with this reminder: "you know what instructions we gave you through the Lord Jesus" (4:2).

Paul's moral exhortation was conveyed under the authority of Jesus. The reminder commanded attention. In the Pauline paraenesis, the title "Lord" has significant rhetorical force. The term itself connotes authority. Invocation of the "*Kyrios* – Lord" appeals to listeners to stand up and take notice. It conveys an implicit but forceful warning. Just after he reminded the Thessalonians of his previous instructions, Paul wrote: "The Lord is an avenger in all these things, just as we have already told you beforehand and solemnly warned you" (4:6). The verbal hendiadys is significant. Paul employs two compound verbs, "*proeipon* – to tell beforehand,"[201] and "*diamartyromai* – to warn solemnly"[202] in such a way that the one qualifies the other. Taken together, they remind Paul's readers that he and his companions had *already* conveyed a warning (threat?) and that they had done so in a *solemn* fashion.[203] Not only had they told the Thessalonians that Jesus the Lord was the authority in whose name the apostles were spelling out some implications of what it mean to be a Christian; they had also told the Thessalonians that the Lord[204] himself would provide the sanction for the moral instruction that had been given.

Jesus as Our Lord

In the introduction to his paraenesis in 4:1-2, Paul twice identifies Jesus as "*Kyrios* – Lord." In the warning at 4:6, Jesus is likewise called "*Kyrios* – Lord." In three of the four passages in which Paul makes mention of the coming of Jesus as parousiac Lord, he speaks of Jesus as "*Kyrios hēmōn* – our Lord" (2:19; 3:13; 5:23). The use of the first-person plural pronoun, "*hēmōn* – our," in this regard is significant. It bespeaks the special relationship that bound the Thessalonians to

Jesus, the parousiac Lord. Jesus' coming was something for which the Thessalonians hoped (1:3), precisely because he was their Lord and would deliver them from the wrath to come (1:10). For them the coming of the Lord Jesus Christ, that is, of "our Lord," was the expectation of a salvific event (5:9). Some five of the seven times that Paul adds the qualification "*hēmōn* – our" to "*Kyrios* – Lord" occur within contexts wherein the use of the pronoun identifies the coming of Jesus as Lord as the object of the Thessalonians' hope.[205]

Since the Thessalonians were expecting the coming of their Lord Jesus to occur in the relatively near future and since they were expecting him to deliver them from the wrath that was coming, it is clear that they likewise expected the manifestation of God's wrath[206] in the relatively near future. This realization may provide the reader of 1 Thessalonians with a useful approach to the problematic phrase "God's wrath has overtaken them at last" (2:16).[207] The phrase is so difficult to understand that some interpreters have claimed that the phrase represents a later interpolation into Paul's letter.

The verb "*ephthasen* – has overtaken,"[208] in the indicative aorist, implies that something has already occurred. In what sense can the experience of God's wrath be said to have already occurred? In what sense can God's wrath be said to have already overtaken those about whom Paul is writing? Is the manifestation of God's wrath a reality of the past? Or is it an essentially future reality whose impending manifestation is so certain that it already begins to impinge upon the present? The imminence of the coming of the deliverer seems to imply that, in Paul's view of things, the latter is the case.

Difficulties Ahead

The Thessalonians could and did expect that they would be delivered from the imminent wrath of God through the agency of Jesus who had been raised from the dead, but they should not have expected to be saved from all affliction. The Thessalonians to whom Paul wrote were in a difficult situation. It was, in fact, Paul's anxiety about their situation that prompted him to send Timothy to Thessalonica (3:2) "so that no one would be shaken by these persecutions" (3:3).[209]

Twice Paul employs an explanatory "*gar* – for" as he writes to the Thessalonians about their situation. He explains: "Indeed [*gar*], you yourselves know that this is what we are destined for. In fact [*kai gar*], when we were with you, we told you beforehand [*proelegomen hymin*] that we were to suffer persecution [*mellomen thlibesthai*]; so it turned out, as you know" (4:3-4). While there may be some discussion as to whether the most correct rendering of Paul's *thlibesthai* is "to suffer persecution"[210] – some editions render his expression as "to suffer hardship" or "to undergo affliction"[211] – there can be no doubt that Paul had forewarned the Thessalonians about the difficult situation that they were about to face. The impending afflictions were part of the message that Paul had delivered to the Thessalonians.

There was a certain inevitability about their fate. Affliction was to be their destiny (3:3).[212] The Thessalonians were not, however, alone in suffering affliction. Paul and his companions were to suffer affliction along with the Thessalonians. As a matter of fact, Paul and his companions had already suffered affliction before arriving in Thessalonica.[213] Affliction was the common lot of Paul, his companions, and the Thessalonians. The first-person plural verb of 3:3 embraces the Thessalonians as well as the senders of the letter. There was a certain commonality – and solidarity – in the afflictions that all of them were to face. The Thessalonians had begun to suffer when they received the word of his message (1:6). These afflictions were but harbingers of things to come.

What Paul had told the Thessalonians was that they were about to suffer difficulties. His *"mellomen* – were to" suggests the proximate future,[214] a future that would bring its own adversity. Paul had not only told the Thessalonians about their difficult future; he had told them this beforehand (*proelegomen hymin*). He had told them this so that they might be prepared for their future. Paul's use of a compound verb with the implication of *fore*-telling (*pro-elegomen*) reminds today's reader of 1 Thessalonians that two things that Paul had foretold to the Thessalonians were the inevitability of their afflictions (3:3–4) and the Lord's future vengeance (4:6). It is only in these two passages that Paul uses a verb of speaking with the compounding preposition "*pro* – beforehand."[215]

Summing Up

Because of their own suffering and mistreatment in Philippi, Paul and his companions had to be emboldened to speak to the Thessalonians, and speak they did. They proclaimed their message, which Paul describes as "the gospel of God." The apostles had been entrusted with this message. In this sense, the message came from God. Yet their message was also, to a very large extent, a message about God. From Paul's references to his oral proclamation to the Thessalonians, it appears that he and his companions had spoken about God who had raised Jesus from the dead. They had spoken about God who was Father and Jesus who was Son. They had spoken about God who was living and true. They spoke about the kingdom of God.

The temporal framework of the story that they told was, however, future-oriented. They spoke of Jesus who was awaited and a Lord who would avenge. The future would be a time of salvation and a time of wrath. That future was imminent and seems to have impinged on the present.

As part of the message, Paul and his companions spoke of the call of God. God was calling those whom Paul addressed to live in a manner that was worthy of God himself. Moral exhortation was part and parcel of the message. The horizon against which Paul announced the call was the future that was about to appear. Paul foretold that life would hardly be rosy until the future came. There were to be suffering and afflictions. In the midst of these trials, those called were to live in such a manner as to please God. The call that he addressed involved some rather specific directives coming from Paul and his companions. The directives touched upon such things as sexuality, love for others, and an energetic self-sufficiency. It was apparently a call for a new socialization, which implied that God was Father.

How did the Thessalonians respond to this message and its implicit call? It is to that issue that the next chapter of this book will be addressed.

∽ 3 ∾

The Life of the Thessalonians

What happened to the Thessalonians as a result of Paul's preaching the gospel of God among them? In his letter to the Thessalonians, Paul rehearses some things that he remembered about them, he tells us about some things that people other than the Thessalonians had to say about them, and he himself tells us something about what he knows of the Thessalonian situation. Before moving on to the situation of the Thessalonians, as this may be inferred from Paul's letter, it will be useful to look at the things that he explicitly stated with regard to the Thessalonians' situation. Words of remembering, saying, and a variety of verbs in the indicative mood are the clearest markers that direct the reader to what happened at Thessalonica.

Paul's Reminiscence

After greeting the Thessalonians in appropriate fashion (1:1), Paul tells them about his prayer of thanksgiving. Its focus was Paul's memory of the Thessalonians.[1] What he remembered in his prayer was "your work of faith and labor of love and steadfastness of hope in our Lord Jesus Christ" (1:3). This oldest example of the classic Christian triad of faith, hope, and charity[2] succinctly describes what Paul remembers about the Thessalonians. Their life was one of faith, hope, and charity. The reality of the Thessalonians' situation provided Paul with an occasion and subject for his prayer of thanksgiving, but, as he was just beginning his letter to the Thessalonians, his synthetic description of the Thessalonians' situation served rhetorically as a *captatio benevolentiae*, an expression of goodwill.

Just what did Paul mean when he wrote about the Thessalonians in this fashion? He wrote about their "work of faith," their "labor of love," and their "steadfastness of hope."[3] This is not quite the

72

same as if he had written about their "faith, hope, and charity." In fact, the direct object of Paul's reminiscence was their work, their labor, and their steadfastness. "Faith, love, and hope" are, in Paul's Greek language, in the genitive case. They serve as modifiers. Technically the qualifiers serve as epexegetical or appositive genitives.[4] This kind of genitive enables a reader to look at one and the same reality from two vantage points. So, Paul is really writing about the active faith, the laboring love, and the patient hope[5] that he so well remembered.

Work of Faith

What is their "work of faith"? From time to time, various commentators have read Paul's "*ergon* – work," as if he had written "*erga* – works." "Work of faith," one commentator noted, refers to "all the moral acts of the Christian who does everything under the light and inspiration of faith."[6] In fact, "*ergon* – work" suggests activity rather than acts. It evokes action itself. Indeed, in Paul's own usage "*ergon* – work" sometimes is used in contrast with "*logos* – word," as if to focus on reality in contrast with mere words.[7] Faith implies an orientation of life turned toward God. "*Tou ergou tēs pisteōs* – work of faith" expresses the dynamism and vitality of that faith.

Faith that is real is faith that is alive. That this is so is apparent in the first few sentences of Paul's communication with the Thessalonians. Paul will write about their "faith in God," using a repeated article in Greek ("*hē* – the") to clearly state that it is both their faith and a faith that is in God. Paul, however, does not actually write about their faith "in God." Rather than "*en theō* – in God," he writes about their faith "*pros ton theon* – toward God." Used with the accusative, Paul's choice of the preposition properly connotes motion toward.

The dynamism implied by Paul's succinct formulations is spelled out as Paul writes about the Thessalonians "turning [*epeststrepsate*] to God" from idols and their "serving [*douleuein*] a living and true God." To "turn" (*epistrephō*) and to "serve" (*douleuō*) are verbs with an active connotation, the latter implying serving as a slave. When Paul describes the Thessalonians as having become "an example to all the believers in Macedonia and Achaia," he writes about the word of the Lord "sounding forth" (*exēchētai*) from them.[8] "To sound forth" (*exēcheō*) evokes the image of the movement of sound. Paul's words capture the flavor of what he means by a "work of faith." It is the Thessalonians' relationship with God in all its vitality and dynamism.

Labor of Love

Accompanying their active faith as a characteristic of the new situation
of the Thessalonians is their labor of love.[9] What is a laboring love?
It seems to be an arduous love, a "hard love." Paul's "*kopos* – labor"
was commonly used in Greek as a way of speaking about a beating.
Generically, it had the connotation of suffering or fatigue. Of all the
New Testament authors, it is Paul who most often uses this word. It
became almost a buzzword for his apostolic labors, frequently within
situational catalogues where it appears among generic descriptions
of the difficulties of life.[10] Later in this letter Paul will write about
his own labor, first reminding the Thessalonians of his own labor and
toil among them, using language that evokes the hardship and effort
involved (2:9), then speaking of his hope that his labor would prove
not to have been in vain, using language that speaks of his personal
investment in his activity (3:5). For Paul, "labor" is not something that
comes easily, nor is it something superficial. It costs, it sometimes
hurts, and it somehow involves a person to the very depths of one's
being.

The labor in which the Thessalonian Christians were involved was
a labor of love. Before bringing his letter to a close, Paul was to repeatedly exhort the Thessalonian Christians to love one another. Their love
for one another was the object of his wish and his prayer: "may the
Lord make you increase and abound in love for one another and for all,
just as we abound in love for you" (3:12).

The paraenesis of 4:9–10 is equally instructive: "Now concerning
love of the brothers and sisters, you do not need to have anyone write
to you, for you yourselves have been taught by God to love one another; and indeed you do love all the brothers and sisters throughout
Macedonia. But we urge you, beloved, to do so more and more."

The wish prayer and the exhortation show that, for Paul, the Thessalonian Christians' fellow Christians were the primary object of their
love. There is, in fact, a familial quality that affects the love that is
theirs. Paul writes about their "love for one another" (3:12; 4:9)[11]
and their sibling love (4:9).[12] Yet this love is not restricted, in nar-
row fashion, to the Christians of Thessalonica. It is extended to all
those in Macedonia with whom the Thessalonians are bound in a relationship of sibness. The Thessalonian Christians love all the brothers
and sisters throughout Macedonia (4:10). Indeed Paul prays that they
may have love "for one another and for all," (3:12) presumably for
all Christians.[13] Thus there is an expansive quality to the love of the
Thessalonian Christians for one another; it extends beyond those who
actually gathered in Thessalonica to other Christians as well. It should
be noted, nonetheless, that if Paul exhorts the Thessalonians to love

one another, he specifically challenges them to esteem very highly in love (*en agapē*) those who have charge over them.

If one can speak about the expansive quality of the Thessalonians' love for one another, one should probably draw equal attention to its dynamic quality. The love of the Thessalonian Christians was legendary. Paul could write enthusiastically about their love for one another and for all Christians throughout Macedonia (4:10). Their love was, in fact, part of the good news itself (3:6). It was proclaimed by Timothy.[14]

The Pauline paraenesis as well as the apostle's prayer indicate that there is room for increase and growth in the Thessalonians' love for one another and for all the Christians of Macedonia. The apostolic prayer is "that the Lord make you increase[15] and abound in love for one another and for all" (3:11). In this context the abundance of the Thessalonians' love is pointed to by means of the characteristic verb "*perisseuō* – abound,"[16] the very same term that occurs in Paul's exhortation to love: "you do love all the brothers and sisters throughout Macedonia. But we urge you . . . to do so more and more [*perisseuein mallon*]" (4:10-11).

As a point of reference for the intensity of love to which they were called, the Thessalonians have the example of Paul himself. In his prayer, he had prayed that they should abound in love for one another, "just as we abound in love for you" (3:12).[17] The reader who comes upon these words is already well aware of the intensity of the love that Paul and his companions had for the Thessalonians. The repeated use of kinship language (1:4, etc.), the explicit affirmation of intense affection (2:8), the urgency of the desire to be with them (2:17-3:1) all bear witness to the intensity of the love with which Paul and his companions loved the Thessalonian Christians.

Not only did these Christians have the experience of the apostles' love as a motivation for their own love, but they had also been God-taught[18] to love one another. Most probably this was a reference to the baptismal catechesis in which love for one another was presented as a hallmark of Christian existence.[19] All of this did not make their love for one another something easy. Their love for one another was, in the words that Paul used in his first rehearsal of the topic, a "labor of love."

Steadfastness of Hope

The third quality that came to mind as Paul reminisced about the Thessalonians was the steadfastness of their hope (*tēs hypomonēs tēs elpidos*). "Steadfastness – *hypomonē*"[20] evokes a sense of almost heroic stick-to-itiveness, a dogged perseverance in spite of the obstacles. In his classic commentary on Paul's letter, Martin Dibelius, with reference to 4 Macc 1:11, simply states that steadfastness is heroism.[21] It evokes notions of inward strength and outward difficulty, the latter fully implied by Paul's repeated reference to the "persecution" of the Thessalonian Christians (1:6 and 3:3).

Constancy in the face of difficulty was a quality of the Thessalonians' hopefulness. Their hope focused on "our Lord Jesus Christ" in such a way that one can say that the Lord Jesus Christ was the object of the Thessalonians' hope. Yet Paul never clearly defines nor fully describes what he means by "*elpis* – hope." Since Paul was a Jew, it is interesting that he specifies "our Lord Jesus Christ" as the object of the hope that he and his companions share with the Thessalonian Christians. For a pious Jew – such as Paul was and continued to be – God himself was the object of hope.[22] The hope of the Jews focused on God as savior and judge. Now, for Paul, hope centers on the Lord Jesus Christ.

Before attempting to elucidate the object of the Thessalonians' hope any further, it might be good to note that the hope about which Paul writes is both discriminatory and eschatologically focused. It is discriminatory insofar as there are those who hope and those who do not (4:9). From this point of view, hope is a distinctive quality that characterizes Christian existence over and against other forms of human existence.

Hope is, moreover, eschatologically focused. In each of the subsequent passages in this letter in which Paul explicitly returns to the theme of hope, the eschatological referent is patent (2:19; 4:13; 5:8).[23] In 1:3 the eschatological referent is epitomized in the terse formula "our Lord Jesus Christ." In this context the formula clearly means the appearance of Jesus Christ as "our Lord." That Jesus was the Christ is taken for granted; it is almost as if the title "*Christos* – Christ" has lost its formal significance and is used simply as an identifying marker that sets Jesus known as Christ off from other Jesuses or Joshuas, who might be otherwise identified.

The appearance of this Jesus as "our Lord" is the formal object of the hope of the Thessalonians. "Lord" is Paul's favorite christological title; yet it is a title whose point of reference is eschatological.[24] The semantic referent is Jesus as eschatological Lord. It evokes notions of Jesus, the parousiac Lord, as savior (5:9) and judge (4:6).[25] In a word, the object of the Thessalonians' hope is somewhat different from the focus of the typical Jew's hope. Whereas the Jew hoped for the manifestation of God as savior and judge, the Thessalonians hoped for the appearance of Jesus as savior and judge. Ultimately, however, these two expressions of hope fuse into one. It is God who will be the principal agent in the eschatological drama in which Jesus will appear as savior and judge; at the parousia Jesus will act as God's agent, assuming divine functions. In this respect he is properly to be called "Lord."

Faith, Love, and Hope

The three qualities of life that attracted the focus of Paul's memory have been so arranged that the emphasis falls upon the steadfastness of their hope. Not only is this element placed last in the series, and therefore underscored according to the typical procedures of Hellenistic rhetoric, but it is also the element that is expanded beyond the simple "two nouns in the genitive" construction. Hope is further qualified insofar as it is related to "our Lord Jesus Christ."

A similar triadic expression occurs in the Pauline paraenesis of chapter 5. There Paul exhorts the Thessalonian Christians to "put on the breastplate of faith and love, and for a helmet the hope of salvation." This description of the panoply is taken from Isa 59:17: "He put on righteousness like a breastplate, and a helmet of salvation on his head."[26] The reference is one with which Jewish Christians readers might be familiar, but it is one that Paul's Gentile Christian readers presumably would not catch. In any event, the allusion is one that Paul does not exploit; in his letter the biblical imagery simply functions as a potent metaphor to describe the defensive weapons with which the Thessalonian Christians should face life. The use of military imagery is consistent with the description found in 1:3, where the life of the Thessalonians is described as hard work within a context of some difficulty.

The biblical allegory describes Yahweh, previously identified as the sole savior of Israel (Isa 59:16), as dressing up with the qualities required for victory. The imagery is rooted in Israel's conviction that God is the savior of Israel. It is to be located within the holy war tradition, which serves as an expression of that article of faith.[27] Paul transposes the referent of the metaphor from God to the Thessalonians and modifies the allegory. In place of the biblical "righteousness" (*dikaiosynē*), an all-embracing description of appropriate behavior, Paul has "faith and love." It is almost as if "faith and love" fills out and specifies righteousness for the new age in which Paul is writing. In place of the biblical "salvation" (*sōtēriou*), Paul writes about "the hope of salvation" (*elpida sōtērias*), that is, the hope that has salvation as its focus and object. When this imaginative element of Paul's exhortation is compared with his recollection in 1:3, the reader cannot help but note Paul's consistency in his use of the triplet, faith, love, and hope, to describe the Christian life.

The Christian life affects a dynamic quality. According to 1:3, faith, love, and hope are exemplary aspects of the life of the Thessalonian

Christians, yet from 5:8 we learn that the Thessalonians must strive for faith, love, and hope. Our brief analysis of Paul's understanding of the love of the Thessalonians has indicated that, although love is characteristic of their life (1:3; 4:9-10), their love must continue to expand. What is said about love can also be said about faith. The Thessalonians have faith (1:3, 8; 3:[5], 6, 7); they are believers (2:10, 13).[28] Yet their faith needs to be strengthened and they need to be encouraged (3:2, [5], 10; 5:8). The same kind of thing can be said about hope. The Thessalonians have a steadfast hope (1:3); yet they apparently need to be exhorted to hope (5:8).

As a matter of fact, the exhortation to hope comes as the third element in the triadic expression of 5:8, just as it does in 1:3. Placed last, it occupies the position upon which the emphasis lies.[29] Indeed, if there is room for growth in the Thessalonians' life of faith and love, there is need for Paul to encourage the Thessalonians, lest they fall into hopelessness and lose something of the quality of their life that sets them apart from others (4:13). That is the burden of the exhortation in 4:13-18, to which 5:1-11 is appended as an explanatory clarification.

In Paul's use of the military metaphor, faith and love are joined together as the elucidation of righteousness. Faith and love form one unit of thought and the hope of salvation another. "Faith and love" follow one another in 1:3. They occur together in 3:6. This pairing of the elements of faith and love, implicit in 1:3 and quite explicit in 3:6 and 5:8, suggests that the two constitute a dyad, whose members belong together. Even though the situation of the Thessalonians is such that Paul must place specific emphasis upon hope, it is their faith and love that specifies the Thessalonians' life as truly Christian. In one of his later letters Paul will write about faith that works through love (Gal 5:6).[30] Faith is a power that manifests its energy in the love that Christians have for one another.[31] In the words of F. F. Bruce, "faith is viewed as the root, love as the fruit."[32]

The classic pairing of faith and love is reflected in Philemon 5. In a thanksgiving report similar to that of 1 Thessalonians 1, Paul speaks about Philemon's love and faith with regard to which he had received an oral report. The two-part description[33] attests to the Christian life of Philemon and serves as a kind of ad hominem argument that grounds Paul's subsequent plea. Love and faith are found in an order inverse to that of the classic pattern,[34] but this may be a stylistic inversion dictated by the nature of Paul's epistolary rhetoric.[35]

In 1 Thessalonians, however, the faith-love expression occurs in its usual sequence, but it is complemented, both in 1:3 and 5:8, with a reference to hope.[36] Although both passages are terse in their expression, both ultimately incorporate a threefold description of the Christian life. The threefold description focuses upon three aspects of a single life. As a result, each triadic expression should be taken as a unit. The unit sums up the life of the Thessalonian Christians, such as that situation can be inferred from Paul's letter. The three themes are the warp and woof of the letter.[37] The triadic description of the wish prayer (1:3), for example, anticipates the report that is cited in 1:9–10, faith, love, and hope effectively preparing the way for the report about conversion, service, and expectation.[38] The threefold description is, in the words of Günther Bornkamm, "the quintessence of the God-given life in Christ."[39]

The truly theological horizon of Paul's threefold description of the Thessalonians' situation is summed up in a simple prepositional phrase, "before our God and Father." A reading of 1 Thess 1:3 in the NRSV and most of the most recent translations of Paul's letter into English gives the impression that the phrase qualifies the verb "remembering,"[40] as if the verb with its modifier meant something like "remembering in my prayers your work of faith...," or, as the New Translation has it, "as we come to our God and Father." If the phrase were to be taken in this sense, the phrase has virtually a cultic sense and Paul's "*emprosthen* – before" might conceivably reflect the Hebrew "*liphne* – before," with its cultic nuance.

There are, however, some twenty words in Paul's Greek text between the verb "remember" and the "*emprosthen* – before" phrase. In this situation, it is quite unlikely that the prepositional phrase really modifies the verb "remember."[41] Some authors, therefore, take the phrase as a reference to existence at the parousia, so that it principally pertains to the steadfastness of hope.[42] In favor of this latter interpretation is the fact that the same phrase occurs with an eschatological referent in 3:13, while similar "*emprosthen* – before" phrases occur in 3:9 and 2:19, where their reference to parousiac existence is quite obvious.

There are, however, good reasons to think that the phrase refers to the present existence of the Thessalonian Christians. Coming at the end of the clause it naturally qualifies all that proceeds it. There is no reason to separate hope from other aspects of Christian existence in this regard.[43] It is, says Bruce, "natural to suppose that the Thessalonians' work, labor, and patient hope are exercised in the presence of God."[44] Christian existence is an existence before God. This not only suggests that the horizon of Christian activity[45] is God but also evokes the notion of what would later be called divine providence.[46] In the words of Buzy, "God is a Father who watches over his children and vigorously helps them in their difficulties."[47]

The God in whose presence Thessalonian Christians live their lives, the God who watches over them in providential fashion is "*our* God and Father." The pronoun suggests that there is some solidarity in this type of Christian existence, not only among the Thessalonian Christians themselves but also between Paul and his companions and the Thessalonians. This is explicitly the case with regard to love, when Paul can speak of the abundance of the love that he and his companions had for the Thessalonians. It is no less true with regard to faith and hope, for they share a common faith and a common steadfastness while waiting for the appearance of our Lord Jesus Christ.

The Reports

In addition to reminiscing about the faith, love, and hope of the Thessalonians, Paul twice mentions reports about their situation that had been brought to his attention. One report came from "all the believers in Macedonia and Achaia": "the people of those regions report [*apaggellousin*] about us what kind of welcome we had among you, and how you turned to God from idols, to serve a living and true God, and to wait for his Son from heaven, whom he raised from the dead – Jesus, who rescues us from the wrath that is coming" (1:9-10). The other report came from Timothy, who had been sent to Thessalonica to strengthen and encourage the Thessalonians for the sake of their faith. Upon Timothy's return to Corinth, the place from which 1 Thessalonians was presumably written,[48] Paul writes that, "he has brought us the good news [*euaggelisamenou*] of your faith and love. He has told us also that you always remember us kindly and long to see us – just as we long to see you" (3:6-7).

Paul uses each of these verbs of announcement just once in 1 Thessalonians. Enthusiastically, Paul tells about the report of all the believers scattered throughout Macedonia and Achaia. People from all over Greece had been talking about the reception that Paul received in Thessalonica. They also talked about the conversion of the Thessalonian Christians. These Thessalonians had abandoned their idols and turned to God.[49] Now they were serving the living and true God and waiting for the parousia. These other Greek Christians were talking about the faith, the love, and the hope of the Thessalonians. They characterized these Thessalonians as an expectant group of people. They were waiting for Jesus, the deliverer.[50]

What Timothy brought with him was the good news of the Thessalonians' faith and love. It was, indeed, something to be talked about. Timothy also reported about something else, namely, the enduring bond of affection between the Thessalonians and Paul and his companions. The language of verse 6b, "you always remember us kindly" (*echete mneian hēmōn agathēn pantote*) echoes the language of 1:2, "we always [*pantote*] give thanks to God for all of you and mention you [*mneian poioumenoi*] in our prayers." There is reciprocity in the affection that they bear for one another. It really was good news!

While there is little reason to doubt that the reciprocity of affection was indeed genuine – knowledge of the Thessalonians' warm memories of him and his companions seems to have elated Paul![51] – one must not overlook the fact that in the letter, mention of this mutual affection serves an epistolary and rhetorical function. "*Mneian poiesthai* – to mention" is a phrase commonly found in ancient letters, where it often has a philophronetic function,[52] that is, it serves to express the friendship existing between the sender and the addressees. As an expression of friendship, it serves the rhetorical purpose of the letter. It prepares for the series of paraenetic exhortations that are to follow.[53]

Not only did the Thessalonians have fond memories of Paul and his companions, they also yearned for their return: "you ... long[54] to see us – just as we long to see you" (3:6c). The elliptical expression of reciprocity harks back to the earlier protracted expression of Paul's desire to visit with the Thessalonians (2:17–3:1a). In Timothy's report, Paul was reassured of the Thessalonians' warm memories of himself and his entourage and was informed of their own desire to be visited by the apostles.

A Matter of Fact

As one peruses Paul's letter to the Thessalonians in an attempt to glean from it knowledge of the Thessalonians' situation, one finds, in addition to the reminiscences and the reports that are cited, a number of passages in which their condition after Paul's departure is described in matter-of-fact fashion. The first of these statements is to be found in 1:6–8: "And you became imitators [*mimētai egenēthēte*] of us and of the Lord, for in spite of persecution you received the word with joy inspired by the Holy Spirit, so that you became an example to all the believers in Macedonia and Achaia. For the word of the Lord has sounded forth from you not only in Macedonia and Achaia, but in every place your faith in God has become known, so that we have no need to speak of it."

What did Paul mean when he indicated that the Thessalonians had become imitators of himself and his companions and of the Lord"? It is hardly likely that Paul was suggesting that the Thessalonians had imitated him – and still less that they had imitated the Lord! – in receiving the word. It would seem that the point of comparison is concentrated in the phrase, "in persecution with the joy of the Holy Spirit."[55] Paul's language is terse. To render Paul's Greek, *dexamenoi ton logon en*

thlipsei pollē meta charas pneumatos hagiou, the NRSV has introduced a few words of interpretation ("in spite of," "inspired by") into
each of Paul's prepositional phrases. For stylistic reasons it has placed
the participial clause "having received the word" between the two
prepositional phrases, which are juxtaposed in the Greek text. By doing so the NRSV has separated what Paul has joined together and has
somewhat skewed the reading of Paul at this point.

Joy coming from the Holy Spirit is an eschatological reality. So, too,
is affliction. According to the categories of Paul's Jewish apocalypticism, affliction is a penultimate reality. It is part of the final adversity
that precedes the ultimate inbreaking of the rule of God. Paul had told
the Thessalonians about the inevitability of the afflictions that he and
his companions were to face (3:3-4).[56] Having become aware of the
persecution of his beloved Thessalonians, Paul affirms in 1:6 that there
is a commonality in their suffering. Like Paul and his companions, the
Thessalonians have been subjected to some persecution;[57] they and
the apostles share a common fate of suffering.

Paul could affirm[58] that their suffering was similar to that of
the churches of Judea: "you, brothers and sisters, became imitators
[*mimētai egenēthēte*] of the churches of God in Christ Jesus that are
in Judea" (2:14). The Thessalonians had experienced persecution at
the hands of their own compatriots just as the Jewish Christians in Ju-
daea had been persecuted by some of their fellow Jews. Indeed some
of those Jews had killed Jesus, whom Paul identifies as "*Kyrios – Lord*"
(2:15). Indeed since solidarity in suffering is the hallmark of Paul's imitation theme, it could be said of the Thessalonian Christians that they
were imitators of the Lord. Paul says this in no uncertain terms in 1:6:
the Christians of Thessalonica had become "imitators[59] of us and of
the Lord."[60]

If one includes the pain that Paul experienced because of his separation from the Thessalonians as part of his suffering, as some authors
do,[61] then one should probably include the grief of the Thessalonians
as part of their suffering. Even though Paul does not affirm that the
Thessalonians were grieving, his exhortation that "they not grieve as
others do who have no hope" (4:13) suggests that they were in danger
of being overcome by grief. The Stoics considered grief (*lypē*)[62] to be
one of the passions or emotions that destroyed human well-being.[63]
The Thessalonians' imminent grief was undoubtedly due to the fact
that some of their number had died.

If Paul twice affirms that the Thessalonians had become imitators
(*mimētai egenēthēte*), respectively of the apostles and of the Lord
(1:6) and of the churches of Judea (2:14), by reason of their common
sharing in persecution, his paraenesis gives him occasion to make
other statements about the situation of the Thessalonians. He affirms

that they are living as they ought to and, by so doing, they please God (4:1). He affirms that they love all the brothers and sisters throughout Macedonia (4:10). He affirms that they are encouraging each other and building up one another (5:11).

Each of these affirmations about the behavior of the Thessalonians is made by means of a brief phrase that confirms that they are already engaged in the path toward which his exhortatory remarks are directed. His affirmation serves as a motivation for them to heed his exhortation. Thus, in regard to their living as they should, Paul states, "as, in fact, you are doing" (*kathōs kai peripateite*) and goes on to say, "you should do so more and more" (*hina perisseuēte mallon*). In regard to their love of fellow believers throughout Macedonia, Paul writes, *kai gar poiete auto*, literally, "for indeed you are doing this." He continues his exhortation with "do so more and more" (*perisseuein mallon*). Finally, with regard to their mutual encouragement, Paul states, "as indeed you are doing" (*kathōs kai poiete*).

While these pithy resumptive formulas differ from one another, there are marked similarities of style and vocabulary that tie them together. In each instance, the principal verb is the present tense of the second-person plural. Paul is making a statement in direct address about the present condition of the Thessalonians. In addition to this common feature of the three formulas, one might note that "*poiete* – do" is twice used as the resumptive verb (4:10; 5:11), that "*kathōs kai* – just as" is twice used as the comparative expression (4:1, 10), and that "*perisseuein mallon* – continue to do so" twice encapsulates Paul's exhortation (4:1; 5:11). Paul is obviously pleased with the behavior of the Thessalonians. All the same he experiences the pastor's need to encourage them.

Much can indeed be learned about the real situation of the Thessalonians from Paul's own reminiscences about them, from his rehearsal of the reports that he had received, and his own explicit statements about them. There are, however, other indications of the real-life situation of the Thessalonian Christians. To some significant degree, this situation is reflected in the formulas of address that Paul uses as he writes to the Thessalonians. To a large extent their situation may be summed up under the simple rubric, "the church of the Thessalonians."[64]

The Church of the Thessalonians

Paul's letter is addressed to "*tē ekklēsia Thessalonikeōn* – the church of the Thessalonians." The formula is significant, and quite different from the formulas of address found in Paul's later letters.[65] Among Hellenists an *ekklēsia* was simply an assembly or gathering, but the term was frequently employed in a specific political sense to denote an assembly of citizens regularly assembled and/or a legislative assembly.[66] The assembly to which Paul was writing consisted of Thessalonians, inhabitants of the city of Thessalonica.

Election

It was quite obvious that Paul was not writing to all the Thessalonians. His relatively short stay in the city did not provide him with the kind of receptive audience he would have needed were he now to presume that his letter was going to be read to the entire citizenry of the city. Moreover it is clear from his remark in 2:14 that some of the Thessalonians were quite opposed to their own compatriots,[67] the Thessalonians to whom Paul was writing. Paul was writing only to some of the Thessalonians. His Greek genitive should be taken as a partitive genitive so that the expression "the church of the Thessalonians" really means "an assembly of some Thessalonians," or "a gathering from among the Thessalonians."[68]

The selectivity of those to whom Paul was writing is further highlighted and nuanced when Paul writes that "God has chosen them" (*tēn eklogēn hymōn*, 1:4). The language is taken from Paul's theological vocabulary,[69] but it does underscore the notion that the Thessalonians to whom Paul was writing were indeed a select group. They were distinct from other gatherings of Thessalonians. In his epistolary address Paul further specifies that distinction by describing the group to whom he was writing as a gathering "in God the Father and the Lord Jesus Christ" (1:1). This qualification sets them apart from other groups of Thessalonians who might gather together. Not only did they recognize the fatherhood of God; they also acknowledged that Jesus Christ was Lord. In sum, they gathered because they had accepted the gospel that Paul and his companions had proclaimed.

This affirmation of the distinct identity of the gathering to which he was writing is confirmed throughout the letter. The people of Macedonia and Achaia had reported how they had turned from idols to God (1:9) and Paul had taken note of the fact that some of their compatriots had turned against them (2:14). That they formed a distinct group is also manifest from the tenor of Paul's paraenesis.

Mention has already been made of the fact that sanctification is the theme that ties together into a single unit the paraenesis of 4:3-8.[70] When one looks beyond the content of the exhortation to the rhetoric that Paul employs, one is struck by the contrast that Paul draws between those who live as God's people and those who do not. Sanctification language inherently makes distinctions. Those who are holy are those who have been set apart.

While exhorting the Thessalonian Christians to a pattern of (sexual) conduct that is consistent with their status as a group set apart, Paul identifies those from whom the Thessalonians are distinct as "the Gentiles who do not know God" (*ta ethnē ta mē eidota ton theon*, 4:5).[71]

Paul's social universe is remarkably simple. There are Gentiles who do not know God and there are those who are holy, those who are God's people. The division of humanity into but two groups reflects Paul's essentially Jewish vision of things. By distinguishing the Thessalonians from the Gentiles who do not know God, Paul has defined *ethnē* in a religious sense. Implicitly the Thessalonians have been coopted into God's covenanted people; somehow they are Jews.

This realization brings the distinguishing phrase of 1:1, "in God the Father and the Lord Jesus Christ," into still sharper focus. Although it must be granted that Paul has a distinctively Christian understanding of the paternity of God, a simple "in God the Father" would have set those to whom Paul was writing apart from those who did not acknowledge God. The additional "the Lord Jesus Christ" serves to distinguish Paul's addressees from others who belong to God's people. The church of the Thessalonians in God the Father and the Lord Jesus Christ is not simply another Jewish synagogue.[72]

Distinctiveness

The identity of the Thessalonian Christian community as a distinct social group is also reflected in the contrast that Paul offers between them and "others [*hoi loipoi*] who have no hope" (4:13). These "others" are to be found again in 5:6 as Paul exhorts the Thessalonian Christians, "let us not fall asleep as others do, but let us keep awake and be sober." Since both of the passages in which the "others" appear are in pericopes in which Paul is expositing the implications of waiting for his Son from heaven (1:10), it is clear that the others are lacking in the steadfastness of hope extolled by Paul in 1:3.

The "others" form a contrast group for the community of Thessalonian Christians. They are distinct from the "one another" who are the members of that community. Those identified as "one another" (*hoi allēloi*) stand over and against "the others" (*hoi loipoi*). The contrast is drawn in each of the apocalyptic units of 1 Thessalonians.[73] Having distinguished those to whom he was writing and "the others" (4:13; 5:6), Paul concludes each of these units with an exhortation to "encourage one another" (*parakaleite allēlous*, 4:18; 5:11).

The reciprocity inherent in "*allēlous* – one another" is fleshed out in the exhortation to mutual encouragement. That reciprocity receives further expression when Paul writes about the Thessalonian Christians' love for one another (3:12; 4:9) and when he encourages them to seek to do good to one another (5:15). The use of "*allēloi* – one another" points to the mutual service that characterizes the relationship among the Thessalonian Christians. They are bound together by a hard love, the labor of love (1:3). Their hard love is a sibling love (*philadelphia*), as Paul reminds them in 4:9.

Bonding

If the Thessalonian Christians are socially distinct from others, they are bound together by a social cohesiveness that is epitomized in "love." The most striking indication of the group's cohesiveness may not, however, be *agapē* and its cognates; the strongest indication of the cohesiveness of this group is that Paul calls them "brothers and sisters." This form of vocative address occurs in 1 Thessalonians with a density that exceeds that of any of his later correspondence.[74] The expression identifies the type of relationship that exists between Paul and the Thessalonian Christians, but it also points to the bonds that unite them among themselves. They are bound together by ties of kinship.

Once again we must note that the natural situs for kinship language is the home. In this respect it is useful to reflect once again on Paul's greeting. His letter is addressed to the gathering (*tē ekklēsia*) of Thessalonians in God the Father and the Lord Jesus Christ. "Gathering" has temporal and spatial connotations. People assemble at given moments in time and in well-defined places. Gatherings take place. The very notion of *ekklēsia* implies locality.[75] In terms of sociopolitical space it is easy enough to say that the "church of the Thessalonians" gathered in Thessalonica. Yet one must be more specific than that. The gathering to which Paul's letter was to be read (5:27) was hardly diffused throughout the city. One must think of some form of architectural space in which the gathering of Thessalonians actually took place. In all probability, that space was a Christian home, for it is there that kinship language belongs.

The words *oikos* and *oikia*, "house" and "household," do not appear in 1 Thessalonians, as they do in many of Paul's later letters, but one significant expression belonging to the same word group does appear in the letter to the Thessalonians. This is the verb *oikodomeō*, whose proper connotation is "to build a house." The verb was commonly used in the general sense of erecting a building, but it also had the metaphorical sense of "building upon" or "founding upon."[76]

In 1 Thessalonians Paul uses the term in another metaphorical sense with the meaning of "building up" or "edifying." The verb appears in the paraenetic injunction that brings to closure Paul's reflections on night and day (5:1–11): "therefore encourage one another and build up each other." "Build up each other – *oikodomeite heis ton hena*"[77] repeats and explains what Paul means by "encourage one another."[78] Coming at the end of a passage in which Paul has used sociologically excluding language in the form of repeated references to "the others" (4:13; 5:6), Paul's use of the upbuilding metaphor may reflect socioecclesiological considerations, as it does in later New Testament writings when this kind of metaphorical usage of "*oikodomeō* – build" will become relatively common.[79]

The suggestion that the Thessalonian Christians gathered in a home may shed some light upon the way Paul identifies their distinctiveness in 4:12. He exhorts them to "behave properly toward outsiders (*pros tous exō*) and be dependent on no one." "*Exō* – outside" is properly an adverb of place and an improper preposition. When Paul describes those who do not belong to the Thessalonians' company as "the outsiders" (*hoi exō*) in 4:12, it would appear that he is using the adverb in a metaphorical sense. Such a use of the adverb appears not to be attested before New Testament times; within the New Testament it first appears in 4:12.[80] Yet one might ask whether "*hoi exō* – the outsiders" really is metaphorical language. Might it not reflect the fact that the outsiders were truly considered to be outside the house setting within which the gathering of the Thessalonian Christians took place?[81]

A Holy Kiss

To bring to closure this brief reflection on the identity of the "Thessalonians" as a relatively well-defined group, aware of its own identity and its social cohesiveness, it might be good to look at Paul's final exhortation, "Greet all the brothers and sisters with a holy kiss" (5:26), followed by the unusual command, "that this letter be read to all of them" (5:26–27).[82] While discussion must be entertained as to the context within which the greeting was to be conveyed as well as on the identification of those to whom the exhortation is addressed, some preliminary thought should be given to the kiss as a social gesture.

The kiss is an especially intensive gesture; it expresses some form of social union. Used with a variety of purposes, both within the family and outside the family circle, a kiss expresses love and respect. Although it sometimes served as a gesture of reconciliation or served to seal a contract, it always expressed significant social bonding. In Paul's finale it is clear that the gesture was considered to be a gesture expressive of at least quasi-family ties since he exhorts the Thessalonians to "greet all the brothers and sisters with a kiss." The use of "*adelphous* – brothers and sisters" is a significant sign of what Paul wanted the kiss to mean. It was to express the bonds of kinship that bind Christians together. In some of his later letters Paul will encourage Christians to greet "one another" with a kiss.[83] This alternative formulation indicates that in Paul's personal *lexis* "brothers and sisters" and "one another" are, in fact, interchangeable expressions – a fact that is not without significance for understanding 3:12; 4:9, 18; 5:11, 15, the five places in 1 Thessalonians where "*allēlōn* – one another" occurs.

The kiss that is to be exchanged among the Thessalonians is described as a "holy kiss," as it will be in Paul's later writings (Rom 16:16, 1 Cor 16:20, and 2 Cor 13:12).[84] Such a kiss is hardly commonplace. There is a kind of exclusiveness attached to a holy kiss. It is a gesture to be exchanged among those who have been called "in holiness," who belong to God's holy people.[85] As a symbolic gesture the "holy kiss" expresses the relationship that exists among Christian brothers and sisters and sets them apart from those who do not know God. Recognition of this function of the holy kiss must certainly be had before the reader of 1 Thessalonians begins to entertain any questions as to when and how Christians exchanged a holy kiss among themselves.

All the Brothers and Sisters

Paul's final exhortation – in some ways the most intense exhortation of the entire letter, for it is an "adjuration"[86] – is that the "letter be read to all the brothers and sisters."[87] This short formula brings into focus many aspects of the self-conscious identity of the Thessalonian Christians as a distinct community as well as of Paul's awareness of them as a distinct community.

To begin, we can once again examine the "*pasin tois adelphois* – all the brothers and sisters" formulation. This, like the appearance of the formula in the previous verse, is one of the relatively rare places in 1 Thessalonians where Paul uses "*adelphoi* – brothers and sisters" other than as a form of address.[88] It had been Paul's custom to address the Thessalonians as "brothers and sisters." As he brings his letter to a close, he presumes that they know who their brothers and sisters are, for they are expected to adopt specific behavior with regard to the brothers and sisters. These brothers and sisters obviously constitute a well-defined group: Paul can write about "all of them." As a matter of fact, in each of the three instances in which Paul writes about the "brothers and sisters" (4:10; 5:26, 27), he qualifies his language by adding an "all." "All the brothers and sisters" is language that is both inclusive and exclusive. None of the brothers and sisters are to be left out; but the brothers and sisters are different from those who are outside the family group.

Such language suggests that the number of the brothers and sisters is rather limited. So, too, does the fact that the letter is to be read to all these brothers and sisters. In the ancient world, reading was a public act. It was not a privatized visual experience such as it is in modern, literate times, when the population is characterized by a high degree of literacy.[89] In ancient times there was one who read, and those who listened to the reading. This was the situation that Paul had in mind as he commanded that his letter be read to all the brothers and sisters. To imagine the situation in this fashion is to raise questions as to who, when, and where.

The third of these questions is, at least initially, the easiest to address. We have already indicated that early Christians gathered in homes and that Paul's letter to the Thessalonians gives evidence of the fact that a home was the typical venue for the gathering of Thessalonian Christians. That his letter was to be read to a home gathering is confirmed by 5:27, which uses kinship language and presupposes that the number of those bound in the kinship relationship was rather limited. This would concur with the suggestion that Paul intended that his letter be read to a home gathering.

One might ask whether Paul intended that his letter be read to a single gathering in someone's home or whether he desired that it be read to more than one assembly. Some commentators believe that Paul intended that his letter be read to more than one gathering, whereas others believe that Paul thought that the letter would be read in one home session, at which all would be present. What is, in other words, the import of the *"pasin* – all" of 5:27? Paul obviously wants the entire *ekklēsia* – church to hear what he has written. Would they hear it at a single time and in a single place? Or was there more than one house church in existence at Thessalonica at the time that Paul wrote his letter to the Thessalonians?

Given the paucity of data, it is difficult to respond to these questions. The fact that Paul uses the term *"ekklēsia* – assembly" in the singular in 1:1 as well as the likelihood that the letter was written within a relatively short time after Paul's visit leads me to think that there was but a single house gathering in Thessalonica at the time when Paul wrote his letter, but of this I cannot be entirely sure.

If this letter was to be read in a Christian home, the where question suggested by verse 27 is satisfactorily answered. There remain, however, the who and when questions. As regards the who question, it is obvious that there was a reader and those who listened to the reading. This has led Charles Masson to suggest that Paul's letter was written to the leaders of the assembly.[90] His suggestion leads us to the larger issue of the organization of the community at Thessalonica. How was it structured? What was its social organization?[91]

The question as to when the letter was to be read leads to a consideration of the activities of the community at Corinth. On what occasions and for what reasons did they gather together? The language may be anachronistic, but would it be legitimate for a contemporary reader of Paul's letter to imagine the letter being read within the context of what would today be called a liturgical assembly?

A Structured Community?

To reflect on the organization of the Christian community at Thessalonica and the possibility of its having had something akin to an identifiable liturgical activity requires yet another look at the paraenetic elements of Paul's letter. We can begin by returning to the conclusion to Paul's relatively long reflection on Christian existence, where metaphor is mixed with exhortation: "therefore encourage one another and build up each other, as indeed you are doing" (5:11). In context, "building up each other" serves to interpret the mutual encouragement to which Paul is exhorting the Thessalonian Christians by giving a concrete reason why Paul thinks it important for them to encourage one another.

Building Up One Another

To some degree Paul's exhortation was unnecessary – just as the communication of his thoughts on the times and the seasons was unnecessary (5:1). Paul's addressees were already doing what he was encouraging them to do. They were, in fact, encouraging one another and building one another up (5:11b-c). As unnecessary as Paul's exhortation may have been, his pastoral attitude prompted him to encourage those to whom he was writing.[92]

The fact that Paul so encourages the members of the community is a clear indication that he is writing about their present experience. Indeed, the whole section that is brought to closure by the exhortation of 5:11 focuses on the present – in sharp contrast with the preceding section that was so clearly oriented to the future and sought to calm whatever anxiety concern for that unknown future might provoke (4:11-18). Continuing his pastoral exhortation about the here and now, Paul exhorts his addressees to "encourage one another and build up each other." The exhortation is not addressed to the leaders of the community; it is addressed to all members of the community. While present among the Thessalonians, Paul and his companions had encouraged each of them (*hōs hena hekaston hymōn...parakalountes hymas*, 2:11-12); now he exhorts the Thessalonians to encourage one another. The mutual responsibility of all the members of the community for one another is patently clear in Paul's use of "*allēlous* – one another" and "*heis ton hena* – each other," that is, "one on one." One cannot help but notice Paul's concern that each and every member of the community be involved in the mutual encouragement that he is promoting. There is a note of commonality and individuality[93] in Paul's paraenesis. Commonality characterizes both the subject and the object of the encouragement.

When the exhortation of 5:11 is compared with that of 4:18, with which it shares many common features,[94] it appears that 5:11's "and build up each other, as indeed you are doing" corresponds to "with these words" (*en tois logois toutois*) in 4:18. The latter expression is retrospective. It points to what Paul has just written, including his rehearsal of the creed and the word of the Lord. The Thessalonians are urged to pass along Paul's words of encouragement. In contrast, "build up each other" does not look back. It looks forward. In its epistolary context, the expression serves as a transition to the paraenesis of 5:12-22.[95] As such it provides a perspective from which the entire body of subsequent paraenesis should be understood.

Apostolic Labor

The transition is completed as Paul begins the exhortation with, "but we appeal to you, brothers and sisters." While clearly marking the beginning of a new train of thought, Paul's choice of words, "*erōtōmen de hymas* – we appeal to you" is, in terms of the choice of verb and its mood,[96] less forceful than was Paul's earlier use of "*parakaleō* – encourage." Paul's appeal is that the Thessalonian Christians "respect those who labor among you, and have charge of you in the Lord and admonish you" and that they "esteem them very highly in love because of their work" (5,12b-13a).[97]

The exhortation prompts the modern interpreter to ask three questions: (1) What kinds of activity did Paul have in mind as he wrote about laboring, being in charge, and admonishing? (2) Within the community who was it that did those kinds of things? (3) What did Paul mean when he encouraged the Thessalonians to respect and esteem those who were involved in these activities? This group of questions ultimately focuses upon the nature of leadership – and therefore upon the structure – of the Thessalonian Christian community.

1. What kinds of activity is Paul describing? Part of the problem in answering this question is that each of the participles, with the exception of the third, that Paul uses to describe those who labor, have charge, and admonish is used but once in this letter and the third

participle is used but twice (5:12 and 14). On the other hand, the fact that Paul uses participles is in itself a significant fact. He is not so much writing about offices within the community as he is writing about activity within the community.[98] His frame of reference is not so much the structure of the community as its functional well-being.

What then are the functions to which Paul refers? "*Kopiaō* – labor" is a verb that, of itself, suggests a great deal of effort resulting in tiredness. It is related to the noun "*kopos* – labor," which Paul used both of his own manual labor among the Thessalonians (2:9) as well as of his apostolic activity among them (3:5). Both of these activities were, as has been noted, factually intermingled with one another. We cannot separate Paul's life-sustaining labor from his preaching because the two activities were truly related to one another.

When Paul now writes about those who were laboring among the Thessalonians, it would seem that he is referring to those who were presently doing the same kinds of things that he and his companions had done while they were among them. Those about whom Paul was writing were continuing where he and his companions had left off. That this was indeed the case becomes all the more likely when we realize that, early on within the Christian movement, both the noun, "*kopos* – labor," and the verb, "*kopiaō* – to labor," became preferred vocabulary to describe apostolic and evangelical activity.[99] It was obviously something in which the various members of the Thessalonian community were already engaged (cf. 1:3).

Being in Charge

The meaning of "*proïstēmi* – to have charge" is a bit more difficult to determine. The root meaning of the verb is to be in a forward position. Thus, the verb was frequently used of those who were in leadership positions. In the deutero-Pauline first letter of Timothy,[100] the term is used in reference to the management of a household (1 Tim 3:4, 5, 12; 5:17). Paul himself, however, at least insofar as we know, used the term on only one other occasion. That was when he was writing about the various gifts or charisms given to the members of the Christian communities in Rome. In his list of seven gifts, he writes about the "leader"[101] who is exhorted to exercise the gift "in diligence" (*proïstamenos en spoudē*). Since this mysterious gift is sandwiched between two other participial expressions that have to do with compassionate care, many commentators hold that Paul is writing about some form of caritative care in Rom 12:8. Consequently many suggest that it is a similar kind of care that Paul had in mind when he wrote to the Thessalonians as he did in 5:12.

There is some similarity between the "shotgun paraenesis"[102] of

5:16-22 and the various exhortations that Paul will proffer in Rom 12:3-21. In both instances church order is of the moment. As far as specifics are concerned one can note the exhortations to love (5:13; Rom 12:9, 10), to be at peace with one another (5:13; cf. Rom 5:16), to avoid vengeance (5:15; Rom 12:17), to rejoice (5:16; Rom 12:12), to pray (5:17; Rom 12:12), to discern between good and evil (5:21; Rom 12:9), and to avoid evil (5:22; Rom 12:21), as well as the references to prophecy (5:20; Rom 12:6). Given these similarities of context and content, it would seem legitimate to infer something about the meaning of what Paul meant by "having charge" in 1 Thess 5:12 from what he would later write in his letter to the Romans.[103]

In his later letters, including Romans, Paul's rhetoric uses a variety of nontaxative lists, for example, lists of virtues, vices, circumstances, household responsibilities, and charisms.[104] Many of these lists feature vocabulary that is not otherwise or rarely found in the New Testament. This leads to the conclusion that Paul is borrowing material from a traditional topos, but makes it difficult for the modern interpreter to determine precisely what Paul had in mind – if indeed he had anything specific in mind! – when he cited one or another item on his list. It is precisely this situation that creates a dilemma for the modern interpreter who wants to understand what Paul means by "*proïstamenos* – having charge" in Rom 12:8.

Given the fact that "*proïstamenos* – having charge" is in a participial form, commentators are virtually unanimous in affirming that Paul is referring to a function rather than to an office within the Christian community at Rome.[105] Some interpreters focus more on the etymology of the participle, while others derive their remarks more from Paul's placing this participle between two others that have to do with charitable activity within the community. Thus the interpretations run the gamut from those that center on leadership[106] – and one must note that Paul has carefully distinguished leadership within the Christian community from other forms of leadership by qualifying "*proïstamenos* – having charge" with a characteristic "*en kyriō* – in the Lord"[107] – and various modes of presidency[108] to those that highlight charitable activity.[109] Some interpreters try to combine the idea of leadership with that of caring by suggesting either an administrator in charge of the community's charitable work[110] or a patron of the community who might look after those who stood most in need of care and protection, for example, widows, orphans, slaves, and foreigners.[111]

Although the terminology of 1 Thess 5:12 is similar to that of Rom 12:8, the participial verb is in the singular in Romans, but in the plural in 1 Thessalonians. Although responsibility for fulfilling the function may have circulated among members of the Roman community,[112] the language of 1 Thessalonians suggests that it is to be fulfilled by more than one person. Given the fact that the letter was written shortly after Paul's departure from Thessalonica, and that the community was rather small, it is not unlikely that Paul has in mind a kind of leadership in which all of the members of the community share.

The third member of Paul's descriptive triad is the participle "*nouthetountas* – admonish.*" This role receives subsequent specification when Paul exhorts the member of the community to "*noutheteite tous atarktous* – admonish the idlers" in verse 14. The *ataktoi* are not so much idlers, as they are those who generally engage in anti-social conduct.[113] They are the disorderly members of the community who disturb its peace and welfare. The exhortation appears "to admonish the idlers" is clearly addressed to the "brothers and sisters,"[114] that is, all the members of the community. It calls for admonition to be given when one or another member of the community has grown slack vis-à-vis his or her responsibilities toward the community.

The element of mutuality in admonition can be inferred from what Paul writes in 1 Thess 5:14. It is explicit in Rom 15:14,[115] when Paul writes about his confidence that the Romans "*dynamenoi kai allēlous nouthetein* – are able to instruct one another." Although the NRSV renders the *nouthetein*[116] of Rom 5:14 as "instruct," thus bringing it into relationship with the "knowledge" to which Paul had just made reference, what Paul has in mind would really seem to be a matter of correcting what is amiss.[117] It is, to echo a comment by Johannes Behm, a reciprocal ministry of the members exercising pastoral oversight with a sense of community obligation.[118] They take responsibility for the behavior of one another.

"*Noutheteō* – admonish" is the strongest term within the range of Pauline terms that have "exhortation" as their general connotation.[119] The exhortation that follows immediately upon the injunction to "admonish the idlers" in 5:14 makes use of a verb that belongs to the same lexical range, but is less harsh. Paul exhorts the members of the community to "encourage [*paramytheisthe*][120] the faint-hearted." He continues to urge the community to care gently for those who are weak as he exhorts them to "help the weak" and "be patient with all."[121] The four exhortations of verse 14 constitute a single group of "four rules."[122] They are introduced by a common lemma, "And we urge you, brothers and sisters."[123] The final rule, "be patient with all," sums everything up and brings the small unit to closure. It parallels the exhortation that Philodorus, the Epicurean philosopher, directed to speakers.[124]

Those identified as being in need of the care of the community are generally identified by means of their psychic disposition; only the "idlers" are identified by means of their behavior. David Black has argued that Paul's call for the nurturing of the idlers, the faint-hearted, and the weak makes reference to people to whom Paul addresses his various exhortations in the letter, that is, the idlers in 4:9-12,[125] the faint-hearted in 4:13-18,[126] and the weak in 5:1-11.[127] Other commentators argue, correctly I believe, that the "idlers" constitute the only truly distinct group of Thessalonians identified by Paul.[128] When Paul wrote his letter to the Thessalonians, the community was of too recent foundation for it to have developed the type of diversification and stratification postulated by Black.

Who's in Charge?

2. When we ask who among the Thessalonians were doing the kind of labor, leading, and admonishing that Paul commends to the respect of the Thessalonians, we are in fact asking a pair of questions. The first is whether it is possible to distinguish three groups of leaders within the community at Thessalonica. Were, in other words, those who labored among them a group distinct from those who are described as being in charge and were both of these groups still different from those who had responsibility for admonishment within the community? A related question is whether those who had leadership responsibilities were somehow distinct from the rest of the community, as, in the church of later centuries, the clergy would be distinct from the laity.

To begin, one must note that this first of Paul's letters does not offer any clear evidence that the community at Thessalonica was as neatly structured as were those to which the first letter to the Corinthians and the deutero-Paulines were addressed and that, apart from the incidental reference to "apostles" in 2:7, the technical language used to designate various "offices" in the early church (that is, not only overseer, elder, and servant,[129] but also apostle, prophet, teacher, and evangelist) is absent from 1 Thessalonians.

It is, moreover, quite clear that Paul is writing about functions and activities within the community in 5:12, and not about offices. His use of verbs in the form of participles, rather than nouns, is patent evidence that he is writing about activity. Laboring, being in charge, and admonishing are three kinds of activity in which the leadership at Thessalonica is involved; they do not necessarily designate three different groups of leaders. In fact the solitary article (*tous*) with which the series of three participles begins is grammatical evidence for the fact that Paul is writing about a single group of persons who are engaged in three kinds of activity.[130]

Who are these persons? Is it possible to identify them as a distinct group within the community of Thessalonica, a kind of leadership cadre set apart from the rest of the community?[131] This is a second structure-focused question that arises from an examination of 5:12. Who was it that did the kinds of things to which 5:12 refers?

In response, one must first of all recall that the following exhortation is directed to the whole community,[132] those whom Paul addresses as "*adelphoi* – brothers and sisters" (5:14). The exhortation urges the entire community to bear responsibility for mutual admonishment. Just as the members of the community are, as a group and individually, to seek to do good, to rejoice, to pray and give thanks always, and to avoid vengeance, so they have a common responsibility to admonish one another, that is, specifically, to admonish those members of the community who are engaged in unruly behavior. Moreover, in 4:18 and 5:11, all the members of the community have been exhorted to encourage one another and thus build up the community. So it would seem that at least one of the functions to which 5:12 refers is a function that devolves upon all members of the community.

Something similar can be said apropos those "who labor among you." Paul and his companions had labored (*kopon, ergazomenoi*) among the Thessalonians with an intensity that was commensurate with the love that they had for the Thessalonians (2:5–12). All the Thessalonians are urged to work (*ergazesthai*) in such a way that they would be dependent on no outsider (4:11–12). Their mutual love was memorable. Paul wrote about it at the very outset of his letter, when he described their loving activity as a "a labor [*kopou*] of love" (1:3). It was the entire community whose labor was known to Paul. The activity of those who labor (*popiōntas*) among the Thessalonians is simply called their work (*to ergon autōn*) in 5:13. Thus it would appear that a second of the leadership functions identified in 5:12 devolved upon the entire community.

The etymology of "*proïstamenos* – having charge," with its prefixed *pro-*, might lead the interpreter to think of those who stand out as leaders within the community. Paul has, in any case, not identified one such leader. His participle is in the plural. Those who lead are also those who labor and those who admonish. Since responsibility for these latter two activities falls on all members of the community, it seems reasonable to assume that Paul would attribute some leadership to each of the members of the community. He does not distinguish those who exercise "pastoral care" from those who generally receive it. He does not give us reason to think that there existed a specific leadership group within the community at Thessalonica; rather all the members of the community were leaders insofar as they labored and admonished. All are engaged in what Abraham Malherbe has called "mutual nurturing."[133] There is a mutuality in leadership and service that would later be recognized as a hallmark of the communities founded by Paul.

Recognition and Leadership

3. Paul called upon the Thessalonians to respect and esteem highly those who were involved in these activities. Paul first calls for the recognition of the service that these members of the community were giving. He asks the community to "know," that is, to recognize and appreciate,[134] those in their midst who were rendering service. Paul's threefold use of "you" (*hymin... hymōn... hymas*) underscores the notion that the Thessalonians have been the beneficiaries of the activities of those who have labored among them. Accordingly they are to recognize what has been done on their behalf and those who have rendered this service.

The responsive character of the Thessalonians' appreciation of the leadership exercised among them is further highlighted when Paul continues his call for appreciation with the specification that they "esteem them very highly in love because of their work" (5:13).[135] These people are to be esteemed for what they have done within the community. They are to be esteemed "*en agapē* – in love." Just as there is a Christian character associated with leadership in the community ("*en kyriō* – in the Lord," v. 12), so there is a Christian quality that characterizes the appropriate response to that leadership ("*en agapē* – in love," v. 13).

Leadership is to be exercised "in the Lord." What would subsequently prove to be one of Paul's favorite expressions is used to identify authority in the name and by the power of whom leadership is to be exercised within the community. That leadership is "work" (*ergon*), that is, apostolic activity. Is it appropriate, although perhaps anachronistic, to speak of that leadership as charismatic leadership? After all, Paul will later begin his reflection on charisms by stating that: "there are varieties of activities [*energēmatōn*], but it is the same God who activates [*ho energōn*] all of them in everyone" (1 Cor 12:6).

Charismatic Gifts

The intertext with 1 Thess 5:12-22 that is found in Paul's letter to the Romans speaks of the "gifts that differ according to the grace given to us" (Rom 12:6). The Greek wording of Paul's communication with the Romans constitutes a nicely turned phrase, virtually a play on words, which closely relates the gifts to the grace of God. They are *charismata kata tēn charin*, gifts according to grace. The grace that is given provides Paul and his readers with a perspective (cf. Rom 12:3), from which Paul can discourse on the body of Christ and the functional roles that devolve upon the various members of the church as it is built up into the body of Christ.

The language of Romans 12 clearly reflects the kind of language which Paul typically uses to describe various functions within the church. In 1 Corinthians 12 Paul attributes these *"charismata —* gifts"[136] to the Holy Spirit. Generally speaking, the gifts fall into two categories, speaking and serving,[137] but no two of Paul's lists of these gifts are exactly alike.[138] Thus Paul seems not to have had in mind clearly defined functions within the church; rather he seems to have envisaged various responses to the movement of the Spirit within the church and its members such that the latter exercise complementary functions within the community.

The only gift that appears on all four of Paul's lists of charisms is the gift of *"prophēteia —* prophecy" (Rom 12:6; 1 Cor 12:10, 28, 29).[139] This term appears in 1 Thess 5:20, where it is closely associated with the Spirit:

> Do not quench the Spirit.
> Do not despise the words of prophets. (1 Thess 5:19-20)

The pair of verses is structurally united[140] by a *parallelismus membrorum,* a kind of parallelism recognized by today's readers of the Bible as a feature of Hebrew poetry.[141] The parallelism is enhanced by the presence of an assonant *"mē —* not" within each member, an example of Paul's use of the rhetorical device technically known as paramoia. The pair of verses (5:19-20) is, in turn, antithetically related to the three verses that immediately follow:

> But test everything;
> hold fast to what is good;
> abstain from every form of evil. (1 Thess 5:21-22)

These three verses are closely related to one another. An adversative *"de —* but" links these three units of thought (vv. 21-22) with the preceding pair (vv. 19-20). The paired exhortation was formulated negatively; each member of the subsequent trio is expressed in positive fashion. Such expression enhances the unity of the passage and accentuates the rhetorical contrast marked by Paul's use of the adversative *"de —* but." All five expressions should be seen within the context of Paul's shotgun paraenesis, which reaches a frenetic or staccato pace in verses 16-22:

> [16]Rejoice always,
> [17]pray without ceasing,
> [18]give thanks in all circumstances;
> for this is the will of God in Christ Jesus for you.
> [19]Do not quench the Spirit.
> [20]Do not despise the words of prophets.

[21]But test everything;
hold fast to what is good;
[22]abstain from every form of evil.

Robert Estienne's 1551 division of this passage, consisting of only thirty-four words in Paul's Greek text, into seven verses accurately reflects the quick movement of Paul's thought and leads to the characterization of these verses as having something of a staccato rhythm. The absence of connectives – asyndeton, in technical parlance – further points to the shotgun character of the exhortation.

There is, nonetheless, a certain unity in the material, which Frank Witt Hughes has identified as a group of seven rules.[142] The editors of N-A[26] have printed verses 17-22 in indented fashion. This arrangement expresses their unity and highlights their evidently formal structure.[143] The two connectives that Paul has used, namely, the "*gar* – for" of verse 18 and the adversative "*de* – but" of verse 21, contribute to the unity of the passage. So, too, does the universal perspective that embraces the entire unit. Paul employs a kind of *inclusio*, fashioned from the use of the root "*pant* – all"; he begins his rapid exhortation with "*pantote...panti* – always ... all" and brings it to closure with "*panta...pantos* – everything ... every." Within this unified passage, verse 18b, with its explanatory "*gar* – for," marks a transition.

The first unit of material, verses 16-18a, need not long detain us, except insofar as it points to the real-life situation of the Thessalonian community, with regard to which Paul is making a concrete exhortation. The triadic unit consists of three parallel clauses, whose essential synonymity is readily apparent.[144] One might categorize Paul's thought in terms of the rhetorical category of *repetitio*, but the category of synonymous parallelism might be equally apropos. For the present there is no need to distinguish one clause from the other, but one must note that Paul has appended an explanatory clause to his repetitious exhortation "for this is the will of God in Christ Jesus for you" (v. 18b).

The Will of God

The verse is clearly transitional, but one must ask whether the transition is effected by Paul's bringing to closure verses 16-18a (transition by closure) or whether the transition is effected by Paul's use of an explanatory clause to move from one exhortation to another (transition by introduction). These alternatives are reflected in the capitalization and punctuation of the various versions. I, however, would suggest that verse 18b, albeit functioning, both grammatically and really, as the provision of grounds for the preceding exhortation, effects a more complete transition by introducing a second series of exhortations.

The verse lacks any expressed verb (one would normally expect the presence of a copulative "*estin* – is"). Otherwise, it is a virtual reprise of the formula found in 4:3, "For this is the will of God, your (sanctification)" (*touto gar estin thelēma tou theou...hymōn*). The formula used in 4:3 has the form of an explanation – one cannot overlook the presence of the demonstrative "*touto* – this" and the explanatory "*gar* – for." These same features are found in 5:18b: "for this is the will of God...for you" (*touto gar thelēma theou eis hymas*).

The repeated explanatory phrase introduces the motif of the "will of God," a major motif in Judaism,[145] into Paul's paraenesis. God's will was the ultimate norm of and motivation for community-conforming behavior, that is, for the conduct that expressed the ethos of God's people.

In the paraenesis of 4:1-8, Paul's "for this is the will of God" looks back to the brace of introductory verses (4:1-2), which recalls the halakah that Paul had previously imparted and looks ahead to the specific instructions that follow – a series of five infinitives having the force of an imperative, of which the first is "*apechesthai* – abstain." The introductory verses speak of God and the Lord Jesus; the paraenesis that follows talks about a specific aspect of life in the Spirit.

There is a parallelism, both structural and thematic, between the discursive paraenesis of 4:1-8 and the staccato paraenesis of 5:16-22.[146] The following elements can be identified: the use of the "*touto gar thelēma theou* – this is the will of God" formula as a hinge element (4:3a; 5:18b), reference to a Christian attitude to God prior to the transitional formula (4:1; 5:16-18a) and a series of five imperatives after the transitional formula (4:3c-6; 5:19-22).[147] The paraenesis consequent to the transition in 4:3 focuses on inspirited life, that is, holiness and the gift of the Holy Spirit (4:8), while the Spirit is a focal point of the exhortation in 5:16-22 (cf. v. 19).

The transitional formula of 5:18b differs significantly from that of 4:3a insofar as Paul has introduced a qualifying "*en Christō Iēsou* – in Christ Jesus" into the transitional formula of 5:18b. The expression provides a christological reference for the paraenesis of 5:16-22 (cf. 4:1, 2, 6), a feature that Paul otherwise omits from his staccato paraenesis.

Prophecy

Paul spares his words as he formulates his paraenetic exhortation: "Do not quench the Spirit. Do not despise the words of prophets.

But test everything; hold fast to what is good; abstain from every form of evil." What does Paul mean by *"prophēteias* – the words of prophets" (v. 20)? *"Prophēteia* – prophecy" can connote either the gift of prophecy or prophetic utterances. In his first letter to the Corinthians, the letter in which Paul uses *"prophēteia* – prophecy" most frequently, he uses the term in both of its senses.[148] Thus there arises a question as to what Paul actually meant when he urged the Thessalonians not to despise "prophecy." That the word appears in a plural form in Paul does not provide a real clue as to the meaning of the term, because it is possible to think of different forms of the gift of prophecy[149] or of a similar gift given to different persons.

The editors of the recent English-language translations of verse 20 disagree among themselves as to what is the correct understanding of *"prophēteia* – prophecy" in this verse. The NIV, RNAB, REB, and the New Translation[150] agree with the NRSV in taking it as a reference to prophetic utterance, while the NJB takes it to mean the gift of prophecy. Because the word is in the plural and lacks an article, one might be inclined to accept "prophetic utterances" as the better rendering, but even that rendition implies that there were "prophets" in the community at Thessalonica, as the NRSV's translation, "the words of prophets," clearly indicates. A prophet is, of course, not someone who so much tells about the future as he or she is one who speaks from the heart, where God alone discerns,[151] and who speaks on behalf of God. In common Greek parlance, *"prophēteia* – prophecy" was the gift of interpreting the will of the gods.[152] The gift was one that Paul apparently valued as the most important of the gifts of the Spirit for a local church community.[153]

With this in mind and while recognizing that Paul's staccato paraenesis does not allow for the discursive reflection about the role of the Spirit and the gift of prophecy in the local community that he would later proffer in 1 Corinthians 12–14, it is clear that the pair of parallel verses in 1 Thess 5:19-20 moves from the general to the particular[154] or, perhaps better yet, from the source to its manifestation. Thus we might identify the parallelism as akin to Semitic synthetic parallelism. There is an identifiable movement of thought within a brace of parallel expressions.

The Spirit

Taking cues from Paul's occasional use of *"pneuma* – spirit" to connote the human spirit[155] and a text in which Plutarch uses a fiery metaphor in reference to the *pneuma*,[156] W. C. van Unnik interprets verse 19 of an individual Christian's personal charismatic zeal and verse 20 of the charismatic activity of others.[157] He sees the pair of verses as an injunction addressed to the members of the community urging them not to suppress charismatic "enthusiasm,"[158] that is, neither in themselves nor in the other members of the community.

Prior to verse 19 Paul had always used the term "*pneuma* – spirit," which has a manifestly anthropological connotation in 5:23, in reference to the divine spirit. In each instance (1:5, 6; 4:8), Paul had qualified "*pneuma* – spirit" by "*hagion* – holy." There is little reason to suggest that, in verse 19, Paul departs from this earlier and consistent usage of "*pneuma* – spirit." The parallelism between 5:16–22 and 4:1-8 confirms that the "*pneuma* – spirit" of 5:19 is the divine spirit.[159]

What could Paul possibly mean by "do not quench the Spirit"? The verb "*sbennumi* – quench or extinguish" is hapax in Pauline usage. It is properly used in reference to extinguishing a fire, as it is in the rest of its New Testament occurrences (Matt 12:20; 25:8; Mark 9:48; Eph 6:16; and Heb 11:34). Plutarch, as has been noted, used a cognate of this verb in reference to the spirit.[160] Early Christian literature, following a biblical tradition, often used fire as a metaphor for the spirit, as a symbol of divine power and action.[161] The power of God was to be made manifest in the coming of his kingdom, the in-bringing of the new age. Paul's worldview was basically framed within the categories of Jewish apocalyptic thought. For him the kingdom was on the point of being realized.

These ideas will be further fleshed out in the course of the present study, but some reference to them must be made at the present time since they provide a background for Paul's understanding of the spirit. Fire could serve as a potent and evocative symbol of God's power. Hence, Paul could exhort the Thessalonians not to quench the spirit. The aforementioned citation from Plutarch indicates that Paul's words would have been meaningful for his Hellenistic audience. To a modern reader Paul's words might recall the Jewish paraphrase of Num 11:24, that of Targum Neofiti 1, which rendered the biblical text as "do not take the Spirit away from them."[162]

The Thessalonians had already experienced the power of God at work among them (1:5-6). Now they were being urged not to impede the present activity of God among them. Specifically they should not disdain prophetic utterance. Paul's reference to the Spirit and its manifestation in 5:19-20 recalls his earlier references to the Spirit, not only in 1:5-6, but also and especially in 4:8, where he concludes an exhortation bearing some similarity with 5:16-22 with "whoever rejects this rejects not human authority but God, who also gives his Holy Spirit to you." A similar perspective shapes the paired exhortation of 5:19-20, "Do not quench the Spirit. Do not despise the words of prophets." Whoever rejects the expression of divine *exousia*,[163] rejects that authority itself.

Testing the Gifts

Verses 19-20 are adversatively linked to the following triad, "test everything; hold fast to what is good; abstain from every form of evil" (5:21-22). Once again Paul's language is comparable to that of Plutarch, who also uses the language of "*dokimazontōn* – testing" and "*kalēn* – good." This language appears when the philosopher refers to the process of distinguishing between authentic and counterfeit coins as a useful simile in his moral reflection.[164]

Although it may be tempting to read verses 19-20 merely as an ethical injunction, it is preferable to consider them as part of Paul's continuing exhortation on charismatic activity within the church.[165] The Pauline paraenesis of 1 Thessalonians is, after all, socially rather than individually oriented. These verses are, moreover, linked to the preceding pair of verses by the connective "*de* – but,"[166] albeit in adversative fashion. There is a close connection between verse 20 and verse 21a: "Do not despise the words of prophets, but test everything." The following exhortation (vv. 21b-22) spells out the implications of the testing process: "hold fast to what is good; abstain from every form of evil."

Within this frame of reference, it is clear that Paul's "*panta* – everything" includes the words of the prophets. Apropos Paul's "test everything," Wayne Grudem[167] repeatedly notes that the apostle is not exhorting the community at Thessalonica to distinguish true prophets from false prophets in the manner in which Israel of old was challenged to discern between authentic and false prophets.[168] Neither is Paul appealing to some individual within the community who has the gift of the discernment of spirits à la 1 Cor 12:10. Paul is rather engaged in exhorting all members of the community in a fashion similar to that in which he exhorted the Corinthians when he wrote: "Let two or three prophets speak, and let the others weigh what is said" (1 Cor 14:29).[169]

In verses 19-20 Paul calls upon the community to discriminate among prophetic utterances. These verses belong to a paraenetic unit (vv. 12-22) whose primary purpose is to order community life and relationships. Paul assumes the presence of one or more prophetic figures within the community at Thessalonica and, further, that these generally speak on God's behalf. Nonetheless, not everything that a prophet says is *eo ipso* to be taken as a word from God. The community itself must discern that which is good from that which seems to be evil, presumably, that which builds up (see 4:18; 5:11) from that which does not.[170]

Paul does not use the language of office[171] in his exhortation to the community at Thessalonica. The language of charism is yet to appear in his written text. It is therefore somewhat anachronistic to speak of the charismatic structure of the community at Thessalonica. Nonetheless the kinds of activity that Christians are exhorted to exercise on behalf of one another are similar to those that Paul will identify, in later letters, by means of the category of charism. Being in charge and prophesying are to be recognized as charismatic gifts. In one sense "laboring" is likewise to be recognized as a charismatic activity since Paul uses the term, almost in a technical sense, to describe the apostolic activity of himself and his companions, and the "apostolate" is certainly to be ranked among the charismatic gifts.[172] In any case the community of Christians at Thessalonica was a tightly knit group, whose members were comparable to a family unit, bound together with bonds of sibling love. In later reflections[173] Paul will identify love as the fundamental and highest gift.

Distinguished from outsiders, the members of the small Christian group at Thessalonica were expected to render mutual service to one another. Mutuality is the hallmark of a charismatically organized community.[174] Toward the beginning of his reflection on charisms in 1 Corinthians 12–14, Paul tells his readers that "there are varieties of gifts, but the same Spirit; and there are varieties of services, but the same Lord; and there are varieties of activities, but it is the same God who activates all of them in everyone" (1 Cor 12:4–5). The triadic language of this passage will make a significant contribution to the church's later reflection on the trinitarian God. In the passage Paul affirms that, from different points of view, the individual charisms are, at one and the same time, gifts, services, and activities. Something similar can be said apropos the various activities to which Paul refers in 1 Thess 5:12–22, where reference is similarly made to *"theos* – God," *"kyrios* – Lord," and *"pneuma* – Spirit."

In sum, the kind of interrelated service that Paul intimates to have existed at Thessalonica, along with the authoritative referents in his exhortation as an indication of his theological context, allow us – albeit *avant la lettre* – to affirm that the Christian community at Thessalonica was charismatically structured. Its characteristic features were not office and individuality, but service and mutuality.

The Gathering of the Community

Since Paul wrote "to the church of the Thessalonians," it goes without saying that the Thessalonian Christians gathered together from time to time. The church is, in fact, a gathering. It takes place in the gathering together of those who actually assemble. It would be interesting to know what the Christians of Thessalonica did when they came together. Paul does not describe for us what actually happened in the assemblies of the Thessalonian Christians, but the modern reader would like to know whether any of their gatherings affected what today would be called a liturgical quality. Does Paul's letter contain any clues to satisfy the curious?

Listening

To be sure, one thing that the Thessalonians did when they gathered was to listen. Their gathering was a gathering of listeners. When Paul and his companions were among them, they heard the word that had been preached (2:13). Later they were to gather to hear the letter that Paul had written to them (5:27). They gathered to hear the spoken word; they gathered to hear – at least on one occasion – the written word. Since Paul's letter contains no clear citation of the Jewish scriptures and since the community was composed of those who had been pagans (1:9), it is difficult to make the case, on the basis of possible analogies with Jewish synagogal services, that the community at Thessalonica gathered to listen to a reading from the Torah.

Praying

Some authors suggest that community prayer was another activity in which the Thessalonians were engaged when they came together. Within the staccato paraenesis of 5:12–22, whose primary purpose is to order community life and relationships,[175] there is the injunction to "rejoice always, pray without ceasing, give thanks in all circumstances." This is yet another example of the triadic exposition of Paul's thought. The notion of "always," with the root *pant-*, serves to bind the three injunctions into a single unit of thought by a sort of *inclusio*.[176] Commenting upon Paul's injunction to "pray without ceasing" (v. 17), Wanamaker notes that Paul expects "his converts to remember continually to pray for their own needs and the needs of others. This was presumably to be done both privately and in the corporate prayers of the church."[177]

The language in which Paul phrases his exhortation recalls the words with which he began his letter. The significant words of

5:16–18a, apart that is, from the mention of joy,[178] are found in Paul's opening rehearsal: "we always [*pantote*] give thanks [*eucharistoumen*] to God for all [*pantōn*] of you and mention you in our prayers [*proseuchōn*], constantly [*adialeptōs*] remembering…" (1:2). In recalling his own thanksgiving, Paul uses verbs in the plural, recalling thereby the common thanksgiving of himself, Silvanus, and Timothy. The prayers that he mentions are prayers of invocation, prayers in which the name of the Lord is invoked. In Paul's estimation, thanksgiving is the expression of a basic Christian disposition. Everything comes as a "*charis* – grace" of God; it is received by the believer with "*charis* – thanks."[179]

In Paul's world prayers were vocal and appropriately accompanied by bodily gesture. This makes it quite reasonable to assume that he was indeed writing about public and common thanksgiving. This is all the more reasonable in that a term like "*eucharistērion* – expression of gratitude" was commonly used in reference to the Egyptian cults of his day.[180] In any event, Paul's "*en panti* – in all circumstances"[181] represents an expression of paraenetic hyperbole, typical of his paraenesis on prayer. Similar hyperbolic qualifications are attached to the other exhortations in Paul's little triad: "Rejoice always; pray without ceasing." The latter injunction generally pertains to all invocatory prayer, but the formula, with a wording similar to that of 5:25, might suggest that Paul really has petitionary prayer in mind.[182]

The first element of the triad, "rejoice always," most likely represents an exhortation in regard to worship, just as much as do Paul's exhortations on thanksgiving and invocatory prayer. "Joy" is a term typically used to describe an attitude of receptiveness in the presence of God. In Paul's own Jewish tradition "joy" is a cultic term. The expression seems to have retained its cultic overtones when Paul wrote, "How can we thank God enough for you in return for all the joy that we feel before our God because of you?" (3:9). "Before our God – *emprosthen tou theou hēmōn*,"[183] that is, in the presence of our God, echoes a cultic formula.[184]

In 3:9 Paul writes redundantly of "joy." His "for all the joy that we feel" is literally "for all the joy that we enjoy" (*epi pasē tē chara hē chairomen*[185]). He associates joy with thanksgiving. In 3:9, as in 5:16, Paul writes enthusiastically about joy. One who gives thanks to God can only do so with joy, because he, she, and they have experienced God's "*charis* – grace." Those who experience God's presence are, as it were, overwhelmed by the experience. In sum, the exhortation to "rejoice always" is, formally and in terms of its content, an integral element of the triad of injunctions in verses 16–18a. All three bear upon the community's life of prayer.

Thus, while 1 Thess 5:16–18a hardly provides an order of worship,[186] it does provide a series of exhortations relative to the community's life of prayer. It is likely that the community was expected to respond to these as a community. These injunctions on community prayer are linked to the exhortations on the Spirit and its manifestations. Together they constitute what Hughes has called "a group of seven rules."[187] The modern reader, for whom 1 Corinthians 12-14 provides a helpful analogue, can legitimately presume that Paul's injunctions relate to the manifestations of the Spirit as the community gathers together for worship.[188]

If the seven rules of 5:16-22 provide one opening through which to catch a glimpse of the Thessalonians' worship, other passages in the letter provide various echoes of their common prayer and liturgy. Louis Monloubou has written that traces of the Christian liturgy are to be found in 3:11-13 and 1:9-10, where the hieratic character of Paul's language betrays its cultic origin.[189] Essentially his claim is that Paul's epistolary language has been shaped in the life-setting of Christian worship. This may be particularly true of the wish prayers, of which 3:11-13 provides a classic example. Gordon Wiles has suggested that not only does Paul's personal devotional practice lie behind such prayers, but also that their language must have been modified according to the usages of the early Christian assembly.[190]

Baptism

This is not to suggest that the wish prayers of 3:11, 3:12-13, and 5:23-24 were prayer formularies in use at Thessalonica. It is simply to suggest that the language of these prayers echoes that of Christian worship. Other echoes of Christian liturgy appear here and there throughout Paul's letter.[191] Commentators typically affirm that formulae such as *"en Christō* – in Christ"[192] and *"en Kyriō* – in the Lord"[193] derive from a pre-Pauline baptismal tradition.[194] Gerhard Friedrich believed that he could identify elements of a Jewish-Christian baptismal hymn in 1:9-10.[195] Ceslas Spicq held that the "taught by God" of 4:9 referred to the day of Christian initiation, inferring that the call of God was concretized in the baptismal catechesis.[196]

The section of 1 Thessalonians that most seems to evoke early Christian baptismal practice is 5:4-11.[197] The passage contains a metaphorical description of Christian existence, with general exhortations that are likewise imaginatively phrased. The contrast between light and darkness, the description of Christians as children of the light and children of the day[198] – a contrast existence – forms one of the leitmotifs of Wolfgang Harnisch's important study of baptismal themes reflected in Paul's paraenesis.[199] The contrast between light and darkness, day and night, is a common motif in various forms of religious

literature. The evocative description that Paul gives of the life situation
of Christians is appropriate for baptismal catechesis, so appropriate
in fact, that some of its elements have entered into the post-Pauline
baptismal catechesis.[200]

Paul exhorts the neophyte Christians at Thessalonica to "be sober,
and put on the breastplate of faith and love, and for a helmet the hope
of salvation" (5:8). The call for sobriety is a commonplace in Hellenistic moral exhortation, but Paul's metaphorical appeal to don military
apparel appears, as we have seen, to reflect Isa 59:17. The biblical
allusion may well have escaped those hearers of the letter who had recently turned from idol-worship, but it would have been meaningful
for Paul, reared as he was in the biblical tradition. Both the biblical text
and Paul employ the verb "*enduō* – put on," a verb that later Christian
literature, including Paul's own letters to the Romans and Galatians,
used in a baptismal context.[201]

The manifold allusions to a baptismal catechesis, and perhaps to
a baptism ritual, albeit clarified only by reference to later literature,
suggest that the Thessalonians engaged in a baptismal practice that –
today at least – would be called liturgical.

Worship

There are other indications in this letter that suggest that the Christians of Thessalonica came together for worship. The initial salutation
is one such indication. Scholars have long noted that Paul's greeting,
"grace to you and peace," while similar to the common epistolary
greetings of his culture, is a bit unusual. It seems to combine elements that reflect a Hellenistic greeting ("*charis* – grace," assonant
with the typical Hellenistic epistolary greeting "*chairein* – greetings") and those that reflect a Semitic greeting ("*eirēnē* – peace,"
the *shalom* of biblical tradition and the familiar Semitic greeting).
This unusual formula may echo a typical opening sentence for a
Christian assembly come together for worship.[202] The unusual formulation may have arisen in the Christian community at Antioch,
where Christians of different cultural heritages came together for
worship.[203]

Another hint that the Christians of Thessalonica came together for
worship can be gleaned from the wish prayer of 5:23, "May the God
of peace himself sanctify you entirely; and may your spirit and soul
and body be kept sound and blameless at the coming of our Lord Jesus
Christ." This prayer appears at the end of Paul's letter,[204] just before
the final greetings. Its language is that of the apostle and its themes
echo those of the letter. So the prayer can safely be assumed to be a
Pauline composition *ad hoc*, rather than a formulaic prayer already

known to the Thessalonian Christians.[205] The prayer has the form of a
homiletic benediction.[206] Form corresponds to function. The function
of such homiletic benedictions, reminiscent of those used in the assemblies of Jews, is to bring to closure an assembly that had gathered
for prayer and study.

In sum, both the opening of Paul's letter and its conclusion appear
to reflect a tradition of Christian worship. Together they give the impression that Paul intended his letter to be read to a community that
had gathered for worship. It has been argued that the prayers, a "holy
kiss," and grace are sufficient indication to warrant the conclusion
that the reading of Paul's letter to the Thessalonians was immediately
followed by the celebration of eucharist.[207] The case of those who
hold that Paul's letter was read immediately before the eucharist, at
the conclusion of the synaxis, is, to a large extent, based on the contention that the "holy kiss" of 5:26 is a liturgical gesture[208] and that the
most likely setting for the liturgical prayer-kiss-greeting sequence is at
the point of transition between synaxis and eucharist.[209]

In my judgment, Paul's "greet all the brothers and sisters with a holy
kiss" is an epistolary formulation. Hellenistic letters of Paul's time typically were brought to closure with a request that the recipients "greet"
others on behalf of the one who had written the letter.[210] In 5:26 Paul
is asking that his greetings be extended to those Christians to whom
his letter was not specifically addressed and who would, presumably,
not hear it read. Indeed, there seems to be no explicit reference to the
celebration of eucharist in this earliest of Paul's letters.[211]

Problems in Thessalonica

Reflecting on the situation of his beloved Thessalonian believers, Paul
says that they had become imitators of the churches of God in Christ
Jesus. He then went on to explain what he meant: "for you suffered
the same things from your own compatriots as they did from the Jews,
who killed both the Lord Jesus and the prophets" (2:14–15). Much
has been written about Paul's statement and his explanation. Could
he, who boasted of being an Israelite (Rom 11:1),[212] have been so anti-
Semitic as to write in this fashion? Many twentieth-century scholars
are convinced that Paul could not have written these words. So they
expunge them from their "critical version" of Paul's letter, ascribing
them to the hands of a later interpolator.[213]

The arguments of those who would, as it were, rewrite Paul's letter are unconvincing. The manuscript tradition consistently includes
this passage within the letter. There is, however, far more than the external evidence to be considered. Not only does Paul write about his

own experience (vv. 15b-16a), but he also writes in a prophetic vein. To a large extent his themes are a reprise and further development of thoughts introduced in 1:6-7. The ideas expressed are consistent with Paul's apocalyptic insights and a (Jewish) theology of martyrdom, which was hardly foreign to him.[214]

The passage provides a frame of reference within which Paul intended the Thessalonian Christians to understand their suffering. They were not alone in their suffering. They shared a fate similar to that of the apostles, the prophets, the churches of Judea, and Jesus himself! As difficult as their situation was, there was nothing unusual about it. Indeed Paul had forewarned the Thessalonian believers about the persecutions that would befall them (3:4). They should have expected to live in a contrary situation; 2:14 and 3:4 indicate that they did so.

That the Thessalonian Christians were a persecuted group is one of the factors that enabled them to be cited as a "model" for groups of believers throughout Macedonia and Achaia (1:6-7). References to the persecution of the Thessalonians are scattered throughout the letter,[215] so much so that one can hardly escape the conclusion that persecution was the epistolary *statsis* of our letter.[216] Their afflictions troubled Paul.[217] His own circumstances prevented him from going personally to the Thessalonians as he should have liked to do (2:18-3:3a).[218] He feared lest they lose confidence in him and apostasize from their faith. Satan, most likely through some form of human agency,[219] frustrated Paul's desire to go to Thessalonica. His disquiet finally led him to send Timothy as an emissary who would find out about the Thessalonians and their faith.

Good News

The news with which Timothy returned was "good news." The Thessalonian Christians had remained steadfast in their faith and love, that is, in their Christian way of life. For Paul such news was part of "the gospel."[220] Paul expected that mention of the sufferings of the prophets and Jesus, the churches in Judea, and the apostles would help to sustain the Thessalonians in the midst of their persecutions (2:14-15). News of their steadfastness was to sustain Paul and his companions in their own distress and persecution (3:7-8). Not only was there mutuality in their suffering of persecution, there was also mutual support and encouragement to be had from the knowledge that others were steadfast in their faith despite the persecution that they were enduring.

This good news was for Paul and his companions a source of joy (3:9). Their joy was, in a way, similar to the joy inspired by the Spirit (1:6) that the Thessalonians had experienced when they received the good news from Paul and his companions. Paul's rehearsal of the results of Timothy's debriefing (3:6-9) bears, in fact, more than one similarity with his description of the coming of God's word to the Thessalonians (1:5-6). In both passages we recognize the themes of good news, faith, joy, and persecution – all within the perspective of thanks addressed to God. The joy experienced by Paul is God's gift.[221] It is a response to his experience – mediated by Timothy's announcement – of God's continuing activity within the Thessalonian community. In the constancy of their faith could be found an indication of the dynamic presence of the Spirit among them. Paul's labor had not been in vain.[222]

A Severe Ordeal

We would like to know more about the real situation at Thessalonica. In the Acts of the Apostles Luke has written a stylized account that mentions the Jews' engaging a band of ruffians who set the city in an uproar, attacked a home, and dragged those upon whom they had set before the crowds and the magistrates. His is an account of violence and unruliness, an appeal to the mobs and the authorities. Luke's account may be stylized, but it cannot be totally disregarded. His mention of the politarchs (Acts 17:6), whose role in the governance of the city has been verified by archeological discoveries,[223] indicates that Luke had some knowledge of sociopolitical conditions in Thessalonica.[224]

Paul will later write about the "severe ordeal of affliction" (*en pollē dokimē thlipseōs*) that occurred in the churches of Macedonia, including presumably the church at Thessalonica, which was a model in regard to suffering.[225] Paul is not graphic in describing the persecution of the Thessalonians. He does, however, remark that the persecution came from their very own compatriots (*hymeis hypo tōn symphyteōn*, 2:14). The most obvious meaning of "compatriots" (*symphyletoi*) is those who belong to the same race (*phylē*). In this case, Paul would be noting, with regard to the largely Gentile community at Thessalonica, that a group of Gentile citizens were responsible for their suffering. Some commentators, however, are of the opinion that, in 2:14, the words have a local rather than a racial connotation.[226]

The intensity with which Paul writes of those Jews who killed the prophets and Jesus alike is, in fact, more readily understandable if Paul were writing about a group of Thessalonians, hostile to Christians, whose numbers included Jews as well as Gentiles.[227] The community of Christians at Thessalonica seems to have consisted of Gentile Christians for the most part,[228] but Paul considers them to be among the chosen, among those who know God.[229] In a sense they were no longer Gentiles. Because of this, it is not impossible that such opposition as came their way might have come from troublemaking Jews, incensed at the new definition of the *ekklēsia,* chosen and beloved by God.[230]

On balance, however, the more likely reading of "compatriots" would lead one to think of Gentiles who were opposed to the Christians at Thessalonica.[231] We can only infer the reasons for the persecution. It might have been the distinctive socialization of the new Christian community with its concomitant disturbance of the prior social relationships with the "compatriots."[232] It might have been the offense caused by their abandonment of traditional and local cults as they turned from their idols to the service of the one God.[233] It might have been that the acknowledgment of Jesus as Messiah was not politically correct insofar as this acknowledgment might have seemed to take away from allegiance owed to Caesar — *kaisaros.*[234] Indeed the expectation of the *"parousia* — coming,"[235] which would have evoked the image of the return of a triumphant conqueror in the Hellenistic world[236] and the idea of a coronation on that occasion,[237] might well have caused no small amount of fear and antagonism, indeed outright opposition, to be directed toward the Christians who spoke in this fashion.

We should not necessarily think that this persecution was systematically or officially organized, nor even that it was officially sanctioned.[238] Sporadic outbreaks of violence or oppression would have been sufficient to lead Paul to write about the persecution of his beloved Thessalonian Christians.

The violence may even have led to the deaths of some Christians. The obvious point of comparison between the situation of the Christians at Thessalonica and those to whom reference is made in 2:15 is that all suffered at the hands of racial homologues. Paul's analogy, however, did make reference to the death of Jesus and the prophets at the hands of their persecutors. Thus it cannot be excluded that some Christians at Thessalonica had died as a result of the persecution.[239]

At the very least the persecution consisted of some sort of social oppression,[240] which, as Wayne Meeks has suggested,[241] may well have contributed to the social bonding of the Thessalonian community itself. Groups attacked from without tend to cohere from within.

The good news brought by Timothy did not in any way diminish Paul's desire to visit the Thessalonians. In fact in seems to have intensified his desire. His thanks to God gave way to a prayer of petition: "Night and day, we pray most earnestly that we may see you face to face and restore whatever is lacking in your faith: Now may our God and Father himself and our Lord Jesus direct our way to you" (3:10-11).

Paul has not only told the Thessalonians about his prayer, he has also given an example of it for their benefit. His prayer continues the thought of 2:17–3:5. It springs from the depths of Paul's involvement and his anxious concern about the situation in Thessalonica.[242] Even Timothy's report was not sufficient to assuage Paul's desire to visit – the "*hodos* – way" of verse 11 recalls the "*exodos* – welcome/coming" of 1:9; 2:1 – the Thessalonians. He wanted to see them face to face and prayed earnestly that the opportunity might be realized.[243] The earnestness of his desire, expressed in a prayer of petition, resulted not only from his longing to be with those whom he so loved (3:12); it also resulted from his desire to restore whatever was lacking in their faith. Paul had sent Timothy "to strengthen" the Thessalonians with regard to their faith (3:2). He prayed to God "to strengthen" them (3:13).[244] There was, however, something that was missing in regard to their faith. What was Paul to do?

4

Writing a Letter

After Timothy's return from his visit to the Christians of Thessalonica, Paul and his companions who had been waiting in Corinth still experienced a burning desire to visit the Thessalonians. They wanted to restore whatever was lacking in the faith of the Thessalonians (3:10), but they could not do so. Satan, who had earlier prevented Paul again and again from visiting the Thessalonians (2:19), apparently continued to impede Paul from realizing his desire. The times were, nonetheless, critical. At Thessalonica there was the difficulty arising from the persecution and questions about those who had died.[1]

Paul viewed the situation as one of some urgency. Satan, the tempter, was already at work (2:18; 3:5). The eschatological showdown between the forces of God and the forces of ultimate evil was at hand.[2] *"Ho telos,"*[3] the climactic end, was in sight. The Lord Jesus was about to come with all his saints (3:13; 4:15).

A Real Letter

In those times of ultimate decision, how could Paul fulfill his desire to restore the things that were lacking in the Thessalonians' faith? Given the impossibility of his own return to Thessalonica, recourse to a letter was a possibility. In ancient times, as in our own day, one of the major functions of a letter was to extend one's personal presence. Sending a letter was a way of being present when, perforce, one was physically absent.

In the Hellenistic world in which Paul lived *"parousia – presence"* was one of the functions of the personal letter.[4] The letter was a way of turning *"apousia – absence"* into *"parousia – presence."*[5] In his letter Paul writes, more than once, about his desire to be personally[6] present with the Thessalonians. His letter is, above all else, a letter whose predominant (epistolary) function is personal contact.[7]

The immediate occasion for the letter was Timothy's return from Thessalonica and Paul's continuing anxiety about the situation there, notwithstanding the reassurance that he had received from Timothy regarding the faith and love of the community. Paul was well aware of the Thessalonians' continuing affection for him (3:6b). A letter was a way of continuing the prior conversation between Paul and the Thessalonians.

Was it also a response to a letter that the Thessalonians had sent to Paul, using Timothy as their courier? It is as difficult to answer this question as it is to state definitively that this was the first letter that Paul had written to this or to any other church. There is no reason for us to assume that each and every one of Paul's letters has been preserved by posterity. In fact, his correspondence with the church at Corinth seems to indicate that at least two of his letters to that church have been lost.[8]

Paul's first letter to the Corinthians is, in any event, part of an ongoing correspondence between Paul and the Christians of Corinth. It is a response to a letter that they had written to him.[9] The letter of the Corinthians to Paul might have been delivered to Paul by Stephanas and his companions on the occasion of the visit mentioned in 1 Cor 16:17. Timothy's return to Paul from Thessalonica created a situation in which he could have brought a letter from the Thessalonians to Paul. Some scholars have argued that Paul's use of a formulaic *"peri (de)* — concerning"* in 4:13 and 5:1[10] is an indication that Paul was responding to concerns about which the Thessalonians had written.[11]

The use of a formulaic *"peri (de)* — concerning"[12] appears in Paul's letter, where it is but one of a number of epistolary conventions and clichés that one finds. Many of these focus on the correspondents' personal relationship. They are similar to the kinds of things that ancient Hellenists said when they wrote to one another, but they are hardly dissimilar to the kinds of things that we moderns say when we write to our friends. In this regard Malherbe,[13] draws attention to thoughts about physical absence and spiritual presence (2:17; 3:10; 3:1) and the idea of loneliness, expressed in Paul's feeling like an orphan (2:17) and being left all alone (3:1).[14] One might also note that, in his letter, Paul uses his own name, thereby interrupting the flow of thought with a personal aside (2:18).

When people write letters, they frequently mention how much they long to see their friends and how much they remember them. They mention their friends' needs and their own desire to be helpful. Since Paul writes about the Thessalonians longing to see him and of their fond remembrance of him (3:6), it is quite likely, observes Mal-

herbe, that the Thessalonians had written to Paul.[15] References to the
needs of the Thessalonians about which Paul has "no need to write,"
but in fact does – to familial love in 4:9 and to the times and seasons
in 5:1 – would make sense in a response to a letter that had spoken
about such needs. Paul also writes about his joy and is full of thanks
(3:9). These are typical attitudes of anyone, whether of today or of
times long ago, who receives a letter.

On the basis of Paul's expression of thoughts such as these Malherbe concludes that "it is quite possible that he [Paul] had written
to them when he first sent Timothy to them and it is highly probable
that they in return wrote him for advice."[16] Malherbe's conclusion is
tentative, as it must be. His argument is intriguing, even if not altogether probative. The ancients used the *peri-* formula to list topics to
which they have been invited to respond by letter. They also used the
very same term simply to introduce a new topic or to respond to various aspects raised in an oral report.What is certain is that Paul did
write a letter to the Thessalonians. Malherbe suggests that the letter
was written hardly more than eight months after Paul's first visit to
the Thessalonians.[17]

It Looks Like a Letter

Letter writing was a well-established form of communication in Paul's
Hellenistic world.[18] It was taught in schools for scribes. There were
theorists like Pseudo Demetrius and Pseudo Libanius who composed
manuals for use in the schools[19] and rhetoricians such as Dionysius of Alexandria, Apollonius Dyskolos, and Theon of Alexandria
who expressed their opinion about letter writing. The theorists commended brevity in a letter. By their standards,[20] and in comparison
with extant letters of the Hellenistic era,[21] Paul's letter to the Thessalonians was a fairly long composition, but it certainly looked like a
letter.

Ancient letters, like modern ones, had a standard epistolary form.
Its first element was the salutation, consisting of the identification of
the sender of the letter, the name of the recipients, and a greeting.
"Isidora to her brother Asklas greeting and may you always be well"[22]
was typical of the way Hellenists began their letters. In Paul's "Paul,
Silvanus, and Timothy to the church of the Thessalonians in God the
Father and the Lord Jesus Christ: Grace to you and peace," we can recognize an expanded version of the typical salutation of the Hellenistic
letter.[23]

Paul does not express a concern for his correspondents' health,
although the health wish was a standard feature of Hellenistic letters.[24]
Such a wish may even have seemed out of place in a letter written to

a group of people whose situation was as precarious as that of the Thessalonians.

Saying Thanks

After the health wish came an expression of thanks. In a letter to his father Epimachus, Apion, a young soldier, once wrote, "I give thanks to the lord Serapis because when I was endangered at sea... (*eucharistō tō kyriō Serapidi hoti...*)."[25] Such expressions of thanksgiving to a god (or the gods) are to be found in many, but not all, Hellenistic letters. Often the papyri Hellenistic letters have a supplication[26] after the health wish, the latter providing an easy transition to the former as it does in Apollonarios's letter to his mother, "Before anything else I wish that you are well, making obeisance on your behalf to all the gods" (*to proskynēma sou poiōn para pasi tois theois*).[27]

From the standpoint of its formulation, there is some similarity between Paul's "we also give thanks to God" (*eucharistoumen tō theō*, 2:1) and Apion's expression of thanksgiving. There is even greater formulaic similarity between what Apion wrote and Paul's expression of thanksgiving in 2:13, "we...give thanks to God for this, that..." (*eucharistoumen tō theō...hoti...*). There are other formulaic similarities between what Paul has written in 1 Thessalonians and what is to be found in some of the extant Hellenistic letters. Two of them, for example, employ a "*mneian poieō* – making mention," formula,[28] just as Paul does in 1:2. Given these similarities, it is hardly surprising that in a classic study of Paul's expressions of thanksgiving, Paul Schubert wrote that "Paul's epistolary thanksgivings must be considered genuine examples of a definite and widely used Hellenistic epistolographical pattern."[29]

In general, the thanksgivings of the extant papyri letters are relatively short. The expression of thanksgiving of 1 Thessalonians is, however, rather long. It constitutes a substantial portion of Paul's letter (1:2–3:13) and contributes notably to the unusual length of his missive. As a matter of fact, two somewhat distinct, but related, and certainly relatively long expressions of thanks can be identified in the letter, 2:1–2:12; 2:13–3:13. The second of these thanksgivings starts with "We also constantly give thanks to God for this" (*kai dia touto kai hēmeis eucharistoumen...*). An emphatic "*hēmeis* – we" and the duplicated "*kai* – and,"[30] reflected in the NRSV's "also," provide a juncture between the two thanksgiving periods. In Paul's joyous outburst at 3:9, we find a hint of even a third thanksgiving.

Paul's two thanksgivings are long, or at least seem to be. The letter actually contains three relatively short expressions of thanksgiving. All three expressions are contained in short, self-contained sentences,

1:2–5; 3:13; and 3:9–10. The first two thanksgivings are presented in the same schematic fashion, that is, with (1) the principal verb *"eucharistoumen* – we give thanks"; (2) the mention of the one to whom thanks are addressed, *"tō theō* – to God"; (3) an adverb of duration, "always" or "constantly"; and (4) a mention of the motivation for the thanksgiving, the "who" or the "why," expressed in the form of a prepositional phrase or causal clause.[31]

The reason for Paul's repeated expression of thanks was the success of the proclamation of the gospel among the Thessalonians. Paul's third "thanksgiving" has another format. It is a rhetorical question, "how can we thank God enough for you...?" (3:9). Phrased in that fashion, this mention of Paul's thanksgiving does not incorporate an adverb of duration as did the thanksgivings previously reported upon. In any case, this outburst is a one-time response to the one-time event of Timothy's return. Timothy returned to Paul as the bearer of good news (3:6). Thus, even in 3:9, Paul's thanksgiving is a response to the proclamation of the gospel. God is at work when the good news is proclaimed (1:5; 3:13). The proclamation of the gospel leads to faith (1:6–7; 3:13; 3:6) and calls for thanksgiving.

The thanksgiving, renewed at 3:9 and leading to the prayer of verses 11–12, was prompted by the reassurance that Paul had received relative to the perseverance of the Thessalonians in the faith. His earlier thanksgivings were motivated by the remembrance of his own visit to the Thessalonians and the recognition that they had accepted God's word for what it truly was. When more closely examined, these two thanksgivings are not really prayers of thanksgiving. Prayers were not to be found in ancient Hellenistic letters. They seem to lie beyond the pale of the genre of the Hellenistic letter. So Paul's "thanksgivings" are, appropriately, reports about Paul's prayers of thanksgiving. The joyous outburst at 3:9 led, however, and almost spontaneously, to the wish prayer(s) of 3:11–13. In 3:11–13 Paul actually prays, just as he will later do in 5:23. There can be no doubt that Paul really was in a thankful mood as he wrote his first letter to the Thessalonians.

Ancient letters typically contained but a single expression of thanksgiving. Paul's letter to the Thessalonians is redolent with thanksgiving. The thanksgiving period is long (1:2–3:13). In addition to its three specific expressions of thanksgiving (1:2–5; 3:13; 3:9–10), there are various "expansions, digressions, and interruptions."[32] Some scholars, impressed by the comparative long length of the first letter to the Thessalonians, explain that the two thanksgivings initially belonged to two separate letters of Paul to the Thessalonians and that the present text is a composite of some of his correspondence with the Thessalonians.[33] In my judgment, the arguments advanced by these scholars are not substantial enough to justify the conclusions that they have drawn.

In contrast with this separation of what Paul had joined together there is the seminal work of Paul Schubert. Having passed in review the opinions of the major early twentieth-century commentators on the letter, who variously suggest that the end of the thanksgiving period might be located at 2:16, 3:10, or 3:13, Schubert argued that there is but one long thanksgiving period, twice repeated.[34] 3:13 then provides "the ultimate eschatological climax of the entire thanksgiving."[35]

The letter then takes a new turn as Paul continues, "Finally, brothers and sisters, we ask and urge you in the Lord Jesus that ... " (4:1). Paul's "*loipon oun* – finally" does not really mean that Paul has come to the end of his letter. It is a typical epistolary formula that, although frequently appearing at the end of a letter,[36] basically means that the writer is changing his or her train of thought. In this respect, the use of this formula is not very different from the way that we speak and write today.

The Body of the Letter

What Paul begins in 4:1 and ends in 5:24 has a rather different character from the first three chapters of the letter. Should we then conclude from the marker ("*loipon oun* – finally"), which Paul has introduced in 4:1, that the body of the letter begins at this point, with the result that Paul's letter should be classified as a paraenetic letter,[37] albeit with a lengthy introductory thanksgiving which serves as a sort of *captatio benevolentiae?*[38] Or should we draw as a conclusion from the transitional elements found in 4:1 that the paraenesis of 4:1–5:22 is a conclusion to the letter and that the real "body" of the letter is the thanksgiving itself?[39]

The function of the body of a letter is to convey the principal message of the letter. This is the *homilia* of Heikki Koskenniemi's analysis.[40] Inspired by Schubert's work, John L. White has distinguished the body-opening, the body-middle, and the body-closing within the letter and finds these elements in 1 Thessalonians, respectively in 2:1–4, 2:5–16, and 2:17–3:10, with 3:11–13 serving as the eschatological climax to the whole.[41] On the other hand, Jack Sanders has contended that Paul's letters give evidence of a formal transition from the epistolary thanksgiving to the body of the letter.[42] According to Sanders's analysis, the thanksgiving of 1 Thessalonians was brought to closure in 3:11–12 with a prayer formula loosely analogous to the Jewish *berakah*. He opines that a formula of injunction (4:1) introduces the body of the letter. This pattern of transition, according to Sanders, would become commonplace in the Pauline correspondence.

Sanders has clearly and correctly identified the prayer formula in 3:11-12 and the formula of injunction in 4:1 as transitional elements. It remains to be seen whether the presence of these elements in 1 Thessalonians represent a clear marker of Paul's transition from an introductory thanksgiving to the formal body of his letter.

In this first of his letters – and in subsequent letters as well – he uses a variety of transitional formulae. White, for example, writes about Paul's use of disclosure formulae (e.g., "we do not want you to be uninformed, 4:13), the request formula (e.g., "we ask and urge you..., 4:1), the expression of joy (e.g., "how can we thank God enough for you in return for all the joy that we feel," 3:9), the expression of astonishment, and the statement of compliance.[43] Roberts has summarized all of these under the single rubric of "expressions of a personal nature" and has added to White's list Paul's use of credal statements, doxologies, eschatological references and request statements, but has pointed out that these are scattered throughout Paul's letters.[44] They represent a shift in the expression of Paul's thought, but not necessarily a transition from one formal part of a letter to another formal part.

As a matter of fact, there is some artificiality in the discussion about the transition from Paul's thanksgiving to the body of his letter. In Paul's Hellenistic world the letters that were actually written did not exactly follow the patterns spelled out by the theorists. There was never perfect correspondence between practice and theory.[45] In this respect there is not a great deal of difference between letter writing today and letter writing in the ancient world. Our schools teach sharp distinctions between the form of the business letter and the form of the personal letter. They teach the conventions of language that are appropriate to each kind of letter. In practice, however, actual letters often contain a certain amount of business and some measure of personal communication. There are standard conventions and departures from and modifications of these conventions. The situation was quite the same in Paul's Hellenistic world, as one gathers from even a cursory reading of extant Hellenistic papyri letters. Once this is recognized it becomes unrealistic to write of transitions from a thanksgiving to a letter body.[46] Accordingly, Bruce Johanson suggests that the real body of 1 Thessalonians is to be found in 1:2-5:24. In Johanson's estimation, the body of the letter is the whole letter, apart, that is, from its obvious prescript and postscript.[47]

Paul's Other Letters

In any discussion of the form of Paul's letter to the Thessalonians, the discriminating reader should pay attention to what and when Paul actually wrote. The issue is important insofar as a comparison of Paul's letter to the Thessalonians with his other letters might shed some light on just how Paul wrote. To be sure, Paul wrote letters and he wrote during Hellenistic times, but scholars are not in agreement among themselves as to which of the letters traditionally attributed to Paul were, in fact, written by him. Today there is a virtual consensus that only the letter to the Romans, the two letters to the Corinthians, the letter to the Galatians, the letter to the Philippians, and the letter to Philemon, along with the "first letter to the Thessalonians," were surely written by Paul.[48] As to when Paul wrote, there is an emerging consensus that his letter-writing activity – at least insofar as it is known to us – was concentrated in a period of just more than a decade's duration, that is, from 50 to 62 C.E., if the period of his letter writing lasted even that long.[49] Romans is arguably the last of Paul's letters and the letter to the Thessalonians presumably the first.

Of perhaps greater importance than determining the actual dates within which Paul's letter writing occurred is the determination of the relative chronology of his letters, that is, the sequence in which they were written. To what extent should Paul's later correspondence be used in an attempt to understand how he wrote the first of his letters? Many of those who study the form of Paul's letters do so by comparing all of his letters among themselves, sometimes including those that most scholars judge not to have been written by Paul himself.

Some insight into Paul's letter- writing habits can be gained from comparing what Paul has written to the Thessalonians with what he has written to others, but some methodological caution is necessary. As a matter of principle, one should not introduce the non-Pauline letters too readily into the discussion.[50] One must also be open to the possibility of some development and evolution in Paul's letter-writing techniques. Paul was a real letter writer. Those who write letters with some frequency are not the slaves of conventional techniques; rather they are communicators who respond to the needs of the moment and enter into communication with those to whom they are sending their letters.

As a letter writer, Paul lost none of the freedom of speech, the *parrēsia*, that characterized his oral communication at Philippi and Thessalonica.[51] His letter to the Thessalonians gives ample evidence of a high degree of authorial creativity.[52] "Paul is," as Lambrecht says, " . . . anything but a slave of a schematic pattern. He freely varies words as well as constructions. He can omit elements; he breaks off, interrupts, and repeats; he changes the order."[53]

Moreover, when Paul composed 1 Thessalonians a "formal ortho-doxy" in letter writing did not yet exist. Even if it had existed, it is hardly likely that Paul would have been in slavish conformity to it. As all letter writers, he enjoyed a kind of epistolary freedom.[54] As a mat-ter of fact, the epistolary theorists urged such freedom of expression in letters, particularly in letters of friendship.[55] Hence there is more than a little value to be gained in studying 1 Thessalonians as an act of communication. Paul was, after all, a flesh-and-blood person who wrote true-to-life letters.

Paul's Goodby

Before beginning a study of 1 Thessalonians as an act of communi-cation, it might be good to look at the end of Paul's letter to the Thessalonians, 5:25-28. It is a conclusion that evokes family ties. Three times in just three verses (vv. 25-27) Paul writes about his "brothers and sisters." The NRSV editors have covered up the redun-dancy by rendering the repetitive *adelphoi* as "beloved... brothers and sisters... of them." The translation has been stylistically en-hanced, but the forcefulness of Paul's own expression has been thereby diminished. As Paul brought his letter to the Thessalonians to a close, his tone was warm, friendly, and familial.

Ancient Hellenistic letters typically ended with a standard saluta-tion, "*errōso* – goodby"[56] in letters in which the format of "X to Y, greetings" appeared in the opening salutation. A variant, "*eutychei* – farewell," appears in letters in which the recipient's name appears as the first word in the correspondence.[57] Paul's letter to the Thessalo-nians includes neither of these standard expressions, but it is clearly brought to closure in 5:25-30. The postscript or eschatocol to the let-ter follows upon the wish prayer of 5:23, to which the affirmation of 5:24 has been appended. The wish prayer, with its telltale "God of peace," serves as prima facie evidence that Paul is bringing his letter to closure.

The postscript of Paul's letter includes an epistolary formula of greetings, "greet all the brothers and sisters with a holy kiss"[58] (v. 26) and an epistolary reflection. A request that greetings be conveyed was typical of personal letters in the Hellenistic era. The epistolary convention not only conveyed a request; it also brought the letter to closure.

The warm tone of Paul's closing remarks is interrupted by verse 27: "I solemnly command you by the Lord that this letter be read to all the brothers and sisters." Paul tells his correspondents what he wants to be done with his letter, namely, that it be read to all the Christians of Thessalonica – an expectation that Paul has forcefully expressed. He has given his request the form of a solemn injunction.

Paul's postscript also includes a prayer request, "Beloved [literally, "brothers and sisters"], pray for us" (v. 25). The prayer request concretizes the exhortation to pray found in Paul's earlier paraenesis at 5:17. It personalizes that request and gives further expression to the relationship that exists between the senders and recipients of the letter. Indeed, for the final time in Paul's letter his beloved Thessalonians are addressed as "*adelphoi* – brothers and sisters."

The link between this request for prayers and the wish prayer that comes just before it cannot be overlooked. In his wish prayer, Paul and his companions prayed for the Thessalonians. Before bringing the letter to closure, Paul asks that the Thessalonians reciprocate by praying for him and his companions. Their relationship as brothers and sisters included their mutual prayer for one another.

Paul's letter concludes with a final salutation, "the grace of our Lord Jesus Christ be with you" (5:28), which harks back to the opening salutation (1:2) and brings the entire letter to closure. Paul began with a word of greeting and ends his communication on the same note. The greetings form an epistolary *inclusio* making Paul's letter a single act of communication.

Writing a Letter

Paul was well aware that he was writing a letter. His reference to the letter in 5:27 is the only instance in 1 Thessalonians where the term "*epistolē* – letter" is actually used. It is the first known mention of a letter written by a Christian author.[59] Paul was clearly aware that what he had done was to write a letter.

Secretaries

One might ask whether it was Paul himself who actually wrote the letter. Did he pen the letter himself or did he employ a scribe to do so? In the Hellenistic world scribes were commonly employed as letter writers, but there were occasions when the letter writers served as their own scribes.[60] Occasionally errors of grammar and orthography are indications that the senders of the letters served as their own scribes. A difference in the script of a letter indicated that a scribe had been employed.[61] In most instances, the calligraphic change comes at the end of the letter just as the final series of greetings is about to be expressed.

These changes in the visual appearance of the letter can be compared to similar phenomena in our times. Letters that are dictated to secretaries generally bear the personal signature of the one who had "written" the letter. Often the "writer" adds a handwritten postscript to a letter that has been typed or word-processed.

We do not have the autograph copies of any of Paul's letters. Therefore we do not have the visual proof that the handwriting has changed in any of them, but we do know that Paul employed amanuenses or scribes to compose some of his later letters.[62] A man who once served as Paul's scribe identifies himself as "I, Tertius, the writer of the letter" (*egō Tertios ho grapsas tēn epistolēn*) in Rom 16:22. Paul's affirmation that "I, Paul, write this greeting with my own hand" at the end of his first letter to the Corinthians and his reference to writing in large letters in his own hand in Gal 5:11[63] are likely indications that Paul appended a few words in his own hand to letters that had been transcribed by an amanuensis.

We neither possess the autograph copy of Paul's letter to the Thessalonians nor do we have evidence such as that provided by Rom 16:22, 1 Cor 16:21 (cf. 2 Cor 13:10), and Gal 5:11[64] to indicate that Paul used a scribe to do the actual writing of 1 Thessalonians. Some scholars, however, are of the opinion that the switch from the first-person plural to the first-person singular in 5:27, "*I* solemnly command you," indicate that Paul himself has taken up the pen at this point.

Some scholars speculate that Silvanus or Timothy might have been responsible for the actual writing of 1 Thessalonians.[65] Of this we cannot be sure. Something of which we can be relatively sure is that the senders of the letter are consistently identified in the plural. They are Paul, Silvanus, and Timothy.[66] It is possible that the letter might have been penned by any one of these three, but it is not at all impossible that a professional scribe had been engaged for the writing of this first letter.[67]

Sending the Letter

Similarly we can only conjecture as to how the letter to the Thessalonians was actually delivered to them. In Paul's world, scribes were sometimes hired to deliver letters as well as to write them.[68] At other times letters were delivered by passing travelers. Apollinarios's correspondence with his mother mentions that the letter was to be delivered by someone who was traveling in her direction and suggests that she might make similar use of a passing traveler in order to respond: "When I found someone who was journeying to you from Cyrene, I thought it a necessity to inform you about my welfare; you must inform me at once, in turn, about your safety and that of my brothers. . . . If you do not find someone coming to me, write to Socrates and he will transmit it to me." Lack of such travelers, fortuitously found, seems to have provoked some frustration on the part of Apollinarios as he later wrote to his mother, "Please write me a letter about your welfare and that of my brothers and of all your people. And, for my part, if I ever find someone [to carry the letter], I will write to you. . . ."[69]

Christian missionaries traveled the ancient trade routes, benefitting from the hospitality of Christian households along the way.[70] It is not unlikely that Stephanas, Fortunatus, and Achaicus made use of these conditions to bring the letter to which Paul responded in his first to the Corinthians. Perhaps Timothy retraced their journey in order to deliver Paul's letter to the Christians at Corinth (1 Cor 16:10, 17).

While it is an epistolary artifact,[71] "Paul's" deliberation as to whether to send Artemas or Tychicus to Ephesus (2 Tim 3:12) points to a decision to be made as to who would be best suited to deliver the so-called second letter to Timothy. Timothy had served as the intermediary between Paul and the Thessalonians (3:2, 6; cf. Acts 18:5), but the letter to the Thessalonians does not indicate that he served as the postman in the delivery of the letter. Neither does the schematized history of Paul's activity found in the Acts of the Apostles suggest an opportunity in which either Timothy or Silvanus served as the designated deliverer of the letter to the Thessalonians.

Conversation in Written Form

Paul's letter was a real letter. Among his contemporaries, letters were easily identifiable by means of their postscripts and their prescripts. No matter what may be the theoretical discussions as to the extent of the body of Paul's letter, its opening (1:1) and its closing (esp. 5:26–28) clearly type it as a letter.

Koskenniemi has identified the expression of friendship, *philophronesis*, as one of the principal functions of the Hellenistic letter. The epistolary theorists known in Paul's time considered the friendly letter to be the highest form of correspondence. They suggested that the letter was essentially a form of personal conversation. The Pseudo Demetrius, Demetrius Phalereus, for example, reports that Artemon, the editor of Aristotle's letters, compared letters with conversations (*dialogoi*) – at least to one half of a conversation – and suggested that letters should be written in a manner similar to that in which conversations are engaged.[72]

A letter, like a conversation, is a kind of familiar dialogue among friends. Thus it was considered rather appropriate for a letter, and particularly the letter of friendship, one of twenty-one types of letters identified by the Pseudo Demetrius,[73] to truly engage the correspondents in dialogue. Not only should the writer reveal something of his or her affect and spirit in a letter, but he or she should also evoke the recipient's presence in the letter that is written. This expectation was particularly applicable to letters of friendship, but it was, in fact, expected in all of the letters that Hellenists wrote.

It is difficult to imagine how a letter could manifest its philophronetic character more fully than did Paul's letter to the Thessalonians.[74] Paul's frequent use of the vocative *"adelphoi* – brothers and sisters"[75] serves to highlight the special relationship that existed between the author and those to whom he is writing. The use of parental imagery as an evocative simile (2:7, 12) highlights the nature of the relationship, as does the reverse image of the orphan (2:17), which poignantly expresses the intensity of the pain of separation from the Thessalonians that Paul and his companions were suffering.

As the epistolary theorists had suggested, Paul was transparent in writing to the Thessalonians about his mood and that of his companions, about their affect for those to whom they were writing. He speaks of their almost unbearable separation (3:1, 5), noting that, if separation was virtually unbearable for the band of three, it was almost more unbearable for Paul than for the others. He wrote of his desire to be with the Thessalonians, and, in a prayer uniquely addressed to God and the Lord Jesus, Paul expressed a wish that his path might be directed to them (3:11).

Throughout his letter, Paul consistently employs the first-person plural. He writes about the common experience of himself and his companions. When he writes about the pain of separation from the Thessalonians and his desire to be with them, he attributes to himself an affect that is attributed to the entire little group of apostles. Only twice in his letter does Paul use the first-person singular pronoun.[76] That is when he speaks of his desire to go to the Thessalonians (2:18) and about the pain of separation from them, which was so personally his (3:5).

Paul also writes about the (fond) memories that he and his companions have of the Thessalonians (1:3). He writes about their overflowing love for those to whom they were writing (2:8; 3:12)[77] and talks about the joy provoked by news of the Thessalonians (3:9). Paul boastfully describes the Thessalonians as his "hope and joy and crown" (2:19). They are truly his "glory and joy" (2:20). The warm positive regard exuded by the author as he wrote reflects the affect that Paul and his companions had for the Thessalonians when they were present among them. During their visit they had showed themselves to be mother and father to the Thessalonians (2:7, 12). At that time they gave of their very selves to the Thessalonians (2:8). This posture was not merely with respect to the Thessalonians as a group; it was a posture that Paul and his companions had adopted vis-à-vis each and every one of the Thessalonians (2:11).[78]

Paul recalled the personal integrity demonstrated by his companions and himself when they were among the Thessalonians (1:5; 2:3-4, 10). He recalls the boldness or freedom that was theirs as they proclaimed the gospel to the Thessalonians (2:2). The results of that heartfelt disposition were clearly known to the Thessalonians. In his letter Paul writes about the disposition itself.

In a sense, Paul was rather transparent, and intended to be transparent, when he wrote to the Thessalonians. This personal transparency is more than mere epistolary self-commendation;[79] it is a way for Paul to be fully present to his addressees, to share with them his very self, as he had shared himself with them when he was physically present among them (2:8).

A Matter of Pronouns

A particularly striking indication of the philophronetic character of Paul's letter to the Thessalonians is his significant use of pronouns. Many commentators have drawn attention to the frequency and singular use of personal pronouns in this first of Paul's letters. Indeed three features of Paul's use of personal pronouns cannot be overlooked. First of all, there is the fact that, in sharp contrast with the friendship letters of his day, Paul's letter to the Thessalonians manifests a marked preference for the use of "we" rather than "I." He prefers to use the first-person plural rather than the first-person singular. This preference is manifest both in the declension of the verbs and his use of pronouns.

There are only three instances in the entire letter in which the first person appears.[80] The first is 2:18, where Paul's parenthetical "certainly I, Paul, wanted to again and again"[81] underscores the depth of his personal concern for the Thessalonians and his desire to visit them once again. The second is in 3:5, "when I could bear it no longer, I sent to find out about your faith." Here, a triple use of the first person in the form of an emphatic use of the personal pronoun, a participle in the first-person singular, and a verb in the first-person singular[82] emphasizes both Paul's emotional involvement with the Thessalonians and the depths of his loneliness[83] as he was about to send Timothy, his confidant and support (3:2), to the Thessalonians. The first-person singular occurs for the third time in the letter's final paraenesis, where Paul appeals to his apostolic authority as he commands that the letter be read to all (5:27).

In terms of Paul's epistolary style, these three passages are striking indeed. The use of the first-person singular is clearly an exception to the general style of the letter. As such it provides evidence that Paul has carefully chosen his pronouns. He uses the first-person plural when appropriate and a first-person singular when necessary. His use of the first-person plural is a self-conscious one. Paul's letter does more than merely bear the greetings of Silvanus and Timothy along with himself (1:1) – for that a cursory greeting in the eschatocol would have been more appropriate.[84] Rather, the letter may be presumed to contain the thoughts and sentiments of Silvanus and Timothy as well as those of Paul.

The fact that the first-person singular does occasionally occur in the letter attests to the fact that the letter is, indeed, the work of a single author. It is Paul's letter[85] even though Silvanus and Timothy are fully associated with him in the sending of the letter, just as they had been fully associated with him in preaching the gospel of God to the Thessalonians. Strikingly, Paul's use of the first-person singular reveals that he did reveal his own soul in his letter, just as the Pseudo Demetrius had suggested.[86] He revealed the depth of his affect for the Thessalonians, the intensity of his longing to be with them, and the loneliness that was his when he was without the presence of Timothy, his brother.

Paul's manifest preference for the use of the plural form of expression in the first person reveals his soul. His preferred style manifests his understanding that he is not alone in his work of evangelizing, whether in preaching or in sending letters. That is a corporate endeavor, not the work of Paul alone. Later generations might reflect that Paul's understanding of Christian ministry is that of a "team ministry," but that kind of reflection remains for the far distant future, a future of which Paul, who lived in the expectation and hope of the reversal of the then present world order, never even dreamed.

Apropos Paul's use of pronouns, there is, as a second striking feature of the epistolary style of 1 Thessalonians, an extraordinarily large number of passages in the letter where Paul uses a pair of pronouns, "*hēmeis* – we" and "*hymeis* – you," within a single epistolary setting. The interfacing of these pronouns begins with the "our [(*hēmōn*] message of the gospel to you [*hymin*]" in 1:5, continues through 1:9; 2:1, 2, 13, 17, 19; 3:2, 3, 6, 7, 9, 11, 12, 13, and concludes with 5:28.[87] This use of pronouns contributes significantly to the dialogic nature of Paul's letter. There is a constant interaction between "we" and "you."

Paul's use of "*hēmeis* – we" has another function in 1 Thessalonians, a third noteworthy feature of Paul's use of personal pronouns. In the series of texts just mentioned, it is to identify the "we" in dialogue with "you." In another series of texts the "*hēmeis* – we" encompasses the senders and addressees in a single group. Together they constitute a single "us," which may then be compared to outsiders. Many of these texts are particularly striking, beginning with 1:10. After having mentioned "what kind of welcome we had among you [*peri hēmōn...pros hymas*]," Paul writes about Jesus "who rescues us" (*hēmas*) – that is, not only Paul and his companions but also the Thessalonian Christians, now formed into a single community of faith with Paul and those who had accompanied him – "from the wrath to come."

Reaching Out

In sum, Paul's letter is full of expressions of a personal nature. These expressions are not only self-revelatory; they also constitute an outreach to the Thessalonians. This reaching out is expressed in Paul's use of personal pronouns, but it is also manifest in a number of other expressions that dot Paul's letter such as "you know" (2:1, 2, 5, 11; 3:3, 4; 4:2; 5:2; cf. 1:4; 4:4), "you remember" (2:9; cf. 3:6), and "you are witnesses" (2:10).[88] Paul's letter was to jar the memory of the Thessalonians. In Paul's world remembering was a way to make present. Paul's desire to reach out to his correspondents was also reflected in his writing about their needs, albeit in oblique fashion (1:8; 4:9; 5:1),[89] and his desire to dispel their ignorance by letting them know something they needed to know. "We do not want you to be uninformed – *ou thelomen de hymas agnoien,*" he writes (4:13). His words recall the kind of disclosure formula typically found in Hellenistic letters, to wit, "I want you to know that – *ginōskein se thelō hoti.*"

In his epistolary outreach, Paul writes about the experience and the affect of the Thessalonians. He writes of their joy (3:6), their fond memories (*mneian hymōn agathēn,* 3:6), and of their longing, which is similar to the longing experienced by Paul and his companions (3:6). While he recalls their faith, love, and hope, he can also talk about what they have become – imitators of Paul and his companions, the Lord, and the churches in Judea (1:6; 2:14). He writes about what others have to say about the Thessalonians (1:9-10) and how exemplary they have become (1:5). He recalls that they have been chosen by God (1:5) and that God's word continues to be a powerful force among them (2:13). Indeed he commends them for the way in which they live, for they live so as to please God (4:1), and for the love that they have for the Christians scattered throughout Macedonia (4:9-10).

The baring of Paul's soul and the personal outreach that so permeates the letter to the Thessalonians reveals that this letter is truly a piece of personal communication. The initial greetings and epistolary closing enable it to be characterized as a letter. Any number of the conventional phrases and epistolary clichés[90] that punctuate the entire composition confirm that its literary genre is truly that of the letter.

We find a variety of formulas of personal address, especially "*adelphoi* – brothers and sisters," which appears in this letter so frequently that it might almost be called its constant refrain. We hear a disclosure formula, such as "we do not want you to be uninformed" (4:13). Paul is exuberant in his expression of thanks (1:2; 2:13; 3:9). He expresses confidence in the Thessalonians (4:1; 9-10; 5:1). Nonetheless he appeals to them to adopt a reasonable pattern of conduct – or to continue the sensible way of life that they have been living. He asks (*erōtaō*, 4:1; 5:12) and urges (*parakaleō*, 4:1, 10, 18; 5:11, 14) them to adopt specific modes of behavior. Paul makes use of a typical formula indicating that one is coming to the end of a letter ("*loipon oun* – finally" in 4:1) and uses "*peri* – concerning" with the genitive to take up some of the topics that he wants to consider, particularly various aspects of the exhortation that he includes in the letter (4:9, 13; 5:1).

What Kind of a Letter?

While these various epistolary conventions clearly show that Paul is writing a letter in the style in which his Hellenistic contemporaries were wont to write,[91] they pose a problem for many modern commentators who want to be more specific about the type of letter that Paul has written.

The Diplomatic Letter

Some years ago Carl J. Bjerkelund took a careful look at the way that Paul used "*parakaleō* – urge" as a formula of exhortation.[92] Paul uses the expression in 4:1, 10 and 5:14. While the appearance of such a formula in a letter is not unusual, Bjerkelund has shown that it is particularly typical of the diplomatic letter, wherein an authorized legate makes an authoritative demand in the name of another, albeit in a tactful manner. One can hardly claim that Paul's letter to the Thessalonians enjoys the status of being a diplomatic letter in the technical sense of the term; nor can we even be sure that Paul had seen diplomatic letters. Nonetheless, the fact that Paul presents himself as some kind of official legate (2:4, 7) and appeals to the authority of the Lord Jesus in his exhortation (4:1; 5:12)[93] makes the comparison between Paul's letter and the diplomatic correspondence of his Hellenistic world a truly evocative enterprise.

A Letter of Consolation

Pseudo Demetrius included the letter of consolation, the *typos para-mythētikos*, among the twenty-one epistolary styles that he identified. The letter of consolation also appears on Pseudo Libanius's list of forty-one epistolary styles.[94] Paul's letter does seem to have had as its purpose, or one of its purposes – letters in the ancient world, as now, can be multivalent! – to console those who were grieving the loss of some of their dead (4:13, 18; 5:11). It is therefore to be expected that Paul's letter will evidence some similarity with Hellenistic letters of consolation. Those letters of condolence, as well as ancient epitaphs, compare death to sleep, urge those who read to grieve not, and assure them that one day they too will be united in the presence of the gods. Similar expressions appear in 1 Thessalonians, whose frame of reference is, however, patently monotheistic.[95]

A Paraenetic Letter

Despite the obvious similarities between Paul's letter and the classic letter of consolation, Juan Chapa's comparative study has led him to the conclusion that the only expression in Paul's letter that is truly at home in the letter of consolation is the exhortation to "encourage one another with these words" (4:18; 5:13).[96] Abraham Malherbe has, on the other hand, repeatedly drawn attention to the paraenetic elements of Paul's letter.[97] One point of comparison is the use of formulae of consolation.

Unlike moral discourse, paraenesis does not blaze new trails; it appeals to traditional norms. In somewhat similar fashion, the moral exhortation that Paul addresses to the Thessalonians repeatedly recalls what they already know and have learned from him. "*Mimēsis* – imitation" was a major theme in rhetorical and epistolary paraenesis.[98] In his letter Paul notes that the Thessalonians had become imitators of himself and his companions (1:6)[99] and draws attention to the similarity of their fate (3:3).

His exhortations to mutual edification (4:18; 5:11), avoiding adultery (4:6), living quietly (4:11), and friendship, albeit in the specifically Christian form of "*philadelphia* – sibling love," are similar to the well-known *topoi* familiar to the Hellenistic moralists. Paul uses the identifiable vocabulary of moral exhortation, a noun like "*paraggelia* – instruction," similar to the moralists' *paraggelma* or *praeceptum*, and an entire range of verbs, including "*parakaleō* – urge" (2:12; 3:2, 7; 4:1, 10, 18; 5:11, 14), "*erōtaō* – appeal" (4:1; 5:12), and "*paramytheomai* – encourage" (2:12; 5:14). He also uses the verb "*noutheteō* – admonish" (5:12, 14), and we cannot forget that the

Pseudo Demetrius had identified the *typos nouthetētikos,* the letter of admonition, as a specific epistolary style.

Because of the frequent recourse to paraenetic language through-out the letter and the rhetorical quality of Paul's appeal, Malherbe has identified the first letter to the Thessalonians as a paraenetic let-ter.[100] He notes that the consolation motif is a kind of paraenesis[101] and claims that his identification of the letter's epistolary genre is all the more substantiated should one take 4:1–5:11 as the body of the letter and interpret 4:1–2 and 4:10b-12 as articulating the principal point in Paul's correspondence.[102]

A Paraclectic Letter

Malherbe's choice of a model by means of which to analyze Paul's letter to the Thessalonians has by no means won the approval of all scholars. Karl Donfried, though not denying the paraenetic character of much of the letter, calls attention to the fact that the verb *paraineō* does not appear in the letters whereas the *parakal-* root is manifest throughout.[103] Hence he prefers to describe the letter as a paraclectic letter, a letter whose genre is that of the *consolatio.* In his words, the first letter to the Thessalonians is a *"logos paramythētikos* to a Christian church suffering the effects of persecution."[104]

Paul's Use of Rhetoric

Paul obviously wanted to be effective in communicating with the Thes-salonians. His sending of Timothy and subsequent sending of a letter are but two indications of that desire. The rejoinder at 5:27 is a re-minder of just how strongly he felt about his message being conveyed to them. His letter is, for the present, his chosen form of communi-cation. In recent years, several scholars have undertaken to examine Paul's letter as a communicatory act, through the prism of Aristotle's rhetorical categories.[105]

Genre

In his *Rhetoric,* Aristotle distinguished three basic types of com-munication. These were the epideictic, forensic (or judicial), and deliberative genres. The focus of epideictic rhetoric is on the present as the communicator attempts to persuade an audience to maintain or reaffirm a particular point of view with a mixture of praise and blame. The focus of judicial rhetoric is on the past as the orator seeks to per-suade an audience to make a judgment about the past. The focus of deliberative rhetoric is on the future as the speaker tries to move an audience to adopt a specific course of action for the future, often the proximate future.

George A. Kennedy views Paul's letter as a composition in the deliberative genre.[106] He regards it as an exhortation to stand fast in the Lord (3:8). The paraenesis of chapters 4 and 5 provides specific advice to the Christians of Thessalonica. It instructs them about how they should live. The narrative that proceeds this varied exhortation principally serves to establish Paul's ethos. From this perspective, Kennedy's assessment highlights many of the features to which Malherbe has drawn attention by identifying the text as a paraenetic letter. Although different in its approach, Kennedy's analysis finds support in the judgment of contemporary epistolary theorists who claim that the body of the letter begins at 4:1.

Charles Wanamaker has criticized Kennedy's characterization of Paul's letter on the grounds that so much of Paul's communication serves to praise the Thessalonians' exemplary behavior (1:2-3, 6-10; 2:13-14, 19-20; 3:6-9; 4:1-2, 9-10).[107] Robert Jewett had claimed that Paul's letter was a composition in the epideictic rhetorical genre, and purely so.[108] Following his lead and that of George Lyons,[109] Wanamaker judges Paul's letter to be a composition in the epideictic genre. With the ebb and flow of its praise and its blame and with thanksgiving to God as one of its principal motifs, Jewett opined that the rhetorical genre of the letter was closer to the epideictic than either of the other two classical genres.

Wilhelm Wuellner has chosen a subgenre of the epideictic genre, namely, the paradoxical encomium (*paradoxon enkomion*), as the most fitting category for identifying the genre of the letter.[110] In Wuellner's opinion the paradox of 1:6, "in spite of persecution you received the word with joy," provides the leitmotif for the entire letter. The body of the letter amplifies and seeks to resolve the paradox. Indeed Wuellner writes of the doubly paradoxical experience of the three parties involved in Paul's communication, namely, himself, the Thessalonians, and "all the brothers and sisters."[111] One paradox is the experience of affliction as validating their service to the living God and one another. The other is the fullness of their sanctification in the present while they wait for its fuller completion at the parousia of the Son from heaven.

Unity and Argumentative Structure

While the determination of the genre of discourse is important for rhetoricians, the fashion in which the discourse is organized into a unified structure[112] is almost as important. Typically rhetoricians make

use of a schema that is especially pertinent to judicial discourse, that
is, the *exordium,* which seeks to attract the audience's attention and
gain a favorable reception, the *narratio,* which conveys background
information by way of a rehearsal of the pertinent data, the *argumentatio,* or exposition of the argument, which the orator seeks to
prove, and, finally, the *peroratio,* which summarizes the argument and
seeks to move the audience to make the hoped-for decision or take
the appropriate action. In fact the *argumentatio* can be somewhat
complex. Often it consists of an opening statement, the *propositio,*
the point that the orator wishes to make, the *partitio* or division of
the issue, the *probatio,* or proof of the argument, a *refutatio,* the
rebuttal of opposing points of view, and a *digressio,* wherein the
speaker makes an exposition of attendant circumstances or pertinent
motivation.

Applying this schema to Paul's letter,[113] Wuellner identifies an *exordium* (1:1-10), wherein verses 9-10 articulate the *propositio,* or
central theme of the letter, an *argumentatio* in two parts (2:1-3:13;
4:1-5:22), and a *peroratio* (5:23-28).[114] Wuellner's schema clearly
identifies 2:1 as the beginning of Paul's argument. In this respect,
Wuellner disagrees with Bruce Johanson, who describes the function
of 1:2-3:13 as that of a *captatio benevolentiae,* in which some of
the rhetorical strategies normally associated with the *exordium* and
narratio are to be found. Johanson identifies 4:1-5:24 as a functional
text-sequence in which elements of *exhortatio, argumentatio,* and
peroratio can be discerned.[115]

Somewhat similar to the latter's point of view is that of Frank
Witt Hughes, who describes the argument of the letter by means
of an *exordium* (1:1-10), *narratio* (2:1-3:10), *partitio* (3:11-13),
a three-part *probatio* (4:1-8; 4:9-12; 4:13-5:3), *peroratio* (5:4-11),
and *exhortatio* (5:12-22) pattern.[116] Hughes, therefore, takes effective issue with his major professor, Robert Jewett, who has identified
1:1-5 as the *exordium,* 1:6-3:13 as the *narratio,* 4:1-5:22 as the
probatio, and 5:23-28 as the *peroratio.*[117]

Theory and Practice

To a large extent this division among the authorities as to the identification of the structure of Paul's letter to the Thessalonians centers
around the issue of whether it is 1:2, 2:1, or 4:1 that is to be identified as the real beginning of Paul's argument. This discussion among
those who take a rhetorical approach to the letter is akin to the
discussion among the epistolary theorists as to where the body of
the letter begins. The diversity of opinion illustrates the difficulty
of applying in too simple and/or too rigorous a fashion categories

that have been worked out in a (somewhat) theoretical fashion. Reality never quite fits into the neatly abstract categories of the theoreticians.

Part of the discussion as to which of the classic rhetorical genres is the most appropriate model from which to analyze Paul's letter focuses upon the presence of patterns of consolation[118] and consolation motifs within the letter. Part of the problem is the simple fact that consolation motifs are found in ancient compositions that are best categorized as belonging to the epideictic genre as well as in writings that are best understood from the perspective of the deliberative genre. On the other hand the letter of consolation (*typos parētikos*) was well known in antiquity. 1 Thess 4:13-5:11 evinces a number of similarities with the letter of consolation.[119] In 4:13 Paul urges the Thessalonians to grieve not; later he will urge them to encourage one another (4:18; 5:11).[120] Thus it is not surprising that some of the Fathers of the Church who were familiar with the classical rhetorical categories considered Paul's letter to be akin to a letter of consolation.[121]

Topoi

It is, in fact, the identification of topics (*topoi*) that an orator treats and the patterns of speech, stylistic devices, and modes of proof that he or she uses that allow for an identification of the rhetorical genre to which a composition belongs as well as for the identification of its structure. In the case of Paul's letter to the Thessalonians it is easy to identify the autobiographical confession of 2:1-12,[122] the treatment of sanctification in 4:3-8, the exhortation on love in 4:9-12, and the apocalyptic disclosures of 4:13-18 and 5:1-11 as specific *topoi*. Various stylistic devices, not to mention characteristic vocabulary, set these passages off as identifiable units within the totality of Paul's composition. *Inclusio, preteritio,* and the use of disclosure formulae enable the reader of today to identify these several topics as readily as did the audience of old to which this letter was first read.

Within these passages as well as elsewhere in the letter Paul uses various rhetorical devices to advantage. We recognize his use of metaphor (2:7, 11; 2:17, 19; 4:4; 5:2, 3, 4-8, 19), repetition (1:5; 2:3, 10, 12, 19; 3:2, 7; 4:1, 6; 5:12, 14, 23), alliteration (5:16-22), antithesis (*contradictio,* 1:5, 8; 2:1-2, 3-4, 4, 8, 13, 17; 4:7, 8; 5:4, 9, 21-22), parallelism (5:21, 23), oxymoron (1:6; 2:13?), and apostrophe,[123] in addition to the aforementioned *preteritio* (1:8; 4:9; 5:1). While the use of metaphor and oxymoron give verve to his letter, Paul's use of repetition, antithesis, and apostrophe allows him to express his thought with an emphatic flair.

The Form of His Appeal

As far as Paul's mode of argumentation is concerned, the major form of *probatio* of which he makes use in 1 Thessalonians is *ethos*,[124] the persuasive power of example. In the *ethos* mode an orator seeks to establish credibility for what is said because his audience trusts the speaker as a good person or expert on the topic. In 1 Thessalonians, Paul constantly seeks to establish his goodwill toward the readers and to affirm his own virtue. Indeed, 1:2-10 is often considered to be an extensive *captatio benevolentiae*.[125] The pastor's praise for his flock (1:8-9; 3:6-10; 4:1,[126] 10; 5:5, 11) is a repeated expression of his good-will toward them. The autobiographical confession of 2:1-12 is an extended rehearsal of the integrity and personal qualities of Paul and his companions. Paul strengthens the authority of his communication by appealing to the Thessalonians' own experience of himself and his companions (1:5; 2:1-2; 5-7, 9-12). In 2:4 and 5 Paul invokes the authority of God. Paul does not present only himself and his companions as examples (1:6); he also draws upon the exemplarity of the Lord Jesus (1:6; 2:15), the prophets (2:15), and the mother churches of God in Christ Jesus that are in Judea (2:15). These are paradigms whose experience has in some way been replicated among the Thessalonian Christians.[127]

The *pathos* of argumentation appeals to the emotions of the audience. In an attempt to win their support, the orator plays upon their feelings. In the letter to the Thessalonians Paul rarely plays to the emotions of his audience, but there are occasions when he does so. He does so when he writes "we were gentle among you, like a nurse tenderly caring for her own children. So deeply do we care for you that we are determined to share with you not only the gospel of God but also our own selves, because you have become very dear to us. You remember our labor and toil . . . we worked night and day. . . . we dealt with each one of you like a father with his children" (2:7-9, 12). And again, "when we could bear it no longer, we decided to be left (all) alone . . . when I could bear it no longer. I was afraid that somehow the tempter had tempted you . . . " (3:1, 5). "You . . . long to see us – just as we long to see you" (3:6).[128] The threat of judgment expressed in 4:6 also represents a use of the *ethos* mode of argumentation. To this short list Johanson would also add the power of persuasion inherent in 2:17-20 and 3:9-13.[129]

In Paul's Hellenistic world, a logical form of appeal (*logos*) could be of the inductive[130] or deductive type. Typical of the latter form of argumentation was the use of the enthymeme, that is, a statement with its supporting reason(s). An implied syllogism stands behind the enthymeme, but the syllogism is not formalized as it is in the *epicheireme.* The use of "*gar* – for" or "*hoti* – because" frequently serves as a textual indicator of this second kind of logical argument. Although it is difficult to characterize Paul's argument in the simple terms of Aristotelian rhetoric, a case may be made that the argumentation in Paul's autobiographical confession is characterized by a quasi-logical type of appeal.[131]

From this point of view, "our coming to you was not in vain" (2:1) serves as a statement of the proposition to be argued.[132] A telltale "*gar* – for" occurs three times (2: 3, 5, 9) as the argument is developed. This cuing particle occurs some five times (4:14, 15; 5:2, 5, 7)[133] in the apocalyptic disclosures (4:13–5:11), where Paul's argumentation is largely based on enthymemes.[134] It might also be suggested that Paul has employed a quasi-logical kind of argumentation in 1:4–5 where he appeals to the experience of the Thessalonians that they have been chosen and then seeks to explicate[135] why they know that they have been chosen. In short, Paul's letter to the Thessalonians gives ample evidence of the type of argumentation proposed by classical rhetoricians.

Orator and Letter Writer

All these similarities, which provide modern scholars with the opportunity to analyze Paul's letters according to the well-known categories of Greek rhetoric, do not mean that Paul had formally studied Greek rhetoric.[136] Indeed, his undisputed claim that he had been a righteous Pharisee in regard to the law (Phil 3:5–6) makes it quite likely that he had never attended a Hellenistic school. On the other hand, knowledge of rhetoric so permeated Hellenistic culture that it is inconceivable that anyone who was as familiar with Hellenistic culture as was Paul would have been immune to the insights proposed by the rhetoricians.

Preacher, Writer, Speaker

To further pursue the issue of the possible influence of the classical rhetoricians on Paul, we might look at four short passages that, on a thematic reading of the letter, hardly gain much attention. These are the passages in which Paul uses the rhetorical device of *preteritio* (1:8; 4:9; 5:1) and his strongly phrased request "that this letter be read to all the brothers and sisters" (5:27).[137]

The fact that Paul repeatedly says – for emphasis' sake! – that there are some topics about which he has no need to write (4:9; 5:1) indicates that he was self-consciously composing a written text. His epistolary prescript and the fact that he calls his text "this letter" (*tēn epistolēn*) shows that he knew full well that his composition was indeed a letter. As a matter of fact, this first of Paul's letters is the only one of his extant letters that he explicitly describes as a letter.[138] There can then be little doubt that Paul knew what he was doing as he wrote his letter.

The first of Paul's *preteritiones,* "so that we have no need to speak about it" (1:8) is contained in the laudatory narration of 1:2–10. It highlights the reputation that the community of Christians at Thessalonica enjoyed among the faith communities of Macedonia and Achaia. At a first reading, the *preteritio* might suggest that, since others had spoken so highly of the Thessalonian Christians, there was no need for Paul and his companions to speak of them as well. On another reading, a reading that is contextual and epistolary, it is obvious that Paul is actually emphasizing his praise of the Thessalonians' faith.[139] While used for emphasis' sake, the *preteritio* of 1:8 indicates that Paul understands that what he is doing is "speaking" (*lalein*), "speaking," that is, in the form of a letter. From his own epistolary discourse we learn that Paul intended to "speak" to his "brothers and sisters" in this letter.[140]

The forceful injunction with which Paul brings his letter to closure in 5:27 shows that he understands his letter to be addressed to a community to whom it would be read. The presence of a "homiletic benediction"[141] also serves as an indication that Paul intended his letter to be read to the Thessalonians. Paul does not urge that his letter be read *by* all the brothers and sisters; he requires that it be read *to* all of them. He understands full well that his communication will be delivered to the community in oral fashion. In a word, Paul considers his letter to be a medium of oral communication. It is a means by which he can communicate orally with those from whom he is separated by physical distance and that set of circumstances which he attributes to Satan (2:18). His letter is a form of discourse.[142] Had he lived in our times, might he have made use of an audio- or videotape?

The observation that Paul's letter is a discourse in the textual form of a letter suggests that it is indeed useful to approach his composition both from the point of view of its epistolary character and from the point of view of its rhetorical composition. When we regard the epistle from the latter point of view, the modern reader must acknowledge that Paul, when writing his letter, employed various stylistic devices known to ancient rhetoricians. He was well aware of the impact that his communication would have upon his audience. The subtle interaction of his pronouns (and pronominal verbal declensions), the frequency of the recall motif, and the manifest use of apostrophe reveal that Paul had his audience very much in mind as he was writing his letter.[143]

An Evangelist's Letter

We cannot forget that Paul was an effective preacher and orator. This is the legacy of Christian tradition to which the Lukan chronicle (Acts) is an early and somewhat stylized witness. In his letter Paul himself repeatedly recalls that he had communicated with the Thessalonians in oral fashion. Moreover, he repeatedly draws attention to the success of his preaching (1:4-10; 2:13-16;[144] 3:6, 9; 4:1). In a word, Paul thought of himself as a relatively successful preacher/orator.

If Paul was as successful a preacher as he seems to have been[145] and if this letter to a community is innovative, as 5:27 seems to imply,[146] then it stands to reason that many of Paul's oratorical skills will make their imprint upon the letter that he has written. This would certainly be the case if Paul's letter had been dictated, as well it might have been. In this case, Paul would have expressed his thought in words that he spoke out as he was "writing." He wanted, moreover, his thought to be conveyed to the Thessalonians in oral fashion. Little wonder, then, that his letter shows evidence of certain rhetorical skills, even if Paul had not been formally schooled in Greek rhetoric. An orator composed the letter to the Thessalonians, and he considered his letter to be a discourse in literary format.

This reflection puts into some focus the discussion among modern exegetes as to whether it is preferable to consider Paul's letter from the standpoint of its rhetorical composition or that of its epistolary form. From the standpoint of the Hellenistic epistolary theorists one cannot really choose the one over the other. Epistolary composition was taught in the rhetorical schools and the letter was indeed one side of a conversation, as Paul deems his own letter to have been. Their theory finds expression in Paul's letter to the Thessalonians. The apostle is well aware that he is writing a letter; but he is equally aware that he is speaking to the Thessalonians through his letter and he intends to communicate *effectively* with them by means of the letter that he wrote.[147]

An Innovative Letter

Those who study theory often find that theory is initially restrictive. Fully integrated, it becomes a useful means and a liberating force. Such is the case with those who have mastered the theory of letter writing. Once mastered, the theory of letter writing allows the writer to develop his or her own art of letter writing. Hellenistic epistolary theorists urged that letters be composed with a certain amount of freedom. It is hardly likely that the one whom Christian tradition has canonized

as the apostle of freedom would have been limited by theoretical con-
straints, even if he had been aware of them. In any case the Paul known
to us through the legacy of his letters is a creative spirit.[148] By virtue of
his own creativity and in keeping with the accepted epistolary theory
of the day, we should expect Paul's letter to be truly creative. It was
not to be restricted by the bonds of rhetorical or epistolary theory.

Every letter that is written is, in fact, a unique communication.
Those who reflect on the epistolary genre make full capital of the
fact that a letter is an occasional composition, which cannot be fully
understood apart from the set of circumstances within which it has
been written – a set of circumstances that are analogous to what the
rhetoricians call the rhetorical *stasis*. In writing to the Thessalonians,
Paul has created a form of communication that is truly new. Consider-
ing the letter from the vantage point of its rhetoric, Thomas Olbricht
describes this new form of communication "church rhetoric."[149] What
Paul has written is, after all, as a communication with a church. Taking a different tack, Helmut Koester has described Paul's letter as an
"experiment in Christian writing."[150]

Thessalonians is indeed an experiment in Christian writing, not in
the sense that it was an activity to be tried out, but in the sense that it
was something new. Insofar as we know, no genre of Christian letter
yet existed. Paul had no model to follow, not even – again insofar as we
know – the personal experience of having written a previous letter to
a gathering of Christians. His rhetorical skill was being put to new purpose; his epistolary talents were applied to different kinds of topics.
Traditional rhetorical and epistolary models were being stretched to
new frontiers.

A Manner of Presence

This stretching out to new frontiers is perhaps most readily apparent
when we consider that Paul was writing a letter within the framework
of Hellenistic culture. One of the primary purposes of the Hellenistic letter was to serve as an expression of *parousia*, presence in the
context of absence. Paul writes about his absence and his desire for
presence in 2:17-3:6. Paul had been constrained from going to the
Thessalonians by Satan himself. Paul was separated from his beloved
Thessalonians and had experienced the separation quite profoundly.
Note the *pathos* of 2:17-3:1, 5!

Paul claims that his absence was merely physical. His theme is
presence in the midst of absence. He claims that his absence was
in outward appearance only; it was not in his heart: "in person, but
not in heart" (*prosōpō ou kardia*, v. 17). The antithetical expression
bespeaks the depth of Paul's desire to be with the Thessalonians. It

is, however, reflective of two different anthropologies.[151] *Prosōpon* is the face; by extension the term connotes outward appearance. *Kardia* evokes the Hebrew *leb,* the very depths of the human being, there where only God can scrutinize (2:4).[152] Presence in the depths of his heart was one modality of his presence with the Thessalonians.

Nonetheless, Paul expressed a manifest desire to be present with the Thessalonians physically, that is, "to see them face to face" (literally, "to see your face"). The horizon of his wish is other than that of mere physical presence. Satan impeded Paul's face-to-face presence with the Thessalonians; a kind of presence to be achieved at the coming of the Lord Jesus (2:18-20). The type of presence that Paul desires to have with the Thessalonians is not simply physical presence, that of his and their *prosōpon.* He desired to be present to the Thessalonians because he was anxious about their faith. His desired presence is in function of their faith.

Such is the burden of the prayer about which he reports in 3:10, "Night and day we pray most earnestly that we may see you face to face and restore whatever is lacking in your faith." Paul's prayer that he be reunited with the Thessalonians had an apostolic purpose. He prayed that he might be with them in order that what was lacking in their faith be restored. Earlier in his letter, as Paul wrote about the way in which he coped with the experience of physical separation from the Thessalonians, he had mentioned *"pistis* – faith" three times: "we sent Timothy, our brother and co-worker for God in proclaiming the gospel of Christ, to strengthen and encourage you for the sake of your *faith.* . . . I sent to find out about your *faith.* . . . Timothy has just now come to us from you, and has brought us the good news of your *faith* and love" (3:2-6).

The type of presence for which Paul yearns is an apostolic presence.[153] Because he could not personally go to the Thessalonians, Paul sent Timothy, his brother and God's co-worker. The credentials of Timothy are fully spelled out. The relationship between Paul and Timothy is clearly articulated. Timothy is the "brother" who will go in Paul's stead. He is, moreover, fully qualified to represent Paul with regard to the faith of the Thessalonians. He, too, was tested and found to be qualified (2:4). Like Paul's, his is an apostolic presence (cf. 2:7). His mission to the Thessalonians is a worthy substitute for Paul's own going to the Thessalonians. As God's co-worker in the gospel of Christ, he is fully qualified for the task.

Paul's letter was yet a third way of being present to the Thessalonians. His letter to the Thessalonians, as all letters, old and new, substitutes for personal presence. Paul's letter has an official function. His relationship with the Thessalonians is not simply that of friendship. He and his companions came to them as "apostles of Christ." His relationship with them continues to be that of an apostle.

The theme and vocabulary of *parousia* (presence) are common-place in epistolary literature. In his letters Paul himself writes about the *parousia* of himself or one of his emissaries (1 Cor 16:17; 2 Cor 7:6, 7; Phil 1:26; 2:12). *Parousia* is often contrasted, explicitly or implicitly, with *apousia* (absence), as it is in Phil 2:12. In 1 Thess 2:17–3:10, the horizon against which Paul speaks of his coming is that of the coming (*parousia*) of the Lord Jesus: "We wanted to come to you . . . but Satan blocked our way. For what is our hope or joy or crown of boasting before our Lord Jesus Christ at his coming [*en tē autou parousia*]" (2:18-19).

From a structuralist point of view, there is a kind of slippage be-tween the coming of Paul and the coming of the Lord Jesus Christ.[154] The *parousia* of Paul gives way to the *parousia* of the Lord Jesus. There is, Elizabeth Struthers Malbon suggests, "a parallel between the 'apostolic *parousia*' and the *parousia tou Kyriou:* both aim to reestablish relationships, to fill an absence with a 'presence.' "[155]

There is, nonetheless, something more than a mere parallel; the absence of Paul gives way to a presence – not the presence of Paul, but the eagerly expected presence of the Lord Jesus. This contributes to the paradoxical quality of Paul's letter. "The sorrow and concern caused by the absence of the Apostle is therefore," writes Helmut Koester, "not overcome by the joy that will be brought with Paul's presence (be it in his personal arrival, or through an emissary or through his letter), but by the outlook to the expected coming of the Lord."[156] While Paul's absence may be compensated for by his presence in heart, by emissary, and by letter – all extensions of Paul's personal presence that compensate for his absence – his presence as an apostle of Christ cedes before the coming (*parousia* or presence) of the Lord Jesus. From a twentieth-century perspective there is a sig-nificant span of time between the historical time of Paul's possible coming and the eschatological time of the coming of the Lord. That is, however, from a twentieth-century perspective. Paul lived in es-chatological time. The resurrection of Jesus as Lord had already taken place, the afflictions (*thlipsis*) of the final times were already being experienced, and the coming of Jesus as Lord was eagerly and immi-nently awaited.[157] From this perspective Paul's presence is relativized by the expected presence of the Lord. That Paul himself, by means of his letter, causes his own *parousia* (presence) to recede in the light of the coming triumphant *parousia* of Jesus as Lord is all the more striking if it was Paul himself who first used the term *parousia* as a technical designation for the eschatological coming of Jesus, the Lord.[158]

And Love

A second major function of the Hellenistic letter was *philophronesis,*
the expression of friendship. Friendship comes to verbal expression
in Paul's letters so often and in so many different ways. Some of these
linguistic elements have already been passed in review. We have re-
hearsed Paul's fond memories of the Thessalonians, described the
letter as a friendly letter, drawn attention to *pathos* as a mode of argumentation, and noted the singular frequency of *"adelphoi –* brothers
and sisters"[159] as the linguistic marker of his use of apostrophe. Classical rhetoricians may consider the expression of such thoughts as
"so deeply do we care for you that we are determined to share with
you not only the gospel of God but also our own selves, because
you have become very dear to us" (2:8) and "we longed with great
eagerness to see you face to face" (2:17) as belonging to the *ethos*
mode of appeal. Paul seeks to establish his affection for the Thessalonians as a ground for his authority. His words express, nonetheless,
the intensity of Paul's relationship with the Thessalonians, as do his
poignant familial metaphors, mother (2:7), father (2:12), and orphan
(2:17).

Twice in his letter Paul comes right out and says that he loves the
Thessalonians, namely, in 2:8 and 3:12. He says, *expressis verbis,* "you
have become very dear to us" (*agapētoi hēmin egenēthēte,* 2:8), and
he prays, "And may the Lord make you increase and abound in love for
one another and for all, just as we abound in love for you" (*perisseusai
tē agapē...hēmeis eis hymas,* 3:12).[160] The former passage affirms
that the Thessalonians were beloved by Paul and his companions.
The latter affirms that the apostles continue to have deep affection
for them. In some respects, the prayer formula is tantamount to a
mild oath[161] affirming Paul's love for the Thessalonians. The prayer
places the apostle's love for the Thessalonians within a theological
and eschatological context. His love for them was an eschatological
sign.[162]

The expression of *philophronesis* is characteristic of the Hellenistic letter. What is striking about Paul's letter is that the very first
expression of love for those to whom he was writing was not an affirmation of his own love for them. Rather he has first assured them
of God's love for them and has given thanks to God for that love (1:4).
Indeed his first apostrophic use of the characteristic *"adelphoi –*
brothers and sisters" is one in which he declares them to be beloved by
God.[163] He does not first address the Thessalonians as those who are
dear to him; rather he addresses them as those who are dear to God.[164]

Paul's personal *philophronesis* for the Thessalonians must be seen
within the larger perspective of God's love for them. The philophro-

netic character of Paul's Hellenistic letter has been transformed in the
light of God's eschatological love for the Thessalonian Christians.

A New Kind of Letter

Paul's letter to the Thessalonians is not simply a personal letter, as
is the typical letter of the Hellenistic era. Paul's letter is an unusual
letter of the Hellenistic period. It appears to be something new. It
is what Helmut Koester has called a "Christian letter."[165] It could be
just as appropriately called an "apostolic letter," for it is in his capacity as an apostle that Paul has written to the Thessalonians.[166] "No
longer," writes Koester, "is the letter a substitute for physical presence for friendship's sake, but a medium through which both writer
and addressees are bound together in the eschatological perspective
of a new message."[167]

The new perspective is reflected both in Paul's epistolary prescript
and his final salutation. Together they form an *inclusio* around this
new kind of letter: "To the church of the Thessalonians in God the
Father and the Lord Jesus Christ: Grace to you and peace ... The grace
of our Lord Jesus Christ be with you" (1:1; 5:28). Both Paul's greeting
as well as his final word represent a departure from typical Hellenistic
usage. "Grace," "the Lord Jesus," and "you" provide the encompassing framework for his letter. Reference to the Lordship of Jesus clearly
imparts an eschatological perspective to his words. That perspective
is reinforced by the "peace" greeting. From Paul's Jewish perspective *shalom — eirēnē* sums up the fullness of God's benefaction to his
people, not excluding his eschatological reign.

In the following chapter we will examine the new message. There
we will summarize Paul's letter in terms of its *homilia*, the specific
message that Paul wished to convey to the Thessalonians by means of
his letter. Before we do so, it would be well to recall that *homilia* or
dialogos is the third function of the Hellenistic letter.

Two additional issues relative to the composition of Paul's letter
to the Thessalonians should be considered before we move on to a
rereading of the letter in order to glean some of the specifics of its
Christian message. Rhetorical analysis of the letter will prove helpful
in both instances.

The Unity of the Letter

One of the perennial problems faced by scholars who study Paul's
letter to the Thessalonians in some detail is whether or not the letter as we now have it is the letter such as it was written by Paul.[168]

Almost from the very beginning of the historical-critical era of New Testament scholarship there have been some scholars who have questioned whether one or another part of 1 Thessalonians was actually written by Paul.[169]

Insertions?

A perennial crux is 2:14-16. The heart of the problem is the harsh things that Paul has to say about the Jews "who killed both the Lord Jesus and the prophets, and drove us out; they displease God and oppose everyone" (v. 15). Almost as problematic is his affirmation that "God's wrath has overtaken them at last" (v. 16). Many critics find in this affirmation an allusion to the destruction of Jerusalem. This occurred after the death of Paul. Accordingly many of these scholars opine that this part of the verse, or the entire pericope, is a posthumous interpolation into Paul's text.[170]

As far as the passage as a whole is concerned, its vituperative tone would seem to be out of character with the Paul who wrote Rom 9-11, especially Rom 9:4-5, and the Paul who so prided himself on his Jewish heritage that he could write about himself as he did in Phil 3:4-6. In evaluating the claims that 2:14-16, in whole or in part, is a later addition to the Pauline text, one must not overlook the dominant place that Paul's letter to the Romans has hitherto had in the interpretation of Pauline literature.[171] The letter to the Romans has functioned as *the* hermeneutical key in Pauline scholarship until very recent times. For those who held that Romans expressed the canon of Pauline orthodoxy, the discordance between 2:14-16 and Rom 9-11 provided a major reason for doubting the authenticity of 2:14-16. In fact, the letter to the Romans is as much an occasional composition as was Paul's letter to the Thessalonians. Its expression of thought was similarly contingent.[172]

In any case, as far as the composition of Paul's letter to the Thessalonians is concerned, rhetorical analysis of the *taxis*, or arrangement, of the letter has shown that it is quite possible to explicate the extant text of 1 Thessalonians as a unified composition.[173] Moreover, one cannot overlook either the fact that *digressio* is a typical rhetorical device or the fact that the *ethos* and *pathos* modes of argumentation contained in 2:14-16 are types of argumentation that are not only rhetorically appropriate but also that Paul himself uses both forms of argumentation in his letter.

As far as the discordant allusion in 2:16 is concerned, specifically, the affirmation that "God's wrath has overtaken them at last," greater attention needs to be paid to the apocalyptic genre of writing than many of those who would willingly excise this passage from Paul's letter are wont to do. The imaginative and symbolic use of language typical of apocalyptic frequently clouds and/or avoids reference to any specific event or person. Moreover, apocalyptic has its own fashion of dealing with time. Written against the background of an apocalyptic framework, Paul's letter to the Thessalonians shows evidence of an apocalyptic understanding of time.

The fact that Paul has an apocalyptic understanding of time is also important to bear in mind when one comes to the crux constituted by 5:1-11. Those who argue that the passage did not belong to Paul's letter as it was initially composed by the apostle himself[174] argue from the fact that, within the body of Paul's letter, the pericope is formally redundant with 4:13-18, its vocabulary is somewhat unusual, and the deletion of it from the letter would not generally interrupt the letter's flow of thought.

Once again rhetorical analysis of the *taxis* of the letter indicates that the letter can well be understood as a unified composition that includes 5:1-11. One must, moreover, be attentive to the function of the apocalyptic genre. 4:13-18 is blatantly an expression of consequent eschatology within an apocalyptic framework. It speaks of a future that is yet to come. 5:1-11 constitutes the other piece of Paul's apocalyptic dyptic. It urges his hearers to live in a way that is fitting for those who are already caught up in the eschatological scenario. If the eschatological future is imminently expected, the coming of that day impinges on the historical present. 5:1-12 uses apocalyptic language to speak of the implications of that future for the present.

A Composite Text?

If some scholars have attacked the integrity of the extant first letter to the Thessalonians on the grounds that 2:14-16 and/or 5:1-11 are later interpolations into Paul's original letter, some scholars ask whether the letter as we now have it was originally written by Paul as a single composition. These scholars generally hold that our extant "first" letter of Paul to the Thessalonians was put together at the time when Paul's letters were collected and "published" in a codex edition. This kind of attack upon the integrity of Paul's letter came first of all from a number of German scholars, among whom Walter Schmithals[175] and Rudolf Pesch[176] are preeminent, but their point of view is beginning to be reflected in some English-language studies of the letter.[177]

As a context of the discussion, one must take into consideration the fact that Paul's letter is unusually long in comparison with typical first-century Hellenistic letters. Indeed Schmithals's pioneering efforts to prove that various letters in the canonical Pauline corpus are composites began with a study of Paul's longer letters, especially the two letters to the Corinthians, where references to earlier (and presumably lost) letters make the discussion particularly interesting.

With regard to the textual indications that conceivably suggest that our present 1 Thessalonians is a composite text, there is the indisputable fact that the letter contains two thanksgiving periods (1:2-2:12; 2:13-3:12).[178] Accordingly Schmithals has divided 1 Thessalonians into two "letters" – or letter fragments since the extant text contains but a single epistolary salutation and one set of final greetings. These are 1:1-2:12; 4:2-5:28; and 2:13-4:1. Schmithals holds that the second letter (2:13-4:1) was written shortly after the first (1:1-2:12; 4:2-5:28). Earl Richard divides 1 Thessalonians in essentially the same fashion,[179] but considers that 2:13-4:2 is a short missive that has been inserted into a longer and later letter. Pesch espouses a view that is similar to that of Richard, but he holds that the earlier letter is a bit longer (2:13-4:8) than Richard claims.[180]

Arguments drawn from rhetorical criticism are not the only ones that should be brought into consideration. They are, however, pertinent. Arguments drawn from classic rhetoric consider that ancient texts have been self-consciously composed by their authors. In particular, classic rhetoric draws attention to the arrangement, or *taxis*, of a text. From this standpoint, the recent rhetorical analyses of Paul's letter to the Thessalonians by Johanson, Hughes, and Wuellner indicate that the text as it now stands can well be understood as a unified composition. Until stronger arguments to the contrary are established, I find no reason for doubting that our extant first letter to the Thessalonians represents the letter such as it came from the Apostle himself.[181]

Paul's Choice of Language

One element to which classic rhetorical analysis draws attention and which has not yet earned especial mention in this study is Paul's *lexis*, or choice of vocabulary. To be sure, an analysis of Paul's choice of language is what enables rhetorical critics to make their judgment with regard to Paul's style and mode of argumentation, but there is more to consider than merely those aspects of his choice of language.

By way of entrée, we might consider an antithetical expression found in the "apostolic parousia" at 2:17. Paul's poignant claim that he wanted to be with the Thessalonians included the heartfelt claim that he was absent from them "in person, not in heart." We have already noted that the language of the antithesis is not entirely consistent. The first expression, "person," is a perfectly acceptable Greek term. Its use is appropriate to Paul's phrase and reflects good Hellenistic anthropology. The contrasting term, "heart," while an acceptable Greek term (*kardia*), seems to reflect a Semitic anthropology and might well be considered an example of "translation Greek."[182]

Paul's opening greeting was "Grace to you and peace." There are reasons to believe that this was not originally an epistolary greeting. "To you" is redundant with "to the church of the Thessalonians." Both are in the dative case, and "to the church of the Thessalonians" can hardly be taken as being in apposition to "to you." This suggests that "grace to you and peace" may well be a formula that Paul has coopted for his letter from some other source.

"Grace to you and peace" is not at all a Hellenistic epistolary greeting. In Hellenistic letters we find a simple "greetings" (*chaire* or *chairete,* depending on the number of recipients of the letter). Granted that Paul's "grace" (*charis*) is more or less homophonous with "greetings" (*chaire*), it is hardly the same. Paul's salutation is, in other words, an epistolary trove. Did Paul compose the salutation as he was writing to the Thessalonians? The redundancy of "to you" makes it hardly likely that this was the case. Rather it would seem that Paul has taken the formulation over from some previous use known to him.

The case has been made that the formula might well have been a typical formula of greeting used in the assemblies in which Christians gathered. If such, it may well have been used at Antioch in Syria, where Paul was a regular visitor. The combination of Hellenistic (*charis* – grace) and Semitic (*etrēnē* – peace) terms in a single greeting would be consistent with the bicultural situation of the Christian community at Antioch.[183] This life-setting of the salutation formula used by Paul in 1:1 would be consistent with the setting envisioned in the eschatocol of the letter (5:23–28). It would indicate that Paul has borrowed various bits of Christian tradition and assumed them into the first of the letters that he wrote. Finally, it would indicate that his language has both a Hellenistic tone and a Semitic ring.

This latter point deserves further elaboration. Paul has addressed his letter "to the church of the Thessalonians." To a Hellenistic audience, such as that of the Christians who gathered at Thessalonica, "the church" was an assembly. Paul's language made good sense as he attempted to communicate well with his Thessalonian "brothers and sisters." Yet the fact that Paul later writes about "the churches of God" (2:14), using a classic biblical expression and one that suggests the unique status of Christian assemblies, suggests that the terminology that Paul used in his letter had a connotation other than that which might emerge on a first reading of his text. "Church" had an obvious meaning for those who read Paul's letter; its connotations were somewhat other for the one who wrote the letter.

Something similar might be said apropos Paul's mention of the "courage" with which he spoke (2:2). Paul's terminology evokes the boldness of the political orator or that of the philosopher who is engaged in a struggle for the truth. That Paul qualifies his oratory as taking place "in spite of great opposition," using the language of the classic *agōn*- motif indicates that he is well aware that he is communicating with Hellenists. Yet the fact that Paul qualifies his boldness as "in our God" and says that what he uttered was a message from and about God indicates that Paul is making use of more than mere Hellenistic metaphor as he was writing to the Thessalonians. His language suggests the courage of the biblical prophets.

Perhaps one should think of two levels in Paul's language, that of his Semitic (biblical and Christian) background and that of his Hellenistic foreground. He was writing from his own experience, which he had conceptualized in familiar terms; he was writing to people who had shared an experience with him, yet whose total experience was not the same as his. To reflect in this fashion is simply to take seriously the fact that Paul was trying to communicate with the Thessalonians through the medium of language, of language in written form, of language in the written form of a letter.[184] The nature of human language is such that the connotations of language used by a communicator are not quite the same as the connotations of that same language as it is perceived by those who receive the communication. Such is the experience of every human being. Paul and the Thessalonians were humans and he made every attempt to communicate well with them.

It is not my intention here to attempt to enter into the Pauline psyche. Nonetheless, we must seriously take into consideration the fact that Paul's letter to the Thessalonians is an act of communication. Classic rhetoric drew attention to the composition of texts, that from which they came; the new rhetoric draws attention to texts as acts of communication with those to whom they are addressed.[185] Accordingly we must be attentive to both the background of Paul's language and the foreground of that language. There are sufficient Semitisms in Paul's letter to the Thessalonians to indicate that the letter has been written by a person with a Semitic background; there are sufficient Hellenistic elements in Paul's letter that manifest characteristic features of a Hellenistic text[186] to indicate that the letter was written to people with a Hellenistic culture. What he had to say in his letter will be the focus of the following chapter.

∽ 5 ∽

Paul's Message

The third major function of the Hellenistic letter was *homilia* or *dialogos,* its specific message. What was it that Paul wanted to say to the Thessalonians? Various textual markers provide the clues.

A Faith to Be Complemented

In 3:9 Paul reports that it is not only the Thessalonians who have received good news with joy. Paul and his companions have also received good news – the good news of the Thessalonians' faith and love (3:6). The good news provided Paul and his companions with needed moral support, but it also brought them joy.

Joyful Prayer

They experienced joy in the very presence of God (*emprosthen tou theou hēmōn*). This descriptive phrase bespeaks Paul's conviction that the Christian life is lived in the presence of God.[1] The God in whose presence Paul and his companions have experienced joy is, as Paul says, "our God" (*tou theou hēmōn*). The God of Paul and his companions is also the God of the Thessalonians.

Paul's joy spontaneously leads to thanksgiving and to a prayer that he shares with the Thessalonians. He writes that his constant prayer is that "we may see you face to face and restore whatever is lacking in your faith" (3:10) and continues: "Now may our God and Father himself and our Lord Jesus direct our way to you" (3:11). The formulation of the latter prayer is unique. It is addressed to our God and Father and our Lord Jesus Christ and the verb "direct" (*kateuthynai*) is in the singular, as if God and the Lord Jesus Christ were expected to act in concert in bringing Paul and his companions to the Thessalonians.

Paul's prayer is that he and his companions be able to be present with the Thessalonians so as "to restore whatever is lacking in their faith" (*ta hysterēmata tēs pisteōs hymōn*).

What are the "deficiencies of faith" that call for Paul's presence and elicit a heartfelt expression of his desire to be present with them? Since his letter is a way of being present with them, it is quite likely that Paul would have tried to compensate for the Thessalonians' lack of faith in the very text that serves as a substitute for his presence.[2]

What Paul Wrote

Between the prayer in which he prays that he might be able to compensate for the deficiencies in the Thessalonians' faith and the paraenesis with which he brought his letter to closure, Paul formally addresses four specific topics: sanctification (4:(1)3-8), love of the brothers and sisters (4:9-12), those who have died (4:13-18), and the times and seasons (5:1-11). The first *topos,* sanctification, is introduced by a pastoral formulation in which Paul reminds the Thessalonians that he has already taught them how to live and commends them for living as they do. Another two topics, sibling love and the times and seasons, are introduced by way of *preteritio.* Although used for emphasis' sake, Paul's phraseology nevertheless indicates that the topics are already known to Paul's audience.

This leaves the fourth *topos* as the only one of the four that is not introduced by a formula that explicitly recalls that the Thessalonians know something about it. Moreover, this fourth topic, those who have died, is the only one of the four that is introduced by a disclosure formula, reinforced with an apostrophic use of "brothers and sisters": "we do not want you to be uninformed, brothers and sisters, about those who have died" (4:13).

Not only does this presentation of the topic contain the only obvious disclosure formula in the entire letter, but the topic is treated in a very logical fashion. It is in this passage of the letter that Paul's argument is most clearly based on enthymemes, the sign of a quasi-logical form of presentation.[3] This seems to suggest that what was lacking in the Thessalonians' faith has to do with the fate of those who have died.[4]

The Thessalonians' Faith

Confirmation that this is so can be had when we read what Paul has to say about faith (*pistis*).[5] When compared with Paul's other letters, the letter to the Thessalonians has an unusual concentration of talk about faith.[6] Paul calls the Thessalonians "believers" (2:10, 13)[7] and observes that their faith is legendary (1:8), an example to others (1:7).

Talk about faith, as indicated by Paul's use of words with the root
pist-, is singularly concentrated in that section of Paul's letter in which
he writes about Timothy's visit to the Thessalonians and his return
(3:1-10). In this passage we find five of Paul's eight uses of the noun
"*pistis* – belief."[8] Paul sent Timothy to encourage the Thessalonians in
their faith (v. 2). He sent him to inquire about their faith (v. 5). Timothy
brought good news about their faith (v. 6). Paul has been encouraged
because of their faith (v. 7). Nevertheless he is concerned because
there is something missing in their faith (v. 10).

After talking about faith so much and stating his desire to go to the
Thessalonians so as to be able compensate for the deficiency in their
faith, Paul stops talking about faith. The next time that he broaches
the subject is in 4:14, where he grounds his argumentation[9] in the
belief that Jesus died and rose: "we believe," he writes, "that Jesus
died and rose again." It appears that Paul is here quoting a traditional
credal formula. This is not the only time that Paul makes reference
to a credal formula in his letter. He has already done so in 1:10; he
will do so again in 5:9-10.[10] It is only in 4:14, however, that Paul
specifically appeals to the faith of the Thessalonians and his own –
not to mention the faith of other believers! – by introducing the
credal formula in a formal manner: "we believe that" (*pisteuomen
hoti*).[11]

The use of the credal formula provides Paul with a way of speaking
about the content of the faith (*pistis*) that unites all believers. In 3:10
Paul poignantly affirms that there was something lacking in the Thessalonians' faith; in 4:14 he proclaims the belief that they share with
other believers. Thereupon he proceeds to spell out the implications
of that faith. The implications deal with the situation of the dead with
respect to the parousia of the Lord Jesus Christ.

Hope, the Complement of Faith

Further confirmation that what is lacking in the Thessalonians' faith
really has to do with those who have already died can be gleaned from
some of the other ways in which Paul writes about the faith of the
Thessalonians.

More than once in his correspondence Paul writes about "faith and
love."[12] As Paul began his letter to the Thessalonians, he called to mind
their "work of faith and labor of love" (1:3). In a later exhortation he
appealed to them to "put on the breastplate of faith and love" (5:8). In
the latter instance, Paul has taken a metaphor from Isa 59:17, where
the prophet's disciple had described the Lord as one who "put on
righteousness like a breastplate and a helmet of salvation on his head."
In self-conscious fashion Paul has transformed the imagery so that it

is not the Lord himself, but Christians who are to arm themselves for the fray.[13]

In place of the biblical "righteousness," Paul uses the faith and love dyad to describe how the Thessalonians ought to live. "Faith and love" serve, so to speak, as Paul's exegesis of the traditional theme of "righteousness." The pairing of faith and love probably took place before the composition of 1 Thessalonians. Faith bespeaks the believers' relationship to God; love evokes the relationship that binds them to one another in community. Faith is the basic situation of those who are oriented toward the one God; but their faith is worked out in love, that is, in their relationships with God's people.[14]

When Paul speaks about faith and love in 1:3 and 5:8, Paul complements his reference to faith and love with a mention of the Thessalonians' hope. In each passage the reference to hope seems to be a deliberate and self-conscious addition to the traditional pair. In both cases, hope is cited in the third instance, in the emphatic position of the triad. In 1:3, the traditional dyad of faith and love appears in the form of epexegetical genitives, "work of faith and labor of love." Hope appears within a more complex expression, "steadfastness of hope in our Lord Jesus Christ." In 5:8, the biblical text had talked of the breastplate of righteousness and the helmet of salvation. Paul has divided the metaphor and added hope as a third referent, "the breastplate of faith and love, and for a helmet the hope of salvation."

The way that Paul writes about faith and love in 1 Thessalonians in these two passages (1:3; 5:8) makes it all the more striking when he reports on the good news brought by Timothy. The good news, which so elated Paul (3:6-9), was the good news of their faith and love (3:6). Paul made nary a mention of their hope. Then, in the prayerful expression of his joy, Paul says that there is something lacking in their faith.[15]

Faith and Expectation

Another time that Paul writes about the faith of the Thessalonians is also significant. In his first rehearsal of the visit to the Thessalonians, Paul praised the legendary faith of the Thessalonians: "in every place your faith in God has become known, so that we have no need to speak about it" (1:8). In this *captatio benevolentiae,* hyperbole and *preteritio* are used to highlight the nature of the Thessalonians' faith. Paul explains why it is that their faith is so widely renowned: "For[16] the people of those regions report about us what kind of welcome we had among you, and how you turned to God from idols, to serve a living and true God, and to wait for his Son from heaven, whom he raised from the dead – Jesus who rescues us from the wrath that is coming" (1:9-10).

Paul has clearly affirmed that their faith is in God[17] and that this entails their conversion to the living and true God.[18] That much of Paul's affirmation represents the traditional language of Jews who were speaking about the conversion of Gentiles.[19] Paul immediately adds, however, something that comes to him from the Christian tradition, namely, that the Thessalonian believers "wait for his Son from heaven, whom he raised from the dead – Jesus, who rescues us from the wrath to come" (1:10).

This verse is Paul's appropriation of bits of Christian tradition. He has cited a credal formula, namely, "whom he raised from the dead."[20] He uses the name of Jesus absolutely, without the juxtaposition of a qualifying epithet. Such usage is unusual for Paul, apart, that is, from formulaic contexts, where Paul's language harks back to early Christian traditions.[21] Yet another indication that Paul is echoing Christian tradition is the fact that he attributes to Jesus the title of "Son" (*Huios*). The attribution is a unique occurrence in this letter, but it is to be found, again with reference to the resurrection, in Rom 1:4, that is, in a passage that many authors believe to have a traditional credal origin.

According to Hans-Heinrich Schade 1:10 represents the dominant christological affirmation of the entire letter.[22] The insight is quite accurate. The verse is singularly important not only because it is the oldest literary witness to the resurrection of Jesus from the dead, but also because of the way in which Paul presents the faith of the Thessalonians as culminating in their expectation of Jesus as eschatological savior. It is sometimes said that a letter's initial formulation, including its expression of thanksgiving, foreshadows the expression of the author's basic message. This would certainly be true of 1:10.

The similarities between 1:10 and 4:14-17 cannot be overlooked. In one and the other instance there is the rehearsal of at least a fragment of a credal formula. In each case there is an absolute use of the name "Jesus" to which a title has been added. The titles, "Son" in 1:10 and "Lord" in 4:15, 17, proclaim the belief that Jesus is the risen one. In both instances there is reference to the "dead" (*hoi nekroi*). In each case there is a reference to the appearance of the risen one "from heaven" (*ek tōn ouranōn* in 1:10; *ap'ouranou* in 4:16). In each instance there is a movement from the credal affirmation that Jesus is the risen one to the expectation of his eschatological appearance. In both cases the eschatological appearance is described in apocalyptic language. Finally, in each instance there is mention of the salvific function of the risen one, "rescues us from the wrath that is coming" in 1:10; "through him" and "with him" in 4:14, 17.[23] In essence, 4:14-17 unfolds and makes more precise, by application to the case of those who have died, what Paul has already affirmed in his thanksgiving.[24]

The Threefold "peri – concerning"

Yet another indication that it is in 4:13-18 that we find the *homilia* of Paul's letter is the presence of the topical *peri* in 4:13. *"Peri"* is, as has been noted, an epistolary formula. It is used to indicate the various topics that an author wishes to address in a letter, sometimes the topics about which he had been queried in previous correspondence. In Paul's letter to the Thessalonians a topical *peri* occurs just three times, that is, in 4:9, 4:13, and 5:1.[25] Respectively they introduce sibling love, those who have died, and the times and the seasons as the topics about which Paul will have something to say. What he has to say is that he has no need to write about sibling love (4:9) or about the times and the seasons (5:1-2), and in each instance he explains why he has nothing to say. In the first instance, he has no need to write because they have been taught by God; in the second instance, he has no need to write because they already know about the day of the Lord.[26] By implication, he has something to write about those who have died. What he has to write about that topic is found in 4:14-17, for which verses 15 and 18 provide an encompassing frame.

Paul's threefold use of the topical *peri*[27] calls for yet another reflection. His description of the life of the Thessalonian community in 1:3 indicates that their life is one of faith, love, and hope in the presence of our God and Father. "Faith and love" is the traditional pair. A faith-relationship with God entails a relationship with those who have a similar relationship with God. This corresponds to the Jewish covenantal pattern.[28] Relationship with God entails relationship with God's people. In Paul's letter God's people are called "brothers and sisters," that is, they are brothers and sisters to Paul, but they are also brothers and sisters to one another.

Faith works itself out in love;[29] hope is the posture that faith takes in the face of the future. Since the Thessalonian Christians have concerns about the eschatological future, Paul writes about their faith, love, and hope (1:3; 5:8). Love and hope are, as it were, two different expressions or implications of faith. They are the form that faith takes with regard to others who have faith and with regard to the future. In 3:10, Paul tells the Thessalonians that, although he has been elated by the good news about their faith and love, he nonetheless has concerns about their faith because there is something lacking in it (3:10). The implications of faith are taken up in 4:9-5:11, where the topic is divided for purposes of discussion.

The topical *peris* introduce the three subtopics. Concerning love
of fellow believers, there is no need to write since they have been
well taught and have effectively responded (3:9-10). In contrast, there
is something to say about those who have died. There is something
about which Paul "does not want them to be uninformed," lest they
be like people who have no hope. Thus, in 4:13, Paul formally and
specifically introduces his topic. In fact, it is the third element of the
faith-love-hope triad. The topic at hand is hope, but Paul explicitly
writes about hope only by way of contrast: the Thessalonians must not
be like those "others" who have no hope (*hoi loipoi hoi mē echontes
elpida,* 4:13). The Thessalonians are faithful (4:14); their love is super-
abundant (3:10). In order that they might be full of hope as well, Paul
writes as he does in 4:14-17.

The Times and the Seasons

The third topical *peri* (5:1) introduces the final movement in Paul's
reflection about the faith of the Thessalonians (5:1-11). This passage
serves as a significant complement to what Paul has written in 4:13-
18. It is the other panel in Paul's epistolary diptych, the companion of
4:13-18. The parallelism and similarities between 5:1-11 and 4:13-18
are readily apparent.[30]

Both units are introduced with a formal announcement of the topic
to be considered and conclude with a paraenetic exhortation. Both
passages incorporate apocalyptic motifs, both make use of a credal
formula, both allude to an authoritative dictum (the word of the Lord
in 4:15, a prophetic utterance from Isaiah in 5:8), both make reference
to the living and the dead (4:13, 14, 15, 16, 17; 5:10), both speak about
being with the Lord (4:14, 17; 5:10) as a manner of talking about salvation, and both make reference to hope (4:13; 5:8). Rather than being a
redundant repetition of 4:13-18,[31] 5:1-11 functions as its useful and
necessary complement. "*De* – but" (5:1) loosely links the two passages
together; "*elpis* – hope" (4:13; 5:8) creates a loose *inclusio* making a
unit of the two passages.

What had been lacking in the faith of the Thessalonians concerned
those who had died. Paul talks about what God's future has in store
for them in 4:14-17. That future is in God's hands. The eschatological
future has, however, implications for people in the present. The eschatological future impinges on the present, because that future has
already begun to be realized.[32]

The day of the Lord is yet to come, yet Christians are already children of the day (5:5).[33] Christians are not only those who await the
parousia; they already live in the eschatological future. The paraenesis of 5:2-10, beginning with the *pathos* appeal of 5:2, is addressed

to their present situation. God is responsible for the consummation of the eschatological future; his people have responsibility in the eschatological future made present in Jesus' resurrection from the dead. 4:13-18 speaks of what God will do; 5:1-11 speaks of what Christians have to do.

The exhortation that Paul addresses to the Thessalonians in 5:1-11 is an elaboration upon a topic about which he need not have written (5:1). Nothing needed to have been written about sibling love (4:9). Paul, nonetheless, picked up the topic and elaborated on it by means of a paraenesis that contrasted the Thessalonian Christians with "outsiders" (4:12) and encouraged them to continue in the way of life that was already theirs.

In similar fashion, Paul appended an exhortation to his *preteritio* on the times and seasons. The elaboration is an exhortation that antithetically contrasts the children of light and the day with the children of night and darkness (5:4-8) and encourages the Thessalonians to continue in the way of life that was already theirs. His "and build up each other, as indeed you are doing" (5:11) is an addition to the hortatory conclusion that echoes 4:18; it is an addition that recalls the pastor's reflection in 4:10.

The Wish Prayers

The complementarity between Paul's parallel reflections on the eschatological future and the eschatological future-made-present that is found in the two-part eschatological disclosure (4:13-5:11) is also expressed in the closing wish prayer at 5:23: "May the God of peace himself sanctify you entirely, and may your spirit and soul and body be kept sound and blameless at the coming of Jesus Christ."

This wish prayer, which Langevin calls a "synthesis blessing," sums up the main thoughts of the letter, with its emphasis on sanctity (3:13; 4:3-8), the encouragement of the Thessalonians (4:18; 5:11, 14) and the horizon of the parousia (2:19; 3:13; 4:13-5:11).[34] The prayer should be read as a two-part blessing, whose structure is characterized by synthetic parallelism in chiastic form:

> May the God of peace himself
> sanctify you entirely;
> and may your spirit and soul and body
> be kept sound and blameless[35]
> at the coming of our Lord Jesus Christ.

Paul's blessing has a Semitic form.[36] This is consistent with its Semitic themes. It contains an apocalyptic mention of the parousia. The "God of peace"[37] speaks of the giver of all good gifts, especially his covenant blessings. The passive voice of *"tērētheiē* – be kept" is a divine or theological passive. Coming from a tradition that tried to avoid the explicit use of God's name – so great was the conviction of God's transcendence – the theological passive implies that the real agent is God himself.

Much has been written about the anthropology of the second stich. Since the blessing seems to have been composed by Paul for this letter, a question has been raised as to whether Paul was proposing, or perhaps writing on the basis of, a trichotomous anthropology, that is, an understanding of the human being as composed of three parts, spirit, soul, and body. Most commentators are of the opinion that Paul did not intend to divide the human person into three constituent parts. The real problem seems to be the presence of the "spirit – *pneuma.*" Soul and body (*hē psychē kai to sōma*) is a perfectly adequate description of the human being in its vitality and its corporeality.

In his letter Paul had heretofore used the term "spirit – *pneuma*" in reference to the divine spirit.[38] The "spirit – *pneuma*" of 5:23 has, however, been taken to denote some kind of superior force in the human being[39] or as the moral disposition.[40] Jewett considers that its presence in Paul's prayer is polemical. He holds that Paul was confronting his libertinist opponents by affirming that it is not only the spirit but also the soul and body that are to be kept holy until the parousia.[41]

Jewett's explanation supposes that Paul's letter was written to a community that had been troubled by ecstatic manifestations and dualistic tendencies close to Gnosticism.[42] Wiles takes a different tack, suggesting that, whereas Paul was focusing on the community in the first stich of his prayer, he may be referring more to individuals in the second.[43] The kinds of sophisticated anthropological considerations advanced by Jewett and Wiles, to name but two approaches to the problem, are unnecessary and foreign to Paul's basic argumentation. Moreover, I find no need to postulate an epistolary situation such as that envisioned by Jewett.

Paul's anthropological terms must be taken in a wholistic sense. In 5:23 he makes use of the literary device of (a triadic) *repetitio* to emphasize that it is the whole human who is to be found blameless at the parousia. As he brings his letter to a close, the wish that Paul expresses in the form of a prayer and blessing is that God effect even now, in the eschatological present, the sanctification of the Thessalonian Christians, and that, in his constant fidelity, he bring that sanctification to completion at the time of the parousia. This summary blessing and wish prayer of 5:23 is akin to the wish prayer of 3:11–13:

Now may our God and Father himself and our Lord Jesus direct our way to you. And may the Lord make you increase and abound in love for one another and for all, just as we abound in love for you. And may he so strengthen your hearts in holiness that you may be blameless before our God and Father at the coming of our Lord Jesus Christ with all his saints.

Despite their obvious similarities, there are interesting differences between the two prayers.[44] The summary blessing brings Paul's final paraenesis (4:1-5:22) to closure with a recapitulation of its major themes. The wish prayer of 3:11-13 flows from Paul's expression of thanksgiving and alludes to Paul's experience of separation from the Thessalonians. It is closely linked with the prayer report of 3:10 and introduces, with its reference to holiness,[45] the exhortation on holiness that follows almost immediately afterward (4:3-8). Appropriately, therefore, does Johanson speak of the "terminal-transitional" functions of 3:(10)11-13.[46]

Within the wish prayer 3:13, "and may he so strengthen your hearts in holiness that you may be blameless before our God and Father at the coming of our Lord Jesus with all his saints," functions as a "third petition."[47] It is not isolable from the prayer of which it is a part. That prayer forms a single semantic unit with the preceding prayer report (3:10-13).

It is, however, only in its third and final petition that the prayer of 3:11-13 reveals a close similarity, in content, if not in form,[48] with the wish prayer in 5:23. As 5:23, it speaks of holiness and blamelessness against the horizon of the parousia of the Lord Jesus Christ. The focus on the parousia provides a perspective for what will follow in Paul's letter. When attention is paid to the transitional function of 3:11-13 and the summary function of 5:23, it is clear that the intervening 4:1-5:22 is "framed," as it were, by the parousia of our Lord Jesus Christ. The entire paraenesis is encompassed by the thought of the parousia. At the center of the discussion is Paul's reflection on the relationship between those who have died and the parousia of the same Lord Jesus Christ. It is given for the sake of information (see v. 13) and for exhortation's sake (v. 18).

In reading the final two chapters of Paul's letter, one might even note the chiastic development of his exposition, following an A, B, C, D, C', B', A' pattern. This would be (A) a prayer for blamelessness with the parousia as its horizon (3:11-13); (B) paraenesis pertaining to relationships among Christians, grounded in the will of God and focusing on the work of the Spirit (4:1-8); (C) paraenesis on the Christian life introduced by a "there is no need to write" expression of *preteritio* (4:9-12); (D) the relationship between the parousia and the fate of those who have died (4:13-18); (C') paraenesis on the Christian life introduced by a "there is no need to write" expression of *preteritio* (5:1-11); (B') paraenesis pertaining to relationships among Christians, grounded in the will of God and focusing on the work of the Spirit (4:1-8); (A') a prayer for blamelessness with the parousia as its horizon (5:23).

We Do Not Want You to Be Uninformed

These various indications point to the disclosure period of 4:13-18 as Paul's attempt to compensate for what was lacking in the Thessalonians' faith.[49] The pericope is central to Paul's argumentation and may be construed to be the focus of the message that the letter, a substitute for his personal presence, was intended to convey. This passage has been subject to more rigorous scrutiny than any other passage in Paul's first letter.[50] Nonetheless it might be useful to pass it in review once again in order better to appreciate the articulation of Paul's thought.

The passage consists of (1) a statement of the topic and the author's statement of purpose for introducing the topic (v. 13); (2) the initial argumentation, that is, the reiteration of a credal formula with a statement of its implications (v. 14); (3) an interpretation for which a word of the Lord serves as formal authority (vv. 15-17); and (4) a final exhortation (v. 18). These four units are linked by appropriate connectors, "*gar* – for," "*gar* – for," and "therefore." Paul's logical arrangement provides unity for his exposition, including the three-verse third subunit. In this subunit the connectives "*hoti* – for" and "*epeita* – then" give logical and narrative coherence to Paul's explanation.

Statement of Topic and Purpose (v. 13)

The disclosure formula and the *hina-* clause ("so that . . . ") indicate Paul's purpose in writing about his topic. He wants to dispel the ignorance of his addressees so that they might not grieve as others do. His social perspective is the distinction between those to whom he is writing and others who grieve and have no hope. Since those to whom he is writing have been characterized as persons of faith, love, and hope, it is clear that Paul writes as he does so as to maintain his addressees within the Christian, that is, the hopeful, family. Hence he addresses them apostrophically as "brothers and sisters." Because he takes up the topic in this fashion, it is clear that Paul's subsequent reflections are an expression of his pastoral care.

The topic is "those who have died." These are *hoi koimēthentes*,[51] literally, "those who have fallen asleep." The metaphorical use of the verb *koimaō* in the passive or middle voice to describe the sleep of death was not unknown in Paul's Hellenistic world.[52] One might ask whether Paul's choice of a metaphor to introduce the topic, rather than identify the dead by a nondescript "*hoi nekroi* – the dead," implies a theological critique.[53] They may well be "dead in Christ" (*hoi nekroi en Christō*, 4:16) but they have only "fallen asleep."[54] The death of those about whom Paul is writing is not the end of their story.

Who were those who have died? How many were they? These are questions for which interpreters of Paul's letter would like definite answers. Such answers are not to be had. Paul's letter is the only source of information and the information that he provides is spotty. Since his letter was written shortly after his visit and since the community at Thessalonica was presumably not very large, it is likely that the numbers of those who had died were not very large. It may not, however, be presumed that Paul's reflections pertained only to those who had died in Thessalonica. The situation of the church at Thessalonica was known to other churches (1:8-9). Relationships existed between the Thessalonian Christians and other Macedonian Christians (3:10). Hence the concern of the Thessalonians, to which Paul responds, might have been the death of Macedonian Christians from several communities.

That the concern had regard to Christians who had died is evident from Paul's description of them as "the dead in Christ."[55] This is Paul's first use of the "in Christ" formula,[56] which will become a commonplace in his later writings. Does the formula in this context signify simply the union[57] between those who have died and Christ as if Paul's expression simply meant "Christian dead," that is, believers who have died? Or does it mean those who have died because of Christ, that is, those believers who have suffered death as a result of their faith in Christ?

Recent studies on Paul's letter have tended to take Paul's frequent use of "*thlipsis* – affliction" as a social commentary. To these scholars, "*thlipsis* – affliction" is not primarily an expression that has come from Paul's theological reflection, in which "*thlipsis*" would designate eschatological woes, nor is it an expression used to describe the inner psychological turmoil of Paul's neophyte Christian community. Understood from a social, rather than from a theological or psychological point, the term *thlipsis*[58] indicates that members of the community were being persecuted. In that case, "the dead in Christ" might well be those who died as the result of some sort of persecution.[59] It is interesting, in any case, to take note of Paul's use of the "*Christos* – Christ" title, as a designation of Jesus, when he writes about the "dead in Christ." That particular christological title evokes the memory of Jesus who had died.[60]

A situation of Christians having died because of their faith in Christ would be particularly problematic for Paul's young community of believers. Their death would easily have led the other members of the community to doubt the reality and/or the imminence of the coming triumph of God, to lose faith in Paul, and to have concerns about their own fate. Will not those who have died be deprived of an opportunity to participate in the parousia? And isn't that all the more tragic if those who have died did so precisely because of their faith? If Christians have died, how will it be possible for them to take part in the glorious parousia of Jesus the Lord? It is in 4:13-18 that Paul gives his answer. His purpose was to console those to whom he was writing.

A Confession of Faith

Paul begins his reflection, introduced by an argumentative "*ei gar* — for since," with an affirmation of the traditional faith of believers: "we believe that Jesus died and rose again." The formal introductory lemma, "we believe that," identifies the credal formula as an expression of faith. Its "we" encompasses not only Paul and the believers but also other believers. The credal formula that follows the introductory phrase is traditional. Signs that the formula predates Paul are its absolute use of "Jesus" and the presence of the verb "*anestē* — rise again." Paul himself normally uses the verb *egeirō* in the passive voice to talk about the resurrection of Jesus as Lord.[61]

Although the verb "*anestē* — rise again" might at first sight seem to suggest that Jesus rose under his own power, its parallelism with "*anastēsontai* — will rise" in verse 16 shows that this is not the case. It is God who is the agent in the entire apocalyptic scenario, as Paul's parallel use of the verb "*egeirō* — raise" in the passive and the inference that Paul draws from the credal affirmation clearly show.

From the creed, Paul draws this conclusion: "even so, through Jesus, God will bring with him[62] those who have died." Were Paul's text to be read as it is in the Codex Vaticanus, a tenth-century manuscript at Athos,[63] and a few other minuscules, Paul's inference would be even stronger. According to these manuscripts, Paul's words read: "thus, through Jesus, God will also bring with him those who have died." On either reading of the text, although more emphatically in the latter case, Paul is affirming that God will so act that the fate of those who have died will be similar to that of Jesus.

The emphasis is on what God has done for Jesus and on what he will similarly do for those who belong to Jesus and/or who have died for the sake of their faith. Paul identifies Jesus by his "human" name, without any christological title, as he tries to respond to the Thessalonians' concern. By emphasizing what God has done on behalf of Jesus, the man, who died, Paul attempts to confirm the hope of the Thessalonians. He affirms that their salvation will be "with Jesus" and because of Jesus ("through Jesus").[64] In effect, from the credal attestation of the resurrection of Jesus, Paul infers that the dead will be saved, in similar fashion, by God's action.[65] How can this be? Paul explains (note the explanatory "*gar* – for" at the beginning of v. 15) in verses 15-17.

An Explanation

Well aware that it is not on his own authority that he speaks,[66] Paul affirms that his explanation is based on a "word of the Lord." Paul's explanation is based on an appeal to authority, to the highest authority, in fact. Students of rhetoric would say that Paul's is an *ethos* appeal. Exegetes have long debated as to (1) what Paul means "by word of the Lord" and (2) what is the content of the word of the Lord.[67] As to the first issue, the question is whether the "word of the Lord" refers to a word of the historical Jesus (perhaps preserved in another form in one of the canonical gospels?[68]), to a word of the risen Jesus, or to a prophetic statement.

My judgment is that Paul is here making reference to a statement of Christian prophecy[69] whose original form might have been something like: "the son of man, with a cry of command, with the archangel's call, and with the sound of God's trumpet, will descend from heaven and those who are left will be caught up in the clouds to meet the son of man in the air."[70] Paul has actualized the traditional logion so that it fits his purposes in writing to the Thessalonians. By calling it a "word of the Lord," he has highlighted the authority of the tradition.[71]

With the Lord as his authority, Paul declares that those who are still alive at the time of the parousia will not have an advantage over those who have died.[72] The introductory formula, "*touto gar hymin legomen* – this we say to you" (v. 15), indicates that Paul is formally drawing an inference from the creed (note the explanatory *gar,* not translated in the NRSV). It indicates that the explanation is addressed to the Thessalonians ("*hymin* – to you"). The explanation is in the form of discourse ("*legomen* – we say"), which contrasts neatly with the references to writing in the encompassing pericopes (4:9; 5:1). Finally, Paul draws attention to the content of his discourse with the demonstrative "*touto* – this."

Paul's declaration deals, in fact, with the respective fates of the living and the dead. It may be that he embarks on his explanation in the way that he does because of a Jewish conviction, to which some apocryphal writings bear witness,[73] that those who are alive at the day of the Lord will be in a better situation than those who have died. This raises the issue of whether Paul had preached about the resurrection of the dead to the Thessalonians.[74] There are those who hold that he did; and those who hold that he did not.[75]

If Paul had preached about the resurrection,[76] the issue that concerns the Thessalonians is whether those who are still alive at the parousia will be in a situation preferable to that of "the dead in Christ." Would they take part in the events attendant upon the parousia of the Lord, whereas those who have died would not because they had not yet been raised from the dead? The matter would be all the more urgent if the dead in Christ had been Christian martyrs.

Paul responds to the concern of the Thessalonians by affirming that those who are alive at the time of the parousia will not have any advantage over those who have died and grounds his affirmation on the word of the Lord. That declaration, a statement of principle, demands further explanation. By way of explanation,[77] Paul describes the future scenario in apocalyptic terms.[78]

The language of apocalyptic is not so much descriptive as it is poetic and evocative.[79] It describes the indescribable in imaginative terms. In his letter, as he imaginatively describes how those who have died in Christ will, nonetheless, be able to participate in the parousia, Paul unfolds a sequential scenario in which everything takes place upon the divine initiative and according to the divine plan.[80] The periodization of events, that is, the presentation of "events" in a well-ordered sequence, is characteristic of Jewish apocalyptic thought. So, too, is the conviction that God is fully in control and the agent of all that transpires. Indeed the view that things happen according to plan is an expression of the faith-conviction that it is God who is making and who will make things happen.[81]

It is appropriate that Paul should have recourse to the language of apocalyptic as he responds to the Thessalonians' concern about those who had died.[82] The resurrection of the dead is an apocalyptic motif, as is the coming of the kingdom of God that Paul had preached at Thessalonica (2:12). The language of apocalyptic is, moreover, the only language that is adequate to describe what will happen to the dead in the future. It is only through the medium of (religious) imagination that one can talk and write about that which has not yet taken place.

Contemporary readers of Paul's letter should not fail to recall that the function of apocalyptic discourse is to console those who are suffering affliction. Often apocalyptic was used to provide hope for those suffering persecution. That is apparently the situation of those to whom Paul was writing. He intended that his message be one of consolation (4:18) and of hope (4:13).

The language of apocalyptic is symbolic.[83] Paul draws upon a number of the stock motifs[84] as he unfolds his scenario: the descent of the Lord from the heavens, the archangel, the sound of the trumpet, the resurrection of the dead, clouds as a means of transportation, and the encounter with the Lord – the Lord who, according to the scene evoked in 3:13, will come with all his saints. While the symbols are classic, every author who writes in the apocalyptic mode makes use of them in a unique literary configuration. Paul himself has done so.

The motifs that he has chosen for use in verse 16 have been so woven together as to show how it is possible for those who have died in Christ to take part in the parousia. Some Jewish apocalyptic texts[85] attest to a tradition that held that some people, God's chosen ones, are translated to heaven or some other kind of paradise after their life on earth.[86] Paul considers ultimate salvation to be a matter of being with Jesus (4:9, 17; 5:10).[87] Translation for a meeting with Jesus is the way in which Paul graphically portrays the salvation for which he hopes.[88] How can those who have died participate in salvation described in these terms?

Paul answers: because they will have been raised from the dead, as Jesus has been raised.[89] As Paul describes the scenario in apocalyptic terms, the archangel's call and the sound of the trumpet might serve as much as a signal to rouse the dead in Christ from their mortal slumber as it is a signal that the eschatological drama is about to begin. The dead in Christ will come to life before they are rapt into the air where they will meet the Lord.[90]

In his response to the Thessalonians' concern, Paul draws from two apocalyptic traditions, the rapture motif and the motif of the resurrection from the dead. What is perhaps most innovative in the response is that Paul brings both traditions together into a single scenario in order to formulate his pastor's response to a problematic situation.[91]

In the twentieth-century discussion of Paul's response to the Thessalonians' concern, two questions constantly arise. One concerns "we who are alive" (*hēmeis hoi zōntes*, vv. 15, 17). The other concerns the background against which Paul paints his picture of the eschatological scenario.

As far as the first question is concerned, it is probably Paul himself who inserted the "*hēmeis* – we" into whatever traditional material he was working with.[92] The identification of "*hoi zōntes* – the living" as "*hēmeis* – we" is not crucial to Paul's argument. Per se, the identification is not part of the argument. The situation is rather that the identification simply expresses Paul's expectation that he and his companions would be alive at the time of the parousia.[93]

The other point that has stimulated scholarly inquiry has to do with the background of Paul's description of the scenario. In what environment was his religious imagination working? Did his graphic description arise from a Hellenistic cultural context? Or did it derive

exclusively from Jewish apocalyptic? *"Apantēsis* – meeting" (4:17) is
a rather common word in day-to-day Greek. Of itself it bears no special
connotations. It was used for quite ordinary meetings. It is, however,
quite obvious that Paul had something special in mind as he wrote
about the dead who had been raised and "we the living" as having a
"meeting" with the parousiac Lord "in the air."

Some commentators believe that Paul had in mind the portrayal of
an imperial visit to a Hellenistic town, an occasion of state, when the
Emperor – *Kyrios* comes to town with his armies and appropriate fan-
fare, there to be publicly welcomed by the citizenry.[94] Others believe
that Paul is responding to the Thessalonians' concern from an essentially Jewish frame of reference, with apocalyptic motifs and themes
drawn from the biblical description of the theophany at Sinai (Exod
19:10–18) or the gathering of exiles (Isa 52:12, etc.).[95]

The discussion continues to be joined, but in some respects the
dilemma is a false one. The question is, moreover, more complicated
than it might seem at first sight because of the very nature of apocalyptic literature. Apocalyptic literature frequently makes use of biblical
themes – allusions to the scriptures abound in our extant apocalyptic
writings – but recasts them in a new mode because different circumstances require a new kind of literature with a different purpose. To
the extent that biblical motifs are reflected in 4:13–18, it must be acknowledged that they have been recast by Paul. The whole scene as it
now stands is a Pauline creation.[96]

Has Paul created the scene on the basis of a Hellenistic cultural
experience or has he created it on the basis of Jewish tradition? Phras-
ing the question as if it were a matter of either-or is a bit too simple.
Paul was writing from his own experience. In his own experience he
was thoroughly immersed in the Jewish tradition and Jewish apocalyptic, but he was writing to a Hellenistic audience in a Hellenistic
mode and was fully conscious of the fact that he was trying to convey
a message to them. Within this perspective, it is most likely that Paul
was drawing on Jewish motifs as he created a scene, but the scene
that he created would be one that would make sense to a Hellenistic audience. In 1 Thess 4:14–17 we have an instance of Paul's use
of dual-level language. Thus it would seem appropriate to write about
Paul's Hellenization of Jewish tradition.[97] For Paul, Jesus-Lord is truly
the *Kyrios.*

Christology and Paraenesis

If 1 Thess 4:13–18 constitutes the core of Paul's *homilia,* his message
is hardly restricted to this relatively short passage. We have already

commented upon much of what Paul had to say in his letter to the Thessalonians as we reflected on his remembrance of his visit to them and what he had heard about the visit, his comments upon the gospel that he preached, and the way of life that his correspondents adopted as a result of his apostolic visit.

Our exposition of the letter's epistolary composition and the rhetorical impact of Paul's language have given us occasion to touch upon other facets of the content of Paul's communication with the Thessalonians. There is, therefore, no need to rehearse these matters once again. Nonetheless it might prove helpful to take "christology and paraenesis" as a rubric under which may be gathered many of the points that Paul makes in his letter. Christology and paraenesis, for instance, serve as the foci of the summarizing wish prayers found in 3:13 and 5:23. Similarly, the paraenesis of 4:13-18 and 5:1-11 is, to a large extent, grounded on a credal formula with a christological focus (4:14; 5:10). The encompassing paraenetic units, 4:1-12 and 5:12-22, are grounded on the will of God (4:3; 5:18), but Paul notes that this is "the will of God in Christ Jesus" (5:18), and has recalled that his earlier oral exhortation had been given through the Lord Jesus (4:2, cf. v. 1).

Christology

Christology, as Marinus de Jonge reminds us, is always christology in context.[98] Christology is never developed in a vacuum. This is, a fortiori, true of the christology of Paul, in general, and specifically of the christology to which 1 Thessalonians bears witness. Paul did not have a fully elaborated christology; rather he worked out his christology in response to the situation in which he was involved, specifically, the situation that faced the Thessalonians as Paul wrote to them. The christology that he developed is at once a partial expression of who Jesus the Christ was and a reflection on Jesus in the light of the situation in which Paul was writing.[99]

Theology and Christology

In a work such as this it is impossible to develop fully the christology of 1 Thessalonians,[100] but some elements are worthy of emphasis.[101] First and foremost one should note that 1 Thessalonians, and certainly the earlier preaching of Paul and his companions to the Thessalonians, had a theological[102] rather than a christological focus.[103] The christology of 1 Thessalonians is subordinate to and in function of Paul's essentially theological frame of reference.

This is evident from the opening salutation in which Paul places the gathering to which he is speaking through his letter in the context of its relationship with God, who is described as Father. Only thereafter does Paul speak about Jesus as Lord (1:1). As the first chapter unfolds one sees that God is Father in relationship with Jesus who is the Son, so constituted and revealed by the resurrection (1:10). The theocentric focus of Paul's letter is likewise in evidence in Paul's final blessing as he prays for the sanctification of the Thessalonian Christians "at the coming of our Lord Jesus Christ" but addresses his prayer[104] to the God of peace and, in a comforting Amen, reassures the Thessalonians that God will do it, for he is faithful (5:23-24).

Sanctification is, in any event, the work of the Father, albeit accomplished through our Lord Jesus Christ (5:9). The parousiac drama described in 4:14-17 is one in which God takes the initiative. Moreover the three traditional credal formulae that Paul has incorporated into his letter have Jesus as their content but God as their focus. In their Pauline usage, they point to what God has done to and through Jesus: "whom he raised from the dead, Jesus (1:10)...Jesus died and rose again, even so, through Jesus God will bring with him (4:14)...God has destined us not for wrath but for obtaining salvation through our Lord Jesus Christ who died for us (5:9-10)."

Particularly significant, at least in respect of the christological formulations of more recent vintage, is the confession of faith cited in 1:10. There it is clearly affirmed that it is God who raised Jesus from the dead. It is God who began the sequence of eschatological events that will reach its culmination in the resurrection of those who have died in Christ (4:16).

Faith and Soteriology

A second focus in Paul's christology is the relationship between christology and faith.[105] The credal formulae cited by Paul bespeak the traditional faith of the church. The presence of these formulae in Paul's letter show that faith had a credal component, which had already been cast into terse expression and had become traditional by the time that Paul wrote. The formula of 4:14, the ground of the argumentation in Paul's *homilia,* is a bipartite formula, formally expressing in simple form[106] the belief that Jesus had died and had been raised. From this faith confession about Jesus, Paul draws the conviction that those who have died in him will be raised and participate in the parousia.

In contrast with the two-part formula of 4:14, the formula of 1:10 focuses exclusively on the resurrection of Jesus, to which Paul attributes soteriological significance. Having affirmed that God raised Jesus from the dead,[107] Paul identifies Jesus as the one who rescues us from the wrath to come. Paul's attribution of this salvific function to Jesus indicates that he understood Jesus' resurrection as having soteriological significance. Jesus' resurrection is related to the salvation of those who are waiting for him. For Paul to have attributed to Jesus this salvific role is for him to have attributed to Jesus a function that properly belonged to God according to his own Jewish tradition.

The formula of 5:10, finally, focuses on the death of Jesus. In this instance alone, a phrase indicating the soteriological significance is clearly part of the traditional formulation, to wit, "*hyper hēmōn* – for us."[108] According to Henk de Jonge, this dying formula harks back to the "exhortatory homily of the earliest, Greek-speaking, Christian community, which may well have been that of Jerusalem in the early thirties."[109] From this perspective, Paul's reprise of the creed not only is an expression of his reaching back into very early Christian tradition, but it also sheds further light on two otherwise problematic passages in Paul's letter, namely, 1:6 and 2:15, both dealing with the *mimēsis* motif.

The credal formulation, to be sure, presupposes an interpretation of Jesus' death as vicarious and atoning. It expresses that conviction by means of Jewish Hellenistic martyrdom terminology. The imitation of the Lord motif – which is not a matter of ethics, but of Christian existence[110] – in 1:6 expresses Paul's conviction that the afflicted Christians of Thessalonica are like the Lord in their suffering. In 2:15 he notes that those same Christians have a fate similar to that of Christians in Judea whose fate in turn was similar to that of the Lord Jesus and the prophets, killed by "the Jews."[111] In 5:14–16 he affirms that those who have suffered like the Lord will be raised like him and will experience salvation "with him."

Paul expresses what he understands the Jesus who has died and been raised to be by means of the christological titles that he attributes to Jesus. These titles, "*Huios* – Son," "*Christos* – Christ" and "*Kyrios* – Lord," give succinct expression to Paul's resurrection faith. The christology that they symbolize is a functional christology.[112]

Among the three titles, some priority can be accorded to the title of Son. This christological title is used but once in Paul's letter (1:10), but it lies on the horizon of Paul's description of the community that gathered at Thessalonica (1:1). This title expresses the theological focus of Paul's vision insofar as it indicates the close relationship between Jesus and God.[113] It shows that Jesus is "qualified" to assume divine functions, specifically, salvation. The relationship between the Father and Jesus has been made manifest in the death and resurrection of Jesus to which the Christ title draws particular attention. It is, moreover, a title that puts Paul's understanding of Jesus and his salvific function within the Jewish tradition of which Paul is heir.

Within his letter, nevertheless, Paul has principally exploited the title of Lord. It designates Jesus as the one upon whom divine functions devolve, the one through whom salvation is mediated, the one who delineates the church and is the object of its expectation, the one to whom allegiance is owed, the one with respect to whom is proclaimed the good news about Christ.

The Parousia

The community at Thessalonica was awaiting the coming (*parousia*) of the Lord Jesus with all his saints. The parousia of Jesus as Lord, so eagerly awaited by Paul and the Thessalonians, provides another perspective from which to look at the christology of Paul's letter. Scott Sinclair has identified four literarily significant passages that express the basic christology of the letter.[114] These are 1:6-10; 3:11-13; 4:14-17; and 5:23. All have the parousia as their focus. The parousia is the central theme in Paul's *homilia*. It is also the object of his prayer.[115]

To a large extent Paul's choice of "*Kyrios* – Lord" as his preferred christological title manifests the centrality of the parousia in his christological expression. That title designates Jesus as parousiac Lord. Eleven of Paul's uses of this title clearly evoke this image of the eschatological Lord.[116]

Paul also writes about "the Lord" in 4:6, when he describes the Lord as an avenger in all these things. The phrase has a biblical ring and seems to evoke the image of God in Ps 94:1. Among exegetes it is a moot point whether Paul is referring to God or to Jesus in 4:6, but the case can be made that Paul is making reference to the Lord Jesus.[117]

This is the other dimension of Jesus the eschatological Lord. In Paul's *pathos* appeal, he cites the Lord who sanctions, in a fashion somewhat akin to the way he had twice invoked authority of the Lord (4:1, 2) as he introduced the paraenesis of 4:1-12. Mention of the Lord in Paul's paraenetic discourse calls for an acquiescing response on the part of those to whom the discourse is addressed. The Lord is Lord and will sanction the appeal made in his name: "*because* the Lord is an avenger in all these things" (4:6).

On the other hand, Paul refers to the parousia as "the coming of *our* Lord [*tou Kyriou hēmōn*] Jesus Christ" (2:19; 3:13; 5:23).[118] The pronoun is significant. It separates those who can claim Jesus as their Lord from those who do not. It suggests that those over whom Jesus is to manifest his Lordship are those who, with Paul, his companions, and the Thessalonian Christians, acknowledge Jesus as Lord. The significance of that relationship will come to full expression at the parousia, for then those who belong to Jesus will meet him and be with him forever. Jesus is "our Lord" insofar as he is the eschatological savior.

Christology and Paraenesis

In his first thanksgiving, Paul recalled that the Christians of Thessalonica, who lived in the presence of our God and Father, had a lifestyle that was characterized by their work of faith, their labor of love, and the steadfastness of their hope in our Lord Jesus Christ (1:3). Their existence was defined in terms of their expectation of the Lord Jesus Christ. That the coming of the Lord Jesus bears upon the Christian way of life is further expressed in Paul's wish prayers, when he prays that they remain blameless until the coming of the Lord Jesus Christ (3:13; 5:23). The coming of the Lord provides horizon and sanction for the Christians' way of life and Paul's exhortation and instruction thereto.[119]

The authority and sanction of Paul's exhortation comes with the invocation of the Lord Jesus. This is nowhere as much in evidence as it is in 4:1-8, when Paul writes: "we ask and urge you in the Lord Jesus ... for you know what instructions we gave you through the Lord Jesus ... the Lord is an avenger in all these things" (4:1-8). Appeal to Jesus is also made in Paul's final paraenesis as he argues: "this is the will of God in Christ Jesus for you" (5:18).

Invocation of the name of Jesus is inherent to Paul's paraenetic appeal. The Lord Jesus is invoked in both Paul's *ethos* appeal and in his *pathos* appeal. Many commentators are so disheartened by Paul's description of the Jews in 2:13-16 that they are inclined to excise the passage from his text. These commentators forget, perhaps, that Paul's manner of speaking about his people is similar to the way in which many prophets of old had spoken about God's people. It is regrettable that Paul's remarks may have contributed to anti-Semitism.[120] This was not his intention; his remarks had an epistolary and paraenetic function. He did not write to the Christians of Thessalonica in order to condemn or vilify those Jews who did such as they did to the Lord and to the prophets. His was a situational and occasional letter. He wrote as he did in 2:13-16 in order to commend the Christians of Thessalonica who were in a situation of manifest affliction and to remind them that "the end" was near. Paul's *pathos* appeal had a paraenetic purpose.[121]

Paul's Exhortation

On reading Paul's letter to the Thessalonians one gets the impression that Paul's exhortation begins in earnest at 4:1. His *"loipon oun — finally"* marks an epistolary transition. Another direct appeal to the Thessalonians as his "brothers and sisters" confirms that a shift has taken place. The formal "we ask and urge you in the Lord Jesus" bespeaks a kind of earnestness that has not hitherto been heard in the letter. Indeed, there is such a change in tone and content in Paul's letter as of 4:1 that one can almost say that his letter begins again at this juncture.

The epistolary transition indicates that what is to follow will be an exhortation. As a matter of fact, from that point on, Paul's letter is an extended exhortation with several parts. The exhortation continues on until the final wish prayer begins to bring the letter to closure (5:23–24).

Paul's paraenetic units cannot, however, be separated from what has preceded them. Paul's rhetorical strategies, including his use of the recall motif and his *ethos* and *pathos* appeal, strengthen the formal exhortation that he will make as of 4:1. Nor should one overlook, as one looks at the first part of Paul's letter, the not so subtle paraenesis that is associated with his use of the imitation motif in 1:6 and 2:14 and other such devices.

Much of Paul's paraenesis has already been discussed in passing. Hence we need not dwell at length upon it, but, as with Paul's christology, it might prove worthwhile to note one or another of its features.

4:3–8

In the first paraenetic unit (4:3–8), whose unifying theme is sanctification, Paul takes the opportunity to address a specific issue, that is, the avoidance of "*porneia* – unchastity." The *topos* is treated in such a general manner that one need not presume that Paul was aware of the existence of a specific sexual problem among his beloved Thessalonians. It is more likely that Paul was writing on the basis of a Jewish bias, the presumption that Gentiles tolerated a sexual ethos that was simply unacceptable to Jews.[122]

Paul's exhortation to his neophyte converts was from the perspective of the divide that separated the way of life of those who did not know God from the way of life of those who were God's holy people. Hence, he exhorts them to avoid unchastity and gives practical advice as to how this is to be done and what it means. Unfortunately Paul's Greek is somewhat cryptic and raises problems of interpretation for the modern interpreter.

The first problem can be readily seen when the NRSV's translation of 4:4 is compared with that of the RSV: "each of you know how to control your own body in holiness and honor" (NRSV) and "each one of you know how to take a wife for himself in holiness and honor" (RSV).

The problem is that Paul is using a metaphorical expression that lit-

erally means "get a dish" (*skeuos ktasthai*). I have previously argued
that the referent of Paul's metaphor is marriage[123] and that Paul is urging the Thessalonians to get married and enjoy sexual relationships
within marriage as a way to avoid unchastity.[124] Such an exhortation
would be thoroughly consistent with the way in which marriage and
sexuality were valued within Judaism.

The second *crux* apropos this paraenetic unit is the issue of
whether Paul is addressing two different matters or a single topic.
The issue revolves around the phrase "that no one wrong or exploit a
brother or sister in this matter" (4:6). Paul's language is generic and
ambiguous. Some commentators take it to mean that Paul is urging the
Thessalonians to avoid defrauding their fellow Christians in business
matters. The epistolary situation of such an exhortation would include
the fact that Jewish authors frequently made use of catalogues of vices
to castigate the avarice of the Gentiles. Paul's choice of language is,
in fact, similar to the language that is sometimes used in these lists
of vices.

Other commentators, however, I among them,[125] are of the opinion
that the entire unit (4:3–8) has but a single topic, namely, the avoidance of unchastity. From this perspective, the "matter" with regard
to which Christians must not exploit their fellow Christians is sexuality. Specifically, Paul would be exhorting the neophyte Christians at
Thessalonica not to treat their Christian "brother" unjustly insofar as
sexuality is concerned. Practically speaking, this means not to violate
a fellow Christian's marriage by committing adultery.

In this case the *adelphon,* literally, brother, of 4:6 must be rendered
in the masculine only. According to traditional Jewish norms, adultery
was committed when a married woman had sexual intercourse with a
man other than her husband. In that patriarchal culture, adultery was
considered to be an offense against the cuckolded husband. In sum,
for the holy people of God who were now the Thessalonian Christians,
Paul's exhortation as to how they might avoid unchastity and live in
holiness was relatively simple. It came down to "get married and do
not commit adultery."

4:9–18

The pastoral attitude with which Paul introduced his paraenesis pervades the second exhortative unit, the shortest of the five (4:9–12). As
Paul encourages the Thessalonians to continue in that mutual love that
is characteristic of the Christian way of life, he continues to maintain
the distinction between Christians and "others," a distinction that he
had introduced into his first paraenetic unit (4:12; 4:5). The passage
has additional ecclesiological significance since it portrays the Chris-

tians of Thessalonica as being in relationship with other Macedonian Christians, to whom their kinship bonds and sibling love are likewise to be extended.

Paul's third paraenetic unit (4:13-18), to which reference has already been made, continues to maintain the distinction between Christians and others (4:13). While instructive, insofar as Paul was seeking to dispel the ignorance of the Thessalonian Christians, it was also exhortative insofar as it concludes – note the "*hōste* – therefore" of verse 18 – with the injunction that Christians are to encourage one another.

5:1-11

The fourth paraenetic unit (5:1-11) is the other side of the exhortation contained in 4:13-18. 4:13-18 affirms that the future is in the hands of God and that Christians should draw consolation and hope from that knowledge. 5:1-11 affirms that Christians must live as Christians in the present. They are to live a life of faith, love, and hope (5:8; cf. 1:3). By doing so, they will build up the Christian community (5:11).

Attention has already been drawn to the similarities between these two paraenetic units (4:13-18; 5:1-11) and the links that bind them together. As the *lexis* of 4:13-18 is symbolic, so the language of 5:1-11 is thoroughly imbued with metaphor. Paul writes figuratively about the thief in the night, the labor of the pregnant woman, the light and the darkness, the day and the night, being awake and being asleep, vigilance and drunkenness, and the soldier's armor.

To a great extent, these metaphors are commonplace in Jewish and Hellenistic literature. The Jewish scriptures speak of thieves and Jeremiah refers to thieves in one of his similes.[126] Later Christian writings will speak about thieves and compare the coming of the Lord to a thief in the night.[127] Homer[128] and other Greek writers used the image of the woman in labor, as did many Jewish writers. The latter group includes not only the authors of the biblical text, but also the authors of apocalyptic texts and the Qumran literature.[129]

The contrast between light and darkness, day and night is a well-known figure of speech, used in Hellenistic paraenesis and Jewish literature as well. The contrast between being awake and being asleep, accompanied by the graphic imagery of drunkenness and sobriety, appears in biblical and later Christian literature.[130] The panoply that Paul has adapted from Isa 59:17 appears in other literature as well.[131] Paul's use of rich metaphorical language links the exhortation of 5:1-11 with the preceding exhortation phrased with the symbolic motifs of Jewish apocalyptic thought.

Paul's metaphors allow him to evoke graphically various aspects of eschatological existence and to encourage the Christians of Thessalonica to engage themselves in that kind of existence. To begin, the metaphors of the thief in the night and the woman in labor express Paul's conviction that the future day of the Lord – a traditional biblical motif to which Jewish prophets from Amos to Joel and the Qumran literature[132] attest – will come unexpectedly and inevitably. That inevitable future, whose precise arrival cannot be known, hangs over the present and impinges an eschatological quality to it.[133] The series of contrasting metaphors that follows colors the Christian condition as an "eschatological existence."[134]

The apocalyptic dualism that thoroughly pervades Paul's description of eschatological existence colored Paul's understanding of his own situation and contributed to the writing of his letter. He presents Satan as the one who had prevented him from going in person to the Thessalonians (2:18). He prayed, on the other hand, that the Lord, acting in concert with the Father, enable him to attain to the Thessalonians. In the apocalyptically colored interim what Paul could do was write a letter.

Paul has woven the four antithetical formulations of 5:1-11, darkness-light, day-night, sleeping-awake, sober-drunk, into a complex and interlocking pattern. The first pair of antitheses, darkness-light and day-night, speaks of the Christian condition; while the second pair, sleeping-awake and sober-drunk, speaks of the appropriate response to that condition. In their antithetical formulation the series of metaphors continues the contrast between those who are Christian and those who are not, which provided a similarly dualistic perspective for the earlier paraenetic units (4:3-8; 9-12; 13-18).

Within this fourth paraenetic unit, the contrast between those who are Christian and those who are not comes to further expression in 4:3, "when they say, 'There is peace and security.' " Who are "they"? The anonymous "they" are contrasted with the "you" to whom Paul writes. You, writes Paul, have no need to have anything written to you about the times and the seasons. They, in contrast, misconstrue the times as times of peace and security, because they, presumably, are unaware that the coming of the day of the Lord has changed the quality of the times and the seasons.

When Paul writes about "them," the language seems hardly to be his own: "When they say, 'There is peace and security,' then sudden destruction will come upon them . . . and there will be no escape" (4:3). Their slogan has a formulaic, almost proverbial, ring.[135] "*Eirēnē* – peace" has a connotation that it does not usually have in Paul, who typically writes about peace as the epitome of God's gift of salvation.[136] "*Aiphnidios* – destruction" and "*ephistatai* – will come" are words that do not appear elsewhere in Paul's writings. The slogan is introduced by an impersonal "they say" (*legousin*), atypical for Paul, but common in apocalyptic writing.[137] In short, Paul's description of "them" and what will happen to "them" seems likewise to be drawn from apocalyptic motifs.

On the basis of the classic contrasts that he has used, Paul has created a description of Christians as "children of the day" (5:5) – a phrase heretofore unattested in ancient literature.[138] That situational description of the condition of Christians grounds the exhortation that follows in 5:8, "*since we belong to the day*, let us be sober, and put on the breastplate of faith and love, and for a helmet the hope of salvation." The military metaphor not only recalls, at least for contemporary readers, the Isaian text;[139] it also identifies Christian existence as a struggle. Such a description is germane to the situation of the Thessalonian Christians involved, as they were, in affliction and persecution (3:3).

Children of the day are destined for salvation through our Lord Jesus Christ; others are destined for wrath (5:9). Once again Paul has used an antithetical formulation[140] to underscore the Christian condition. "*Orgē* – wrath" (see 1:10) again places the reader in the thought world of eschatology and the literary world of apocalyptic imagery. Within that futuristic perspective, "*sōteria* – salvation" evokes a yet-to-be acquired salvation. Paul does not further speculate as to the nature of this future salvation. "To live with him, that is, with our Lord Jesus Christ, is Paul's formulaic trove to describe salvation (see 4:14, 17). Its significance is highlighted in the last contrast of the pericope, which consists of a series of contrasts one after the other. That contrast is: "Jesus died for us . . . we live with him" (5:10).

In order that the Christians of Thessalonica might live with Jesus, Paul makes his direct appeal: "encourage one another and build up each other, as indeed you are doing" (5:18). This summary injunction recalls the exhortation to put on faith, love, and hope. This the Christians of Thessalonica have done (see 1:3). Since they are building up the church, Paul can turn his attention to the upbuilding of the church in his final paraenesis.

5:12–13

The fifth paraenetic unit (5:12-22), as the third, bears upon relationships within the Christian community which is being built up (5:11). Its staccato pace and the absence of quasi-logical argumentation – apart, that is, from the appeal to God's will in Christ Jesus in verse 18 – give it a different tone from Paul's earlier paraenesis. In some ways it returns the audience to the point at which Paul began his letter, namely, the life of the community and the movement of the Spirit within it (1:1-10).

The Matrix of Paul's Thought

A variety of closing conventions brings to a close the text that its author calls a letter (5:27). The letter is clearly Paul's own composition. It expresses his thoughts about a variety of topics, past, present, and future, in a personal and friendly manner. A perennial question in this regard concerns the source of Paul's thought. Where did Paul's ideas come from? Granted his was a creative mind, but even creative minds do not think and write in a vacuum.

The question as to the source of Paul's thinking was most vigorously raised a few generations ago. Then it was common to ask whether Paul and his writings were best understood within the context of the history of religions, and therefore on the basis of Hellenistic models, or within the context of apocalypticism, and therefore on the basis of Jewish models.

Discussion was more sharply joined when Hellenism and Judaism were considered as two distinct realities, with the twain never meeting. Recent studies have shown that too sharp a distinction between Judaism and Hellenism cannot be drawn. The Judaism of the diaspora, of which Paul was a child, was a form of Judaism that was clearly influenced by Hellenistic thought and culture. Even Palestinian Judaism, at least in Paul's day, more or less contemporary with that of Jesus of Nazareth, was not immune to Hellenistic influence. On the part of both Jews and Gentiles, there was passage to and fro between Rome and Jerusalem.

Hellenistic and Jewish

When asking about the background about Paul's letter to the Thessalonians, one may not overlook the significant fact that it is truly a letter and that a letter is an act of communication. Paul was writing to a group of people who had been Gentiles and who were living in Macedonia. To communicate with them he used the medium of the personal letter, which he had adapted to his own purposes. This was a Hellenistic form; its text was written in Greek, the lingua franca of the Hellenistic culture that permeated the Mediterranean basin at that time.

On the other hand Paul was a Jew and proud to be one (Rom 11:10; Phil 3:4-6).[141] The language of his letter to the Thessalonians reflects his Jewish heritage. He writes about the one God, about the Christ (that is, the Messiah), and about the Holy Spirit. His worldview is that of the Jew who divides humankind into those who know God and those who don't (4:5). His *homilia* uses imaginative language that seems best understood within the categories of Jewish apocalyptic.

When one compares what Paul has written in his letter to the Thessalonians with what he writes in other letters, it is hard to escape the conclusion that he is thoroughly imbued with apocalyptic thought. Indeed the formal appeals to the Jewish scriptures in those later letters betray his ongoing Jewishness.

Paul has written a letter to the Thessalonians in self-conscious fashion (5:27). He is clearly desirous of communicating with the Thessalonians so as to compensate for their lack of knowledge (3:10; 4:13). The book of Acts and the imitation of his epistolary style by later authors show the reputation that he would come to enjoy as a master communicator. The first of his letters evinces his desire to communicate effectively as he makes use of acquired skills that are comparable to those of learned orators and rhetoricians. Whether Paul received formal schooling with regard to these skills makes little difference to all but the historian. His words were chosen so as to make an impression, so as to obtain the desired result.

Without his having written so (Paul has written a letter; he has not written a treatise on letter writing) it would seem that Paul considers that he and his message were the bridge between the announcement of God's saving reign, the gospel, and the Hellenistic Gentiles to whom the gospel was addressed. His oral proclamation and his written text were a bridge between Judaism and Gentility, between his biblical heritage and a Hellenistic culture.

To pose the question of the background of Paul's thought in either-or terms is to create a false dilemma. It is not a matter of either-or; it is a matter of both-and. Paul's letter did not simply arise from Judaism; nor did it arise simply out of Hellenism. The expression of his thought was derived from both since it was at attempt to mediate a Jewish belief and hope to people who were or had been Gentiles.[142]

Judaism

What in Paul's letter derives from his innate Judaism? One might begin with his dichotomous worldview, the sharp distinction between those who know God and those who do not. One must add that the God about whom Paul wrote was the one God of Jewish monotheism. Prayer, whether of petition or thanksgiving, addressed to the one God (1:2; 2:13; 3:12; 5:23) is an expression of Paul's Jewish heritage. So, too, is his conviction that knowing God is something more than a philosophical acceptance of monotheism, something more than knowing something about the one God. To know God is to have such an experience of God that people live as God's very own people (1:9; 3:3-8).[143] Specifically, one might note a traditional Jewish association of the marital ethos and living as God's people, which is reflected in

4:1–8. The fashion in which Paul introduces his paraenesis on sexuality is particularly noteworthy. "Learning," "living," and "the will of God" reflect significant motifs in traditional Jewish halakah.[144]

Likewise Jewish is Paul's familiarity with the Jewish scriptures, which he does not use as grounds for formal argument in this letter, but to which he does make allusion. One should also note the theme of election, with which the letter begins (1:4), and the covenantal motifs that pervade the entire composition. A single mention of the archangel (4:16) and a solitary reference to Satan (2:18) point to the variety of motifs familiar to Jewish apocalyptic that have made their way into Paul's composition, particularly in 4:13–5:11. Finally, Paul's own thoughts about himself derive from his Jewish heritage. His self-portrayal evokes the memory of the Jewish prophets of old, especially Jeremiah and the deutero-Isaiah.[145]

Christian Tradition

One can write about the Christian tradition and Paul's letter to the Thessalonians only in a very circumspect manner. The specific language of tradition (*paradosis*) is not present in the letter.[146] The letter was written barely a generation, if that, after the death and resurrection of Jesus. The time span is too short to speak properly about "tradition" in the sense that later generations of Christians speak about it. If one must be guarded in writing about Christian "tradition" and Paul's letter, one must also be careful when one talks about "Christian" tradition and his letter. In the middle of the first century C.E. Christianity was not yet weaned from its Jewish matrix. To a large extent it still was a movement, in which only a limited number of people was involved, within Judaism. Even the Gentiles who had turned to the living God were considered to have been co-opted into God's chosen people.

Paul's letter shows, nonetheless, that Paul was conversant with those who had gone before him believing that Jesus was someone for whom God had destined a special role in the history of humankind.[147] His letter reflects the Christian faith of himself and his companions, a faith shared with the churches of God in Christ Jesus that were in Judea, a faith shared with a nascent Christian community in Philippi.

Paul's is a Christian document, which echoes the traditional kerygma and reflects the christological expressions of earlier Christian communities. There are elements of traditional credal formulae found in 1:10; 4:14; and 5:10. Their language shows that they represent succinct formulations of *what* Christians believe and that the various formulations precede Paul's writing to the Thessalonians. It is the traditional faith of believers that "Jesus died and was raised." The titles of

"Son" and "Christ" (Messiah) attributed to Jesus derive from Christian tradition. A debate has long raged about the origin of the *"Kyrios –* Lord" title, but a very strong case can be made that Paul's favorite christological epithet had been used in Aramaic-speaking Christian circles.[148]

Certainly deriving from Paul's Christian experience is his appeal to the example of the churches of God in Christ Jesus that are in Judea (2:14). It is likely that an early Christian "liturgical" greeting underlies the new form of epistolary greeting found in 1:3.[149] The expectation of Jesus as "Son of Man," which lies behind such passages as 1:10[150] and 4:16–17,[151] also derives from early Christianity, as does Paul's appeal to "the word of the Lord." When Paul appeals to a saying of the Lord in 4:15, one can discern Paul's reference to a traditional saying once formulated by an early Christian prophet and his acknowledgment of the authority that the living Lord Jesus had over the Christian faithful.[152]

By way of summary, Langevin[153] has suggested that the pre-Pauline christological tradition reflected in Paul's letter contained these notions: (1) Jesus, the historical person; (2) the royal Messiah; (3) the Son of God; (4) One raised from the dead; (5) the present and eschatological Lord; (6) the judge and savior; (7) the glorious Lord. Modern Christian readers of Paul's letter might be surprised that Paul does not make reference to the early Christian story, not even specifically to the crucifixion of Jesus. That story had not yet been written. A brief reflection on how it came to be will form part of the next chapter in this book.

Hellenism

Paul lived in the Hellenistic world, in the midst of Hellenistic culture. As a diaspora Jew, he would have been familiar with Hellenism. We should then ask about the extent to which that familiarity is reflected in Paul's letter to the Thessalonians. It is almost self-evident that Paul has written a letter within the Hellenistic tradition of letter writing. Almost as evident is the fact that he made use of communication strategies known to Hellenistic rhetoricians. The studies of Abraham Malherbe make the case that Paul is familiar with the Hellenistic philosophic tradition.[154] Paul's general familiarity with that tradition cannot be discounted. This is not to say that Paul had actually read the philosophers. Neither does the fact that Paul employed common rhetorical strategies indicate that he had attended a school of Hellenistic rhetoric. Familiarity with these traditions and manners of speaking may imply no more than that Paul was an intelligent participant in the culture in which he lived and that he was bent on communicating effectively with those to whom he spoke and wrote.

Paul and his companions preached as they worked (2:9), just as many philosophers, particularly within the Stoic-Cynic tradition, had done. As the philosophers had used the image of the contest, the *agōn-* motif (2:3), to describe what they doing, so Paul employed the same motif to describe the apostles' preaching of the gospel. His description of himself and his companions recalls some political institutions of the day (2:4). Some of his terminology, especially the *parakaleō-* formula (4:1, 10; 5:14), recalls the language of diplomatic correspondence. Paul's description of the coming of the parousiac Lord (4:16–17) evokes the Hellenistic ceremonial attendant upon the solemn visit of the emperor to one of the cities of his empire. In short, there is little doubt that the letter that Paul wrote reflects the Hellenistic world within which he and the Thessalonians lived.

Transformation

The fact that Paul's descriptive scenario of the parousiac Lord, so deeply rooted within the Jewish apocalyptic tradition as it is, is comparable to that of the imperial visit leads us to further pursue notions that have been introduced earlier in this study. It has been suggested that Paul had transformed the form and function of the Hellenistic letter in such a fashion that he had created something new, the apostolic and ecclesiastical letter. It has also been suggested that there is more to Paul's language than might have met the Hellenistic ear.

There is an entire range of Greek words and expressions that appeared in Paul's Greek version of the Jewish scriptures, of whose biblical connotation the Thessalonian Christians were presumably unaware, but which were certainly well known to Paul. The connotations that those expressions had certainly would have influenced Paul's use of the Greek language. The preacher's choice of language for a letter written in Greek was, however, designed to assure the acquiescence of his audience. The images were contextual and were therefore capable of conveying meaning. Awareness of the imperial visit and the experience of the household enabled those who heard Paul's letter to understand what he had written.

When Paul wrote about their afflictions, they knew what they and the members of their community had suffered. When he addressed them as a gathering and spoke about good news, they knew what he was talking about. Hellenists gathered in political assemblies, sometimes called an *ekklēsia.* They eagerly awaited the good news of victory and were elated by the good news of births in the imperial household. They knew the kind of unqualified allegiance that a *"Kyrios* – Lord" could demand.

The coming of an emperor to a city paled, however, before the coming of *the* Lord, who was none other than our Lord Jesus Christ. It was on the basis of the authority of that same Lord Jesus Christ that Paul could ground his paraenesis. The good news that he had previously announced and that he recalled in his letter was good news that came from God, but it focused on that same Lord whom God had raised from the dead.

The Christians who gathered at Thessalonica to hear the reading of Paul's letter were a gathering, an *ekklēsia* (1:1). Their numbers were not as large as were those of the political assembly of freeman, but they did gather to hear good news. They had been assembled together to hear the good news about the Lord, now read from a text. When they gathered to hear the reading of Paul's letter, they gathered as *"ekklēsia* – church." Those who gathered had been chosen; they were to experience salvation. Their experience was somehow analogous to the experience of Paul's forebears in faith who had assembled in the desert, there to experience salvation. That privileged gathering had been called an *ekklēsia* in Paul's Greek Bible.[155]

Paul's letter to the church of the Thessalonians was intended to respond to their concerns and to enable them to encourage one another. Encouragement was necessary since those who had turned to serve the living and true God were suffering *"thlipsis* – persecution." The Hellenists knew that the God whom they embraced was unlike the inert statues that adorned their city. The God of Paul and his companions was unlike Isis and Serapis. For a Jew the description of God as living and true could, however, only evoke the living God of the biblical tradition and the fidelity of the God of the covenant.

Paul's letter of encouragement was written by one who lived in the final times, between the resurrection of Jesus as Lord and his coming as our Lord. Persecution was the inevitable fate of Paul, his companions, and those to whom he was writing (3:3). Paul called those troubles *"thlipsis,"* language once used to describe the afflictions that Israel suffered in Egypt.[156] Psalmists and prophets used similar language to describe afflictions experienced by God's people before their deliverance.[157] Paul and those who listened to his letter were waiting for the coming of Jesus who would deliver them. Did not their experience of persecution appear to an apocalyptic thinker like Paul an experience of eschatological tribulation from which the Savior would deliver them?

The time of Jesus' appearance as Lord was in the hands of God. In the meantime the Thessalonians had to get on with their life of faith, love, and hope. Paul's letter was sent to urge them to do so and to remind them of his presence with them, in heart, if not in person (2:17). It was written by a man of faith to believers, in whose faith there was something lacking. In the transformation of his language and the creation of a new literary genre, Paul intended to further the transformation of the Thessalonians as a community of faith and to participate in that new creation which the faithful God had begun in raising Jesus from the dead.

∽ 6 ∽

The Birth of the New Testament

Almost two thousand years have passed since Paul wrote to the Thessalonians. What did he do when he wrote to them? He wrote a letter, as he himself knew full well (5:27). Yet it was a new kind of letter, one skillfully crafted for a new kind of situation. It was written by one who had come to those to whom he was writing as an apostle of Christ (2:7); it was a way of extending his apostolic presence to them. His was a new creation, the letter of an apostle.

The apostolic letter to the Thessalonians was the first of a new literary genre within Hellenistic literature, the genre of the apostolic letter. It is somewhat anachronistic, nonetheless, to speak of the genre of apostolic letter, except from the perspective of historical retrospect. There were no other apostolic letters at the time that Paul wrote, at least insofar as we know. It was one of a kind, the only one of its kind.

Since Paul's letters were letters to communities, it might be appropriate to say that what Paul did in writing to the Thessalonians was to write a letter to a Christian church. Apparently this was the first text written for a Christian church. Since Paul's letter was the first of this kind of writing, one might call what Paul did in writing to the Thessalonians the creation of ecclesiastical writing.

Paul's Other Letters

Paul's letter to the Thessalonians would not long remain the only one of its kind. Within the space of a few years Paul would write letters to other communities evangelized by himself and his companions. These were the letters to Christians gathered at Corinth and Philippi, in Galatia and in the home of Philemon. These writings were similar to Paul's first letter. They were written to flesh-and-blood communities. They mentioned real people. They dealt with real concerns. The letters were a way of bringing Paul's apostolic presence to meet those concerns, even if that apostolic presence was sometimes unexpected and perhaps even undesired.

A Letter to the Churches of Galatia

Within a few years after Paul wrote to the Thessalonians, he wrote another letter, this time to the churches of Galatia. It is a letter that burns with passion. Paul was disturbed and visibly angry, because the faith of the Galatians had been severely troubled by those Judaizers who believed that circumcision was a necessary expression of one's allegiance to Christ. Paul calls the Galatians foolish and bewitched (Gal 3:1). His anger prompts him to exclaim, "I wish that those who unsettle you would castrate themselves!" (Gal 5:12). A long postscript, a real P.S., sums up Paul's argumentation, with pathos, ethos, and quasi-logical appeal (Gal 6:11-17). His emotion is such that, after an extended epistolary salutation (Gal 1:1-5), he omits the customary thanksgiving and, instead, begins to express his astonishment that the Galatians had so quickly deserted the one who had called them in the grace of Christ (Gal 1:6).

The opening of Paul's letter to the Galatians clearly shows that he was writing an apostolic letter. It begins: "Paul an apostle – sent neither by human commission nor from human authorities, but through Jesus Christ and God the Father, who raised him from the dead – and all the members of God's family[1] who are with me." Instead of the simple list of three names with which the letter to the Thessalonians began (1 Thess 1:1), Paul solemnly identifies himself as an apostle in the opening of the letter to the Galatians and associates with himself not one or two other apostles but *all* the members of God's family."

In his prescript, Paul expands on what it means to be an apostle and incorporates into his exposition a credal formulation. From its opening words, Paul's communication proceeds on the basis of an ethos appeal. He has forthrightly set out his apostolic authority, fully aware that attempts had been made to undermine that authority in the churches of Galatia. How different is Paul's description of himself in Gal 1:1 from the simple mention of his name in 1 Thess 1:1! Paul's companions, Silvanus and Timothy, are likewise mentioned by name in 1 Thess 1:1.[2] In contrast those who are with Paul at the time that the letter to the Galatians was written are identified, not by name, but by an indication of their Christian situation and their relationship with Paul. They are "all the members of God's family who are with me" (Gal 1:2).

The salutation of the letter to the Galatians is also longer than the simple liturgical formulation that Paul had appropriated for his letter to the Thessalonians. There he had greeted the Thessalonians with a simple "grace to you and peace" (1 Thess 1:1). A relatively long greeting, into which elements of traditional Christian formulation and a doxology have been incorporated, opens the letter to the Galatians: "Grace to you and peace from God our Father and the Lord Jesus Christ, who gave himself for our sins to set us free from the present evil age, according to the will of our God and Father, to whom be the glory forever and ever. Amen" (Gal 1:3-5).

The Letter to All the Saints in Philippi

The formal protocol of Paul's letter to the Galatians shows that Paul was self-consciously writing an apostolic letter. His letter to the Philippians is characterized by a less formal, warmer, and friendlier tone. Paul, it seemed, had a warm relationship with the churches of Macedonia. From them he received support in time of need (2 Cor 8:1-6; 11:9). There he had close companions, both male and female,[3] with whom he had worked (Phil 4:2-3).

The letter to the Philippians begins: "Paul and Timothy, servants of Christ Jesus, to all the saints in Christ Jesus who are in Philippi, with the bishops and deacons: Grace to you and peace from God our Father and the Lord Jesus Christ" (Phil 1:1-2). Paul has continued the practice, begun in his letter to the Galatians, of giving a qualifying description of the senders of the letter. In this case, however, it is not the title "apostle," evocative of his authority, but rather the qualification as "servant" that Paul chooses as he writes to his friends at Philippi His salutation is: "Grace to you and peace from God our Father and the Lord Jesus Christ." This salutation will become his standard. The salutation was so typical of Paul that it has even made its way into the manuscript tradition of 1 Thess 1:1, where the salutation had been the more simple "Grace to you and peace."

The Letter to Philemon and the Church in His House

The other authentic letter of Paul from prison is his letter to "Philemon our dear friend and co-worker, to Apphia our sister, to Archippus our fellow soldier, and to the church in your house" (Phlmn 1:2), popularly and in the manuscript tradition simply called the letter to Philemon.[4] It is a letter that Paul wrote to the people who gathered in Philemon's house on behalf of Onesimus, a slave and neophyte Christian (Phlmn 10). Onesimus had apparently availed himself of his legal right to have an advocate plead with his owner on his behalf.[5] Since the letter is clearly addressed to a gathering of people in Philemon's home,[6] an *ekklēsía* or church, even this short letter should be classified as an ecclesiastical letter.

From the standpoint of the new rhetoric, Paul's listing of the addressees is intended to make a powerful impact. He writes to people whom he calls his friends and family members, people with whom he has worked and those with whom he has struggled. Paul appeals to Philemon, not on the basis of his apostolic authority – the letter to Philemon is the only authentic Pauline letter in which the term "apostle" does not appear – but on the basis that he is a prisoner of Christ Jesus (Phlmn 1, 9) and an old man (Phlmn 9).[7] Thus he identifies himself as a prisoner of Christ Jesus (Phlmn 1) and names Timothy "our brother"[8] as he begins the shortest and perhaps the most appellative of his extant letters.

The Letters to the Church of God That Is in Corinth

With the Christians of Corinth, Paul had an extensive correspondence. Passages such as 1 Cor 5:9 and 2 Cor 2:3-4, 9; 7:12, indicate that the apostle sent at least four letters to the Corinthians. Many scholars believe that there were at least five such letters and that several of the apparently lost letters have been incorporated into the canonical second letter to the Corinthians, which reads, in its present form, as a somewhat disjointed composition.[9] Each of the two canonical letters to the Corinthians – whether canonical 2 Corinthians represents a single letter or is a composite of several letter fragments makes little difference to this contention – is a hands-on, ad hoc response to a variety of difficulties that arose within the Christian community at Corinth after Paul's departure therefrom.

Paul learned about these difficulties from his visitors from Corinth, such as those of the household of Chloe (1 Cor 1:11) and Stephanas and those who traveled with him (1 Cor 16:17), as well as from at least one letter that had been transmitted to him (1 Cor 7:1). Among the problems addressed by Paul were the Corinthians associating with immoral people, a variety of issues related to sex and marriage, some relating to food that had been offered to idols, spiritual phenomena within the community, a collection made on behalf of other Christians, the role of Apollos, and the divisions caused by factionalism. There may well have been a real tension between the haves and the have-nots at Corinth.

Paul wrote a number of apostolic letters to this community that was in such disarray. The series of forthright letters apparently came almost one after another in the space of a relatively short span of time, probably less than two years.[10] Although the two canonical texts are lengthy – one of the factors leading to the various compilation theories – each of them is clearly an apostolic and ecclesiastical[11] composition. The first of them begins: "Paul, called by the will of God to be an apostle of Christ Jesus, and our brother Sosthenes, to the church of God which is at Corinth, to those sanctified in Christ Jesus, called to be saints together with all those who in every place call on the name of our Lord Jesus Christ, both their Lord and ours: Grace to you and peace from God our Father and the Lord Jesus Christ" (1 Cor 1:1-3). The protocol of the canonical second letter to the Corinthians similarly begins: "Paul, an apostle of Christ Jesus by the will of God, and Timothy our brother, to the church of God which is at Corinth...."

The Letter to All God's Beloved in Rome

The last letter that Paul wrote may be his letter to the Romans, his last will and testament, in fact, if not by intention.[12] It is one of the longest of Paul's letters and it is certainly the most famous and well-read of all of them. It stands out from the others because it is addressed to a community that Paul had not evangelized and that he himself had not yet visited. As such it is an extended letter of introduction, one that Paul wrote to a community that he intended to visit while he was on his way to Spain (Rom 15:23-24). Presumably he expected to receive support from the Roman church for his various mission endeavors in the West.

Although Romans has been plumbed for its theological insights, especially since the Reformation, to the point that some have considered it be almost a theological treatise, it seems clear that it is a real letter.[13] The letter has its own epistolary situation and an epistolary form. Its protocol clearly reveals that it is an apostolic letter: "Paul, a servant of Jesus Christ, called to be an apostle, set apart for the gospel of God... to all God's beloved in Rome, who are called to be saints: Grace to you and peace from God our Father and the Lord Jesus Christ" (Rom 1:1, 7). In this protocol we recognize Paul's by now familiar epistolary greeting, but the letter lacks any specific reference to a gathering of Romans, to an *ekklēsia* at Rome.

This does not mean that Paul did not know people at Rome. The last chapter of the letter contains an extended series of greetings in which twenty-six people appear, twenty-three of whom are called by name. In the judgment of many scholars this, plus the fact that the letter seems to come to an end in Rom 15:33, makes it unlikely that Romans 16 originally belonged to the letter to the Romans. How could Paul have known so many people in a place that he had not visited? Many of these same scholars note that Rom 16:1-16 seems to be a letter of recommendation for Phoebe, the deacon of the church of Cenchreae. They think that Romans 16 was probably a letter of recommendation, an epistolary genre known to the Hellenists (*typos systatikos*), sent to the church at Ephesus, where Paul had spent more than two years of his life.

The consensus of scholarship on Paul's letter to the Romans had been weighted toward the view that Romans 16, although written by Paul, had been appended to Paul's letter to the Romans. A 1977 study by Harry Gamble[14] has, however, begun to turn the tide of critical scholarship back toward the view that Romans 16 was written to Christians in Rome. In fact, Gamble suggests that the list of persons whom Paul greets in Romans 16 is as extensive as it is precisely because Paul had not yet visited Rome. It would have been to his advantage to mention the names of those Christians at Rome of whom he knew through his apostolic efforts in other churches.

Apostolic and Ecclesiastical Writings

That question remains joined.[15] What is beyond dispute, however, is that the writing of a letter to the church of the Thessalonians began a new chapter in the life of Paul the apostle. It was the chapter of Paul, the writer of apostolic letters. A new genre had really been created — within the space of a single decade.[16] In retrospect the creation of the new genre dates back to the writing of that first letter to the Thessalonians. From that time on ecclesiastical documents, in the form of letters, were part of the Christian story.

So far as we know, Paul himself wrote at least nine letters, 1 Thessalonians, Galatians, Philippians, Philemon, 1-2 Corinthians, and Romans, and the two "lost" letters to the Corinthians. He may have written more than nine letters. We cannot presume that it is only the missing letters to the Corinthians that have not been preserved. On the other hand, if the various partition theories are correct, holding as they do that various letter fragments have been collected together in our canonical Romans, 1-2 Corinthians, 1 Thessalonians, and Philippians, we may actually possess two letters of Paul (Galatians and Philemon) and as many as fifteen letter fragments, that is, portions of fifteen letters written by Paul to various churches.

The Highest Form of Flattery

The letters of Paul were such that they made a significant impact upon the life of first-century Christians. Some of Paul's disciples imitated the master by writing letters in his name. While the biases germane to our current society may look upon these "letters" as forgeries — and they are forgeries in the literary, if not the ethical sense — it must be recognized that within Paul's Hellenistic world it sometimes happened that texts were written in the name of another in order to pay honor to them. Letters that were written in Paul's name are an implicit tribute to his memory. By and large, however, they were not so much written to honor his name, as they were to re-embody his message in a new set of circumstances. The adaptation and actualization of Paul's message was the common purpose behind a new type of Christian literature, the text that looks like a letter, but is not actually a letter. Six of these look-like-letter texts are "Paul's" letter to the Ephesians, his letter to the Colossians, his second letter to the Thessalonians, his two letters to Timothy, and his letter to Titus.[17]

An Epistle to the Saints in Colossae

Of these, the so-called letter to the Colossians probably represents the oldest imitation of the Pauline letter.[18] Its thought, style, and vocabulary are so close to that of the apostle that many scholars continue to hold that Paul himself wrote the letter, but a strong majority has made a convincing case that the letter is pseudonymous and post-Pauline. The style and principal theological notions of Colossians are different from those evident in Paul's authentic letters. The manifest similarity with Paul's theological ideas and his own vocabulary comes from the fact that the letter to the Colossians represents, in great measure, a reworking of Pauline themes for a new situation.[19] It should also be noted that the image of Paul the apostle that emerges from a reading of this text – notably the portrayal of Paul as a minister of the church (Col 1:24-25) – is quite different from that gleaned from a reading of Paul's own letters.

Although pseudepigraphal, the letter to the Colossians has the manifest form of a letter. In its protocol, we find an epistolary address, salutation, and thanksgiving formula: "Paul, an apostle of Christ Jesus by the will of God, and Timothy our brother to the saints and faithful brothers and sisters in Christ in Colossae: Grace to you and peace from God our Father. In our prayers for you we always thank God, the Father of our Lord Jesus Christ, for we have heard of your faith ... and ... love ... (Col 1:1-4). The greeting itself is contained in an expression that is shorter than Paul's standard salutation, but it is obviously dependent upon Paul's typical wording.[20]

The abundance of epistolary conventions with which the "letter" closes (Col 4:7-18) gives evidence of the fact that its anonymous author wants his text to be read as a letter. He calls it a "letter" (*epistolē*). It is, however, a strange letter since it is destined to be read by others than those to whom it is addressed (4:16).[21] It contains greetings from and to, with an abundance of names.[22] The epistolary postscript of Col

4:18 recalls similar formulae in Gal 6:11, 1 Cor 16:21, 2 Cor 10:1, and Phlmn 19. It is undoubtedly a convention introduced into the "letter" to establish its letter form and assure its verisimilitude.

A Letter to the Saints

Further removed from Paul, yet still beholden to him, is the so-called letter to the Ephesians. The non-Pauline style and treatise-like character of the epistle have long been obvious to commentators. One particularly puzzling feature is the manifest similarity between this text and the epistle to the Colossians.[23] Their respective structures, themes, and vocabulary are so akin that it is difficult to escape the conclusion that Ephesians is dependent on Colossians, in which case the epistle to the Ephesians represents a second-generation dependence upon Paul.

What is also striking is the fact that this text, purportedly a letter to a community with whom Paul had long lived, is not addressed to a gathering, an *ekklēsia*. Nor does it exude the warm tone and familiarity that one would expect of Paul in writing to those among whom he had lived and with whom he had worked. While the epistle to the Ephesians contains a recommendation of Tychicus (6:21-22; cf. Col 4:7-9), its closing lines notably omit the kind of greetings that one finds in Romans 16 and 1 Corinthians 16.

In some ways the letter to the Ephesians comes quickly to closure, without much evidence of standard epistolary closing formulae, even though the double salutation of 6:23-24 has a manifest Pauline ring. On the other hand, the Pauline protocol of Ephesians 1 gives clear evidence of its epistolary form: "Paul, an apostle of Christ Jesus by the will of God, to the saints who are in Ephesus and are faithful in Christ Jesus: Grace to you and peace from God our Father and the Lord Jesus Christ." There follows, not the standard epistolary thanksgiving, but an unusual blessing (a *berakah*), very rich in its theological content.

The opening salutation of the letter to the Ephesians is problematic. The manuscript tradition offers abundant evidence of the omission of "in Ephesus" from some transcripts.[24] This has led some commentators to conclude that the "letter" was not intended as a one-time communication with a particular church, but that it was rather intended to be a kind of circular letter that was destined to be read to various communities. In this case, the reader could fill in the blank, as it were, by mentioning the specific community to which the letter was actually being read at the time.[25]

If the epistle to the Ephesians was intended to be an encyclical letter of this sort, it would have been a new sort of ecclesiastical writing. Whereas Paul's letters were written to specific churches, the epistle to the Ephesians would have been a letter "for the churches." A first step in that direction would have already occurred if the author of the epistle to the Colossians had really intended that there be an interchange of letters received between the churches of Colossae and Laodicea (4:16).[26] It is more than likely, nonetheless, that the epistle to the Ephesians was originally intended for Christians living in that Asian metropolis. Subsequently the epistle would have circulated among the churches, as the omission of the geographic designation from its epistolary preface in some of the ancient manuscripts may well indicate. In this regard, Bruce Metzger writes about the "secondary 'catholicing' " of the epistle.[27]

Interestingly, neither the epistolary prescript to the epistle to the Colossians nor that of the epistle to the Ephesians identifies the recipients of the respective texts as an *"ekklēsia* – church." That is undoubtedly in keeping with the ecclesiological understanding manifest in these documents, that *"ekklēsia* – church" is a term appropriately used to identify all believers (the universal church) rather than a specific group of Christians that actually gathers together (the local church). If these texts had been composed for the benefit of Christians other than those residing in the cities of Colossae and Ephesus, then they were epistles for "the church," that is, for the church in this new meaning of the term.

Letters to Timothy and Titus

Within the canonical corpus of Pauline epistles, the first letter to Timothy and the letter to Titus stand out as having a specifically ecclesiastical character. To a large extent each of these texts represents a body of regulations for good order in the church, promulgated in the form of an apostolic letter. Since the regulations for good order in 1 Timothy are more complex than those found in Titus, it has been suggested that the epistle to Titus is earlier than the first letter to Timothy or that Titus was written in order to provide a set of guidelines for a less fully developed ecclesiastical situation than that to which 1 Timothy responds.

The epistle to Titus concludes with several verses that arguably have the form of an epistolary postscript, especially the summary expression of greetings to and from and the final salutation of Tit 3:15, "All who are with me send greetings to you. Greet those who love us in the faith. Grace be with all of you," but not excluding the list of personalized requests in verses 12–14. The first epistle to Timothy is not as blatant as is that to Titus in bringing the text to closure in letter-like fashion. Its "grace be with you" (*hē charis meth'hymōn*, 1 Tim 6:21) is but a vestige of the epistolary form. The pronoun in the second-person plural ("you – *hymōn*) is an indication that the letter is really intended for an audience beyond the sole Timothy of its epistolary prescript. A similar remark can be made apropos the final salutation of the epistle to Titus.

Each of these two epistles has an epistolary prescript, but in neither instance is the salutation followed by an expression of thanksgiving. It is interesting to note that, although each of these epistles is purportedly addressed to Paul's closest friends and co-workers, their epistolary identification of Paul ranks among the most formal in the entire New Testament.

The epistle to Titus begins:

Paul, a servant of God and an apostle of Jesus Christ, for the sake of God's elect and the knowledge of the truth that is in accordance with godliness in the hope of eternal life that God, who never lies, promised before the ages began – in due time he revealed his word through the proclamation with which I have been entrusted by the command of God our Savior, to Titus, my loyal child in the faith we share: Grace and peace from God the Father and Christ Jesus our Savior. (Tit 1:1–4)

The prescript of the first epistle to Timothy likewise presents Paul in solemn fashion, albeit with not as much detail as is found in the epistle to Titus. The thrust of their characterization of Paul is to establish the authority on the basis of which the ensuing regulations were "promulgated." The situation is somewhat different for the second letter to Timothy. Its epistolary format, and ultimate function, are still more obvious than is the case with either of the other so-called pastoral epistles. The epistolary closing contains greetings for Prisca and Aquila, as well as the household of Onesiphorus, and greetings from Eubulus, Pudens, Linus, and Claudia (2 Tim 4:19–21).

The prescript of 2 Timothy is followed by an expression of thanksgiving in typical epistolary form: "Paul, an apostle of Christ Jesus by the will of God, for the sake of the promise of life that is in Christ Jesus, to Timothy, my beloved child: Grace, mercy, and peace from God the Father and Christ Jesus our Lord. I am grateful to God..." (2 Tim 1:1–3).[28] There is no need to analyze the details of either this prescript[29] or the following thanksgiving, but an attentive reader will surely observe that the salutation itself, with its mention of "*eleos* – mercy" represents an expansion of Paul's epistolary greeting. The formula is verbally identical with that found in 1 Timothy, and somewhat different from the greeting of the letter to Titus in which Christ Jesus is somewhat unusually designated as "our Savior," to wit, "grace and peace from God the Father and Christ Jesus our Savior" (Tit 1:4).

The second epistle to Timothy, with its long reflection on Paul

(2:1–4:8), appears to be an epistolary testament that bears some analogy with the farewell discourse. It is virtually a farewell discourse in the form of a letter. The farewell is sandwiched between two sections with personal notes and "biographical" data (1:15–18; 4:9–22), which provide an aura of authenticity and the semblance of a truly personal letter. There are manifest similarities, particularly of thought and expression, between 2 Timothy and the other pastoral letters (1 Timothy, Titus); one must not simply group all three texts together nor presume that they have one and the same author. The literary genre of 2 Timothy is different from that of the other texts, even though all three have a superficial epistolary form. All three originated during the third Christian generation.[30]

Another Letter to the Church of the Thessalonians

While the three pastoral epistles and the epistle to the Ephesians give evidence of some distance from the apostle, all the while being somewhat dependent on him, the last remaining pseudepigraphal Pauline epistle in the New Testament betrays an almost slavish dependence upon 1 Thessalonians. That dependence is most obvious in the epistolary prescript, where the salutation of 2 Thess 1:1–2 is an exact reprise of 1 Thess 1:1, except that the salutation itself is in the longer form to which readers of Paul had become accustomed.

The relationship between the first and second letters to the Thessalonians is so close that, until the 1980s, the majority of biblical scholars were reluctant to characterize 2 Thessalonians as a pseudepigraphal work, yet pseudepigraphal it seems to be. The so-called second letter to the Thessalonians stands out among the pseudepigrapha insofar as it takes into account the fact that Paul had written letters with utter seriousness. The postscript that precedes the final salutation, "I, Paul, write this greeting with my own hand. This is the mark in every letter of mine; it is the way I write" (2 Thess 3:17), imitates what Paul has done in 1 Cor 16:21; Gal 5:11; Phlmn 19. The plea that Paul himself has written this epistle is much too strong – and out of place for a letter that would have been written, had it been genuine, shortly after 1 Thessalonians. As an exaggerated guarantee, it actually points to the fictitious nature of the text's origin.

In 2 Thess 2:1–2 the author apparently seeks to discredit some letters already in circulation which claimed Pauline authorship: "we beg you ... not to be quickly shaken in mind or alarmed, either by spirit or by word or by letter [mēte di'epistolēs hōs di'hēmōn], as though from us, to the effect that the day of the Lord is already here." While ostensibly pleading the case of the genuineness of the text in which it is found, the remark casts doubts on at least one then extant letter attributed to Paul. Some authors have recently suggested that the letter whose importance is thereby relativized is none other than the very first of Paul's letters, the (authentic) letter to the Thessalonians.[31] Even if 2 Thessalonians was not intended to be a replacement for 1 Thessalonians, it does appear to be the work of a late Paulinist who has rethought the kind of Pauline apocalypticism evidenced in 1 Thessalonians. In the name of the apostle himself, it pleads that the coming of our Lord Jesus Christ lies at some moment in an as yet indeterminate future and argues that a whole scenario must run its course before the coming takes place.

The Pauline Collection

In retrospect, Paul's first letter to the Thessalonians appears to have been a seed. For Paul himself it was a first venture into the writing of an apostolic letter and ecclesiastical texts, that is, texts written in the form of apostolic letters to churches. As he himself wrote a variety of such letters during the short span of a single decade, the new form became ever more identifiable. After his death, other writers borrowed his name and his style to produce a new generation of apostolic letters. Although clearly destined for church use, their epistolary situation is different from that of Paul's genuine letters.

Taken as a group, it can be said that their vision of church is different from that of Paul. Whereas he had written to congregating flesh-and-blood churches, with a relatively spontaneous and charismatic church order, the mimetic texts were written for a different kind of church, be it the "universal church" of Colossians and Ephesians, or the "structured church" of the pastorals. By and large, these pseudepigraphal letters – I prefer to call the pseudepigrapha "epistles" and Paul's own writings "letters" – were written in order to allow some of Paul's fundamental insights to be applied to the ecclesial situation of a new generation. That is also the epistolary situation of 2 Thessalonians, unless one is willing to adopt the radical hypothesis that it was actually intended to serve as a replacement for the oldest of Paul's letters.

With so many letters and epistles of Paul in existence, perhaps even circulating from church to church, and with the authority of the legendary Paul coming to ever fuller expression in the third Christian generation, it would have been surprising if some effort had not been made by one or another Paulinist to gather together the works of the beloved apostle. The way in which the author of the second epistle of Peter writes about Paul (2 Pet 3:15-16) seems to indicate that a collection of Paul's letters existed at that time, presumably sometime early on in the second century C.E.[32] Johannes Weiss, Edgar G. Goodspeed, and some few other scholars are of the opinion that the epistle to the Ephesians, so different in its epistolary form from the other Pauline letters, was composed as a summary reflection on the significance of Paul's theology in conjunction with the collection of Paul's letters.[33] It would have served as a preface or epilogue to the collection itself.

The letter collection was a literary genre known in Hellenistic philosophical circles. Collections of letters were also known in Rome, where they were politically important. There exist collections of letters by Cicero, Augustus, Horace, Ovid, Seneca, and Pliny.[34]

The author of the second epistle of Peter talks about all Paul's letters, but he does not indicate just how many there were in the Pauline collection known to him. One such collection appeared in the Chester Beatty codex, P[46], in which we have the oldest remaining fragments of Paul's letter to the Thessalonians. This codex comprises a collection of ten letters to the churches. It includes the epistle to the Hebrews and dates back to the turn of the second century.

Second-century Christians certainly had an interest in collecting the Pauline letters to the churches.[35] Marcion, the Roman heretic, had his *Apostolicon,* a collection of ten Pauline letters, in which he included Galatians, 1-2 Corinthians, Romans, 1-2 Thessalonians, Laodiceans (=Eph)[36], Colossians, Philemon, and Philippians. For organizing the collection in this fashion, Marcion was chided by Tertullian, who says that Marcion failed to recognize the ecclesiastical status (*"de ecclesiastico statu"*) of the epistles to Timothy and Titus and that he included in the collection the letter to Philemon, which, Tertullian notes, was addressed to a single individual (*"ad unum hominem"*).[37]

As Tertullian's remark indicates, the letter to Philemon was popularly considered as a letter to an individual. As a result, it was preserved in the early manuscript tradition together with the other Pauline letters to individuals, namely, the two epistles to Timothy and the epistle to Titus, apparently once read in the order Titus, 1 Timothy, and 2 Timothy.[38] The letter to Philemon was appended to the collection of Paul's letters to individuals, placed after the pastorals according to the stichometric principle, whereby longer works appeared in the first instance, with shorter compositions following thereafter.

In Rome authors had begun to experiment with the use of books (codices) rather than scrolls (*volumina*) for their compositions as of the first century C.E. Apparently Christians had been using papyrus codices for the publication of their literature before the end of the century.[39] The pastoral letters were handed down as a collection, in book form. The oldest known codex is identifiable from a papyrus fragment containing bits of Tit 1:11-15 and 2:3-8 (P[32], ca. 200 C.E.).

At the time that Christians were beginning to gather the letters of Paul into books, their predilection for scrolls was something of a cultural idiosyncrasy. Karl Donfried has launched the intriguing suggestion that it may have been Paul himself who got the early Christians into bookmaking, not papyrus codices, but parchment booklets.[40] Scraps of leather from the shop on the agora would have served as appropriate writing material for a leatherworker who was also a letter writer. His longer letters would have required several pieces of parchment.

Be this as it may, there is little doubt that Paul's writing a letter to the Thessalonians was the start of something quite significant. It led to his writing similar letters to other churches. It led some of his disciples, most, if not all, of whom had never met Paul personally, to write texts for churches in the form of apostolic letters. It led to the gathering of these letters into books. It even led to disputes about which letters should appropriately be included in the anthology.

The disputes arose because letters continued to be written in Paul's name. In some cases the earlier letters and epistles provided the occasion for these new Pauline letters. Sometime in the third century, for instance, a letter to the Laodiceans was written[41] (cf. Col 4:16). This "letter" is actually a pastiche of citations from and allusions to Paul's letters, especially the letter to the Philippians. The Canon of Muratori rejects another, and no longer extant, letter to the Laodiceans, which it attributes to the work of the Marcionites.

The Canon of Muratori likewise rejects from its authoritative collection of Pauline writings a letter to the Alexandrians, again a text that has not been preserved. The late second-century Acts of Paul contains a third epistle of Paul to the Corinthians, which was accepted by Ephraem, the Syrian deacon, and which came to enjoy a degree of popularity within the Armenian church.[42] In Latin there exists an entire correspondence (fourteen epistles) between Paul and Seneca, the Stoic philosopher. Six of the epistles in this collection are attributed to Paul.[43]

Other Christian Writings

Sometime after Paul's death (ca. 62 C.E.) the changing circumstances of the churches led to the writing of another kind of Christian literature. The very first generations of Christians had, by and large, been uninterested in composing any distinctively Christian literature. The oral witness of those who lived with Jesus and the expectation that the parousia of Jesus as Lord was on the immediate horizon made it unnecessary for them to produce documentary reports about him.

The first generations of Jewish Christians, moreover, had their sacred scripture and were able to reflect on the significance of Jesus in the light of these scriptures.[44] They had no real need of other texts. (This situation, of course, did not preclude the writing of letters. Thus it is that the letters of Paul were written before any of the gospels.)

The First "Gospels"

The situation was to change drastically as of 70 C.E. By that time the pillars of the church had died. Personal testimony was no longer to be had from Peter and others who had known Jesus in Palestine. Even some second-generation Christians had died. Jerusalem was under siege and soon the temple itself would be razed. The day of the Lord had still not come with full apocalyptic éclat. The situation was critical and it appeared that Jesus was not soon to appear as the parousiac Lord.

It was in this context that the evangelist known to history as Mark, presumably the sometime companion of Paul,[45] compiled bits and pieces of the oral tradition about Jesus. The fourth-century ecclesiastical historian, Eusebius of Caesarea, states that Papias, a second-century bishop of Hierapolis, had heard the following story:

> When Mark became Peter's interpreter, he wrote down accurately, although not in order, all that he remembered of what was said or done by the Lord. For he had not heard the Lord nor followed Him, but later... he did Peter, who made his teaching fit his needs without, as it were, making any arrangement of the Lord's oracles, so that Mark made no mistake in thus writing some things down as he remembered them. For to one thing he gave careful attention, to omit nothing of what he heard and to falsify nothing in this.[46]

The tradition preserved by Eusebius says that Mark compiled stories that he had heard.[47] These stories had been told in an unordered sequence and in a manner that had been adapted to the audience at hand. These notions are essentially those maintained by contemporary biblical scholars who hold that the first "evangelist" compiled his own narrative, a story about Jesus, on the basis of traditions that he had heard. These scholars hold that Mark created a new genre when he first wrote the story of Jesus, the genre that is today known as the gospel. As Paul, Mark had created a new literary genre. It was a text written for a church in the form of a narrative. Mark's story does not come to a proper end (cf. Mark 16:8), for the story about Jesus was not fully complete as Mark wrote his gospel about the year 70 C.E.

Written as a crisis document, Mark's gospel proved to be inadequate for a Jewish Christian community that was trying to determine its own identity within Judaism whose visible focus of unity, the temple, had been destroyed in the catastrophe of 70 C.E.[48] From that community emerged a new revised edition of Mark, the gospel according to Matthew. Since it is a fully adapted and reworked edition of Mark, it was intended as a replacement for Mark, at least within Matthew's Jewish Christian community.

Matthew's revision brings the story of Jesus to a close with a magnificent scene of the great commission (Matt 28:16-20), in which the risen Jesus, acting with full authority, commands the disciples to make disciples, baptize, and preach throughout the whole world. This new version of the gospel does not claim Matthean authorship, but its subsequent publication in codex form led to its being called the gospel *according* to Matthew. It is good news expressed in written form in yet another version, a Jewish version.

Although some scholars today are of the opinion that Luke, the author of the third gospel, was aware and made use of the Matthean composition, most believe that Luke was acting on his own when he, in turn, rewrote the Markan text as the first century C.E. was drawing to a close. To be sure, he had other sources available to him in addition to the gospel according to Mark. At least one of these sources, a collection of sayings attributed to Jesus, was available to Matthew as well. Luke's revision of the Markan gospel was intended to serve the needs of a Hellenistic audience.

Rather than leave the story of Jesus unfinished as did Mark, Luke completed the story by adding various narratives dealing with apparitions of Jesus in and around Jerusalem and then adding a companion volume, the book of Acts. Looking at Luke-Acts from the author's perspective, we should think of a single two-part work. The preface of Acts 1:1-4 recalls that of Luke 1:1-4, both indicating that Luke has written for the benefit of Theophilus. The repeated story of the Ascension (Luke 24:44-53; Acts 1:4-14) forms a hinge between the two parts of Luke's work.

Johannine Literature

The Johannine community existed in its own world. One can almost speak of its sectarian character. In any case tensions existed between the Johannine community and other Christian churches at the end of the first century C.E.[49] Those tensions are symbolized in the authority accorded to the twelve in the synoptic tradition vis-à-vis the authority accorded to the Beloved Disciple in the Johannine tradition[50] as well as in the competing roles that the latter assigns to the Beloved Disciple and to Simon Peter.[51] Although the gospel of Mark circulated widely within early Christianity, it is not at all certain that it was well known – if known at all – in the Johannine school within which an anonymous evangelist has produced the text that tradition has revered as the gospel according to John.[52]

In some respects the fourth gospel arose from a confluence of factors similar to those that had led to the writing of the gospel according to Mark and the gospel according to Matthew. Its Jewish Christian Johannine community had seen the death of the first generation of revered witnesses (John 11:1-15; 21:18-19, 21-23). The Temple was no more, and the community had to deal with its disappearance (John 2:13-22; 4:19-24; 10:1-5; etc.). In the crisis of its separation from other expressions of Judaism, the community had to define its own existence.[53] Hence, the constant polemic with "the Jews."

To be sure there are many Synoptic-like elements in the fourth gospel. These may be explained in ways other than a direct dependence of the fourth gospel on one or another of the earlier gospel texts. C. K. Barrett has written that, "One would be inclined to call the Fourth Gospel deutero-Pauline, except that it does not use Paul's name and is so rich in fresh and independent thought."[54] The fourth gospel is a new version of the story of Jesus, written for different circumstances, in different times, and for another community.

Some time after the fourth gospel was written the community experienced a need to refine its message and adapt it to somewhat different circumstances. The "message" had to be written because of the kind of schism that was tearing the community apart.[55] In these circumstances the first epistle of John was written. It is a deutero-Johannine text, written around the turn of the century by someone who venerated the Beloved Disciple and did his best to apply his gospel to a particular situation.[56] Tradition calls it an "epistle," but it does not have an epistolary form, nor does it otherwise make any claim to be a letter.[57]

In contrast with this first epistle, which has been called a letter by tradition even though it is not, the second and third epistles of John are real letters.[58] They are one-page letters written shortly after the first epistle by a person who calls himself "the elder." In length and the relative simplicity of their epistolary form these two letters are much like other letters that have been preserved from Hellenistic times. Indeed, the third epistle, written to a person named Gaius, has the character of a truly personal letter. Its philophronetic character is most evident. Alone among the letters of the New Testament it has the health wish (3 John 2), so typical of Hellenistic letters.

The second letter of John is definitely an ecclesiastical composition. While associated with one church, metaphorically called "the elect sister," the presbyter addresses his letter to another church, called "the elect lady and her children." His letter contains instructions for the church. That it represents a new expression of the Johannine gospel is most evident in its reprise of the new commandment motif (2 John 5-6).[59] The letter addressed to Gaius, although personal, also has an ecclesial focus (3 John 10). It urges Gaius to extend hospitality to wandering Christian missionaries, perhaps emissaries of the presbyter. He puts him on guard against an obstreperous person named Diotrephes. Most probably Gaius and Diotrephes belonged to two different Johannine house churches in the same general area.

The relationship between the Book of Revelation and the other works that have come from the Johannine school is difficult to determine.[60] It has sometimes been suggested that this book was composed somewhat before the gospel. Once again, this is something that is difficult to determine with desired certainty. That it was produced within Johannine circles is clear. Its collection of letters to the seven churches, albeit a literary collection composed for the Book of Revelation, has been influenced by the tradition of the ecclesiastical letter that goes back to Paul.

Other "Apostolic" Letters

Among contemporary scholars it is widely believed that the New Testament epistles that go by the names of James, Peter, and Jude are pseudonymous. This is not the place to argue for the pseudonymity of these texts, but this is the position that serves as my working hypothesis. Their pseudonymity makes it difficult to date the texts. One of the most difficult of all to date is the letter of James, which, if it is authentic, is to be dated no later than the early sixties, but which, if it is pseudonymous, may have been written as much as a half century later.

The Epistle of James

The epistle of James is called a letter because it looks like a letter, at least at the beginning. Its epistolary prescript is: "James, a servant of God and of the Lord Jesus Christ, to the twelve tribes in the Dispersion: Greetings" (Jas 1:1). Its patronymic James is certainly "the Lord's brother" (Gal 1:19), who was leader of the Christian community in Jerusalem. A metaphor is used to designate the recipients of the text. The simple salutation, "*chairein* – greetings" having been expressed, the "epistle" loses its epistolary character. Indeed, apart from 1:1 and 2:1, its Christian character is hardly in evidence. Nonetheless it does show some familiarity with the Pauline tradition about justification and faith (Rom 2:9-5:1; Gal 2:15-3:24), with which it takes issue (Jas

2:14-26), even though its author may not have actually read the Pauline letters.[61] That the author attempts to refute a Pauline position and uses the format of a letter, albeit with the greatest superficiality, to do so is yet another indication of the authority enjoyed by the apostolic letter at the turn of the century.

The Letter of Jude, Brother of James

It is likewise the epistolary prescript that allows the epistle of Jude to be typed as a letter: "Jude, a servant of Jesus Christ and brother of James, to those who are called, who are beloved in God the Father and kept safe for Jesus Christ: May mercy, peace, and love be yours in abundance" (Jude 1-2).

The epistolary salutation is a bit strange. While the reference to the intruders in verse 4 and the description of the opponents suggest that the letter enjoyed a definite epistolary *stasis* and was therefore an occasional letter to a specific group, the formal opening does not really indicate who the intended recipients were. The mercy-peace-love wish is likewise unusual as an epistolary formula. The short text that follows this epistolary greeting is unusually rich in its variety of allusions, to the Bible (vv. 5-7), to the *Assumption of Moses* (v. 9), to Jewish tradition (v. 11), to 1 *Enoch* (vv. 14-15).

Letters of Peter, an Apostle

Nothing in the early traditions about Peter suggest that he was a literary man except for the fact that two epistles are attributed to him. The first of these is most visibly a letter, because of its epistolary protocol and eschatocol:

> Peter, an apostle of Jesus Christ, to the exiles of the Dispersion in Pontus, Galatia, Cappadocia, Asia, and Bithynia, who have been chosen and destined by God the Father and sanctified by the Spirit to be obedient to Jesus Christ and to be sprinkled with his blood: May grace and peace be yours in abundance.... Through Silvanus, whom I consider a faithful brother, I have written this short letter to encourage you to testify that this is the true grace of God. Stand fast in it. Your sister church in Babylon chosen together with you, sends you greetings; and so does my son Mark. Greet one another with a kiss of love. Peace to all of you in Christ. (1 Pet 1:1-2; 5:12-14)

The epistolary elements of this prescript and postscript are clear. Sender and recipients are cited and there is a formula of greetings. Contained in the epistolary closing is the identification of the text as a short composition (*di'oligōn egrapsa*). Although this text is shorter than most of Paul's letters, it is longer than most of the deutero-Paulines and far longer than the average Hellenistic letter. Along with its reference to the brevity of the composition, with its implied suggestion that the text is a letter,[62] the epistolary conclusion contains a mention of the scribe (Silvanus), community and personal greetings, the holy kiss, and a farewell salutation.

The abundance of epistolary formulae makes it clear that the anonymous author wants his composition to be recognized as a letter, indeed as an apostolic letter to various Christian communities. He intends that it be read as an apostolic encyclical. Its patronymic ascription to Peter is evidence of the authority enjoyed by Peter at the time (73–92 C.E.). The invocation of Peter's name adds weight and authority to the text even if the sometime fisherman had not actually written it.

Scholars have long debated over the nature of the text. Many have held that it is a baptismal homily or a collection of fragments of such homilies. There is, however, little doubt that the author has intended his final composition to be a letter.[63] This is not to negate the fact that the letter incorporates elements of other literary genres, just as Paul's letters had incorporated credal formulae, wish prayers, hymns, paraenetic *topoi*, and so forth.

The similarity between Paul's letters and the first epistle of Peter does not stop at the fact that the apostolic letter is actually a composite literary form, incorporating elements with other literary forms. The identification of the pseudonymous sender as an "apostle of Jesus Christ" is Pauline and types the document as an apostolic letter. The epistolary salutation, "grace to you and peace," is Pauline, although "be in abundance" is something new. The names of the scribe (Silvanus) and the sender of personal greetings (Mark) are persons known to have been associated with Paul. The holy kiss recalls 1 Thess 5:26 and other Pauline letters. The brevity of the final salutation has a Pauline ring. Furthermore, much of the vocabulary and thought of the letter echoes that of Paul's letter to the Romans.[64] Thus it would seems appropriate to characterize the first epistle of Peter as being simultaneously deutero-Pauline and deutero-Petrine.[65]

The second letter of Peter is a "second letter," as its author claims in 2 Pet 3:1, "This is now, beloved, the second letter [*deuteran epistolēn*] that I am writing to you." It is intended as a sequel to 1 Peter, the protocol of which is recalled in its epistolary prescript, "Simon Peter, a servant and apostle of Jesus Christ, to those who have received a faith as precious as ours through the righteousness of our God and Savior Jesus Christ: May grace and peace be yours in abundance in the knowledge of God and of Jesus our Lord" (2 Pet 1:1–2).

Given its own designation as a second letter, it is obvious that the author, like the author of the similarly pseudonymous 2 Thessalonians, takes letter writing seriously. It is also obvious that the author has somehow been influenced by the Pauline tradition. The patronymic sender is identified not only as apostle of Jesus Christ but also as servant of Jesus Christ (cf. Rom 1:1; Phil 1:1).[66] The Pauline themes of faith and righteousness appear in the epistolary prescript.

In place of an expected epistolary postscript, the second epistle of Peter concludes with a doxology, "To him be the glory both now and to the day of eternity. Amen" (2 Pet 3:18). As a finale to a letter, a doxology is also to be found at Jude 25. Doxologies are also found in Phil 4:20 and 2 Tim 4:18, where the doxologies are placed toward the end of the letter, but before its concluding words.

The stated purpose of the second epistle to Peter is that it is a reminder to remember (2 Pet 3:1-2). Apart from its epistolary prescript, the text most resembles that of the farewell address or testament. In it "Peter" reminds and forewarns the Christians who are to survive him. Its literary form, with concomitant purpose, is thus similar to that of 2 Timothy, which also has a doxology as a concluding formula. One further striking peculiarity of this second epistle of Peter is that its second chapter incorporates virtually the entire epistle of Jude.

Coming after Jude as it does, 2 Peter appears to have been written at some time during the first few decades of the second century.[67] As it is being brought to its conclusion it appeals to the authority of Paul, the letter writer:

So also our beloved brother Paul wrote to you according to the wisdom given him, speaking of this as he does in all his letters. There are some things in them hard to understand which the ignorant and unstable twist to their own destruction, as they do the other scriptures. You therefore, beloved, since you are forewarned, beware that you are not carried away with the error of the lawless and lose your stability. But grow in the grace and knowledge of our Lord and Savior Jesus Christ. (2 Pet 3:15-18)

The writing of those texts that Christian tradition has identified as the New Testament began when Paul wrote the first of his letters, the letter to the Thessalonians. The newest of the texts included in the canonical collection is the second epistle of Peter. It concludes with an exhortation focusing on the collection of letters that Paul wrote. It compares them with the sacred scriptures of old but notes that, nonetheless, there are some things in them hard to understand.

Collections, Apocrypha, and a Canon

In addition to the anonymous author of the second epistle of Peter, other early Christian authors wrote about the letters of Paul. Clement of Rome, Ignatius of Antioch, and Polycarp of Smyrna not only wrote about Paul's letters,[68] they were also influenced by him. They too wrote letters, whose thoughts and language echo that of the Apostle. Typically, these and other Fathers of the Church wrote about Paul's "letters," in the plural. In their works they cited and alluded to several different letters written by Paul. One can only conclude that these early Christian writers knew of a collection of Paul's letters.

Collections

It is likely that the earliest collection of Paul's letters was a collection of letters to seven churches.[69] 1 Corinthians appears next to 2 Corinthians and 1 Thessalonians next to 2 Thessalonians in P[46] and in Marcion's *Apostolicon*. So it is likely that these two collections were envisioned not so much as collections of ten letters as they were collections of letters to seven churches. The genre of "a collection of letters for seven churches" was certainly known in early Christianity, as the Book of Revelation's letters to the seven churches of Asia (Rev 2:1–3:22) and Ignatius's collection of seven letters indicate.

At the time the number seven symbolized wholeness or universality. An anthology of Paul's letters in the form of a collection of letters to seven churches would have symbolized their universal import. The symbolism is explained in the Canon of Muratori:

> For the blessed Apostle Paul himself, following the rule of his predecessor John, writes only by name to seven churches in the following order – to the Corinthians a first, to the Ephesians a second, to the Philippians a third, to the Colossians a fourth, to the Galatians a fifth, to the Thessalonians a sixth, to the Romans a seventh; although for the sake of admonition there is a second to the Corinthians and to the Thessalonians, yet one church is recognized as being spread over the entire world. For John too in the Apocalypse, though he writes to seven churches, yet speaks to all.

That letters, imitative of Paul's apostolic letters to churches, were often circular or encyclical letters, which thereby acquired a universal character, is evident from the manuscript tradition of the epistle to the Ephesians[70] and the epistolary prescripts of Jude and 1 Peter. The collection of Paul's letters into a book[71] would have allowed these letters, as well as their imitations, to be circulated among the churches.

Because they were gathered into books, Paul's letters to churches had became letters for the churches, that is, letters for the church.

It is generally acknowledged that Marcion's collection of Paul's letters was a first step toward the development of an authoritative collection of Christian writings that could serve as a norm of faith.[72] Marcion accepted seven letters to the churches (Romans, Corinthians, Galatians, Ephesians, Philippians, Colossians, Thessalonians, and the church in Philemon's house). For accepting such a small number of letters into his *Apostolicon,* Marcion was criticized by Tertullian and other church authorities.[73] He accepted but one of the written gospels,[74] namely, that of Luke,[75] reputed to have been Paul's companion[76] and physician.[77] For Marcion gospel and letters stood in a significant relationship with each other; the one gave importance to the other, the other clarified the one.

Marcion's views prodded the church to more adequately determine what really belonged to the normative collection of apostolic writings. The church was to develop its canon of scripture to some large extent in reaction to the overly ardent Paulinist that Marcion was. "It was," writes Bruce Metzger, "in opposition to Marcion's criticism that the church first became fully conscious of its inheritance of apostolic writings."[78] Up to this time, the four gospels had circulated independently of one another,[79] but now there was a growing conviction that the four gospels were as one in proclaiming the truth about Jesus.[80] As the number seven, the number four symbolized wholeness and universality. Irenaeus of Lyons, having criticized Marcion for restricting the gospel to the gospel according to Luke,[81] gave classic expression to the emerging view:

> Since there are four regions of the world we live in, and four universal winds, and the church has been thickly sown all over the earth, and pillar and prop of the church is the Gospel and spirit of life; it is only reasonable that she has four pillars, from every quarter breathing incorruption and giving fresh life to people. From which it is clear that the Logos, Artificer of all things, he who is seated upon the cherubim and holds all things together, when he has been manifested to people, gave us the Gospel in four forms but united in one spirit.[82]

The oldest extant manuscript to contain all four gospels is the fragmentary P[45] (Chester Beatty Biblical Papyrus I).[83] Dating from the first half of the third century, it contains Matthew, Mark, Luke, John and Acts. In this papyrus, the second part of Luke's work has been separated from part one, namely, the gospel that he wrote. The church had gained something in its consensus about the unity and universality of the four gospels, but it had lost something as well, namely, Luke's own clearly expressed conviction that the story of Jesus is completed in the story of the church.

This relatively early collection of the four gospels into a single volume was published in the form of a codex. The use of the codex allowed for the symbolic expression of the church's theological conviction about the unity and universality of the gospels.[84] The use of scrolls would have been inadequate to express the belief since no single scroll could contain all four books.

Apocrypha

Prior to the publication of P[45] other "gospels" had been written and had begun to circulate among the churches. The writing of gospels did not come to a halt with Irenaeus's polemics. Other gospels were written for the benefit of various Christian sects. Some of these apocryphal gospels were known to and criticized by various Fathers of the Church; some others have been discovered among the manuscripts of Nag Hammadi.[85] Some of them are well known and have had considerable influence on Christian tradition and piety, such as the proto-gospel of James. Many of these gospels were attributed to apostolic figures, including some with a narrative form, such as the gospel of Peter, the gospel of Nicodemus, and the infancy gospel of Thomas, and others in the form of dialogue or collections of sayings, such as the gospel of Philip, the (Coptic) gospel of Thomas, and, one might add, the gospel of Mary.

In a fashion similar to which there continued to be letters composed in Paul's name, a few other "letters" were written, including the letter of Peter to Philip and the letter of the pseudo Titus. More curious still is the Epistle of the Apostles. Not only is it an encyclical letter purportedly destined for "the churches of the East and the West, the North and the South"; it claims to have been sent by the eleven apostles who remained after the resurrection of Jesus.[86]

"Acts of the Apostles" were written that bear the name of Andrew, Andrew and Matthias, John, Paul, Peter (in Greek), Peter (in Coptic), Peter and the Twelve, Philip, and Thomas. Books of Revelation abound, with such patronyms as James (three different apocalypses), Peter (three different), Paul (two different),[87] and Thomas.

All of this is in addition to various apocryphal texts that bear names other than those of apostles, such as the classic gospel of the Ebionites. From the end of the first century C.E. various churches held in esteem a number of other letters, some of which were not apocryphal because they bore the names of their authors, and other texts that were found useful to the ecclesiastical purpose. Among these can be cited the aforementioned letters of Clement, Ignatius, and Polycarp. There was a letter attributed to Barnabas and a "second" attributed to Clement. Many churches found the so-called Teaching of the Twelve Apostles (the *Didache*) and the Shepherd of Hermas, both of which probably date from the first half of the second century, quite useful for piety and instruction.

Canon

Beginning with the debate prompted by Marcion's *Apostolicon* and lasting for a little more than two hundred years (mid-second century to the mid-fourth century) a variety of controversies prodded the greater church to a more precise awareness of the value of the apostolic writings; it did not accept these other writings attributed to the apostle Paul. It retained the old collection of letters to the seven churches and a smaller collection of letters to three individuals. The former collection was more widely valued than the latter.

As a sort of appendix to the Pauline collection, there came to be added the anonymous text that the codex compilers designated as (the letter) "To the Hebrews." Before the end of the second century, some Christian churches, but not all, had begun to attribute this text to Paul.[88] Hence it came to be added to the "Pauline collection." The corpus was no longer a larger collection of letters to the churches and a smaller collection of letters to individuals, but a collection of fourteen epistles. In these texts, which it deemed worthy of being read in the Christian assembly, the churches found an expression of its normative faith.

In his 367 Easter pastoral, Athanasius, the influential bishop of Alexandria, wrote:

> it is not tedious to speak of the books of the New Testament. These are the four Gospels. . . . In addition, there are the fourteen epistles of Paul, written in this order. The first, to the Romans; then two to the Corinthians; after these, to the Galatians; next, to the Ephesians; then to the Philippians; then to the Colossians; after these, two to the Thessalonians, and that to the Hebrews; and again, two to Timothy, one to Titus; and lastly, that to Philemon. These are the sources of salvation so that whoever thirsts is sated by their eloquence; in them alone is pious doctrine taught.[89]

Shortly thereafter (382 C.E.) from a Synod in Rome came a decree (of Damasus):

> Likewise the order of the writings of the New and eternal Testament, which the holy and Catholic Church supports. Of the Gospels, according to Matthew . . . Mark . . . Luke . . . John. The

Epistles of Paul in number fourteen: To the Romans one, to the Corinthians two, to the Ephesians one, to the Thessalonians two, to the Galatians one, to the Philippians one, to the Colossians one, to Timothy two, to Titus one, to Philemon one, to the Hebrews one. Likewise the Apocalypse . . . And the Acts . . . Likewise the canonical epistles in number seven. Of Peter the apostle . . . James . . . John . . . another John, the presbyter . . . Jude. . . . The canon of the New Testament ends here.[90]

Looking Back

The canon of the New Testament did not end with the Decree of Damasus. Other churches throughout Christendom took their cues from the example of Alexandria and Rome and promulgated official lists of books. These were the twenty-seven books of the New Testament, to be used by the churches down through the centuries for its worship and as a norm for its faith.

With the acceptance of the canon, the birth of the New Testament, in the sense of a recognizable collection of twenty-seven books, was complete. Its story had yet to be written; indeed it continues to be written as the New Testament is taken up by thousands of different individuals and communities in as many different times and cultures. The New Testament took its life from the life of the church(es). It came into being as the New Testament toward the end of the fourth century C.E. In another and more radical sense, the New Testament was truly born when "Paul, Silvanus, and Timothy [wrote] to the church of the Thessalonians in God the Father and the Lord Jesus Christ: grace to you and. . . . "

It was at that moment that the New Testament, as we have come to know it, was born, for it was at that moment that the "gospel," which had theretofore been communicated only in oral fashion, now became good news in written form. The writing of the first letter to the Thessalonians represents a transformation of the medium through which the gospel is communicated to people. This new medium was a way of extending the apostolic presence and witness to those with whom the apostle could not be physically present.

This transformation of the medium of the gospel required the development of something that is seen in retrospect as a new literary genre, the apostolic letter or the ecclesiastical letter. Whether one chooses "apostolic" or "ecclesiastical" to describe Paul's communication with the Thessalonians depends on one's point of view. The first designation highlights the sender of the communication; the second points to the receiver of the communication. Real communication, in any event, requires both a sender and a receiver. Accordingly it is appropriate to call the letter to the Thessalonians both an apostolic letter and an ecclesiastical letter. There cannot be an "either-or," for it is really a matter of "both-and."

When Paul wrote to the Thessalonians, he created not only a new literary genre, but also a new mode of being church. The church of the Thessalonians was the first Christian community that gathered (as *ekklēsia*) to listen to the reading of a Christian text. He commanded that his letter be read (5:27); the *ekklēsia* came into being when it gathered to listen. Later there would be other Christian texts. Throughout the centuries, Christians would gather to listen to the reading of Christian texts and the church would come to be.

When one looks at what it means to be a Christian today, it is no only a matter of faith, love, and hope – and it must certainly be that it is also a matter of gathering for the reading of those early Christian texts that we have come to know as the New Testament. Twentieth century Christians living in a highly privatized and literate community may read the scriptures at home, but still today when they gather as "church" they gather to listen to the reading of the scriptures.

The scripture (*hē graphē*) that Paul wrote, for his letter was something that he wrote (*graphein, graphesthai*, 4:9; 5:1), was a marvelous blending of the old and the new. In his scripture he had captured at least part of the tradition and carried it forward to people who had various questions and concerns. In what Paul wrote to the Thessalonians we hear echoes of the early Christian preaching of the gospel, with its focus on the kingdom of God. We hear of Jesus who had died, been raised, and who is to come with all the saints at the time of ultimate salvation. We read of the titles that men and women of Christian faith attributed to the risen one, known as the Christ, Lord, and Son. We learn of the halakic or catechetical kind of instruction that had accompanied the proclamation, reminding those chosen by God how they were to live, as God's people.

In this sense there was apostolic "tradition" that was given new shape in the form of the apostolic letter. The novelty that was the letter brought that tradition to bear on a new ecclesial situation, namely, the persecuted church of the Thessalonians, which had serious concerns about the fate of those who had died. How was it possible for them to participate in the glorious parousia? Paul's letter was an epistolary experiment to bring the "traditional faith" in response to this new present and its future situation. It was, in fact, something of a mosaic because it contained not only credal formulations along with remnants of preaching and early catechesis, but also because it blended into the new creation consolatory patterns, wish prayers, moral paraenesis, the autobiographical confession, and various kinds of language that can be summed up simply as a "letter writer's jargon."

That Paul has woven so much diversity into a single letter helps us to realize just how difficult it is to type Paul's letter to the Thessalonians in a simple fashion. There are elements in it that console, others that answer questions, others that confirm the faith, others that express friendship and presence, others that encourage, and still others that challenge. Given this situation, there is little wonder that various readers give different responses to what Paul has written. Similarly, it should not be surprising for those who read Paul's letter to appreciate the difficulties that scholars experience in trying to type, by assigning it to one specific category, a new creation that is so obviously a literary mosaic.

The sheer diversity of materials that Paul has incorporated into his one letter helps us to realize what a true letter writer Paul really was, for there are few of us whose letters are of a "pure epistolary genre" or who do not incorporate into our letters material from various sources. Indeed there are few of us who, upon receiving a letter, have not occasionally frowned a bit as we have asked, "What was the *real* purpose of that letter?"

By writing to the Thessalonians Paul had created a textual form of Christian witness; he had expressed the gospel message in the form of a text. Contemporary theorists tell us much about a text. They speak of a text's semantic autonomy and its polyvalence. Once created, a text enjoys its own existence. It simply "is," and those who read it and those who listen to it draw from it what they will within their own cultures and time and according to their own experience. Reading carefully what Paul wrote to the Thessalonians gives us some idea of what he wanted to achieve when he wrote. We have no idea what he achieved at the time. In a sense he had truly given birth. From his own creativity he had produced something new, over which he no longer had control.

Once a child is born, it has its own existence and lives its own life. The umbilical cord has been cut. So it has happened that what Paul began by writing to the Thessalonians has had its own existence. By creating a text from his discourse, Paul gave a kind of permanent existence to his apostolic witness. The church at Thessalonica read and responded to this apostolic witness in new form, presumably in much the same way that it had responded to the apostolic witness in oral form. Previously they had the living memory of the apostolic witness; now they had the apostolic witness in written form, something on to which they could hold, something to sustain them, something that they could discuss and even question – as the second letter to the Thessalonians so clearly demonstrates.

After his experiment in apostolic and Christian writing, Paul continued to write. Others were to write in his stead.[91] The church provided a new life for his letter when it continued to read the letter not only in the church of Thessalonica, but in the churches of Rome and Alexandria, as Marcion and Origen attest. Those who have read the letter have treated it in various ways. The anonymous author of the second letter to the Thessalonians "corrected" his message; the similarly anonymous author of the second letter of Peter commented that it was difficult to understand.

The church gave a new form of existence to Paul's letter to the Thessalonians when it incorporated the letter into an anthology of apostolic and ecclesiastical texts that would be called the New Testament. The very name symbolized the new status accorded to Paul's letter and those other texts that had been collected into the anthology. Those who gathered the texts together did so in order to preserve the apostolic witness for generations who were no longer able to hear the apostles themselves. Thus they preserved the memory of the apostolic witness, allowing it to be a living memory. They decreed that the written apostolic witness should be read in the churches, that is, to all the brothers and sisters, whenever they gathered in solemn assembly. They had found a new way to extend the apostolic memory and presence. They desired that that apostolic witness, now in written form and gathered together, should serve as a standard of the church's faith. The standard was to be maintained and to live.

Prodded by Marcion and challenged by various doctrinal crises, the church had created a New Testament canon, a list of its foundational texts that it deemed to be authoritative and inspirited of God's own Spirit. By so doing the church, too, had created – or, better yet, reformed[92] – a new literary genre, the canon, or list, of authoritative books. The new genre was the church's response to the various crises of faith that had engrossed its attention in the second, third, and fourth centuries.

As Paul had created a new literary genre, to bring the apostolic witness to bear upon the faith of the Thessalonian church, a community suffering affliction and with a faith that was somehow deficient, so the church created a new literary genre, the canon of scripture, to bring the apostolic witness to bear upon the faith of a broader community which, too, had suffered its pain and had likewise to grow in its faith. As Paul had feared lest the Thessalonians lose their confidence in him (3:5), so the teachers of the church of a later time feared lest the church lose its surety and confidence in the apostolic tradition. A letter was a response to the first situation; the canon of the New Testament to the second.[93] The church had made something new out of elements that were old. It, too, created unity out of diversity.

Those who inserted Paul's letter to the Thessalonians into this authoritative and liturgically useful anthology caused it to be read in a new way. They caused Paul's letter to the Thessalonians to be read as part of the New Testament, as part of scripture. The letter to the Thessalonians was no longer simply the letter to the Thessalonians; it would forever be valued as one of Paul's letters, and a part of the New Testament.

They created a situation in which Paul's letter would forever after be read in intertextual fashion. Hereafter the text would not be read so much as an occasional composition as it would be as part of a collection, from which readings would be taken "on occasion." In many respects, the various writings came to be esteemed more for their unity than for their individuality. People who listened to readings from the collection or read from it themselves have responded, nonetheless, in diverse ways to its message, phrased, in fact, in many different ways according to its various literary forms and compositional situations. To say that each one takes from the scripture what he or she wants may be an exaggeration, but there is more than a small measure of truth in the affirmation that a polyvalent collection bears a multitude of meanings.

In the churches Paul's letter to the Thessalonians and the other items in the canonical collection have been valued as God's gift, his legacy to his people, the word of God, a sign of God's love. This common insight was not so far removed from Paul's own vision when he first wrote the good news. As he wrote he assured those to whom he was writing that the good news that he shared was good news that he had received from God (2:4, 8). He wrote to them of God's love, of which his own was but a sign.

Those who included Paul's letter in their literary anthology laid the groundwork for what might be called a canonical reading of the text.[94] A letter that Paul wrote for a church gathered in a specific time and space became a letter for the church, transcending times and spaces. His letter to a church had become an epistle for the church. It would continue to be read in Christian gatherings, but no longer as a one-time communication. Gathered into the New Testament it acquired a degree of transtemporality. Taken from the time and space in which it was written, Paul's letter to the Thessalonians lost, in the popular mentality at least, its letter character to become simply scripture. In fact, it is scripture because it was written — written, that is, as a letter.

Naming comes after birth. Having written to the Thessalonians, Paul called what he had done a letter (5:27). The church would call it (part of) the New Testament. He commanded that his letter be read. We read it accordingly, for in a very real sense the New Testament was born when that first letter of Paul was written.

Notes

Introduction

1. See Jerome D. Quinn, "P⁴⁶ – The Pauline Canon?" and Young Kyu Kim, "Paleographical Dating of P⁴⁶ to the Later First Century."

2. The text of these leaves was first published in 1934. The text was again published in 1936, when the entire extant group of eighty-six became accessible. A facsimile of Beatty's ninth and tenth leaves was published in 1937. See Frederic G. Kenyon, *The Chester Beatty Biblical Papyri: Descriptions and Texts of Twelve Manuscripts on Papyrus of the Greek Bible*, vol. 3: *Pauline Epistles and Revelation. Text*, 14-15; vol. 3: *Supplement: Pauline Epistles. Text*, 155-56; *Plates*, ff. 94r, 94v, 97r, 97v.

3. See, for example, Jorge Sanchez Bosch, "La chronologie de 1 Thessaloniciens et les relations de Paul avec d'autres églises." Johanson, however, repeatedly makes the point that although 1 Thessalonians is the earliest extant letter of Paul, it is not necessarily the first letter that he wrote. See Bruce C. Johanson, *To All the Brethren: A Text-Linguistic and Rhetorical Approach to 1 Thessalonians*, 60, n. 304 and *passim*.

4. The text was published by Bernard P. Grenfell and Arthur S. Hunt, *The Oxyrhynchus Papyri*, XIII (London: Egypt Exploration Fund, 1919), 12-14.

5. See Vittorio Bartoletti, *Papyri della Società Italiana* 14 (1957): 5-7.

6. A notable exception to the singular lack of importance to be attributed to the scattered readings of P⁶⁵ is its reading of "babes" (*nēpioi*) in 1 Thess 2:7. P⁶⁵ is the oldest witness to the *"nēpioi* – babes" reading in this much disputed passage.

7. See L. Casson and E. L. Hettich, *Excavations at Nessana*, vol. 2: *Literary Papyri* (1950), 119.

1. A Visit to Thessalonica

1. Strabo (cf. fragment 24) suggests that Thessalonica was built on the site of Therme, but no artifacts older than the fourth century B.C.E. have as yet been discovered on the site of ancient Thessalonica.

2. See Strabo, 7. Fragment 21.

3. Cf. Holland Lee Hendrix, "Thessalonicans Honor Romans" (Harvard Th.D. thesis, 1984), 19–22, 192, 347. Metellus was also honored on a statue dedicated in his honor to Zeus Olympios at Olympia by a Thessalonian, Damon son of Nikanor. See 22–25 and *passim.*

4. It is not clear whether the exemption from taxation was made by Rome itself or whether it resulted from a decision made at the local level. For a discussion of the issue and its consequences in the practical order, see Hendrix, "Thessalonicans," 340–59.

5. In speeches (55 B.C.E.) decrying the deteriorating situation in Macedonia and laying the blame for this on the administrative mismanagement of the proconsul, L. Calpurnius Piso Caesonius, Caesar identifies the Via Egnatia as a "military road" (*via militaris; De Provinciis Consularibus* 2, 4; *In Pisonem* 34, 84). He describes the inhabitants of Thessalonica as dwelling "in the very heart of our power" (*positi in gremio imperii nostri*).

6. See Hendrix, "Thessalonicans," 26–27, 203, 208.

7. Thessalonica is not specifically mentioned in any of the accounts of the Mithridatic Wars. See Hendrix, "Thessalonicans," 201–36, 388–401. Hendrix cites Cicero, *In Pisonem* 38, 61, Livy; *Epitome* 53, 54, 63, 65, 74, 76, 81, 82; Plutarch, *Sulla* 11, 14, 23, 26; Appian, *Illyrian Wars* 5, *Mithridatic Wars* 29, 35, 41–45, 49, etc.

8. Hendrix, "Thessalonicans," 251.

9. Hendrix, "Thessalonicans," 31–33, 155–62.

10. Hendrix, "Thessalonicans," 159.

11. Hendrix, "Thessalonicans," 37.

12. The latter two functions are cited on a now lost fragment of a stele that apparently commemorated the construction of a temple of Caesar. Hendrix calls them civic officers (109). The "architect" may have been some type of commissioner of public works. See "Thessalonicans," 106–9.

13. Cf. G. H. R. Horsley, *New Documents Illustrating Early Christianity,* vol. 2, 34–35, 34, and Bruno Helly, *Ancient Macedonia,* 2:531–44. Schuler and Elliger, however, contend that the office of politarch was instituted during the organization of Macedonia as a Roman province. See C. Schuler, "The Macedonian Politarchs," *CP* 57 (1960): 90–100, 96; Winfred Elliger, *Paulus in Griechenland: Philippi, Thessaloniki, Athen, Korinth,* 93. On the politarchs see, further, Horsley, "Politarchs," *ABD,* vol. 5, 384–89.

14. See the discussion of these inscriptions in Hendrix, "Thessalonicans," 106–15. A list of all the known inscriptions referring to politarchs in Macedonia was published by C. Schuler in "Macedonian Politarchs," 96–98.

15. See Edgar DeWitt Burton, "The Politarchs," *American Journal of Theology* 2 (1898): 598–632, 628. Burton believed that there were five politarchs at the time of Paul. In fact, both of the artifacts studied by Hendrix list only five politarchs.

16. *Anthologia Palatina,* 9, 428. Cf. A. S. F. Gow and D. L. Page, eds., *The Garland of Philip and Some Contemporary Epigrams,* 1 (Cambridge: University Press, 1968), 12–13. See Hendrix, "Thessalonicans," 72.

17. *Metropolis tēs nun Makedonias.* See Strabo, VII, fragment 21.

18. The commentators generally bemoan this fact. As a result, despite the fact that Thessalonica was one of the most important cities of ancient Greece, no thoroughgoing history of ancient Thessalonica has yet been written, whereas histories have been written about other cities in Greece, for example, nearby Philippi. A fortiori a complete history of the religions of Thessalonica has not yet been written and will probably not be written. In this respect, Hendrix's work represents a partial yet pioneering effort. See also Charles Edson's "Macedonia: State Cults of Thessaloniki" (1940).

19. See C. Makaronas, "Excavations at the Serapion," *Makedonika* 1 (1940): 464-65.

20. See especially Charles F. Edson, ed., *Inscriptiones graece Epiri, Macedoniae, Thracae, Schythiae,* 2/1: *Inscriptiones Thessalonicae et viciniae* (Berlin: De Gruyter, 1972).

21. Pace Robert Jewett, who dates the synagogue to the third century B.C.E. in *The Thessalonian Correspondence: Pauline Rhetoric and Millenarian Piety,* 120. See B. Lifschitz and J. Schiby, "Une synagogue samaritaine à Thessalonique"; Emmanuel Tov, "Une inscription grecque d'origine samaritaine à Thessalonique"; James D. Purvis, "The Paleography of the Samaritan Inscription from Thessalonica"; Colin J. Hemer, *The Book of Acts in the Setting of Hellenistic History.*

22. See Acts 16:16-39. Counting the distance between Philippi and Thessalonica as approximately 140 kilometers, Robert Jewett has opined that the journey would take about four days. See Jewett, *A Chronology of Paul's Life,* 60.

23. Acts 17:1.

24. *De Provinciis Consularibus,* 2.4.

25. See also 2:13-14.

26. For example, the RNAB includes all twelve verses in a single paragraph; the New Translation published by the Society for the New Translation makes paragraph breaks at verse 4 and verse 9; the NIV makes a break at verse 7 (which appears as the middle of verse 6 in the published editions) and verse 10; the NJB makes a single paragraph break in the middle of verse 7; and the REB makes its paragraph break at verse 10.

27. It occurs some twenty-three times in 1 Thessalonians alone, i.e., in 1:8, 9; 2:1, 3, 5, 9, 14, 19, 20; 3:3, 4, 9; 4:2, 3, 7, 9, 10, 14, 15; 5:2, 5, 7, 18.

28. Johanson subdivides 1 Thess 2:1-12 into two subsequences, i. e., 2:1-8 and 2:9-12. See Johanson, *To All the Brethren,* 87.

29. In contrast, the RSV translated Paul's *gar* by "for" in all four instances. The particle has its most forceful sense when it introduces the reason or cause for something that has just been described (hence "for" or "since"), but it sometimes introduces an explanation and occasionally serves merely as a connective between two related thoughts. In the latter sense it serves as a rather weak connective, tending to be replaced by *de* in Hellenistic Greek.

30. Elsewhere in 1 Thessalonians, the verb *mnēmoneuō* occurs only in 1:3, where Paul writes about what he remembers in his prayer. Although the use of the verb in 2:9 is unique in the letter, it is part of the pattern of a "recall motif."

31. See " 'The Gospel of Our Lord Jesus' (2 Thes 1, 8): A Symbolic Shift of Paradigm," esp. 430–33.

32. The expression comes from Nils Dahl, who used it in a paper read to the 1972 Society of Biblical Literature Paul Seminar.

33. See also 1:5; 3:3–4 (6); 4:1, 2, 6, 10, 11; 5:2.

34. Abraham Malherbe suggests that the letter was written "not much more than eight months" after the visit. See A. J. Malherbe, *Paul and the Thessalonians*, 2.

35. The designations "first" and "second," per se do not indicate the order in which the texts were written. These adjectives simply indicate the sequence in which the texts are found in the ancient manuscripts, a sequence that is determined by their relative length. Some scholars who held that 2 Thessalonians was written by Paul – certainly the traditional view – thought that 2 Thessalonians was written before 1 Thessalonians. The theory, first proposed by Hugo Grotius in 1640, appears in the writings of some twentieth-century authors, including Johannes Weiss, Wilhelm Michaelis, T. W. Manson, R. Gregson, Robert Thurston, and Paolo Neri.

Some contemporary scholars, notably Robert Fortna and Charles Wanamaker, believe that the only way to maintain the authenticity of 2 Thessalonians is to posit that 2 Thessalonians was written before 1 Thessalonians. See Fortna, "Philippians: Paul's Most Egocentric Letter," 222, 231, n. 12; Wanamaker, *The Epistles to the Thessalonians: A Commentary on the Greek Text*, xiii; P. Neri, "2 Ts: Ovverosia, prima lettera ai Tessalonicesi," *BeO* 32 (1990): 230, 246.

36. See the discussion of this issue in my *Letters That Paul Did Not Write: The Epistle to the Hebrews and the Pauline Pseudepigrapha*, as well as the discussions of various aspects of the issue by Daryl Schmidt, Greg Holland, Franz Laub, and myself in *The Thessalonian Correspondence*, edited by R. F. Collins, 383–417 and 426–40.

37. Cf. 2:10.

38. Cf. O. Nestor Míguez, "La Composición social de la iglesia en Tesalónica," 76–78.

39. See also 2 Thess 3:8, a pastiche of 1 Thess 2:9. See my *Letters*, 219–20. The paired expression appears only in these three NT passages and these are the only NT passages in which the noun *mochthos* ("toil") appears.

40. The use of this expression does not necessarily indicate a Jewish division of time. Although modern Indo-European languages typically speak of "day and night," the ancient Greek, Latin, and Hebrew languages used "night and day."

41. "From sunrise to sunset" is the conventional phrase to describe the length of the workman's day. See the discussion in Ronald F. Hock, *The Social Context of Paul's Ministry: Tentmaking and Apostleship*, 31–32, 75 (n. 38), 81 (n. 55).

42. See the entry *ergazomai* in LSJ.

43. The notion recurs in Paul's "farewell discourse" to the elders of Miletus who gathered at Ephesus. See Acts 20:34.

44. Cf. 2 Thess 3:7–9. With specific reference to 1 Thess 2:3–6, Ehrhard

Kamlah has argued that there is a basic paraenesis that is exemplified by Paul himself. Cf. E. Kamlah, *Die Form der katologischen Paränese im Neuen Testament*, WUNT, 7 (Tübingen: Mohr, 1964), 198.

45. See Acts 18:3. This is, in fact, the only passage in the New Testament where Paul's trade is specifically identified. Other New Testament passages speak more generally about Paul's work. See 1 Cor 4:12; 2 Cor 12:14; Acts 19:11–12; 20:34; and, in the judgment of some exegetes, Acts 28:30. Taken cumulatively, these passages show that Paul worked in Thessalonica, Corinth, Ephesus, and, perhaps, Rome.

46. See, for example, F. F. Bruce, *Paul: Apostle of the Heart Set Free*, 36; Gerd Theissen, *The Social Setting of Pauline Christianity: Essays on Corinth* (Philadelphia: Fortress, 1982), 105.

47. Information about Paul's native city comes from Luke. See Acts 21:39; 22:3.

48. Among the Fathers, Origen, Rufinus, Theodoret, and Chrysostom; among the ancient versions, the Old Latin (h) and the Syriac Peshitta (syrp). See the references in Hock, *Social Context*, 21–22, 72, and R. Silva, "Eran, pues, de oficio, fabricantes de tiendas," *EstBib* 24 (1965): 123–34, esp. 124–26. See also Joachim Jeremias, "Zöllner und Sünder," *ZNW* 30 (1931): 293–300, 299; F. J. Foakes Jackson and Kirsopp Lake, *The Beginnings of Christianity*, I: *The Acts of the Apostles*, 4 (London: Macmillan, 1933), 223; Ernst Haenchen, *The Acts of the Apostles: A Commentary*, 543, n. 3.

49. See especially Theodor Zahn, *Apostelgeschichte des Lukas*, KNT, 5 (Leipzig, Erlangen: Deichert, 1919–21), 632–34; Wilhelm Michaelis, "*skēnopoios*," *TDNT*, vol. 7, 393–94; Ronald F. Hock, "Paul's Tentmaking and the Problem of His Social Class," 55, n. 2; "The Workshop as a Social Setting for Paul's Missionary Activity," 441, n. 8; *Social Context*, 20–21, 66.

50. See K. P. Donfried, "Paul as *Scēnopoios* and the Use of the Codex in Early Christianity," 249–56, esp. 254–55.

51. *m., 'Abot* 2:2.

52. *m., 'Abot* 4:5.

53. *t., Qidd.* 1:11.

54. *b., Qidd.*, 29a.

55. See Rinaldo Fabris, "Il lavoro nel metodo missionario e pastorale di Paolo," 181–82. Fabris sees Paul's manual labor as a means of making visible "God's free and efficacious initiative toward the salvation of every human being."

56. See Leon Morris, "*Kai hapax kai dis.*" Cf. 2 Cor 11:9.

57. Cf. 2 Cor 8:1–2.

58. Cf. 2 Cor 11:9.

59. See 1 Cor 4:12; 9:19; 2 Cor 11:17. While 1 Cor 9:19 is generally presented as an introduction to the verses that follow (1 Cor 9:19–23), it is, in fact, a transitional verse that provides a commentary upon Paul's realized desire to be able to preach the gospel "free of charge" (*adapanon*). See the pertinent remarks of Ronald Hock in "Paul's Tentmaking," esp. 558–62. Hock's exegesis of these passages leads him to the conclusion, contrary to

that of the reigning *opinio communis,* that Paul came from an upper-class society.

60. Musonius Rufus, a philosopher more or less contemporary with Paul, wrote an entire tractate on "What Means of Support Is Appropriate for a Philosopher?" Unfortunately only a portion of that treatise is extant today.

61. See the discussion of this matter in Hock, *Social Context,* 52–59.

62. See Rom 4:4; 1 Cor 3:8, 14.

63. "So that we might not burden any of you," literally, "any one of you" (*tina hymōn*). Paul's choice of a distributive singular is significant. He might have used a simple plural "you" (*hymas*), as he does elsewhere in his letter, or the expression "some of you" (*tines hymōn*).

64. See Phil 4:10–17. Francis X. Malinowski suggests that the reason why Paul ultimately accepted some support from Philippi was that the women of that community, with whom Paul seems to have enjoyed a rather warm relationship, would not take no for an answer to their offer of aid. See F. X. Malinowski, "The Brave Women of Philippi," 62.

65. See Gal 2:10; Rom 15:25–29. Apropos the collection, see especially Keith F. Nickle, *The Collection: A Study in Paul's Strategy,* SBT, 48 (London: SCM, 1966). Sanchez Bosch is of the opinion that Paul may not have made such a collection at Thessalonica because of his short-term ill will toward James and the community in Jerusalem. Cf. Jorge Sanchez Bosch, "La chronologie de la première aux Thessaloniciens et les relations de Paul avec d'autres églises," 346.

66. See Hock, *Social Context,* 56, with references, especially to Diogenes Laertius, cited on 98. Hock cites Menedemus of Eretria and his friend Asclepiades of Phlonta (millers) and Cleanthes (gardener and miller) as earlier examples of working philosophers.

67. Musonius, fragment 11.

68. Cf. Diogene Laertius, *Lives of Eminent Philosophers,* 2, 122.

69. This is the burden of the participial clause in 2:9: "we worked day and night while we proclaimed to you the gospel of God," literally, "working day and night, we proclaimed to you the gospel of God" (*nyktos kai hēmeras ergazomenoi... ekēryxamen eis hymas to euaggelion tou theou*).

70. See Hock, *Social Context,* 57. Hock cites Musonius's rhetorical question, "Is not the one who procures for himself the necessities of life more free than the one who receives them from others?"

71. See Hock, "The Workshop." Luke does not cite the workshop as a site for preaching (but see Acts 17:16), but Hock has demonstrably shown that the workshop ought to be added to Luke's short list of the synagogue, home, and the Areopagus as social situations in which Paul evangelized.

72. See Malherbe, *Paul and the Thessalonians,* 17–20; "Paul: Hellenistic Philosopher or Christian Pastor?" in *Paul and the Popular Philosophers,* 67–78, esp. 69.

73. See the criticism of Malherbe by Florence Morgan Gillman in "Jason of Thessalonica," 48–49.

74. See G. H. R. Horsley, "The Purple Trade, and the Status of Lydia of Thyatira," in *New Documents,* 25–32.

75. For other descriptions of the ideal philosopher, see Epictetus, *Discourse* 3, 22; Lucian, *Demonax;* Maximus of Tyre, *Discourse* 36. See Malherbe, *Paul and the Thessalonians,* 4, n. 8. See further Helmut Koester, "I Thessalonians: Experiment in Christian Writing," 41–42, and D. W. Palmer, "Thanksgiving, Self-Defence, and Exhortation in 1 Thessalonians 1–3," 24–26.

76. According to the translation provided by A. J. Malherbe, in " 'Gentle as a Nurse': The Cynic Background to 1 Thessalonians 2," originally published in *NovT* 12 (1970): 203–17, reprinted in *Popular Philosophers,* 35–48, 45–46. Malherbe offers a different translation of this passage in *Paul and the Thessalonians,* 3–4.

77. The letter was destined to be read aloud. See 5:27.

78. With regards to the triangular relationship elucidated by Paul in 1 Thessalonians, see Albert Vanhoye, "La composition de 1 Thessaloniciens," esp. 84–85.

79. Cf. my "Paul as Seen through His Own Eyes: A Reflection on the First Letter to the Thessalonians," in *Studies on the First Letter to the Thessalonians,* 175–208, esp. 177–80; Hendrikus Boers, "The Form-Critical Study of Paul's Letters: 1 Thessalonians as a Test Case," 150; Giuseppe Barbaglio, "Analisi formale e letteraria di 1 Tess. 1–3," 50–52, 54, 56; A. J. Malherbe, "Exhortation in 1 Thessalonians," in *Popular Philosophers,* 49–66, esp. 52–53, 57.

80. See, however, 2:10.

81. In one of these instances, God is the referent of the reflexive pronoun (2:12).

82. "You have become" (*egenēthēte*) is in the aorist, which indicates a definite action in the past.

83. See also NJB, RNAB, and the New Translation as well as the RSV's "so, being affectionately desirous of you, we were ready to share with you not only the gospel of God but also our own selves."

84. See, for example, the discussion in Paul Ellingworth and Eugene Nida, *A Translator's Handbook on Paul's Letters to the Thessalonians,* 30, and Traugott Holtz, *Der erste Brief an die Thessalonicher,* 83.

85. This fact has apparently led to some confusion in the transmission of the manuscript. N-A[26] lists the variant *imeiromenoi,* which appears in a few late Greek minuscule manuscripts (323, 629, 630, 945, 1881, 2495, etc.), but the variant was not considered sufficiently important to be included in the apparatus of *The Greek New Testament.*

86. The verb also occurs in Symmachus's translation of Ps 63:2. Hesychius, the first-century C.E. lexicographer, treats this rare verb as synonymous with *epithumeō* and defines it as "to feel oneself drawn to something, with strong intensification of the feeling." Cf. Hans-Wolfgang Heidland, "*omeiromai,*" *TDNT,* vol. 5, 176.

87. See Norbert Baumert, "*Omeiromenoi* in 1 Thess 2, 8."

88. Cf. 3:6.

89. Baumert, in fact, sees this as one of two "interruptions" (my term) in the confession in which Paul departs from his reflections about the past in

order to talk about the present. The other such interruption is, according to Baumert, to be found in vv. 3–4. See Baumert, *"Omeiromenoi,"* 561.

90. See vv. 1, 2, 3, 4, 8, 9.

91. "We had courage to declare" (*eparrēsiasametha*), with the participles "already suffered" (*propathontes*) and "been shamefully mistreated" (*hypristhenes*) in v. 2. "We have been approved" (*dedokimasmetha*) and "we speak" (*laloumen*), with the participle "to please" (*areskontes*) in v. 4. "We came" (*egenēthēmen*) in v. 5, with the participles "we seek" (*zētountes*) in v. 6 and "we might have made" (*dynamenoi*) in v. 7. "We were" (*egenēthēmen*) in v. 7. "We were determined," with the participle "deeply do we care for you" (*omeiromenoi*) in v. 8. "We proclaimed" (*ekēryxamen*) with the participle "we worked" (*ergazomenoi*) in v. 9. "Our conduct was" (*egenēthēmen*, literally, "we were") in v. 10, with its modifying participles "urging" (*parakalountes*), "encouraging" (*paramythoumenoi*), and "pleading" (*martyromenoi*) in v. 12.

92. There are ten participles in all. To these may be added the noun *nēpioi* ("gentle") in v. 8. The meaning of this expression is debated. See the discussion below.

93. See Epictetus, *Diss* 4, 1, 91.

94. See 2:18; 3:5; 5:27. See my *Studies on the First Letter to the Thessalonians,* 178–80.

95. On Paul's theology, see my *Studies,* 230–52, esp. "titles and attributes," 230–36.

96. See further my "God in the First Letter to the Thessalonians: Paul's Earliest Written Appreciation of *ho theos,*" esp. 138–41.

97. Paul uses the definite article in twenty-seven of the thirty-six explicit references to "God" in 1 Thessalonians. See 1:2, 3, 4, 8, 9; 2:2 (twice), 4, 8, 9, 10, 12, 13 (twice), 14; 3:2, 9 (twice), 11, 13; 4:3, 5, 7, 8, 14; 5:9, 23. An anarthrous *theos* is to be found in 1:1, 9; 2:4, 5, 13, 15; 4:1, 16; 5:18.

98. Cf. 1 Cor 8:4.

99. While it is obvious that Paul could speak of "our God" in the sense that God was the God of himself and of the Thessalonian Christians at the time that he wrote 1 Thessalonians, his God would not have been their God at the time of his visit. His "our" (*hēmōn*), moreover, corresponds to the verb "we had courage" (*eparrēsiasametha*), which is in the first-person plural and clearly refers only to Paul and his companions.

100. See. Rudolf Bultmann, *Theology of the New Testament,* vol. 1, 220–27; Robert Jewett, *Paul's Anthropological Terms: A Study of Their Use in Conflict Settings,* 305–33, esp. 313–15.

101. See E. Springs Steele, "The Use of Jewish Scriptures in 1 Thessalonians," 12–13.

102. 2:5; 2:10.

103. Cf. Rom 8:8; 1 Cor 7:32; Gal 1:10. The participial form in 2:4 suggests purpose. *Areskō,* a verb commonly used in Hellenistic parlance, means "to please," but with the added connotation of "being at the service of" or "rendering service to."

104. Other present participles are used of God in 1:9 (God who lives), 4:8

(God who gives the Spirit), and 5:23 (God who calls). See my remark in this regard in *Studies*, 240.

105. The phrase occurs only eight times in his authentic letters: Rom 14:17; 1 Cor 4:20; 6:9, 10; 15:24, 50; Gal 5:21; and 1 Thess 2:12. J. Christiaan Beker has suggested that the proleptic presence of the new in the old is the reason for Paul's sparing use of this terminology. See J. C. Beker, *Paul the Apostle: The Triumph of God in Life and Thought*, 146.

106. In *Paul the Apostle* Beker identifies the eschatological triumph of God as providing the coherent element in Paul's thought.

107. On the glory of God in Paul, see Beker, *Paul the Apostle*, 362–63.

108. See my "God in the First Letter to the Thessalonians," 149–53.

109. See my *Studies*, 187–89.

110. This is so true that some scholars consider the noun "approval" (*dokimē*) to be of Pauline coinage.

111. In secular usage *dokimazō* often meant "to assay (metals)."

112. Cf. Rom 1:28; 2:18; 12:2; 14:22; 1 Cor 3:13; 11:28; 16:3; 2 Cor 8:8, 22; 13:5; Gal 6:4; Phil 1:10; 1 Thess 2:4 (twice); 5:21

113. The reader who is generally familiar with Paul's language might have expected him to use the theological passive in v. 4. In fact Paul has added to the verb in the passive voice the qualifying prepositional phrase "by God," an exceptional and striking expression.

114. Cf. Albert-Marie Denis, "L'apôtre Paul, prophète 'messianique' des Gentiles: Etude thématique de 1 Thes., II, 1–6," 287–90.

115. Paul's use of the perfect passive tense of the verb, rather than a construction that made use of the adjective *dokimos*, would indicate that Paul and his companions continue to enjoy divine approval.

116. See "The Faith of the Thessalonians," in *Studies*, 209–29.

117. Cf. Tit 1:3 and my comment in "The Image of Paul in the Pastorals," 151.

118. See 1 Thess 1:5; 2:2, 8, 9; 3:2.

119. Cf. Gal 1:11–12a.

120. See *Studies*, 189–91. With Denis one might note that 2:4 expresses "the real reason for the apostle's activity." See Denis, "L'apôtre Paul," 287.

121. See Beker, *Paul the Apostle*, 6, 10; R. F. Collins, "Paul's Damascus Experience: Reflections on the Lukan Account"; E. Springs Steele, "Jewish Scriptures," 12–13. There is also a strong influence of motifs from the Deutero-Isaian servant canticles on Paul's references to himself as a prophet. Some of those references can be discerned in 1 Thessalonians, as Denis has shown in "L'apôtre Paul."

122. Cf. 2 Cor 11:13, the only other passage in the New Testament where the expression occurs in this form. Although "apostles of Christ" appears in the Greek text of 1 Thess 2:7, some translations, including the RSV, place it in v. 6 for stylistic reasons.

123. Cf. 1 Cor 9:1–20.

124. Admittedly, with some variety. See Rom 1:1, "Paul, a servant of Jesus Christ, called to be an apostle"; 1 Cor 1:1, "Paul, called to be an apostle of Christ Jesus"; 2 Cor 1:1, "Paul, an apostle of Christ Jesus"; and Gal 1:1, "Paul

an apostle...through Jesus Christ and God the Father." Cf. Eph 1:1; Col 1:1; 1 Tim 1:1; 2 Tim 1:1; Titus 1:1.

125. Cf. C. K. Barrett, *The Signs of an Apostle*, 12–16, 31, 45.

126. See *Studies*, 182–83, 276. Paul used the term *apostolos* with a greater range of applicability than did later Christian tradition which tended to limit the use of the epithet to Paul and the Twelve. Cf. Rom 16:7; 1 Cor 12:28; 15:7; 2 Cor 8:23; 11:13; Phil 2:25.

127. On the use of "Christ" in 1 Thessalonians, see my *Studies*, 275–78.

128. In both cases there is some variation in the manuscript tradition as well as among the various Greek translations.

129. See C. K. Barrett, *Signs*, 45–46.

130. Cf. 3:2, 7; 4:1, 10, 18; 5:11, 14.

131. See Carl J. Bjerkelund, *Parakalō: Form, Funktion und Sinn der parakalo-Sätze in den paulinischen Briefen*.

132. Cf. Elizabeth Struthers Malbon, " 'No Need to Have Any One Write'?: A Structural Exegesis of 1 Thessalonians," in *1980 SBL Seminar Papers*, 301–35, esp. 314–16, which were omitted in the *Semeia* revision.

133. Cf. 3:11, 13.

134. The term *psyche* ("life") signifies the life of an individual as life is manifested in behavior. See Jewett, *Paul's Anthropological Terms*, 347.

135. From the first century C.E. *Hōs ean* ("like") became a common substitute for *hōs an*.

136. Elsewhere in the NT it is found only in Eph 5:29, a deutero-Pauline text. In the Greek text of 2:8, the verb is in the subjunctive mood rather than in the participial form suggested by the NRSV translation. The use of the subjunctive suggests a potential that has endured.

137. Pedro Gutierrez has studied the use of the image in the biblical tradition in *La paternité spirituelle selon Saint Paul*, 91–101.

138. Cf. Plutarch, *How to Tell a Flatterer from a Friend*, 69 B.C.E., and Dio Chrysostom, *Discourse* 4.73–139. These citations are given in a brief, but nuanced, treatment of the use of the analogy among the philosophical moralists by Malherbe, in " 'Gentle as a Nurse': The Cynic Background to 1 Thess 2," *NovT* (1970): 203–17, esp. 211–14, reprinted in *Popular Philosophers*, 43–45. See also 53.

Malherbe's identification of the metaphor as characteristic of a *topos* has been criticized by Wolfgang Stegemann and Beverly Gaventa. Cf. W. Stegemann, "Anlass und Hintergrund der Abfassung von 1 Th 2, 1–12," in Gerhard Freund and Ekkehard Stegemann, *Theologische Brosamen fur Lothar Steiger*, esp. 399–401, and Beverly R. Gaventa, "Apostles as Babes and Nurses in 1 Thessalonians 2:7," esp. 198–203. Gaventa identifies the metaphor as significant because of its "reference to an important social relationship – one proximate to kinship itself" (202).

139. The translation (and reconstruction) is by Menahem Mansoor, *The Thanksgiving Hymns*, STDJ, 3 (Leiden: Brill, 1961), 150–51. The similarities between Paul's juxtaposition of maternal and paternal imagery in 2:7b–12 and 1QH 7:20–22 have been profitably exploited by Gert Jeremias, *Der Lehrer der Gerechtigkeit*. SUNT, 2 (Göttingen: Vandenhoeck and Ruprecht, 1963),

190. Otto Betz, Walter Grundmann, and Traugott Holtz have also drawn attention to the similarities between 2:7 and 1QH 7:19-25. See O. Betz, "Die Geburt der Gemeinde durch den Lehrer," *NTS* 3 (1956-57): 314-26, 322; W. Grundmann, "Die *nēpioi* in der urchristlichen Paränese," *NTS* 5 (1958-59): 188-205, 200; and T. Holtz, *Der erste Brief,* 83, n. 342.

140. Cf. 1QH 9:29-32.

141. *Zeus and Osiris,* 364D.

142. See Karl P. Donfried, "The Cults of Thessalonica and the Thessalonian Correspondence," 338-40.

143. See further Beverly R. Gaventa, "The Maternity of Paul: An Exegetical Study of Galatians 4:19," in *The Conversation Continues,* edited by R. T. Fortna and B. R. Gaventa, 189-201.

144. See, especially, A. J. Malherbe, "Gentle as a Nurse."

145. A word found elsewhere in the New Testament only in 2 Tim 2:24.

146. A notable exception is the fifth-century Codex Alexandrinus. On the other hand, on three of the four occasions that Origen refers to this verse he treats it as if it read *"nēpioi* – children," as do many of the Old Latin versions of the text. For a study of the patristic references to the text see Jean Gribomont, "Facti sumus parvuli: La charge apostolique (1 Th 2, 1-12)."

147. *"Nēpioi* – children" is the reading found in N-A²⁶ and *GNT*³. The editors assign a C rating to the reading, indicating thereby that there is a considerable degree of doubt as to which of the two is really the superior reading. Bruce Metzger and Allen Wikgren, members of the editorial committee, have expressed some reservations.

For a survey of the manuscript evidence see K. Aland, *Text und Textwert der griechischen Handschriften,* II, 4, 301-3. For a discussion of the issue and the reasons why *"nēpioi* – children" seems, on text critical grounds, to be the preferable reading, see B. M. Metzger, *A Textual Commentary on the Greek New Testament,* 629-30; B. R. Gaventa, "Apostles as Babes and Nurses," 194-98; and Philip W. Comfort, *Early Manuscripts and Modern Translations of the New Testament,* 162-63.

On the other hand, Traugott Holtz and Helmut Koester argue for the *"ēpioi* – gentle" reading on the basis of internal criteria. See T. Holtz, "Traditionen im 1. Thessalonicherbrief," in *Die Mitte des Neuen Testaments: Einheit und Vielfalt neutestamentlicher Theologie,* 78; H. Koester, "The Text of 1 Thessalonians," 224-25. See also Georg Bertman, *"nēpios, nēpiazō,"* *TDNT,* vol. 4, 912-23, 919.

148. This is not a matter of mere speculation. In the case of the Sinaiticus, Ephraemi Rescriptus, and Claromontanus codices the manuscripts themselves have been "corrected" by a later copyist.

149. See Charles Crawford, "The 'Tiny' Problem of 1 Thessalonians 2, 7."

150. Following Max Black's interaction theory of metaphor, Stephen Fowl has argued that Paul has deliberately introduced the maternal metaphor after the child metaphor in order to supplement and correct the latter. Cf. S. Fowl, "A Metaphor in Distress: A Reading of *NĒPIOI* in 1 Thessalonians 2.7."

151. See Gaventa, "Apostles as Babes and Nurses," 203-7; Gribomont,

"Facti sumus parvuli," 337-38; Malbon, "No Need to Have Any One Write?" 315.

J. J. Janse van Rensburg has argued that the three familial metaphors of 2:7b-12, children, mother, father, are antithetical to the threefold negative description of 2:5-7a. See J. J. Janse van Rensburg, "An argument for reading *NEPIOI* in 1 Ts 2:7," esp. 255-57.

152. The point should not be forced, however, since in Paul's koine Greek the particle was practically synonymous with the more common *kathōs*.

153. There is also a repeated *hōs: kathaper oidate hōs hena hekaston hymōn hōs pater tekna heautou parakalountes hymas....*

154. See Gutierrez, *La paternité spirituelle*, 89-117.

155. See Gutierrez, *La paternité spirituelle*, 91.

156. In Greek the clause does not contain a noun, the verb, and three adjectives; rather it contains the verb *egenēthēmen*, in the first-person plural, modified by three adverbs. "Conduct" is an interpretive addition in the translation.

157. *b., Qidd.*, 29a. According to the Talmud, some rabbinic authorities added "to swim" to this list of duties.

158. See Gutierrez, *La paternité spirituelle*, 30, n.5, who cites Gen 28:1; Tob 14:3, 8; and 1 Macc 2:46-49 in this regard. The idea provides the basic literary theme for the *Testament of the Twelve Patriarchs*. A father's responsibility to provide for the socialization of offspring is also amply attested in the New Testament. See, for example, Eph 6:4 and John 5:19-20a, and my comments apropos this latter text in *These Things Have Been Written*, 143-44.

159. See especially 1 Cor 4:14-15 and Phlmn 10. See, further, 1 Tim 1:2; 2 Tim 1:2; Tit 1:4. See Collins, "The Image of Paul," 160, and Norman R. Petersen, *Rediscovering Paul: Philemon and the Sociology of Paul's Narrative World* (Philadelphia: Fortress, 1985), 128-31.

160. See Dietrich Wiederkehr, *Die Theologie der Berufung in der Paulusbriefen*, 37.

161. In an attempt to use inclusive language, and conscious of the fact that the Christian community was not composed exclusively of males, the NRSV has rendered Paul's *adelphoi* as "brothers and sisters." Proceeding from the same concerns, the REB has rendered Paul's Greek as "my friends," and The New Translation has opted for "dear friends." These latter translations express a sensitivity for inclusive language and reflect the bonds that linked Paul and his companions to the Thessalonians, but they do not reflect the semantic field of kinship language. The NIV, the NJB, and the RNAB have, on the other hand, retained the more literal "brothers" as the appropriate translation of *adelphoi.*

162. With most scholars today, I would consider Romans, 1-2 Corinthians, Galatians, Philippians, 1 Thessalonians, and Philemon to be the only extant authentic Pauline letters.

163. That is, in Romans 10 times (of 19), 1 Corinthians 20 times (of 39), 2 Corinthians 3 times (of 12), Galatians 9 times (of 11), Philippians 6 times (of 9), 1 Thessalonians 14 times (of 19), and Philemon once (of 4). The term

adelphos occurs some 343 times in the New Testament, and 113 of these occurrences are to be found in the authentic Pauline letters. In contrast, the term occurs only twenty times in the deutero-Pauline letters, and nine of these occurrences are to be found in 2 Thessalonians, a text which in many respects is a slavish imitation of 1 Thessalonians. See my *Letters That Paul Did Not Write,* esp. 141, 122.

164. In addition to the fourteen uses of the term as a formula of direct address, the term is used in the plural to describe the Christians of Thessalonica and Macedonia in 4:10; 5:26, 27 (where, for stylistic reasons, it is rendered as "of them" in the NRSV). In 3:2 it is used as an epithet to describe Timothy, and in 4:6 it is used to identify a Christian husband.

165. See 1:4; 2:1, 9, 14, 17; 3:7; 4:1, 10, 13; 5:1, 4, 12, 14, 25. In all but one instance *adelphoi* appears in these passages as an unqualified vocative. In 1:4, the vocative is qualified by the expression "beloved by God" (*ēgapemenoi hypo tou theou*).

166. See my *Studies,* 296–97.

167. Cf. Hans F. von Soden, *adelphos, ktl., TDNT,* vol. 1, 144–46, 146.

168. *Hōsper adelphois,* Jewish War, II, 122. Cf. 1QS 6:10, 22; CD 6:20, 7:1, 2, etc.

169. H. von Soden, *adelphos,* 145.

170. In this regard it is useful to note that whereas the vocative *adelphoi* occurs fourteen times in the relatively short 1 Thessalonians, it occurs only ten times in the much longer letter to the Romans, a letter to a community that Paul did not know. This comparative frequency indicates that the term, especially as employed in the vocation, has more than a generic connotation ("fellow member of a religious brotherhood") in Paul's usage. Similarly one can note that the vocative occurs twenty times in the first letter to the Corinthians, admittedly a long letter, but one whose principal theme is an appeal to greater unity within the community.

171. On the importance of the house church in early Christianity, including, a fortiori, the Pauline foundations, see especially Hans-Josef Klauck, *Hausgemeinde und Hauskirche im frühen Christentum;* "Die Hausgemeinde als Lebensform im Urchristentum"; Jerome Murphy-O'Connor, *St. Paul's Corinth: Texts and Archaeology,* GNS, 6 (Wilmington, Del.: Glazier, 1983), 153–61; Vincent P. Branick, *The House Church in the Writings of Paul;* A. J. Malherbe, *Social Aspects of Early Christianity,* 60–91; along with my own modest contributions to the study of this topic in "The Local Church in the New Testament," *Church* 2 (Summer 1986): 23–28, esp. 26–27; "Small Groups: An Experience of Church," *LS* 13 (1988): 109–36, esp. 109–15; "House Churches in Early Christianity," *Tripod* 55 (1990): 3–6 (in Chinese), 38–44 (in English).

172. See Wayne A. Meeks, *The First Urban Christians: The Social World of the Apostle Paul,* 75.

173. For an overview of some of the positions on this issue, see Jewett, *The Thessalonian Correspondence,* 114–18.

174. Some authors, however, attribute the stereotypical features of Luke's narrative to a use of sources. Buck and Taylor, for example, write of a journey

source that would have as its characteristic formula a Pauline visit to a town where the gospel is unknown, preaching in the synagogue, turning to the Gentiles, incurring the anger of the Jews, and being expelled from town. In addition to the use of such a stereotypical schema, the journey source would have had a specific interest in matters legal and political. Cf. Charles Buck and Greer Taylor, *Saint Paul: A Study of the Development of His Thought* (New York: Scribner's, 1969), 190–95.

175. See Acts 17:10–15; 18:1–17. See, for example, Jack T. Sanders, *The Jews in Luke-Acts*, 77, 272. By means of this schematized narrative structure, Luke, says Sanders, has "drawn a picture of *increasing Jewish hostility and opposition to the gospel*" (his emphasis, 77).

176. Dieter Lührmann, "The Beginnings of the Church at Thessalonica," 241. Lührmann has taken his cue from Acts 17:2, where Luke narrates that Paul entered the synagogue "as was his custom" (cf. 238).

177. See Haenchen, *Acts*, 110, 513–14.

178. Cf. Richard I. Pervo, *Profit with Delight: The Literary Genre of the Acts of the Apostles*, esp. 31, 36.

179. The point has been repeatedly urged by Karl Donfried. See "Paul and Judaism: I Thessalonians 2:13–16 as a Test Case," 247; "The Cults," 342–43; "1 Thessalonians, Acts and the Early Paul," 5. See also, F. F. Bruce, "The Acts of the Apostles Today," 56, and Mark Allan Powell, *What Are They Saying About Acts?* esp. 21–37, 80–95. Edouard Delebecque has suggested that the greater amount of detail found in the Western textual tradition of Paul's account to Thessalonica suggests that the text was revised for the sake of greater accuracy, perhaps by Luke himself. Cf. E. Delebecque, "Paul à Thessalonique et à Berée selon le texte occidental des Actes (XVII, 4–15)."

180. See Donfried, "The Early Paul," 5.

181. In this division, I take issue with Manus, who divides the material into three subunits, vv. 1–4, 5–7, 8–9. See Chris Ukachukwu Manus, "Luke's Account of Paul in Thessalonica (Acts 17, 1–9)," 29–30. Manus's division does not sufficiently take verse 4 into account. Although the faith of some has merited but little interest in Luke's adventure story, mention of that faith is not only a conclusion to the account of the proclamation of the gospel; it also serves as a contrast to vv. 5–7, the rejection of the gospel by the Jews, and as a parallel with vv. 8–10a, the vindication of the gospel.

182. Cf. the use of the formula "Paul and Silas" in the Lukan accounts of the Philippian (Acts 16:19, 25, 29) and Thessalonian (Acts 17:4, 10) visits. Later he pairs Silas with Timothy. They are left behind at Beroea but rejoin Paul in Corinth (Acts 17:14, 15; 18:5).

183. This would have given them legs of about thirty, twenty-seven, and thirty-five miles. See Hemer, *Acts*, 108, 115. On Amphipolis, see Rainer Riesner, "Amphipolis: Eine übersehene Paulus-Station," *BK* 44 (1989): 79–81.

184. See Haenchen, *Acts*, 506.

185. Note the use of the verbs in the singular in vv. 2–3, in contrast with the use of the plural in v. 1.

186. The succinctness of the Lukan account precludes one concluding from the mention of the three sabbaths that he understood Paul's visit to

Thessalonica to have been limited to, at most, three weeks. Phil 4:9 gives one the impression that Paul's visit was longer, as does the intensity of his relationship with the Thessalonians, the expression of which so pervades the entire first letter to the Thessalonians.

187. See Manus, "Luke's Account," 30–31. This argument from scripture is typical of Luke-Acts. See Luke 24:25-35; 44-46; Acts 3:18; 18:28; 26:22-23. For a general overview of early Christian scriptural apologetic, see Barnabas Lindars, *New Testament Apologetic: The Doctrinal Significance of the Old Testament Quotations* (London: SCM, 1961), esp. 251-59.

188. William S. Kurz, "Hellenistic Rhetoric in the Christological Proof of Luke-Acts," *CBQ* 42 (1980): 171-95, esp. 171-80. On Luke's imparting a rational quality to Paul's argumentation, see, further, Dieter Werner Kemmler, *Faith and Human Reason: A Study of Paul's Method of Preaching as Illustrated by 1-2 Thessalonians and Acts 17, 2-4, 11-143.*

189. Jack T. Sanders opines that it is not certain that Luke wants his readers to think of the conversion of some Jews, since, in his view, the pair of genitives in v. 4b, "a great many of the devout Greeks and not a few of the leading women," may be an epexegetical explanation of the "some" of v. 4a. In any case, suggests Sanders, "persuasion" is not the same thing as "conversion." Cf. J. T. Sanders, *The Jews,* 272-73. Bawley, on the other hand, cites Acts 17:4 as one text (see also 13:43, 48; 14:1; 17:11-12; 18:4; 19:10) that indicates that "Paul's preaching consistently bears fruit among both Jews and gentiles." Cf. Robert L. Bawley, *Luke-Acts and the Jews: Conflict, Apology, and Conciliation,* SBLMS, 33 (Atlanta: Scholars, 1977), 77

190. See Acts 17:12.

191. See Pervo, *Profit with Delight,* 81.

192. Manus, "Luke's Account," 31. According to Manus, "what probably appeared as an ethnic squall, has become for Luke a popular agitation."

193. Cf. Acts 6:12 + 7:56-58; 14:4-5; 14:19-20; 16:19-23; 17:13; 18:12-17; 19:21-40; 21:26-22:24; 23:7-10; 25:24. Given the frequency of these scenes and their stereotypical character, it is clear that the mob scene fulfills a narrative function in the Lukan account. See Pervo, *Profit with Delight,* 31.

194. The verb *ochlopoiein* appears in the entire Bible only in Acts 17:5. Most commentators note that its use is hapax in Luke-Acts. However, the lexicographers, e.g., Liddell and Scott, cite only Acts 17:5 as a known usage of the verb. Hippocrates' *ochlonepoiei* is cited as an analogous usage in BAGD.

195. Pervo notes that "if one of Luke's two villains is 'the Jews,' the urban rabble is the other." See Pervo, *Profit with Delight,* 36. However, it must also be noted that Acts 17:5 forms but a single sentence in Greek, whose main verb is "attacked" (*exētoun*). The subject is "the Jews" (*hoi Ioudaioi*), but "the Jews" are qualified by four participles, linked by "and" (*kai*): The Jews, being jealous and...gathering some ruffians and...inciting the mob and throwing the city into confusion, attacked Jason's house. The grammatic construction adds dramatic quality to the account.

196. Cf. Matt 9:23. In its two other New Testament occurrences (Mark 5:39; Acts 20:10) the verb *thorobein* describes human emotions.

197. See Acts 17:7.

198. On Jason, see especially Gillman, "Jason of Thessalonica" and "Jason," *ABD*, vol. 3, 649.

199. See the similar expressions "Jason and some believers" (literally, "some brothers") and "Jason and the rest" in vv. 6 and 9. Apparently these were included among those who say "that there is another king named Jesus" (v. 7). On the other hand, Jason is not reckoned among the Thessalonians who later traveled with Paul. Luke cites only Aristarchus and Secundus in this regard. Cf. Acts 20:4; 27:2.

200. Jason is a Greek name, but Hellenistic Jews living in the Diaspora frequently adopted approximative homonyms as a moniker while dealing with the Hellenistic world, for example, Jason in the case of one named Joshua or Jeshua. Commentators therefore generally assume that Jason was a Hellenistic Jew. See Gillman, "Jason of Thessalonica," 41. Wayne Meeks, however, presumes that Jason was a Gentile. See Meeks, *The First Urban Christians*, 63.

201. Pace Haenchen (*Acts*, 507) and Hans Conzelmann (*Acts of the Apostles*, 135), who take *dēmos* as a synonym of *ochlos*. In my judgment, it is preferable to take *dēmos* in its technical, political sense. See Hemer, *Acts*, 115; Manus, "Luke's Account," 31.

In the New Testament, *dēmos* is a Lukan term, occurring only in Acts 12:22; 17:5; 19:30, 33. The translation of verse 5 in the RSV ("to the people") and NIV is along the lines of the Haenchen-Conzelmann interpretation, while that of the NRSV ("to the assembly"), along with those of the REB, RNAB, and NJB ("the People's Assembly") seems closer to that of Hemer. In any case, Luke makes use of technical political vocabulary in the following verse, where he makes reference to the politarchs.

202. In Acts Luke commonly designates Christians as "*adelphoi*, brothers (and sisters)." See Acts 1:15, 16; (2:37); 6:3; 9:17, 30; 10:23; 11:1, 12, 29; 12:17; (13:15); 14:2; 15:1, 3, 7, 13, 22, 23, 32, 33, 36, 40; 16:2, 40; 17:6, 10, 14; 18:18, 27; 21:7, 17, 20; 22:13; 28:14, 15. In five of these instances, 1:16; (2:37); (13:15); 15:7, 13 Luke calls them "men brothers" (*andres adelphoi*). Apparently Luke has used this latter expression when he wants to indicate that the assembly is a male assembly. Cf. Acts 2:29; 7:2; 13:26, 38; 22:1; 23:1, 6; 28:17.

203. The point is worth noting in the light of Haenchen's comment that "for them the words in v. 6b do not really fit" (Haenchen, *Acts*, 507).

204. The terseness of Luke's narrative, leaving modern readers with the impression that so many significant details have been omitted, clearly indicates that he has composed a summary account of what transpired at Thessalonica. It is more than probable that Luke himself did not know the answer to some of the questions that we are presently raising.

205. See Malherbe, *Paul and the Thessalonians*, 12–17; Gillman, "Jason of Thessalonica," 48–50.

206. This is essentially the same accusation as that brought against Jesus in Luke 23:2. See Walter Schmithals, "Die Berichte der Apostelgeschichte über die Bekehrung des Paulus," *Theologia Viatorum* 14 (1977–78): 145–65, 157; J. T. Sanders, *The Jews*, 365–66, n. 236.

207. On hospitality, see Abraham J. Malherbe, "The Inhospitality of Diotrephes," in *God's Christ and His People: Studies in Honour of Nils Alstrup Dahl,* edited by Jacob Jervell and Wayne Meeks (Oslo: Universitetsforlaget, 1977), 223–26.

208. *Tēn oikoumenēn anastatōsantes.* The verb, used only three times in the New Testament (Acts 17:6; 21:38; Gal 5:12), generally has a pejorative meaning.

209. *Oikoumenē* is, in the New Testament, a Lukan term. Eight of its fifteen occurrences are to be found in Luke-Acts: Luke 2:1; 4:5; 21:26; Acts 11:28; 17:6, 31; 19:27; 24:5. The expression occurs in Luke's special material in Luke 2:1. Its presence in Luke 4:5 (cf. Matt 4:8) and 21:26 (cf. Matt 24:29; Mark 13:25) is clearly redactional. Cf. Matt 24:14; Rom 10:18; Heb 1:6; 2:5; Rev 3:10; 12:9; 16:14.

210. See Acts 1:8.

211. Cf. A. N. Sherwin-White, *Roman Society and Roman Law in the New Testament* (Oxford: University Press, 1963), 103, and, especially, Edwin A. Judge, "The Decrees of Caesar at Thessalonica," as well as the discussions of Judge by Donfried ("The Cults," 342–44), Manus ("Luke's Account," 33–34), and Gillman ("Jason of Thessalonica," 45–46).

212. See Judge, "The Decrees of Caesar," 6.

213. One might note the subtle contrasts between "emperor" (*kaisaros*) and "king" (*basileia*), as well as that between "world" (*oikoumenē*), that is, the ordered world, and the disorder suggested by the verb "turn upside down" (*anastatosantes*). Although Luke refers to the emperor as *Kaisar,* the title "king" (*basileus*) was also used of the emperor in contemporary Hellenism. See BAGD, 135.

214. Cf. Acts 9:23–25 (cf. 2 Cor 11:32–33); 23:23, 31.

215. Literally, "the brothers," as in v. 6.

216. The Greek noun is rendered in the NRSV as "city authorities" in v. 6, but as "city officials" in v. 8.

217. Haenchen writes of the "loose style of the Hellenistic age." Verses 8 and 9 form a single sentence in Greek, whose subject, "they," implied in the Greek verb and its modifying participle, is no longer "the Jews"; it is rather the city officials. See Haenchen, *Acts,* 508.

218. F. F. Bruce concludes that it was the lien placed upon Jason and the others that probably prevented Paul from returning to Thessalonica as he should have liked (1 Thess 2:18). Cf. F. F. Bruce, *Commentary on the Book of the Acts,* 345.

219. Cf. D. Lührmann, "The Beginnings of the Church," 237–41.

220. Lührmann evinces some skepticism as to the existence of a Jewish synagogue in Thessalonica at the time of Paul's visit. See "The Beginnings of the Church," 239.

221. See Acts 17:3, 7.

222. See 1:1, 9; 2:1.

223. See 1:9.

224. Note the use of *thlipsis,* "persecution" (NRSV), in 1:6; 3:3, 7, as well as in the controverted 2:14–16. Apropos the textual controversy regarding

2:14-16, see my *Studies,* 27-28, 101-5. Apropos the situation of distress as presented in Acts 17 and 1 Thessalonians, see Donfried, "Cults," 349-51; Gillman, "Jason of Thessalonica," 42-45; and, especially, Donfried's "The Theology of 1 Thessalonians as a Reflection of Its Purpose."
225. See 3:10.

2. The Gospel of God

1. See 1:5; 2:4; 3:2. Béda Rigaux has given a survey of Paul's use of the term *euaggelion* in 1 Thessalonians in "Evangelium im ersten Thessalonicher-brief," 3-4.
2. See Rom 1:1; 15:16; 2 Cor 11:7. Elsewhere in the New Testament the expression occurs only in Mark 1:14 and 1 Pet 4:17.
3. That is, nine times in the letter to the Romans, eight times in each of the extant letters to the Corinthians, seven times in the letter to the Galatians, nine times in the letter to the Philippians, once in the letter to Philemon, and six times in 1 Thessalonians. An additional twelve occurrences are to be found in the deutero-Pauline letters. Cf. Robert Morgenthaler, *Statistik des neutestamentlichen Wortschätzes* (Zurich, Frankfurt: Gotthelf, 1958), 101.
4. That is, in addition to 1 Thess 3:16, three times in Romans, six in 1 Corinthians, two in 2 Corinthians, and seven in Galatians. A compound form of the verb *proeuaggelizō,* to declare the gospel beforehand, hapax in the New Testament, is to be found in Gal 3:8. In contrast, the verb occurs only twice in the deutero-Paulines, both times in Ephesians. Apropos the significance of this shift in usage, see my " 'The Gospel of Our Lord Jesus' (2 Thess 1, 8): A Symbolic Shift of Paradigm," 428-29, 439-40.
Whereas 63 percent of the occurrences of the noun *euaggelion* occur in the authentic Pauline correspondence, only 35 percent of the occurrences (nineteen of fifty-six) of the verb are to be found in Paul's letters. The verb is one of Luke's favorite expressions, found ten times in the gospel and fifteen times in Acts.
5. Peter Stuhlmacher has described Paul's use of the noun and its cognate verb as an indication of an exceptionally important phenomenon in Paul's thought. Cf. P. Stuhlmacher, *Das paulinische Evangelium,* 57.
6. See Piero Rossano, "Preliminari all'esegesi di 1 Tess 2, 1-12," *BeO* 7 (1965): 117-21, 119, and my *Studies* 24, 184-85. See further Béda Rigaux, *The Letters of St. Paul* (Chicago: Franciscan Herald, 1968), 122; Gérard Therrien, *Le discernement dans les écrits pauliniens,* Ebib (Paris: Gabalda, 1973), 65; and Johannes Schoon-Janssen, *Umstritten "Apologien" in den Paulus-briefen: Studien zur rhetorischen Situation des 1. Thessalonicherbriefes, des Galaterbriefes und des Philipperbriefes,* 39-65.
7. See Willi Marxsen, "Auslegung von 1 Thess 4, 13-18," 24; *Der erste Brief an die Thessalonicher,* 43; *Einleitung in das Neue Testament: Eine Einführung in ihre Probleme* (4th rev. ed.; Gütersloh: Mohn, 1978), 47.
8. "*His* gospel," says Marxsen (*Der erste Brief,* 36). This analysis has

led Marxsen to further reflection on the relationship between the subjective character and the objective content of the message. See *Der erste Brief,* 36–37.

9. *To euaggelion hēmōn,* literally, "the message of us." The NIV, NJB, and RNAB translate the phrase as "our gospel," the translation that appeared in the RSV (cf. the New Translation's "our Good News"). "Our gospel" is more simple than the NRSV's cumbersome rendition of *to euaggelion* as "the message of the gospel," here and in 2:4. Striving for a more fluid translation, the REB offers as a paraphrase "we brought you the gospel," an expression that lessens the intensity of the contrast between the first- and second-person pronouns in Paul's Greek text.

10. See 2 Thess 2:14; 2 Tim 2:8.

11. Cf. Jer 12:3; 17:10; Ps 16:3 (LXX); Prov 17:3.

12. According to Jewett, the *kardia* is "the center of man" (*Paul's Anthropological Terms,* 314). See, further, my *Studies,* 189–90.

13. See 1:5; 2:2, 4, 8, 9; 3:2.

14. See Jewett, *Paul's Anthropological Terms,* 346.

15. They accepted it for what it really was. Cf. 2:13.

16. While the NRSV, NIV, NJB, REB, and the New Translation render the Greek phrase in similar fashion, that is, some variant of "in spite of great opposition," the RNAB offers a more subjective rendition, "with much struggle."

17. Cf. "God gave us the courage to speak" in NJB and the New Translation.

18. See W. C. van Unnik, "The Christian's Freedom of Speech in the New Testament," in *Sparsa Collecta,* 2. NovT Sup, 30 (Leiden: Brill, 1980), 269–89, and "The Semitic Background of *parrēsia* in the New Testament," 290–306. See Albert-Marie Denis, "L'apôtre Paul," 251–59; Stanley B. Marrow, "*Parrhesia* and the New Testament" and *Speaking the Word Fearlessly: Boldness in the New Testament.*

The verb *parrēsiazomai* is frequently used in Acts, but Paul himself uses it only in 2:2. He uses the cognate noun *parrēsia* four times (2 Cor 3:12; 7:4; Phil 1:20; Phlmn 8). Van Unnik renders this noun as "freedom of speech," stating that it became an important element in Christian vocabulary ("Semitic Background," 306) and that it has its place in the missionary practice of the Apostle ("Freedom of Speech," 276). Louw and Nida, however, merely assign the *parrēs-* word group to the semantic domain of attitudes and emotions, under the rubric of "courage, boldness," one of twenty-four categories within this domain. See Johannes P. Louw and Eugene A. Nida, eds., *Greek-English Lexicon of the New Testament Based on Seminatic Domains,* vol. 1, 307.

19. See Denis, "L'apôtre Paul," 252–53; my *Studies,* 191.

20. See Beker, *Paul the Apostle,* 3.

21. See my *Studies,* 185–87.

22. See Marrow, "*Parrhesia,*" 432–36; Ceslas Spicq, "*parrēsia,*" in *Notes de lexicographie néo-testamentaire,* vol. 3: *Supplément,* 526–33, esp. 526–29; Jan Lambrecht, "A Call to Witness by All: Evangelisation in 1 Thessalonians," 326.

23. See van Unnik, "Freedom of Speech," 276, and the REB's "we declared the gospel of God to you frankly and fearlessly."

24. See Victor C. Pfitzner, *Paul and the Agon Motif: Traditional Athletic Imagery in the Pauline Literature*, esp. 111-15; 126-29.

25. See Pfitzner, *The Agon Motif*, 23-37, and the citation of Dio Chrysostom quoted above, 16.

26. See 1:8; 2:1-2, 3-4, 5-7, 13; 4:7, 8; 5:6, 9, 15. To these can be added 5:4-5, which, however, does not use the distinctive "*alla* – but" to underscore the contrast.

27. See 2:3, 5-6, 10, 11; 5:23.

28. The antithetical style is characteristic feature of the Hellenistic philosophers. See above, 16-17, and my *Studies*, 184, n. 57.

29. Because of their choice of the word "conviction" as a translation for Paul's Greek *plērophoria*, the editors of the NRSV along with most modern translators of the text render Paul's third use of the preposition *en* in 1:5b as "with."

In the Greek text, as published in *The Greek New Testament* (3d ed. corrected; Stuttgart: United Bible Societies, 1988), and the *Greek-English New Testament* (2d rev. ed.; Stuttgart: Deutsche Bibelgesellschaft, 1985) – the Greek text popularly known as the twenty-sixth edition of Nestle-Aland (N-A[26]) – the preposition *en* is repeated in each member of the three-part *repetitio*. The editors have enclosed the second and third use of the preposition within brackets, thereby indicating that the presence of the word in the text is disputed. The textual dispute does not affect the sense of Paul's words.

Apparently because of this situation, the editors of *The Greek New Testament* have not cited the grounds for the dispute in the textual apparatus nor is the dispute commented upon by Bruce M. Metzger in *Textual Commentary*. The basis for the dispute, as indicated in the critical apparatus of the *Greek-English New Testament*, is that in the latter two cases the preposition does not appear in several ancient manuscripts, including the Codex Sinaiticus. Since the repetition of the preposition is not necessary for the meaning of Paul's words, it is more likely that scribes omitted it in the second and third instances – to improve the style of the text – than that they added the preposition in these two cases.

Mathaeus Chattuvakulam notes that while the *en* could have instrumental or modal significance, it is the modal meaning that is predominant. See Chattuvakulam, "The Efficacy of the Word of God according to St. Paul," 41.

30. See J. Terence Forestell, "The Letters to the Thessalonians," *JBC*, 229.

31. See Rom 15:18-19; Gal 3:5. See further Barrett, *The Signs of an Apostle*, 42, 122, n. 80.

32. The Christian Community Bible, nonetheless, renders 1:5b as "miracles, Holy Spirit and plenty of everything were given to you," interpreting the verse as an indication of the manifestations that accompanied, and therefore authenticated, the preaching, rather than as an indication of the power of the preaching itself. Such an interpretation is also to be found in a few commentators, for instance, Amiot, Cerfaux, Gutjahr, Tarazi, van Unnik, and Wanamaker. See, for example, Lucien Cerfaux, *Christ in the Theology*

of St. Paul, 286, and Paul Nadim Tarazi, *1 Thessalonians: A Commentary,* 49–52.

More accurate, in my judgment, is the remark of D. E. H. Whiteley: "It was not the power to work miracles, at least not 'miracles' in the sense of healings, etc., but the power to work the 'miracle' of causing the heathen to believe." Cf. D. E. H. Whiteley, *Thessalonians in the Revised Standard Version,* New Clarendon Bible (London: Oxford, 1969), 36. See, further, the discussion in the doctoral dissertation of Chattuvakulam, "The Efficacy of the Word of God," 40–46, and the argumentation of Helmut Koester in "Apostel und Gemeinde in den Briefen an die Thessalonicher," 287–98, 288–89.

33. See 2:13: "God's word, which is also at work [*energetai*] among you." See also Rom 1:16: "the gospel: it is the power of God for salvation."

34. Wanamaker states that "it is difficult to separate 'in power' from the subsequent words 'in the Holy Spirit,' because the source of this power for Paul was the Holy Spirit" (Wanamaker, *Thessalonians,* 78).

35. In this regard Lucien Cerfaux, the eminent Roman Catholic Pauline scholar, wrote: "It goes without saying that the distinction between the person of the Holy Spirit and the divine sphere of the Spirit, which is established in theory, is not an easy thing for the exegete of Paul's writing to apply. . . . It is not always possible, and it is not always of any use to set the limits to a word: it is much better to understand each word or passage in the imprecise meaning which it had in Paul's mind." See Cerfaux, *Christ,* 295–96.

Grammarians such as Nigel Turner and Maximilian Zerwick explicitly state that in 1:5 Paul is simply making reference to the divine Spirit that moves Paul and his companions to proclaim the gospel. Cf. N. Turner, *A Grammar of New Testament Greek,* 3: *Syntax* (Edinburgh: T. & T. Clark, 1963), 175; M. Zerwick, *Graecitas biblica Novi Testamenti exemplis illustratur* (5th rev. and augmented ed.; Rome: Pontifical Biblical Institute, 1966), 59.

36. See Gen 1:2.

37. See Gal 3:2. See further Max-Alain Chevallier, *Esprit de Dieu, paroles d'hommes: le rôle de l'esprit dans les ministères de la parole selon l'apôtre Paul,* 109–10; *Souffle de Dieu: le Saint-Esprit dans le Nouveau Testament,* 230.

38. See F. F. Bruce, *1 and 2 Thessalonians,* 14. See also Denis, who hesitatingly suggests "persuasion" as an alternative translation, even though he later offers "conviction" as an alternative. See Denis, "L'apôtre Paul," 245, 247.

39. See Ernest Best, *A Commentary on the First and Second Epistles to the Thessalonians,* 75–76; B. C. Johanson, *To All the Brethren,* 84; and Charles Wanamaker, who cites Traugott Holtz, whom he seems to have misinterpreted. See Wanamaker, *Thessalonians,* 79, and Holtz, *Der erste Brief,* 47. Johanson writes about the objective and subjective qualities, opining that the third member of the triad constitutes as *ethos* appeal.

40. See Gerhard Delling, *"plērophoria,"* TDNT, vol. 6, 310–11, 311; Bartolomäus Henneken, *Verkündigung und Prophetie im 1. Thessalonicherbrief. Ein Beitrag zur Theologie des Wortes Gottes,* 36.

41. See Béda Rigaux, *Saint Paul: Les épîtres aux Thessaloniciens,* 378;

"Evangelium," 3-10. See also Delling, *"plērophoria,"* 311; Otto Kuss, *Die Thessalonicherbriefe,* 13; Henneken, *Verkündigung und Prophetie,* 36-37; Tarazi, *Thessalonians,* 52-53; Ceslas Spicq, *"plērophoreō, plērophoria,"* in *Notes de lexicographie néo-testamentaire,* vol. 2, 707-9, 707; and Hans Dieter Betz, "The Problem of Rhetoric and Theology according to the Apostle Paul," who notes that the term *plērophoria* has a rhetorical background (22, n. 32).

42. See my "The First Letter to the Thessalonians," *NJBC,* 774.

43. J. Paul Sampley identifies the patterns of Paul's thought and the things for which he gives thanks in prayer as an indication of the realities that matter within Paul's thought world. See Sampley, "From Text to Thought: The Route to Paul's Ways." In *Pauline Theology,* vol. 1, edited by J. M. Bassler, 3-14, 11-12.

44. See the brief discussion by Caroline Vander Stichele in "The Concept of Tradition and 1 and 2 Thessalonians," 502-3, n. 13.

45. In the NRSV the two phrases appear in inverted order: "word of God that you heard from us." Were one of these genitives an objective genitive and the other a subjective genitive, the complexity of Paul's expression would not be so manifest. In fact, however, both genitives are subjective.

46. From *kērrysō,* the verb used by Paul in 2:9. Cf. Rom 2:21; 10:8, 14, 15; 1 Cor 1:23; 9:27; 15:11, 12; 2 Cor 1:19; 4:5; 11:4; Gal 2:2; 5:11; Phil 1:15. The verb is used with some frequency in the Synoptics and Acts, but not in the fourth gospel. In Paul the technical expression "to proclaim the gospel" *(kēryssō to euaggelion)* occurs only in 2:9 and Gal 2:2, but it is also to be found in Matt 4:23; 9:35; 24:14; 26:13 (where it describes Christian missionary activity); Mark 1:14; 13:10; 14:9; (16:15); and Col 1:23. Paul uses the cognate noun *kērygma,* "preaching" or "proclamation" sparingly (Rom 16:25; 1 Cor 1:21; 2:4; 14:14; cf. Titus 4:17) and the cognate noun *kēryx,* "preacher" or "herald," not at all (cf. 1 Tim 2:7; 2 Tim 1:11).

47. "To speak" *(laleō)* and "word" *(logos)* are important terms in the *lexis* of 1 Thessalonians, being used four (1:8; 2:2, 4, 16) and nine (1:5, 6, 8; 2:5, 13 [three times]; 4:15, 18) times, respectively. Curiously, Paul does not use another verb "to speak," *legō,* cognate with *logos,* with the same frequency and force as he uses *laleō. Legō* appears only in 4:15 and 5:3.

48. Elsewhere Paul uses the verb *laleō* in 1:8; 2:4; and 16.

49. On the authenticity of this passage, see my *Studies,* 27-28, 97-106, 124-34.

50. In his little study of the foundation of the church at Thessalonica, which, regrettably, presumes the authenticity of 2 Thessalonians, L.-M. Dewailly repeatedly emphasizes that "speaking" is *the* function of the apostle. See *La jeune église de Thessalonique,* esp. 24, 43.

51. See Gerhard Schneider, *"areskō," EDNT,* vol. 1, 151.

52. See Wanamaker, *Thessalonians,* 96-97.

53. See Plutarch, *Moralia,* 48E-74E. Marco Adinolfi offers a selection of texts from Aristo, Aristophanes, Aristotle, Democritus, Demosthenes, Dio Cassius, Diogenes Laertius, Epictetus, Euripides, Horace, Isocrates, Lucianus, Marcus Aurelius, Musonius Rufus, Plato, Plutarch, Polibius, Seneca, Xeno-

phon, and St. Augustine in order to illustrate the meaning of *parrēsia* in the Greco-Roman world. See Adinolfi, *La prima lettera ai Tessalonicesi nel mondo greco-romano*, 72-78.

54. See M. MacLuhan, *The Medium Is the Message* (New York: Bantam, 1967).

55. Cf. 1:6; 2:2 as well as the remarks of Helmut Koester, referenced above, 41 and 235, n. 32.

56. Cf. 2:7-12 and the discussion above, 25-30.

57. All three terms, *hosiōs, dikaiōs,* and *amemptōs,* are adverbs in Greek. A more literal translation of Paul's words might read: "we were among you in a pure, upright, and blameless fashion."

58. The adverb *hosiōs* is not otherwise found in the New Testament, but the corresponding adjective, *hosios,* is found eight times. The three occurrences of the vocable in Acts are in biblical citations: Ps 16:10 in Acts 2:27; Isa 55:3 in Acts 13:34, 35.

59. See Rigaux, *Thessaloniciens,* 426.

60. See Best, *Thessalonians,* 105.

61. Some authors (e.g., Lightfoot, von Dobschutz, Hauck, Masson, Wanamaker) make such distinctions, almost as if Paul distinguished the *fas* from the *ius* in the Romans' *fas et ius.* It should, moreover, be observed that the two terms were not adequately distinguished in Hellenistic literature. In fact, *hosi* – and *dikai* – seem to constitute a traditional pairing. Cf. Luke 1:75; Eph 4:24.

62. Within the New Testament, outside of Luke 1:6 and Heb 8:7, the term occurs only in Phil 2:15; 3:6; and 1 Thess 2:10; 3:13; 5:23. In the latter two occurrences, the term occurs in a "wish prayer," where it has an eschatological nuance. On the role of these wish prayers, see Gordon P. Wiles, *Paul's Intercessory Prayers: The Significance of the Intercessory Prayer Passages in the Letters of St Paul,* 45-71.

63. See Rigaux, *Thessaloniciens,* 427. Rigaux (427-28) further notes that the three expressions used by Paul in 2:10 occur together in several passages of the Prima Clementis.

64. In Israel's wisdom tradition the pairing of these two terms constitutes a classic portrayal of the just person. Cf. Job 1:1, 8; 2:3; 12:4; 15:14; 22:19; Wis 10:5; 18:20-21 (cf. 10:15). In the book of Job, where *amemptos* occurs thirteen times, it renders nine different Hebrew terms.

65. Cf. Phil 3:6, "as to righteousness under the law, blameless" (*kata dikaiosynēn tēn en nomō genomenon amemptos*).

66. "*Planē* – deceit," can have a passive or an active meaning. Rigaux has opted for an active meaning, "error" (the translation of the RSV) and suggested that there is a progression from "*planē*" to "*dolos* – trickery" (*Thessaloniciens,* 406-8; similarly, Denis, "L'apôtre messianique," 282). Given Paul's *repetitio,* it is preferable to take the term in an active sense, interpreting "*ek planēs* – from deceit" as virtually synonymous with "*en dolō* – trickery." Walter Schmithals offers "fraud" or "deception" as a meaning for the former expression. Cf. Walter Schmithals, *Paul and the Gnostics,* 144.

Regarding the biblical and possibly apocalyptic connotations of the expression, see Denis, "L'apôtre messianique," 272–75; George Lyons, *Pauline Autobiography: Toward a New Understanding*, 193–96.

67. Some interpreters (for example, Rigaux, *Thessaloniciens*, 407; Leon Morris, *The First and Second Epistles to the Thessalonians*, 71; Lyons, *Pauline Autobiography*, 194–96; and Jewett, *The Thessalonian Correspondence*, 105–6) believe that the use of this term indicates that Paul and his companions had been accused of some form of sexual misconduct while in Macedonia, but such an interpretation is unwarranted in view of the literary form of the pericope and Paul's use of the rhetorical device of *repetitio*. See Schoon-Janssen, *Umstrittene "Apologien,"* 58.

68. See Malherbe, "Gentle as a Nurse," 45–47, who cites Dio Chrysostom's *Oratio* 32. The true philosopher speaks "with purity [*katharōs*] and without guile [*kai adolōs*]," "not for the sake of glory [*mete doxes charin*], nor making false pretensions for the sake of gain [*met' 'ep agryrio*]." Unfortunately this passage from Dio Chrysostom, cited by Denis ("L'apôtre Paul," 283) and many authors who have drawn their inspiration from Malherbe, is not cited in Adinolfi's survey of passages (*La prima lettera*, 66–91) parallel to Paul's autobiographical confession. Adinolfi does, however, cite Dio's *Oratioa* at 37, 36 (*La prima lettera*, 70).

The choice of vocabulary in the *repetitio* of 2:3 is classic and typical of moral discourse, but it is rather unusual for Paul to use these terms. "*Planē* – deceit" and "*dolos* – trickery" are hapax in 1 Thessalonians; they occur only once (Rom 1:27) and twice (Rom 1:29; 2 Cor 12:16), respectively, in Paul's later correspondence. Among the three terms in Paul's *repetitio*, only "*akatharsia* – impure motives" occurs again in 1 Thessalonians, namely, in 4:7 (cf. Rom 1:24; 6:19; 2 Cor 12:21; Gal 5:19), where it is antithetical to "*hagiasmos* – holiness." Walter Schmithals interprets the term as "lack of integrity" (*Paul and the Gnostics*, 145).

69. That is, *pleonexia*, another stock item in the catalogues of vices.

70. See the *en hymin di'hymas* ("among you for your sake") of 1:6 and the *hymin tois pisteuousin* ("toward you believers") of 2:10.

71. See 1:5; 2:2, 4, 8, 9; 3:2 and the cognate *euaggelizesthai* in 3:6.

72. See 1:5, 6, 8; 2:5, 13 (3 times); 4:15, 18, and the verb *laleō*, "to speak," in 1:8; 2:2, 4, 16.

73. See 1:8; 2:16.

74. The verb is hapax in Paul's extant writings.

75. See 3:2, 7; 4:1, 10, 18; 5:11, 14. According to Otto Schmitz, "*parakalein* . . . serves in the NT to denote missionary proclamation and also as a kind of formula to introduce pastoral admonition." See Gustav Stählin and Otto Schmitz, "*parakaleō, paraklēsis,*" *TDTN*, vol. 5, 773–99, 799.

76. See 5:14.

77. In the New Testament, this verb is used only by Paul and only three times by him (3:4 and 2 Cor 13:2; Gal 5:21).

78. See 4:2. The noun *paraggelia* ("instructions") is hapax in Paul. The cognate verb, found in 4:11, is also used in 1 Cor 7:10 and 11:17.

79. That is, except for the infinitives of 2:2, 8 in which cases, however, the principal verb is in the first-person plural.

80. Strangely, the verb *akouō*, "to hear," cognate with *akoē*, does not appear in 1 Thessalonians even though it appears in each of the other extant letters written by Paul.

81. Rom 10:14-17 (18); Gal 3:2-5. Apart from 2:13 and 1 Cor 12:17, these are the only two passages in which Paul uses *akoē*, that is, three times in Romans and twice in Galatians.

82. J. D. G. Dunn, *Romans 9-16*, WBC, 38B (Dallas: Word, 1988), 628.

83. See Heinrich Schlier, *Der Römerbrief*, HTKNT, 6 (Freiburg, Basel, Vienna: Herder, 1977), 316.

84. See v. 13 and Dunn, *Romans*, 629.

85. See Rom 10:18. According to Dunn, "the chain is...reduced to one link." See Dunn, *Romans*, 630.

86. See C. E. B. Cranfield, *The Epistle to the Romans*, 2, ICC (Edinburgh: T. & T. Clark, 1979), 533, 535.

87. See also Gal 3:2, 5, where Paul uses the elliptic expression *akoē pisteōs*, "believing what you heard," literally, "the hearing of belief." E. P. Sanders has argued in favor of the accuracy of this sort of translation, but Hans Dieter Betz has rendered the phrase as the "proclamation of faith." See E. P. Sanders, *Paul and Palestinian Judaism: A Comparison of Patterns of Religion* (Philadelphia: Fortress, 1977), 482-83, and H. D. Betz, *Galatians*, Hermeneia (Philadelphia: Fortress, 1979), 133, 136.

Betz comments: "The term *akoē* implies that a message which was received by divine revelation is being proclaimed orally and heard. When heard in the sense of 'accepted' it creates faith because it carries with it a divine power – the 'power of the word' " (133, n. 50). See, further, F. F. Bruce, *The Epistle to the Galatians: A Commentary on the Greek Text*, NIGTC (Grand Rapids, Mich.: Eerdmans, 1982), 149. Bruce suggests that, in Galatians, Paul may have been influenced by Isa 53:1.

88. Cf. Dunn, *Romans*, 629, and Schlier, *Römerbrief*, 316-17, who speaks about the "messianic times."

89. Cf. 1 Cor 12:17, the only passage in which Paul uses the noun *akoē*, apart from 2:13 and the aforementioned Rom 10:14-18 and Gal 3:2-5.

90. This expression, "receive the word" (*dechesthai ton logon*), also seems to belong to the typical kerygmatic language of the early church. Within the New Testament it is to be found especially in Luke-Acts (Luke 8:13; Acts 8:14; 11:1; 17:11). Cf. Jas 1:21. In 2 Cor 11:4, Paul uses *dechesthai euaggelion* as an alternative formulation. Apropos *dechesthai*, see my *Studies*, 214, 218-19.

91. The verb is translated "welcome" in the NJB, REB, NIV, and The New Translation.

92. "Frequently the conception of a *hospitable reception* is present... which can designate theologically *acceptance* of the message of Jesus" (Gerd Petzke, *"dechomai,"EDNT*, vol. 1, 292). In Paul this usage is reflected in 2 Cor 7:15 and Gal 4:14.

93. See above n. 87. On the significance of the Thessalonians' faith, see "The Faith of the Thessalonians," in *Studies*, 209-29.

94. The various commentators understand the dative case (*tois pisteu-ousin*) in a variety of grammatical fashions. See *Studies*, 217, n. 44.

95. Note the use of the article in 1:7; 2:10, 13.

96. "Being a believer," Bultmann once wrote, "is not a static affair. It takes place in the flux of individual life." See Rudolf Bultmann, *"pisteō, ktl,"* *TDNT*, vol. 6, 174-228, 218.

97. *Paralabontes ... edexasthe ... logon theou* ("when you received the word of God, ... you accepted it"). In the reflection that follows I shall attempt to capture the nuance of Paul's use of the participle *paralabontes* "when you received." Paul's use of this participle poses a twofold problem for those who read his text in the NRSV. First, the editors have, for stylistic reasons, translated the present participle as if it were a subordinate clause introduced by a conjunction. In the Greek text a participial clause functions as the grammatical subject of the verb "*edexasthe* – accepted."

Secondly, and this may prove to be a bit more confusing for those who read Paul in English translation, Paul uses two different verbs in v. 13, namely, *paralambanō* – receive and *dechesthai* – accept. These two verbs also appear in 2 Cor 11:4, where they are similarly translated as "receive" and "accept." In 1 Thessalonians 1:6, however, *dexesthai* is translated as "receive" (not "accept" as in 2:13). To further compound matters, *paralambanō* is translated as "learn" (from us) in 4:1. In all other Pauline usages, the editors of the NRSV have translated Paul's *paralambanō* as "receive" (cf. 1 Cor 11:23; 15:1, 3; Gal 1:9, 12; Phil 4:9).

Of these instances 1 Cor 15:1 is particularly noteworthy because Paul writes of "receiving the gospel" (*paralambanō to euaggelion*). See Gal 1:9. In any case, it is important that one distinguish *paralambanō* – receive from *dechesthai* – accept in 2:13. See further the deutero-Pauline 2 Thess 3:6, "the tradition that they received from us" (*tēn paradosin hēn parelabosan par'hēmōn*) and the apropos comments of Caroline Vander Stichele, "The Concept of Tradition," 500-503.

Differences in the translations of *dechesthai* and *paralambanō* comparable to those of the NRSV are to be found in most of the recent English-language translations of 1 Thessalonians. Particularly confusing is the RNAB, which renders all three verbal expressions as "receive." Of those that have been cited in the present work, the NJB is alone in distinguishing *dechesthai* ("welcome") from *paralambanō*. The NJB, however, renders the expression *paralabontes logon akoēs par'hēmōn* as "you heard the word that we brought you," thereby distinguishing the subject of the participle ("we brought") from the subjective genitive qualifying the noun ("you heard"), whereas the Greek suggests a first-person plural subject in both instances.

98. See Vander Stichele, who correctly notes that "In 1 Thes 2, 13 the emphasis lies not on *paralambanō* but on the following *edexasthe*. The fact that the Thessalonians accepted the word of the apostle is what is stressed" ("The Concept of Tradition," 502).

99. See *Studies*, 304; Vander Stichele, "The Concept of Tradition"; and my *Introduction to the New Testament*, 11-12.

100. See Dewailly, *La jeune église*, 29; Richard Howard Davis, "Remem-

bering and Acting: A Study of the Moral Life in Light of I Thessalonians," 183, 250–56.

101. The "speak" (*laloumen*) of 2:4 has essentially the same meaning as does "declare the gospel of God" (*lalēsai to euaggelion tou theou*) in v. 2.

102. See 1:5.

103. Three times, viz., in 2:2, 8, 9. Cf. Rom 1:1; 15:16; 2 Cor 11:7. Interestingly, this expression does not occur in the deutero-Paulines (see, however, 1 Pet 4:17), not even in 2 Thessalonians, where the choice of vocabulary otherwise so slavishly imitates the *lexis* of 1 Thessalonians. See my *Letters That Paul Did Not Write*, 219–21.

104. That is, twice in 2:13. Cf. Rom 9:6; 1 Cor 14:36; 2 Cor 2:17; 4:2; Phil 1:14 (Col 1:25; 1 Tim 4:5; 2 Tim 2:9; Titus 2:5 and Heb 4:12; 13:7).

105. Cf. 4:15 and 2 Thess 3:1.

106. 3:2. Cf. Rom 15:19; 1 Cor 9:12; 2 Cor 2:12; 9:13; 10:14; Gal 1:7; Phil 1:27 (twice). See also 2 Thess 1:8 and my comments in that regard in "The Gospel of Our Lord Jesus."

107. Cf. my *Introduction*, 102–4; Metzger, *Textual Commentary*, 631. For the statistical evidence of the manuscripts whose reading differs from that chosen by the editors of N-A^{26} see K. Aland, *Text und Textwert der griechischen Handschriften*, II, 4, 306–10.

108. See above, 1–3. Since there is no extant papyrus witness to 3:2, the verse is not examined in Philip W. Comfort's *Early Manuscripts*.

109. That the Thessalonians to whom the letter is sent are called "brothers and sisters" (*adelphoi*) by Paul, Silvanus, and Timothy implies that Paul, Silvanus, and Timothy must be considered as their "brothers."

110. See 1 Cor 3:9; 2 Cor 6:1.

111. This "Western" reading is also attested by some of the Latin Church Fathers, especially, Ambrosiaster, Pelagius, and the Pseudo-Jerome.

112. In Rom 16:21, Paul calls Timothy "my co-worker" (*ho synergos mou*). In Phil 2:25, Epaphroditus is called "my brother and co-worker [*ton adelphon kai synergon*] and fellow soldier."

113. A later "corrector" of the Codex Claromontanus emended the manuscript so that it read "our brother and the servant of God and our co-worker" (*ton adelphon hēmōn kai diakonon tou theou kai synergon hēmōn*), a rather awkward reading that retains all the words of the (presumably) original text while purifying it of its theological boldness. This "corrected" reading is found in the majority of the medieval Greek manuscripts of the verse.

114. The KJV reflects the medieval Greek texts on which that version was based.

115. Similar translations are found in the NIV, NJB, RNAB, and REB. The similarity of these translations bears witness to the success of *The Greek New Testament*, a project that was initiated in order to meet the requirements of modern translators of the Bible.

The NJB's translation is not as quite as bold as that of the others. It renders *synergon tou theou* as "God's helper," as did the JB, rather than as "God's co-worker." For stylistic reasons, the NRSV ("in proclaiming"), the NIV and NJB ("in spreading"), and the REB ("in the service of") render the simple preposition *"en* – in" by means of a prepositional phrase. Paul's preposition probably reflects the Hebrew *b,* that is, "with regard to."

116. It is interesting to note that "gospel," from the Old English "god" (good) and "spell" (tale), has essentially the same etymology as does the Greek *euaggelion,* from the adverb *"eu* – well" and the root *"aggel* – to announce." On the meaning of "gospel," see my "Gospel."

117. Cf. 2:13.

118. See 14:15; 1:8.

119. See Söding, "Der Erste Thessalonicherbrief und die frühe paulinische Evangeliumsverkündigung: Zur Frage einer Entwicklung der paulinischen Theologie," 187-96.

120. Note the explanatory *"gar* – for" at the beginning of v. 14.

121. Note the *houtōs kai,* which introduces Paul's deduction. Some of the ancient manuscripts, including the Codex Vaticanus (B), a tenth-century minuscule from Mount Athos (1739), and the Syriac Harclean text, somewhat modify the Greek word order, thereby accentuating that as Jesus was raised from the dead, so God will likewise bring with him those who have fallen asleep, that is, have died. This variant reading is: *houtōs ho theos kai tous koimēthentas dia tou Iēsou axei syn autō.*

122. See 4:17.

123. D. E. H. Whiteley, *Thessalonians,* 39.

124. Cf. 2:13.

125. See 1 Cor 8:4-7(8); 10:19. The only other passages in his letters in which Paul speaks about idols are Rom 2:22; 1 Cor 12:2; and 2 Cor 6:16.

126. Cf. Exod 20:4; Deut 5:8, where the word *eidōlon* appears in the Greek Bible, with the meaning that it has elsewhere throughout the LXX.

127. See Hendrix, "Thessalonicans," 24.

128. See Hendrix, "Thessalonicans," 148-52. On the Cabiros cult, see Edson, "Cults of Thessaloniki," 188-89; Robert Maxwell Evans, "Eschatology and Ethics: A Study of Thessalonica and Paul's Letters to the Thessalonians," 68-71; Jewett, The *Thessalonian Correspondence,* 127-32, 165-70. Jewett's exploitation of the available evidence has been criticized by Koester, in "From Paul's Eschatology to the Apocalyptic Schemata of 2 Thessalonians," 443-45.

129. Hendrix, "Thessalonicans," 155-58. See, further, 159-69 for a discussion of the representation of Thessalonike-Eleutheria and Aphrodite-Honomia on the eral coinage.

130. See Hendrix, "Thessalonicans," 170-77, and "Archaeology and Eschatology at Thessalonica," 115-16. Apropos the imperial cult and the "temple of Caesar" at Thessalonica, see Evans, "Eschatology and Ethics," 65-68; Hendrix, "Thessalonicans," *passim,* but esp. 61-62, 296-302, 326-35, and "Archaeology and Eschatology," 115.

131. See Hendrix, "Thessalonicans," 45-54; "Archaeology and Eschatology," 116-17. Fragments of the statue were discovered in 1939.

132. See Hendrix, "Thessalonicans," 36-37.

133. See Hendrix, "Thessalonicans," 126-29.

134. See Evans, "Eschatology and Ethics," 63-79, and Donfried, "Cults," 337-46.

135. A.P. 9, 59. See Hendrix, "Thessalonicans," 79–80.

136. See Hendrix, "Thessalonicans," 323.

137. See 1:1, 2, 3, 4, 8, 9 (twice); 2:2, 4 (twice), 5, 8, 9, 10, 12, 13 (three times), 14, 15; 3:2, 9 (twice), 11, 13; 4:1, 3, 5, 7, 8, 14, 16; 5:9, 18, 23. In all but nine instances (1:1, 9; 2:4, 5, 13, 15; 4:1, 16; 5:18), *theos* is accompanied by the article. On Paul's notion of God, see "The Theology of Paul's First Letter to the Thessalonians," in *Studies*, 230–52, and "God in the First Letter."

138. Cf. Rom 2:22 and 2 Cor 6:16.

139. For the view that Paul's paraenesis on the avoidance of *"porneia* – fornication" (4:3–8) is an exhortation to the Christians of Thessalonica to turn from the cult of Aphrodite and to be on guard against the insertion of sexual-erotic elements into their religious practice, see Herbert Ulonska, "Christen und Heiden: Die paulinische Paränese in I Thess 4, 3–8." This situation might explain Paul's paraenetic emphasis on the will of God and living as God's people ("sanctification"). In any event, the poet Antipater makes reference to the Thessalonians' devotion to Aphrodite.

140. The verb *epistrephō* is but rarely used by Paul. In its two other occurrences (2 Cor 3:16; Gal 4:9), it is also used of a religious "conversion," albeit in the latter instance of a turning away from God.

141. See 4:5 and Gal 4:8 (cf. 2 Thess 1:8; Titus 1:16).

142. See Jacques Guillet, "Le titre biblique *Le Dieu vivant*," in *Mélanges offerts au Père de Lubac*, vol. 1, Théologie, 56 (Paris: Aubier, 1963), 11.

143. Cf. Johannes Munck, "I Thess i. 9–10 and the Missionary Preaching of Paul: Textual Exegesis and Hermeneutic Reflexions."

144. Cf. Rom 1:25.

145. See Earl Richard, "Early Pauline Thought: An Analysis of 1 Thessalonians," 42, and Joseph Plevnik, "Pauline Presuppositions."

146. See, however, 5:24.

147. Apropos Paul's use of credal formulas to speak about the resurrection of Jesus in 1:9–10 and 4:14 see my *Studies*, 253–63, 339–45.

148. See my *Studies*, 256, 341–42.

149. As for the anti-Semitism of this passage, see the discussion below, 171. It is, in any case, imperative that Paul be understood within the context of Judaism. As for the authenticity of this passage, see below, 145–146.

150. The term *"anamenō* – wait for" is hapax in the New Testament. See Paul-Emile Langevin, *Jésus Seigneur et l'eschatologie: Exégèse de textes prépauliniens*, 67–73.

151. See B. Rigaux, "Vocabulaire chrétien antérieur à la première épître aux Thessaloniciens," 384–85.

152. The relative infrequency of the expression "kingdom of God" in the deutero-Pauline literature confirms the non-Pauline character of the expression. The expression, absent from 1 Timothy and Titus (as well as from 1 Peter), is found but once in Ephesians (5:5) and 2 Thessalonians (1:5) and twice each in Colossians (1:13; 4:11) and 2 Timothy (4:1, 18).

153. See Ulrich Luz, *"Basileia, as, hē,"* EDNT, vol. 1, 201–5, 201.

154. See C. H. Dodd, *The Parables of the Kingdom* (rev. ed.; Digswell Place: Nisbet, 1961), 21.

155. See J. Christiaan Beker, "Recasting Pauline Theology: The Coherence-Contingency Scheme as Interpretive Model," 22-23.

156. John M. G. Barclay writes: "We are fortunate to be able to reconstruct with some confidence Paul's gospel message as he preached it in Thessalonica.... In its outline and in its central focus that picture is unmistakably apocalyptic" ("Thessalonica and Corinth: Social Contrasts in Pauline Christianity," 50).

157. See the brief description of these titles in Earl Richard, *Jesus: One and Many: The Christological Concept of New Testament Authors*, 325-29. Apropos the *"Huios* – Son" title, see my *Studies*, 283-84.

158. See Thomas Söding, "Die frühe paulinische Evangeliumsverkündigung," 187, who argues that the return of Christ is not only the center of the gospel but also that it qualifies Christian existence in its totality.

159. Pace Heinz Giesen, "Naherwartung des Paulus in 1 Thess 4, 3-18?"

160. Cf. Ceslas Spicq, *Agape in the New Testament*, vol. 2: *Agape in the Epistles of St. Paul*, 16.

161. See my *Studies*, 239-40.

162. As 1 Thess 1:4-5 points to a relationship between election and the proclamation of the gospel, the deutero-Pauline 2 Thess 2:14 points to a link between the call and the proclamation of the gospel: "he called you through our proclamation of the good news."

163. See Louw and Nida, *"kaleō, ktl."* in Louw and Nida, *Greek-English Lexicon*, vol. 1, 424.

164. The verb *"douleuō* – serve," appearing later in Romans and Galatians, and once in Philippians, is hapax in 1 Thessalonians, precisely at 1:9.

165. Cf. Eph 4:1; Col 1:10.

166. See Davis, "Remembering and Acting," 183, 253-54, and Vander Stichele, "The Concept of Tradition," 499-504.

167. This is the NRSV translation of *paradidōmi* in 1 Cor 15:1-2, where we find the correlative terms *"paradidōmi* – proclaim" and *"paralambanō* – receive" in a single context.

168. H. Balz, *"hagios, ktl.," EDNT*, vol. 1, 16-20, 20.

169. See *Studies*, 308, and Marco Adinolfi, "La santità del matrimonio in 1 Tess. 4, 1-8," 165-66.

170. See Vander Stichele, "The Concept of Tradition," 502.

171. Although the noun *paraggelia* is hapax within the authentic Pauline corpus at 1 Thess 4:2, the verb *paraggellō*, hapax in 1 Thessalonians at 4:11, also appears in 1 Cor 7:10 and 11:17.

172. Paul uses the adverb *"axiōs* – worthy" only in paraenesis, where it denotes the goal and motivation of Christian action. See Peter Trummer, *"axios," EDNT*, vol. 1, 113.

173. Cf. Georg Schneider, *"areskō," EDNT*, vol. 1, 151.

174. 2:12, 4:7, and 5:24 are the only three explicit references to the "call" of the Thessalonians in the letter. On "calling" in 1 Thessalonians see I. Howard Marshall, "Election and Calling to Salvation in 1 and 2 Thessalonians," 269-70.

175. So Rigaux, *Thessaloniciens,* 515. Most commentators, however, pass over the particle in silence. It is, in any case, absent from some of the ancient manuscripts and has been deleted from the Codex Bezae Cantrabrigiensis.

176. Cf. DBF's explicative *kai* (Par. 442, 9; 229).

177. The use of the repeated article in 4:8, *to pneuma autou to hagion,* contrasts sharply with the simple "Holy Spirit" of 1:5 (*pneumati hagiō*) and 1:6 (*pneumatos hagiou*).

178. On these prayers, see especially Wiles, *Paul's Intercessory Prayers,* 45-71.

179. In the LXX the biblical *emeth* is frequently rendered as "*alēthinos* – true." Cf. Exod 34:6; 2 Sam 7:28; 1 Kings 10:6; 17:24; 2 Chr 9:5; 15:3; Ps 19:9; 86:15; Prov 12:19; Zech 8:3; Jer 2:21; Dan 10:1. Elsewhere in the LXX *emeth* is rendered as "*pistos* – faithful." Cf. Prov 14:25 (comp. 3 Macc 2:11).

180. The point was made more than a half-century ago by Sri Lanka's T. Isaac Tambyah, who, however, curiously identified the *theo-* root as a reference to Jesus and the phrase as a reference to John 13:34; 15:12. Cf. T. I. Tambyah, "*Theodidaktoi:* A Suggestion of an Implication of the Deity of Christ." Without specifying the Jesus reference, Spicq has identified the phrase as an allusion to the love command, a significant segment of early Christian baptismal catechesis. Cf. C. Spicq, *Agape,* 2, 18. See also the discussion of *theodidaktos* in Wanamaker, *Thessalonians,* 160.

181. See the discussion by Abraham Malherbe in Malherbe, "Exhortation in First Thessalonians," 253-54. Malherbe draws attention not only to the fact that the Epicurians urged self-reliance, but also to the fact that they had a self-serving and utilitarian view of friendship.

182. See Calvin J. Roetzel, "*Theodidaktoi* and Handwork in Philo and I Thessalonians," esp. 330.

183. See Rom 12:10, the only other passage where Paul treats the topic with this specific term.

184. Cf. 3:12. In 1 Thessalonians there is, as has already been noted apropos 3:13 and 5:23, some topical similarity between the content of Paul's wish prayers and his moral exhortation. 3:12 can almost be considered a prayerful commentary upon 4:9-12. See Marshall, "Election and Calling," 270-71.

185. "*Adelphoi,*" in form, a masculine plural with the meaning "brothers," can bear the connotation "brothers and sisters." Cf. Gerhard Friedrich, "Die erste Brief an die Thessalonicher," 212-13, and Johannes Beutler, "*adelphos, ktl.,*" *EDNT,* vol. 1, 28-30. In 1 Thessalonians, "*adelphos* – brother" appears some nineteen times, fourteen of which are in the vocative plural, with the meaning "brothers and sisters" (1:1, 4; 2:1, 9, 14, 17; 3:7; 4:1, 10, 13; 5:1, 4, 12, 25). There are three additional plural uses of the noun (4:10; 5:26, 27) and two uses in the singular (1:2; 4:6).

186. The cognate noun "*paraggelia* – instruction," found in 4:2, is hapax within the authentic Pauline corpus. The verb "*paraggelō* – command" is found in 1 Cor 7:10 and 11:17 in addition to 4:2.

187. For stylistic reasons, the NRSV has translated the vocative "*adelphoi* – brothers and sisters" of 4:10 by "beloved."

188. See Bjerkelund, *Parakalō,* 34-108.

189. Paul uses a perfect passive participle, suggesting that a past action continues to have effect in the present. See my *Studies,* 236, 354.

190. Cf. C. H. Dodd, "A Hidden Parable in the Fourth Gospel," in *More New Testament Studies* (Manchester: University Press, 1968), 30–40, and my *These Things Have Been Written,* 143–46.

191. In addition to the rabbinic texts cited by Dodd in "A Hidden Parable," 36–38, see Gutierrez, *La paternité spirituelle,* 15–83, and John W. Miller, *Biblical Faith and Fathering: Why We Call God "Father"* (New York: Paulist, 1989), 69–90.

192. See "On Rewards and Punishments," 157. See Roetzel, *"Theodidak-toi,"* 129–31.

193. See Roetzel, *"Theodidaktoi,"* 330–31.

194. Cf. Rom 15:20; 2 Cor 5:9.

195. See Roetzel, *"Theodidaktoi,"* 330.

196. See my *Studies,* 232–34.

197. See the discussion above, 25–30.

198. According to Daniel Wallace, v. 10 functions as a summary of the eschatological teaching Paul had given, the expansion and explanation of which is to be found in 4:13–5:11. See Wallace, "A Textual Problem in 1 Thessalonians 1:10: *Ek tēs Orgēs* vs. *Apo tēs Orgēs."* Wallace opines that, contrary to the reading chosen for N-A[26]·GNT[3], *apo* is the better reading of Paul's text.

199. Cf. Birger A. Pearson, "1 Thessalonians 2, 13–16: A Deutero-Pauline Interpolation," 81; Alois Stoeger, "Wrath," in J. B. Bauer, ed., *Encyclopedia of Biblical Theology,* vol. 3 (London: Sheed and Ward, 1970), 1010; Anthony J. Tambasco, *A Theology of Atonement and Paul's Vision of Christianity,* Zacchaeus Studies: New Testament (Collegeville, Minn.: Liturgical Press, 1991), 31–34. Romans is the only other letter in the authentic Pauline corpus in which Paul explicitly writes about God's wrath (Cf. Rom 1:18; 2:5, 8; 3:5; 4:15; 5:9; 9:22 (2x); 12:19; 13:4, 5). Cf. Eph 2:3; 5:6; Col 3:6. It is only in 1 Thess 1:10 that Paul explicitly describes God's wrath as *"mellousa* – that is coming."

200. The Greek *parousia* literally means "presence." When contrasted with absence, it can acquire the connotation of "arrival" or "coming." Paul uses the term with its ordinary meaning of "presence" in 2 Cor 10:10 and Phil 2:12 and with the connotation of "coming" in 1 Cor 16:7; 2 Cor 7:6, 7; Phil 1:26. In 1 Thessalonians, however, the term is used in a very particular sense, namely, to designate the coming of Jesus as Lord at the close of the present age. Cf. 1 Thess 2:19; 3:13; 4:15; 5:23 (cf. 1 Cor 15:23). The term is also used in this quasi-technical sense in 2 Thess 2:1, 8, 9, in dependence on 1 Thessalonians, as well as in Matt 24:3, 27, 37, 39; Jas 5:7, 8; 2 Pet 1:16; 34 (cf. 3:12); and 1 John 2:28.

201. Paul also uses this verb in Gal 5:21. Elsewhere in the New Testament the verb appears only in Acts 2:31.

202. Within the New Testament this verb belongs to the vocabulary of Luke-Acts, where it appears ten times. Within the authentic Pauline corpus, it is hapax in 1 Thess 4:6, but it also appears in the deutero-Pauline 1 Tim 5:21 and 2 Tim 2:14 and 4:1. See also Heb 2:6.

203. The NRSV's literal translation, with semantic focus, allows each of these emphases to be underscored (cf. RNAB, the New Translation). The RSV's translation, "as we solemnly forewarned you," with syntactic focus highlights the hendiadic nature of the expression (cf. NIV, NJB, REB).

204. In his review of my *Studies*, Ernest Best (*JTS* 36 [1985]: 454) noted that I had changed my view as to how the "*Kyrios* – Lord" of 4:7 was to be interpreted. In my earlier work (see my *Studies*, 191) I was of the opinion that the referent was God; later (see my *Studies*, 271, 280) I expressed the view that the referent was Jesus. The present analysis confirms the later opinion.

205. It might possibly be argued that in 3:11 the use of "*hēmōn* – our" serves a similar function. The last appearance of the expression "*Kyrios hēmōn* – our Lord" occurs in the final greeting (5:28).

206. Cf. Rom 1:18.

207. See my *Studies*, 97–98, and, more fully, Tjitze Baarda, " 'Maar de toorn is over hen gekomen' (1 Thess 2:16c)" and Ingo Broer, " 'Der ganze Zorn ist schon über sie gekommen': Bemerkungen zur Interpolationshypothese und zur Interpretation von 1 Thess 2, 14-16," esp. 149-54. On the text critical problem, see further T. Baarda, "1 Thess. 2:14-16: Rodrigues in 'Nestle-Aland.' "

208. Cf. Rom 9:31; 2 Cor 10:14; Phil 3:16.

209. Baumert's understanding of the text, after study of the Greek terminology, is that "no one become infatuated and confused in the midst of these persecutions." He relates the phrase to "for the sake of your faith" (3:2), which he takes to mean "with regard to your confidence in us." See N. Baumert, "Brüche im paulinischen Satzbau" and " 'Wir lassen uns nicht beirren.' Semantische Fragen in 1 Thess 3, 2f."

210. Along with the NRSV, the NIV, the Christian Community Bible, and the Jewish New Testament render *thlibesthai* by "suffer persecution." See further the discussion of the "persecutions" of the Thessalonians by Donfried, in "Theology."

211. The NJB and REB offer "to suffer hardship," while the New Translation, having used "hardship" in v. 3, renders *thlibesthai* by "great suffering." The RNAB, along with the RSV, speaks of "afflictions."

212. It is only in 3:3 (cf. 1 Cor 3:11; 2 Cor 3:15; Phil 1:16) that Paul uses the verb *"keimai,"* radically, "to be laid," with the connotation of destiny. See, however, the critical remarks of Baumert, in "Brüche," 8-9. Baumert is of the opinion that the phrase *keimai eis* connotes being found in an unfavorable situation.

213. Cf. 2:2, where Paul uses the verbal hendiadys *"propaschō* – previously suffer" and *"hybrizō* – shamefully treat." *Propaschō* is hapax in the NT, while *hybrizō* is hapax in the Pauline corpus. The latter's cognate noun, *hybris*, is likewise hapax in the Pauline corpus, appearing only in the situational list of 2 Cor 12:10 (cf. Acts 27:10, 21).

214. Cf. 1:10, where Paul writes about the wrath "that is coming."

215. *Prolegō* is hapax in 3:4, just as *proeipon* is hapax in 4:6. Paul uses both verbs in Gal 5:21. Apart from these passages, neither verb appears in the authentic Pauline corpus except for the use of *prolegō* in 2 Cor 13:2.

3. The Life of the Thessalonians

1. The "memory language," from the root *mnē-*, which twice occurs in 1:2-3 is relatively rare in Paul's letters. Apart from 1:3 the verb "*mnēmoneuō* – remember" occurs only in 2:9 and Gal 2:10, with its occurrence in 1:3 being the only instance where Paul actually describes himself as remembering. The noun "*mneia* – memory (or mention)" of 1:2 also occurs in Phil 1:3 and Phlmn 4. In the latter instance, as in 1:2, the noun is the object of the verb "*poieō* – make," an example of a classic turn of phrase, found in Plato and Aeschines. The expression "to make memory of," for example, really means "to mention." Interestingly, the NRSV renders this phrase as "remember" in Phlmn 4, but as "mention" in 1 Thess 1:2. In the latter instance "remember" would create an unpleasant redundancy with the "remember" of v. 3.

2. See 1 Cor 13:13.

3. In a Vanderbilt doctoral thesis Abraham Smith notes that "the readers and listeners of I Thessalonians would have noted an over-all immanent structure which emphasized a love for threes." See A. Smith, "The Social and Ethical Implications of the Pauline Rhetoric in I Thessalonians," 93. Smith makes repeated references to Paul's rhetorical "love for threes."

4. See BDF, 167.

5. These translations come from BDF, 163. In his Westminster commentary, *The First and Second Epistles to the Thessalonians*, E. J. Bicknell had rendered Paul's phrase "your active faith and labour of love and patient hope" (4), apropos of which he gives a commentary (5-6) and a lengthy additional note (9-21). Bicknell's translation has been cited with approval by Rigaux. See Rigaux, *Thessaloniciens*, 363. Lambrecht speaks of the "time dimensions of their existence": "faith relies on the past, love is active in the present, and hope looks to the future" (see "Evangelisation," 325)

6. See Spicq, *Agape*, vol. 2, 104-5. The original French of Spicq's text did, however, focus more on the total moral life ("la réalisation globale de la conduite morale") than on individual moral acts. Cf. C. Spicq, *Agapè dans le Nouveau Testament*, 2: *Analyse des textes*, Ebib (Paris: Gabalda, 1959), 11. Spicq had, earlier in the same paragraph, written about "the 'activities' of the virtues." In this case, the original French, *actes*, suggests individual acts more clearly than does the English translation.

Taking "*ergon* – work" as if it referred to specific acts not only misconstrues Paul's thought in 1 Thessalonians; it also leads to an unnecessary and inappropriate discussion on "faith without works," a topic that arises in the letter to the Romans, when Paul addresses "the Jewish question." See Beker, *Paul the Apostle*, 59-94.

7. See Rom 15:18 and 2 Cor 10:11. Cf. Col 3:17; Luke 24:19; Acts 7:22.

8. An alternative image is offered by Lambrecht, who speaks of a "chain reaction": from God to the apostles, to those who imitate them, and those who imitate the latter group. See Lambrecht, "Evangelisation," 324.

9. Once again the English translation of Spicq's work is act-specific, as the translation mentions "the 'labors' of love." This corresponds, not to a

French expression, but to the simple Greek *kopos* in Spicq's original work. See *Agape,* vol. 2, 104; *Agapè,* vol. 2, 11.

10. See 2 Cor 6:5; 11:23, 27. In 1 Thessalonians Paul uses *"kopos* – labor" of his apostolic activity in 2:9 and 3:5 (cf. 2 Thess 3:8). See also 1 Cor 3:8 and Gal 6:17 (cf. 2 Cor 10:15). Only in 1:3 and 1 Cor 15:58 is *"kopos* – labor" used in regard to those to whom Paul is writing. Apart from these ten – eleven, if 2 Thess 3:8 is included – occurrences, the term appears only seven times in the New Testament.

11. In Paul's Greek text, the two expressions are different. In 3:12 there is a nominal phrase, *tē agapē eis allēlous,* literally, their love which is (directed) toward one another; while in 4:9, there is an infinitive of purpose, *eis to agapan allēlous.*

12. Elsewhere in Paul the term *philadelphia,* "sibling love," appears only in Rom 12:10, *"tē philadelphia eis allēous* – love one another." Cf. Heb 13:1; 1 Pet 1:22; 2 Pet 1:7 (2x).

13. There does not seem to be an understanding of "love for all," such as is implied in the Q-Sermon (Luke 6:27-28, 32 = Matt 5:43-46) or the Lukan parable of the Good Samaritan (Luke 10:29-37), in Paul. On the different approaches to love in the New Testament see my "The Church: A Community of Those Who Love One Another," *Emmanuel* 98 (1992): 94-101, 107.

14. The verb *euaggelizō,* hapax in 1 Thess, "refers to the total task of the apostle in proclamation." Cf. Georg Strecker, *"Euaggelizō," EDNT,* vol. 2, 69-70, 69.

15. *"Pleonazō* – increase" is hapax in 1 Thessalonians.

16. See also 4:1.

17. Paul's own elliptic language has the very terse comparative phrase *kathaper kai eis hymas,* literally, "just as we for you." Because of the elliptic quality of his epistolary language, the use of Greek words with the root *agap-,* "love," in the prayer of 3:12 and the paraenesis of 4:9-10 is not as prevalent as it would appear to be from a reading of these passages in a modern English language translation. The translations do, however, capture the sense of Paul's words.

18. See above, 63-65.

19. See my "The Church: A Community of Those Who Love One Another."

20. See Luke 8:15. Because "work" and "labor" are "activity" words and "steadfastness" is an "endurance" word, Smith notes that Paul is making a distinction between faith and love, on the one hand, and hope, on the other. From this observation as well as from the absence of hope from 3:6, he draws the conclusion that "the chief problem for the Christians at Thessalonica is a loss of hope." See Smith, "Social and Ethical Implications," 127-28.

21. "All people, even their torturers, marveled at their courage and endurance [*hypomonē*], and they became the cause of the downfall of tyranny over their nation." See Dibelius, *An die Thessalonicher I-II: An die Philipper.* HNT, 11 (3d ed.; Tübingen: Mohr, 1937), 3.

22. See Ps 22:10; 28:7; 33:18, 22.

23. The cognate verb *"elpizō* – hope" appears in all six other authentic

Pauline letters, but it does not occur in 1 Thessalonians. This letter uses only the noun *"elpis* – hope."

24. See my *Studies,* 266-74. For a summary overview of the implications of Jesus as "Lord," see my *"The Lord Jesus Christ."*

25. See Hans-Heinrich Schade, *Apokalyptische Christologie bie Paulus: Studien zum Zusammenhang von Christologie und Eschatologie in den Paulusbriefen,* 40-43.

26. Cf. Wis 5:16-22.

27. See Wim Beuken, *Jesaja,* 3A, De Prediking van het Oude Testament (Nijkerk: Callenbach, 1989), 144-45. With reference to the theological conviction see, among other passages, Exod 15:3 and Isa 49:24-25.

28. Cf. 1:7; 4:14. See my *Studies,* 216-19, 294-95.

29. See Rigaux, *Thessaloniciens,* 367, with reference to 187-89.

30. "Faith working through love" (*pistis di'agapēs energoumenē*).

31. See Frans Mussner, *Der Galaterbrief,* HTKNT, 9 (Herder: Freiburg, 1974), 353; Hans Dieter Betz, *Galatians: A Commentary on Paul's Letter to the Churches in Galatia,* Hermeneia (Philadelphia: Fortress, 1979), 263; F. F. Bruce, *The Epistle to the Galatians: A Commentary on the Greek Text,* NICNT (Grand Rapids, Mich.: Eerdmans, 1982), 233.

32. See Bruce, *Galatians,* 232.

33. See further the deutero-Pauline 1 Tim 1:14 and 2 Tim 1:13, which are a later echo of Paul's language. With reference to the dyad in 1 Thess 3:6, see my *Studies,* 221-22.

34. In Greek we have *akouōn sou tēn agapēn kai tēn pistin,* literally, "hearing of your love and faith." The unusual sequence of the bipartite expression might be explained as due to Paul's use of the expression as a sort of *captatio benevolentiae.* Paul has, moreover, abundantly used friendship language in the greeting of the epistle. Although the sequence is well attested in the manuscript tradition, it was apparently so unusual to warrant "correction" in P[61], a few majuscules, and some of the ancient versions.

Paul's Greek phrase is modified by a complex relative clause, whose component elements are frequently separated from one another in the modern translations. Thus the NRSV reads: "I hear of your love for all the saints and your faith toward the Lord Jesus." The NJB, RNAB, and REB, however, provide a translation that retains the "love and faith" expression.

35. With regard to the use of the expression in this epistolary context, see further Norman R. Petersen, *Rediscovering Paul: Philemon and the Sociology of Paul's Narrative World* (Philadelphia: Fortress, 1985), 240-41.

36. See 1 Cor 13:13, where the three terms appear in the faith-hope-love sequence known by most Christians. As a characteristic, unified description of the Christian life the threefold expression occurs not only in 1 Thess 1:3, 5:8, and 1 Cor 13:13, but also in Col 1:4-5. Exegetes are in general agreement that Paul has received the triad from the early Christian church (cf. Holtz, *Der erste Brief,* 44). Apropos 1 Cor 13:13, one can argue the case that, if "love" occupies the climactic position in 1 Corinthians, that is because of Paul's rhetorical situation. 1 Corinthians is just as contextual as is 1 Thessalonians.

In *Paul the Apostle,* J. C. Beker argues that "all Paul's theological thought is contextual-particularist" (38).

37. According to Wiles (*Paul's Intercessory Prayers,* 175) 1:3 announces the main subject matter of the letter.

38. See Johanson, *To All the Brethren,* 86.

39. See G. Bornkamm, *Paul* (London: Hodder and Stoughton, 1971), 219.

40. See Holtz, *Der erste Brief,* 43; Wanamaker, *Thessalonians,* 76.

41. See Bruce, *Thessalonians,* 12.

42. This is the interpretation given by Milligan, Frame, and Findlay in their commentaries on the letter and systematically put forth by Tarazi in *Thessalonians,* 40–41.

43. See Dibelius, *Thessalonicher,* 3–4; Rigaux, *Thessaloniciens,* 367.

44. See Bruce, *Thessalonians,* 12–13.

45. Dibelius (*Thessalonicher,* 3) notes that all three members of the triadic expression formulated by Paul as a description of Christian existence have an "active character."

46. See Ps 33:18–20, "Truly the eye of the Lord is on those who fear him, on those who hope [*elpizontas,* LXX] in his steadfast love... Our soul waits for [*hypomenei*] the Lord."

47. See Denis Buzy, "Epîtres aux Thessaloniciens," 138.

48. See Acts 18:5, 11.

49. See Perkins, "Hellenistic Religious Practices," 327–33.

50. In early Judaism, it was God who was "*ho ruomenos* – the deliverer" (1 Macc 2:60; 5:17; 12:15; Dan [LXX] 3:8; 8:4, 7, 11). Now it is Jesus who assumes the function of eschatological deliverance.

51. In suggesting that Paul was relieved to learn that the Thessalonians still had such fond memories, Wanamaker has proposed that the epistolary stasis may have been one of three situations: (1) Paul's hasty departure from Thessalonica (Acts 4:14); (2) possible resentment on the part of the Thessalonians because Paul would have left them behind to face their "persecutions"; (3) the Thessalonians' disappointment that he had not returned sooner. Cf. Wanamaker, *Thessalonians,* 134.

52. See Johanson, *To All the Brethren,* 70–71. Johanson cites Heikki Koskenniemi, *Studien zur Idee und Phraseologie des griechischen Briefes bis 400 n. Chr,* 146–47, as his principal reference.

53. See Wanamaker, *Thessalonians,* 134.

54. The verb "*epipotheō* – to long" is hapax in 1 Thessalonians. Cf. Rom 1:11; 2 Cor 5:2; 9:14; Phil 1:8; 2:26.

55. See David M. Stanley, "'Become Imitators of Me': The Pauline Conception of Apostolic Tradition," in *The Apostolic Church in the New Testament,* 376–77; Helmut Koester, "Apostel und Gemeinde"; Franz Laub, *Eschatologische Verkündigung und Lebensgestaltung nach Paulus,* 80–84; Holtz, *Der erste Brief,* 48–49; John S. Pobee, *Persecution and Martyrdom in the Theology of Paul,* 69–70; Mary Ann Getty, "The Imitation of Paul in the Letters to the Thessalonians," 280.

Lambrecht and Ware, however, interpret the *mimēsis* motif as a matter of imitating the apostles in their kerygmatic activity. While it cannot be denied that the Thessalonians similarly spoke forth God's word (see 1:8), this interpretation of the *mimēsis* motif recurs in 2:14. See Lambrecht, "Evangelisation," 324; James Ware, "The Thessalonians as a Missionary Congregation: 1 Thessalonians 1, 5-8."

56. According to Wayne A. Meeks, "The interesting thing here is that Paul is reminding the Christians of something they were *taught* [his emphasis] when they were first converted. The expectation of suffering was part of the catechism, so to speak, of the churches in the Pauline mission areas." See Meeks, "Social Functions of Apocalyptic Language in Pauline Christianity," 692. See also Barclay, "Social Contrasts," 51, 53.

57. See Donfried, "Theology" and Thomas Söding, "Widerspruch und Leidensnachfolge: Neutestamentliche Gemeinden im Konflikt mit der paganen Gesellschaft," 137. Söding does not, however, link the theme of persecution with that of the imitation of Christ (see 149-52).

58. On the integrity of 2:14-16, see *Studies,* 27-28, 101-5, and below, 145-146.

59. The noun "*mimētēs* – imitator" occurs but six times in the NT, that is, twice in 1 Thess (1:6; 2:14), twice in 1 Cor (4:16; 11:1) and twice in deutero-Pauline literature (Eph 5:1; Heb 6:12).

60. The *mimēsis* motif appears in each of Paul's letters with the exception of Romans, written to a community that Paul himself did not evangelize. The appearance of the motif generally has a paraenetic function, but that function is not exercised as blatantly in 1 Thessalonians as it is in some of the other Pauline compositions.

61. See Getty, "Imitation," 280.

62. Paul does not use the noun "*lypē* – grief" in 1 Thessalonians (cf. Rom 9:2; 2 Cor 2:1, 3, 7; 7:10 (twice); 9:7; Phil 2:27). He does, however, use the cognate verb "*lypeō* – grieve," which is hapax in 1 Thessalonians, but occurs eleven times in 2 Corinthians and once in Romans.

63. The others were "*phobos* – fear," "*epithymia* – desire" and "*hēdonē* – pleasure." Cf. Epictetus, *Dissertationes,* I, 9, 7; III, 11, 2. Paul exhorts the Thessalonians not to have "*lypē* – grief" in 4:13; previously (4:5) he had exhorted them not to have "*epithymia* – desire."

64. See my "Glimpses into Some Local Churches," and *Studies,* "Ecclesiology," 58-63, "The Church of the Thessalonians," 285-98. The latter essay is largely theological in its approach, but does touch upon some aspects of the Thessalonians' social situation.

65. See "Glimpses into Some Local Churches," 293-94.

66. See LSJ, 509.

67. In 2:14 the word "*symphyletēs* – compatriot," hapax in the New Testament, is used to identify those who were persecuting the Thessalonian Christians. Rhetorically, the expression accentuates the emotional pain of the persecution. The Thessalonians were being persecuted by their very own.

68. See Acts 17:4.

69. See *Studies,* 88-290.

70. See above, 61.

71. See my "God in the First Letter," 143-45.

72. Acts 17:1 contains the only extant attestation to the existence of a Jewish synagogue in Thessalonica at the time. See Lührmann, "Beginnings of the Church," 239.

73. Barclay correctly notes that an apocalyptic worldview reinforces social alienation. See Barclay, "Social Contrasts," 54-56.

74. See especially the fourteen uses of the vocative *adelphoi* (1:4; 2:1, 9, 14, 17; 3:7; 4: 1, 10, 13; 5:1, 4, 12, 14, 25).

75. See "Glimpses into Some Local Churches," 292-94.

76. See LSJ, 1204.

77. The unusual Greek *heis ton hena*, meaning "one another" (*allēlous*, BDF, 247 [4]) or "each other" (*heis ton heteron*, ZGB, 156) may be a Semitism.

78. The "*kai* – and" that joins the two verbal phrases is probably an epexegetical *kai*.

79. See Josef Pfammatter, "*oikodomeō*," *EDNT*, vol. 2, 495-98, esp. 497-98. With particular respect to 1 Thess 5:11, Wanamaker (*Thessalonians*, 189-90) traces the origins of the metaphorical use of *oikodomeō* to the LXX, specifically Jeremiah. He calls attention to the call of Jeremiah (Jer 1:10), but the link between Jer 1:10 and 1 Thess 5:11 is not apparent to me.

80. See Mark 4:11; 1 Cor 5:12, 13; Col 4:5.

81. See LSJ, 600, and Rolf Peppermüller, "*exō*," *EDNT*, vol. 2, 12-13. On the relationship between outsiders and the house in Mark, see Robert M. Fowler, *Let the Reader Understand: Reader-Response Criticism and the Gospel of Mark* (Minneapolis: Fortress, 1991), 211.

82. See *Studies*, 137-39 and 365-70.

83. See Rom 16:16; 1 Cor 16:20; 2 Cor 13:12 (cf. 1 Pet 5:14).

84. In 1 Pet 5:14, the kiss exchanged among Christians is identified as a kiss of love (*philēma agapēs*).

85. In the interpretation of 5:26, one must take note of the significant presence of the *hagi-* root, the "holiness" word group, in 1 Thessalonians. "*Hagiazō* – sanctify" appears in 5:23; "*hagiasmos* – sanctification" in 4:3, 4, 7; "*hagios* – holy" in 1:5, 6; 3:13; 4:8; 5:26 (and 5:27 according to many mss., including, apparently, P⁴⁶); and "*hagiōsunē* – holiness" in 3:13.

Apropos of the "*pasin tois hagios adelphois* – all the holy brothers and sisters" and "*pasin tois hagiois* – all the saints" readings of 5:27, see Metzger, *Textual Commentary*, 633-34.

86. "*Enorkizō* – command" is hapax in the NT.

87. On the text critical problem, see above, n. 85. Although, on text critical grounds, "*pasin tois adelphois* – all the brothers and sisters" is the most likely reading of 5:27, the editors of RNSV have rendered the phrase "to all of them" for stylistic reasons. Their rendering is accurate since the "*pasin tois adelphois* – all the brothers and sisters" of v. 27 repeats the "*tous adelphous pantas* – all the brothers and sisters" of v. 26.

88. In the singular in 3:2 and 4:6; in the plural in 4:10; 5:26, 27.

89. With regard to the social stasis of the Thessalonian Christians, see Míguez, "La Composición social de la iglesia."

90. See Charles Masson, *Les deux épîtres de saint Paul aux Thessa-*

Ioniciens, 79–80. Among some of the Fathers of the Church – Theodore of Mopsuestia, for example – there was a view that Paul turned away from addressing the community in general to address its leaders in v. 14.

91. This is, in fact, one of four basic questions that must be considered in any so-called sociological reading of a biblical text. The others concern the social worldview of the community, the social status of its members, and its social dynamic. Our reading of 1 Thessalonians has tried to be attentive to these issues. On the method itself, see Howard Clark Kee, *Knowing the Truth: A Sociological Approach to New Testament Interpretation* (Minneapolis: Fortress, 1989).

92. See Abraham Malherbe, *Paul and the Thessalonians,* 80–81, 88–89. In this regard the subtitle of Malherbe's book, "The Philosophic Tradition of Pastoral Care," is particularly significant. See, further, my reflections on the "pastoral interlude" (4:1) in *Studies,* 303–305.

93. One ought not to press the point too far, but it might be suggested that *"heis ton hena* – each other" points to the individuality of the experience and that *"allēlous* – one another" highlights its commonality, respectively the "each" and "every" of Paul's exhortation.

94. See Juan Chapa, "Consolatory Patterns," 226–27.

95. See the deutero-Pauline Eph 5:21.

96. See 4:1, where the formula *"erōtōmen hymas"* also appears. The NRSV, sensitive to the less forceful nature of this introductory formula, translates the *"erōtōmen hymas"* of 4:1 as "we ask you."

97. The two clauses are connected by a *"kai* – and" in Paul's Greek, but the editors of the NRSV have chosen to render the *kai* simply by a semicolon.

98. See, with regard to the parallel passage in Romans 12, James D. G. Dunn, *Romans 9–16,* WBC, 38B (Dallas: Word, 1988), 734.

99. These terms were, in technical jargon, *termini technici.* See Adolf von Harnack, *"Kopos (kopian, hoi kopiōntes) in frühchristlichen Sprachgebrauch,"* ZNW 27 (1928): 1–10; Spicq, *"Kopiaō, kopos,"* Notes de lexicographie néo-testamentaire, vol. 3, 404–12, esp. 410–11; and Herbert Fendrich (*"Kopos," EDNT,* vol. 2, 307–8) who writes: *"kopos* becomes a term for missionary labor (1 Cor 3:8; 2 Cor 10:15; 1 Thess 3:5) and for activity in the Christian community as a whole (1 Cor 15:58; 1 Thess 1:3). Eschatological fulfillment is always in view: 'Everyone will receive his own reward according to his *effort'* (1 Cor 3:8); such work is not in vain (15:58) because of Christ's resurrection (cf. v. 14)."

100. With reference to the non-Pauline character of this letter, see my *Letters That Paul Did Not Write,* 88–131.

101. Both the NJB and the REB translate the *proïstamenous* of 1 Thess 5:12 as "leaders." The NRSV translates the *proïstamenos* of Rom 12:8 as "leader," but renders the plural form of this participle in 1 Thess 5:12 as "those who . . . have charge." The RSV had similarly rendered 5:12 as "those who are over you," but had translated Rom 12:8 as "he who gives aid, with zeal," apparently taking as a principal cue for the translation the sandwiching of this participle between two that connote caritative activity.

102. The descriptive expression comes from Roetzel, "I Thess. 5:12–28: A Case Study," 375.

103. The similarities are such that 1 Thess 5:12–22 and Rom 12:3–21 serve as an intertext for one another. See James W. Voelz, "Multiple Signs and Double Texts: Elements of Intertextuality," in *Intertextuality in Biblical Writings: Essays in Honour of Bas van Iersel* (Kampen: Kok, 1989), 27–34, 30.

104. In the literature these various lists are generally identified by means of their classic designations, the catalogue of virtues (for example, Gal 5:22–23; cf. Col 3:12–13; Eph 4:25–31; 1 Tim 6:11; Tit 3:2), the catalogue of vices (Rom 1:29–31; 1 Cor 5:10–11; 6:9–10; Gal 5:19–21; cf. Eph 5:3–8; Col 3:5–9; 1 Tim 1:9–10; 6:4–5; 2 Tim 3:2–5; Tit 3:3; 1 Pet 4:3), the peristatic catalogue or hardship lists (Rom 8:35; 1 Cor 4:9–13; 2 Cor 4:8–9; 6:4–5; 11:23–29; 12:10); and the household code (cf. Eph 5:22–6:9; Col 3:18–4:1; 1 Tim 3:2–7, 8–13; Tit 1:7–9; 2:2–10). The list of charisms is something that is proper to the "Pauline literature," but there are several such listings in the New Testament (Rom 12:6–8; 1 Cor 13:8–10, 28, 29–30; cf. Eph 4:11; 1 Pet 4:11).

105. See, for example, C. K. Barrett, *A Commentary on the Epistle to the Romans*, HNTC (New York: Harper & Row, 1957), 239.

106. In the words of Leon Morris, "*Leadership* is a general term which neatly reflects Paul's word." See Morris, *The Epistle to the Romans* (Grand Rapids, Mich.: Eerdmans; Leicester: Intervarsity, 1988), 442.

107. See (1:1); 3:8; 4:1. Josef Hainz sees in the *en kyriō* formula of 5:12 an indication of the ground of legitimation of the leadership and the source of its authority, while Karl Donfried writes of the formula being used "in an instrumental sense within a larger context of ethical exhortation," but it is not entirely clear as to what he understands by "instrumental sense." According to Hainz, the leaders' authority comes not from Paul but from the Lord. See Hainz, *Ekklesia: Strukturen paulinischer Gemeinde-Theologie und Gemeinde-Ordnung*, 45–46; Donfried, "The Early Paul," 15, n. 31.

108. Bassin, for example, writes about presiding during the gatherings of the community. See François Bassin, *Les épîtres de Paul aux Thessaloniciens*, 165.

109. For example, Malherbe, *Paul and the Philosophers*, 90.

110. See C. E. B. Cranfield, *A Critical and Exegetical Commentary on the Epistle to the Romans*, vol. 2: *Commentary on Romans IX–XVI and Essays*, ICC (Edinburgh: T. & T. Clark, 1979), 626.

111. See Otto Michel, *Der Brief an die Römer*, KEK, 4 (14th ed.; Göttingen: Vandenhoeck and Ruprecht, 1978), 379. Similarly, Ziesler speaks of "the source of funds for poor relief." See John Ziesler, *Paul's Letter to the Romans*, TPINTC (London: SCM; Philadelphia: Trinity Press International, 1989), 300, and, apropos 1 Thess 5:12, Wanamaker, *Thessalonians*, 193.

112. See Barrett, *Romans*, 239.

113. "*Ataktos* – idler" is hapax in the authentic Pauline corpus at 5:14. Elsewhere in the New Testament, it appears only in 2 Thess 3:6, 11, along with the cognate verb *ataktēō* (3:7). This deutero-Pauline text contrasts the state of being *ataktos* with "work" and "labor," hence the translation "idle."

The traditional assumption of Pauline authorship of 2 Thessalonians has undoubtedly led to the translation of *ataktos* in 1 Thess 5:14 as "idle." See Spicq, "Les Thessaloniciens 'inquiets' étaient-ils des paresseux?"; "*atakteō, ataktos, ataktōs,*" *Notes de lexicographie néo-testamentaire,* vol. 1, 157–59; Malherbe, *Paul and the Thessalonians,* 92.

114. For stylistic reasons, Paul's *adelphoi* is rendered as "beloved" in the NRSV.

115. See Michel, *Römer,* 456.

116. Within the New Testament the verb reflects Pauline usage. It is found only in Rom 15:14; 1 Thess 5:12, 14; Col 1:28; 3:16; 2 Thess 3:15, and in a "Pauline address" at Acts 20:31. See Dunn, *Romans 9–16,* 858.

117. See Morris, *Romans,* 509.

118. See Johannes Behm, "*noutheteō, nouthesia,*" *TDNT,* vol. 4, 1019–22, 1022.

119. See Malherbe, *Paul and the Thessalonians,* 91.

120. Cf. 1 Thess 2:12.

121. Once again stylistic reasons have prompted the editors of the NRSV to render Paul's simple "*pantas* – all" as "all of them."

122. See Frank Witt Hughes, "The Rhetoric of 1 Thessalonians," 116. Hughes translates the four in this fashion: "admonish the disorderly, cheer up the downhearted, pay attention to the weak, be bighearted to all." Arguing from the triadic pattern of Paul's expression of thought in 1 Thessalonians, D. A. Black links the fourth injunction "be patient with all" to the exhortation on retaliation and reciprocity in v. 15. He considers the three-part injunction of vv. 14d-15 as bearing upon "responsibilities to those outside the congregation." Black's division of the text neglects the parallelism among the four expressions in v. 14 as well as the grammatical unity of v. 15. See David Alan Black, *Paul, Apostle of Weakness: Astheneia and its Cognates in the Pauline Literature,* 34–35.

123. For stylistic reasons, the NRSV renders Paul's *adelphoi* as "beloved."

124. See Philodemus's fragmentary *On Frankness,* 64, 67, 69. See Malherbe, *Paul and the Thessalonians,* 86, 93.

125. For Black the "idle" of 5:14 are the unemployed of 4:9-12. He echoes the classic commentary that "the presumption of an imminent return of Christ, which Paul himself believed and taught, led to an un-Pauline eschatological 'super-enthusiasm' resulting in the neglect of worldly duties." See Black, *Paul,* 29, 40–41.

126. Black, *Paul,* 29, 41–43.

127. With emphasis, Black writes: "These believers are 'weak' in that they have grown weary of waiting for the End and thus face the danger of being overcome by spiritual sleep" (*Paul,* 46). Cf. Black, "The Weak in Thessalonica: A Study in Pauline Lexicography."

128. Along with Traugott Holtz, Udo Schnelle notes that it is only these unruly persons who are identified as constituting a distinct group within the community at Thessalonica. See Holtz, *Der erste Brief,* 250–51; U. Schnelle, "Die Ethik des 1 Thessalonicherbriefes," 299.

129. My preferred translation of the classic triad, *episkopos, presbyteros,*

diakonos. See my "Pastoral Ministry: Timothy and Titus," *Church* (Summer 1987): 20–24, 21.

130. See, among others, Hainz, *Ekklesia,* 37; Laub, *Eschatalogische Verkündigung,* 70; Bruce, *Thessalonians,* 118; Lambrecht, "Evangelisation," 331.

131. Black (*Paul,* 31–32) thinks that it is "incontestable" that there was such a group. He argues from Acts 14:23 and the notion that the first Christian communities were "in all probability" organized on the model of the Jewish synagogue. Each of these arguments is suspect.

132. Similarly, Heinz, *Ekklesia,* 47.

133. See *Paul and the Philosophers,* 89.

134. See the comparable use of *epiginōskō* in 1 Cor 16:18.

135. On the grammatical issues involved in the interpretation of this clause, see Wanamaker, *Thessalonians,* 194.

136. The expression is virtually a technical term in the Pauline and later Christian literature. Cf. Rom 1:11; 5:15, 16; 6:23; 11:29; 12:6; 1 Cor 1:7; 7:7; 12:4, 9, 28, 30, 31; 2 Cor 1:11; cf. 1 Tim 4:14; 2 Tim 1:6; 1 Pet 4:10 (cf. Eph 4:7, 8, 11). Apparently used for the first time in Paul's first letter to the Corinthians, the terminology may have been coined by Paul himself. See Ernst Käsemann, "Ministry and Community in the New Testament," in *Essays on New Testament Themes,* SBT, 41 (London: SCM, 1964), 64.

137. Cf. 1 Pet 4:11.

138. See D. A. Carson, *Showing the Spirit: A Theological Exposition of 1 Corinthians 12–14* (Grand Rapids, Mich.: Baker, 1987), 35–36.

139. In 1 Cor 12:28, 29 the charism is identified in terms of the charismatic rather than in terms of the gift given. Thus we have the noun "*prophētēs* – prophet" rather than "*prophēteia* – prophecy."

140. See *Verkündigung und Prophetie,* 108.

141. See BDF, 485.

142. See Hughes, "Rhetoric," 116.

143. The verses are not, however, printed in indented fashion in *GNT*[3].

144. Although Smith makes repeated reference to Paul's rhetorical "love for threes," he does not cite 5:16–18a as an instance of this phenomenon. See Smith, "Social and Ethical Implications," 93.

145. See my *Studies,* 308–9, 329.

146. In his analysis of the structure of 1 Thessalonians, Smith notes that it is appropriate "to see 4:13–5:11 as thematically similar apocalyptic material in the middle of two sections with specific social and ethical exhortations. A thematic similarity, of course, would indicate a ring construction pattern. Thus, the audience would not focus on the similar word or order of words between 4:1–12 and 5:12–22, but would focus instead on the similar type of material found in these sections" ("Social and Ethical Implications," 104). He does not, however, draw attention to the specific similarity between 4:1–8 and 5:16–22, nor between 4:9–12 and 5:12–15. Attention to these details would have enhanced Smith's contention that Paul had made use of a ring construction pattern and would have provided a significant horizon for under-

standing the leadership models to which attention is called in 5:12–15 and 16–22.

147. In my judgment the fact that there are *five* such elements in each instance is not of particular significance. It is simply a fact to be noted. It might further be noted that in 4:1–8 the imperatives are in the form of an infinitive, whereas in 5:16–22 they are in the imperative mood.

148. Of the gift in 12:10; 13:2, 8; and 14:22; of the utterance in 14:6. On prophecy and prophets in 1 Corinthians, see Carson, *Showing the Spirit,* 91–100.

149. In his long article on prophecy (*"prophētēs, ktl.," TDNT,* vol. 6, 781–861, 852–53) Georg Friedrich associates prayer with prophecy and makes specific reference to 1 Thess 5:15–20, where, within a tightly structured context, three references to prayer as well as a reference to prophecy are to be found. See further BAGD, 722, which cites 5:20 and 1 Cor 13:8 as a plural indicating "various kinds and grades of prophetic gifts," albeit admitting that "utterances of Christian prophets in the form of a prophetic saying" is the possible meaning. See Henneken, *Verkündigung und Prophetie,* 111.

150. See also David Stern's *Jewish New Testament* and the Christian Community Bible.

151. See Jer 11:20 and 1 Thess 2:4.

152. See LSJ, 1539–40.

153. See 1 Cor 14:1 and the remarks of Marshall (*Thessalonians,* 158), Wanamaker (*Thessalonians,* 202), et al.

154. See Henneken, *Verkündigung und Prophetie,* 109. Cf. Ernst von Dobschutz, *Die Thessalonicher-Briefe,* KEK, 9 (Göttingen: Vandenhoeck and Ruprecht, 1909), 225, and Michael Theobald, " 'Prophetenworte verachtet nicht!' (1 Thess 5, 20). Paulinische Perspektiven gegen eine institutionelle Versuchung," 43–44. Theobald links the kerygma to prophecy as the general to the particular and notes that they have a common source, namely, the Spirit.

155. See Bultmann, *Theology,* 205–9, and Robert Jewett, *Paul's Anthropological Terms,* 167–86, 451.

156. *De Pythiae oraculis,* 17. See Wayne G. Rollins, *"De Pythiae oraculis (Moralia,* 394D–409D)," in H. D. Betz, *Plutarch's Theological Writings and Early Christian Literature,* SCHNT, 3 (Leiden: Brill, 1975), 103–30, 402C, 118, and Adinolfi, *La prima lettera,* 238–39.

157. W. C. van Unnik, " 'Den Geist löschet nicht aus' (I Thessalonicher V, 19)."

158. Van Unnik ("Geist," 269) claims that Paul's *pneuma* is, in terms of its content, identical with Plutarch's *enthousiasmos.* Apropos the latter, see Kathleen O'Brien Wicker, *"De defectu oraculorum (Moralia,* 409E–438E)" in Betz, *Plutarch's Theological Writings,* 131–80, 432DE, 171 (cf. 412A, 139; 438C, 180).

159. Similarly, Donfried, "The Early Paul," 15.

160. See above, n. 156.

161. See E. M. Good, "Fire," *IDB,* vol. 2, 268–69.

162. See Giovanni Rinaldi, "Il Targum palestinese del Pentateucho."

Whether Paul actually knew of this usage is difficult to determine. The parallel shows, however, that the notion was circulating in Jewish circles during Paul's day. A contemporary reader, taking the hermeneutics of intertextuality seriously, must, at the very least, find the parallel enlightening.

163. The word is variously translated "power" or "authority." It occurs with some frequency in 1 Corinthians, less frequently in 2 Corinthians and Romans, but not in the remaining four letters of the authentic Pauline corpus. I use the term here because it seems to capture what Paul is pointing to in 4:8 and 5:19-20. Interestingly, the NRSV introduces the notion of "authority" into its translation of 4:8.

164. *De Stoicorum repugnantiis*, 23 (*Moralia* 1045EF). See Helge Almgvist, *Plutarch und das Neue Testament: Ein Beitrag zum Corpus Hellenisticum Novi Testamenti*, ASNU, 15 (Uppsala: Appelbergs, 1946), 124, and Adinolfi, *La prima lettera*, 239.

165. Similarly, Schnelle, "Ethik," 299.

166. The adversative conjunction is not found in all manuscripts – including the Sinaiticus, *prima manus*. Text critics nonetheless believe that the word does belong to Paul's text.

167. See W. Grudem, *The Gift of Prophecy in 1 Corinthians* (Lanham, Md.: University Press of America, 1982), 63, 105-6, and *The Gift of Prophecy in the New Testament and Today* (Eastbourne: Kingsway, 1988), 75, 104-5. with some verbatim repetition between the two books. Cf. Eduard Schweizer, *Church Order in the New Testament*, SBT, 32 (London: SCM, 1961), 191.

168. Apropos 5:19-22, Donfried says: "Quite clearly the Apostle does not wish the gift of the Spirit to be confused with the excesses of the Dionysiac mysteries; for Paul the Spirit does not lead to 'Bacchic frenzies'... " ("Cults," 342). See also Paul-Emile Langevin, "Conseils et prière," 37. While it is clear that the apostle would have the Thessalonians avoid such confusion (cf. 1 Cor 12:1-3), the entire paraenetic unit seems to focus upon life within the community rather than upon the community's relationships *ad extra*. See Laub, *Eschatologische Verkündigung*, 69-70.

169. See Carson: "Almost certainly the responsibility to weigh what the prophets say rests with the entire congregation, or, more precisely, with the congregation as a whole" (*Showing the Spirit*, 120).

170. In a brief comment, Schnelle draws attention to the relationship that Paul establishes between charismatic phenomena and ethics in 5:19-22. See Schnelle, "Ethik," 299.

171. The German *amt.*

172. It is enumerated as the first (*prōton*) in 1 Cor 12:28 and cited in the first instance in the following verse. Cf. Eph 4:11.

173. See Rom 5:5; 1 Cor 12:31-14:1.

174. See 1 Cor 7 and Käsemann's identification of "to each his own" and "for one another" as summary descriptions of criteria of authentic charisms ("Ministry and Community," 76-77).

175. See Laub, *Eschatologische Verkündigung*, 69-70.

176. Wiles describes these expressions as "a closely knit paraenetic unit" (*Paul's Intercessory Prayers*, 168-69).

177. See Wanamaker, *Thessalonians*, 200.

178. And the preposition "*en* – in."

179. See Albert Vanhoye, "La composition de 1 Thessaloniciens," 83. Still more specifically Rivera has argued that *paraklēsis*, the transforming power of the message, is the proper object of "*eucharistia* – thanksgiving" in 1 Thessalonians and that an interactive flow between message and thanksgiving constitutes the essential structure of the letter. See L. F. Rivera, "Cristianismo existencial y expresión eucarística de la religión: 1 y 2 Tesalonicenses."

180. See Donfried, *Cults*, 353.

181. In fact the interpreter must decide whether "*en panti*" is to be taken temporally ("at all times") or circumstantially ("in all circumstances").

182. See Wiles, *Paul's Intercessory Prayers*, 286. Langevin ("Conseils et prière," 35) notes that prayer moves spontaneously from thanksgiving to petition. The sequence of vv. 17–18a is, however, just the opposite.

183. One must not overlook the fact that Paul consistently uses pronouns and verbs in the plural in those contexts of 1 Thessalonians in which he writes about joy. Joy is a community experience.

184. Cf. 2:19, where we have a similar use of "*emprosthen* – before." Joy is to be experienced in the presence of the Lord. Jorge Sanchez Bosch formally denies that 2:19 evokes "cultic joy" (304), but, despite his many references to the verse and his brief reflections on the subject of joy (304–5), he does not adequately consider the significance of joy in this verse. See J. S. Bosch, "*Gloriarse*" *según San Pablo: Sentido y teología de chachaomai.*

185. 3:9 and 5:16 are the only two passages in 1 Thessalonians in which Paul uses the verb "*chairō* – rejoice." The cognate noun, "*chara* – joy," occurs in 1:6; 2:19, 20 in addition to 3:9.

186. Pace Ralph Martin, *Worship in the Early Church* (London: Marshall, Morgan and Scott, 1964), 135–36, who notes that 5:16–22 "reads as though it contained the 'headings' of a Church service." Cf. 1 Tim 2:1–15 and my comments in this regard in "Image of Paul," 164–65.

187. See Hughes, "Rhetoric," 116.

188. In this regard, Udo Schnelle writes that 5:19–20 makes reference to a strong pneumatic and prophetic element in the community's worship. See Schnelle, "Ethik," 299.

189. See L. Monloubou, *Saint Paul et la prière: Prière et évangélisation,* LD, 110 (Paris: Cerf, 1982), 53.

190. He further comments: "And behind the prayer language of both Paul and the churches to whom he wrote, lay not only the prayer customs of the Hellenistic world, but more directly the liturgical style of the Jewish synagogue and the Old Testament, freely adapted to new purposes by the emerging Christian Gentile communities and by the apostle himself" (Wiles, *Paul's Intercessory Prayers*, 23–24).

191. Henk J. de Jonge situates the dying formula of 5:10, " . . . our Lord Jesus Christ who died for us" within the context of the exhortatory homily, rather than within a eucharistic setting. See de Jonge, "The Original Setting of the CHRISTOS APETHANEN HYPER Formula."

192. 1 Thess 4:16 (cf. 1:1; 2:14; 5:18).

193. 1 Thess 3:8 (cf. 4:1; 5:12).
194. Cf. Ernst Fuchs, "Hermeneutik?" in *Gesammelte Aufsätze*, vol. 3: *Glaube und Erfahrung: Zum christologischen Problem im Neuen Testament* (Tübingen: Mohr, 1965), 116-35, 121, and "Zukunft des Glaubens nach 1 Thess 5, 1-11," in *Gessamelte Aufsätze*, vol. 3, 334-63, 340; Udo Schnelle, *Gerechtigkeit und Christus gegenwart*, GTA, 24 (Göttingen: Vandenhoeck and Ruprecht, 1983), 112; Jürgen Becker, "Die Erwählung der Völker durch das Evangelium: Theologiegeschichtliche Erwägungen zum 1 Thessalonicherbrief," in *Studien zum Text und zur Ethik des Neuen Testaments*, edited by Wolfgang Schrage, 89; Donfried, "The Early Paul," 14. Pheme Perkins has appropriately noted that "baptism and other ritual forms of practice and speech...served to define the community as much as teaching did" ("Hellenistic Religious Practices," 327).
195. See Gerhard Friedrich, "Ein Tauflied hellenistischer Judenchristen."
196. See Spicq, *Agape*, vol. 2, 18.
197. See the discussion in my *Studies*, 142-53.
198. With regard to this Pauline neologism, see Camille Focant, "Les fils du jour (1 Thes 5, 5)."
199. See Wolfgang Harnisch, *Eschatologische Existenz: Ein exegetischer Beitrag zum Sachanliegen von 1 Thessalonicher 4, 13-5, 11*, FRLANT, 110 (Göttingen: Vandenhoeck and Ruprecht, 1973), esp. 116-42. Harnisch built upon the earlier work of Fuchs, his mentor, as well as the contributions of Georg Braumann and Norbert Schneider. Cf. G. Braumann, *Vorpaulinische christliche Taufverkundigung bei Paulus*, BWANT, 82 (Stuttgart: Kohlhammer, 1962); N. Scheider, *Die rhetorische Eigenart der paulinischen Antithese*, HUT, 11 (Tübingen: Mohr, 1970). Although taking issue with Harnisch's contention that 5:1-11 is a later Pauline interpolation into the original letter, Joseph Plevnik looked favorably upon the suggestion that 5:4-10 echoed early baptismal catechesis. See Plevnik, "1 Thess 5, 1-11: Its Authenticity, Intention and Message."
200. See Eph 5:22-24.
201. See Rom 13:12, 14; Gal 3:27. Cf. Col 3:10, 12; Eph 6:11, 14; 1 Pet 1:13. See Laub, *Eschatologische Verkündigung*, 237. Laub does not make specific reference to baptismal catechesis in his commentary on the passage in *1. und 2. Thessalonicherbrief. Die neue Echter Bibel*, 13 (Würzburg: Echter, 1985).
The intertextuality between 1 Thess 5:8 and Eph 6:10-19 is strong indeed, but it is difficult to establish, beyond the shadow of all doubt, that the appearance of the verb "*enduō* – put on" and the use of similar imagery in a paraenetic context necessarily point to a baptismal context.
202. See Gerhard Delling, *Worship in the New Testament* (London: Darton, Longman and Todd, 1962), 48-50.
203. See Rigaux, *Thessaloniciens*, 354. One might also note that Becker opines that the "*en Christō* – in Christ" formula, which he and others identify as a baptismal formula, has an Antiochene origin. See Jürgen Becker, "Zum Schriftgebrauch der Bekenntnisschriften," in *Volkskirche – Kirche der Zukunft? Leitlinien der Augsburgischen Konfession für das Kirchen-*

verständnis heute, edited by Wenzel Lohff and Lutz Mohaupt. Zur Sache, 12-13 (Hamburg: Lutherisches Verlagshaus, 1987), 92-103, 100.

204. The formula is apparently of Christian coinage. See C. J. Cuming, "Service-Endings in the Epistles," 112. Walter Schmithals claims that the formula, with its alternate, "the Lord of peace," typically appears in Paul's epistolary conclusions. See Schmithals, *Paul and the Gnostics,* 131.

205. See Paul-Emile Langevin, "L'intervention de Dieu selon I Thes 5, 23-24," 236-56. Langevin calls this pair of verses a "synthesis benediction" (254).

206. Cf. Robert Jewett, "The Form and Function of the Homiletic Benediction."

207. See especially Cuming, "Service-Endings," and James M. Gibbs, "Canon Cuming's 'Service-Endings in the Epistles': A Rejoinder."

208. See, for example, the argument of Cuming, "Service-Endings," 112-23, who argues that the kiss was "after the prayers" rather than "before the eucharist." Cuming, however, believes that the kiss may have initially been the climax and conclusion to a nonsacramental service.

209. See, for example, James M. Gibbs, who has written that "in at least some churches in the first century C.E. there was a single service consisting of a ministry of word and sacrament. Within this structure the logical place for the reading of an epistle would appear to be in the position of the sermon" ("Canon Cuming's Service-Endings," 546-47). See, further, Hans Lietzmann, *Mass and the Lord's Supper: A Study in the History of the Liturgy* (Leiden: Brill, 1953-79), 186; John A. T. Robinson, "The Earliest Christian Liturgical Sequence," in *Twelve New Testament Studies,* SBT, 10 (London: SCM, 1962), 154-57; Wiles, *Paul's Intercessory Prayers,* 70.

210. Such a request using the word "*aspazomai* – greet" is typical of the papyrus letters collected by John L. White beginning around 40 C.E. See letters Nos. 84 (p. 122), 87 (p. 130), 90 (p. 142), 91 (p. 143), 94 (p. 146), 96 (p. 151), 99 (p. 154), 103 (p. 161), 104 (p. 164), 108 (p. 170), 109 (p. 173), 110 (pp. 174-75), 111 (p. 176), and 112 (p. 177) in John L. White, *Light from Ancient Letters.* All of these examples except letter no. 90 use "*aspazomai* – greet" in the request. Typical is the mid-first-century letter 91, " ... Salute [*aspazou*] the children of Herennia and Pompeis and Syrion and Thaisous and her children and husband and all my friends."

211. Not even the "died for us" formula of 5:10 should be construed as having had a eucharistic setting in the Thessalonian community. See de Jonge, "The CHRISTOS APETHANEN HYPER Formula."

212. Cf. Phil 3:4-6.

213. See, especially, Pearson, "1 Thessalonians 2, 13-16," and Daryl D. Schmidt, "1 Thess 2, 13-16: Linguistic Evidence for an Interpolation." See the discussion of the issue in my *Studies,* 14-15, 97-105.

Significant reflections on the pericope as an integral part of the letter have been offered by Karl Donfried, Ingo Broer, and Traugott Holtz. See Donfried, "Paul and Judaism: I Thessalonians 2:13-16 as a Test Case," 242-53; Broer, "Der ganze Zorn"; Holtz, "The Judgment on the Jews and the Salvation of All Israel: 1 Thes 2, 15-16 and Rom 11, 25-26," 284-94. See also John W. Simpson, Jr., "The Future of Non-Christian Jews: 1 Thessalonians 2:15-16 and Romans 9–11"; "The Problems Posed by 1 Thessalonians 2:15–16 and a Solution."

214. See Pobee, *Persecution and Martyrdom, passim.*

215. References to the persecution of the Thessalonians are concentrated in 1:6–7; 2:14–16a; 3:3–4, but see also 2 Cor 8:1–2 and Acts 17:1–9. In his study of "Persecution and the Thessalonian Church," Donfried finds explicit persecution terminology in 1:6; 2:13–16; 3:3 and 3:4 and implicit persecution terminology in 1:4 ("chosen you"); 1:7 ("example"); 2:18 ("Satan"); 3:5 ("tempter"); and 4:13 ("those who have died"). See Donfried, "Theology," 248–56.

216. See Marxsen, "Auslegung von 1 Thess 4, 13–18," 24; *Der erste Brief,* 25–26.

217. Cf. 2 Cor 11:28.

218. Note the rare use of the first-person singular in 2:18 and 3:5 (see my *Studies,* 178–79). The only other passage in the letter where the first-person singular appears is 5:27.

219. See Donfried, "Theology," 253; Perkins, "Hellenistic Religious Practices," 331.

220. Cf. 1:8.

221. See Rainer Kampling, "Freude bei Paulus," 73–74.

222. See 3:5.

223. See above, 7 and Jack Finegan, *The Archaeology of the New Testament: The Mediterranean World of the Early Christian Apostles* (Boulder, Colo.: Westview; London: Croom, 1981), 108.

224. See the sober reflections of Donfried in "Paul and Judaism: I Thessalonians 2:13–16 as a Test Case," 247–48.

225. See 2 Cor 8:2; 1 Thess 1:7.

226. See, especially, the classic commentary of George Milligan, but also the remarks of J. B. Lightfoot. See Milligan, *St. Paul's Epistles to the Thessalonians: The Greek Text with Introduction and Notes* (London: Macmillan, 1908), 29; J. B. Lightfoot, *Notes on Epistles of St. Paul from Unpublished Commentaries* (London: Macmillan, 1895), 32. Cf. Donfried, "Paul and Judaism," 247–48; Rigaux, *Thessaloniciens,* 443; Holtz, *Der erste brief,* 102; Morris, *Thessalonians,* 82.

227. In the situational list of 2 Cor 11:23–27, Paul distinguishes difficulties coming from Jews (v. 24) from those coming at the hands of Gentiles (v. 26).

228. See 1:9.

229. See 1:4; 4:5.

230. While the evidence of Acts should not be totally discounted, Luke's narrative account describes violence that arose in conjunction with the Pauline mission. The persecution to which 1 Thessalonians makes reference seems to be a persecution that took place, or continued to take place, after Paul's departure.

231. See Haenchen, *Acts,* 513–14; Dennis R. MacDonald, "Apocryphal and Canonical Narratives about Paul," 68. Apart from the semantic issue, there is the historical question of whether there were Jews living in Thessalonica at the time. As has been previously noted, archeological evidence does not

offer any indication that there was a Jewish settlement at Thessalonica at the time. On the other hand, Acts does indicate that there was a synagogue of the Jews in Thessalonica (Acts 17:1) and it is, apriori, likely that Paul would have stopped in communities along the trade routes where he could expect to find some compatriots. Lührmann and others, however, are skeptical about the existence of a Jewish synagogue in Thessalonica at the time of Paul's visit. See Lührmann, "The Beginnings of the Church," 239.

232. See Meeks, "Social Functions," 691-92; Perkins, "Hellenistic Religious Practices," 326.

233. See Barclay, "Social Contrasts," 53.

234. See Donfried, "Cults," 342-52; Perkins, "Hellenistic Religious Practices," 327.

235. See 2:19; 3:13; 4:15; 5:23.

236. See Erik Peterson, "Die Einholung des Kyrios"; Heinrich Schlier, "Auslegung des 1. Thessalonicherbriefe (4, 13-5, 11)" *BibLeb* 4 (1963): 19-30, 24.

237. Cf. 2:19.

238. See Malherbe, *Paul and the Thessalonians*, 46-48, 65-66.

239. See Donfried, "Cults," 349-50, repeated verbatim in "Theology," 254-55, who interprets "about those who have died" (4:13) along these lines. Perkins, "Hellenistic Religious Practices," 333, erroneously refers to Fitzmyer's "Paul and the Law" (186-201 in *To Advance the Gospel* [New York: Crossroad, 1981]) as espousing a similar position. The interpretation has, in fact, arisen from time to time. See, for example, A. H. M'Neile, *Saint Paul: His Life, Letters and Christian Doctrine* (Cambridge: University Press, 1920). Barclay, however, takes issue with this position on the grounds that "Paul would hardly have missed an opportunity to celebrate the deceased as martyrs" ("Social Contrasts," 53).

240. See Holtz, *Der erste Brief*, 102. Hendrix renders Paul's *thlipsis* as "'affliction' and/or 'pressure.'" See Hendrix, "Archaeology and Eschatology," 118.

241. See Meeks, "Social Functions," 692; Perkins, "Hellenistic Religious Practices," 326; and, generically, Söding, "Widerspruch," 146.

242. See Wiles, *Paul's Intercessory Prayers*, 54. Wiles writes that the pastoral anxieties, priestly responsibilities, and parousia hopes of the earlier passage have been transmuted into the intercessory prayer (53).

243. The "*to prosōpon* – face to face" and "*hyperekperissou* – earnestly" of 3:10 echo the "*perissoterōs* – great eagerness" and "*prosōpō* – face to face" of 2:17.

244. These are the only two passages in the authentic Pauline corpus, apart from Rom 1:11; 16:25, in which the verb "*stērizō* – strengthen" appears.

4. Writing a Letter

1. Willi Marxsen judiciously remarks that, formally, the former is a practical problem; the latter a theoretical problem, but that, practically speak-

ing, the two matters were closely related. See Marxsen, *Der erste Brief*, 25.

2. See Pobee, *Persecution and Martyrdom*, 98–101.

3. For the eschatological significance of the expression *eis telos*, literally, "until the end," but rendered by the NRSV as "at last" and, alternatively, as "completely" or "forever," see Donfried, "Paul and Judaism," 250–52. Cf. Matt 10:22; 24:13; Mark 13:13 (comp. Luke 18:5; John 13:1).

4. See Koskenniemi's Oslo dissertation, *Studien zur Idee*, and Klaus Thraede, *Grundzüge griechisch-römischer Brieftopik*, 17ff. and 125ff. William G. Doty has summarized the three functions of the letter identified by Koskenniemi, friendship, presence, and dialogue, in *Letters in Primitive Christianity*, 11–12.

5. See Koskenniemi, *Studien zur Idee*, 38.

6. See the use of the idiomatic "to see your face," *idein hymōn to prosōpon*, in 2:17 and 3:10.

7. See Vanhoye, "La composition," 86.

8. See 1 Cor 5:9, 11; 2 Cor 2:3–4; 7:8. These passages suggest that Paul had written to the Corinthians at some time prior to the writing of the extant first letter to the Corinthians and that there was a "tearful" letter that he wrote to that community at some point between the writing of the two letters that have been preserved.

Some recent commentators suggest, however, that the letters have not been lost. They hold that the two canonical letters to the Corinthians are compilations of various letters that Paul wrote to the Corinthians. In the opinion of these commentators, the passages to which 1 Cor 5:9, 11; 2 Cor 2:3–4; 7:8 refer have been incorporated into the extent letters. See, for example, the exposition of the partition hypothesis by Walter Schmithals in *Gnosticism in Corinth*, 87–101, and the discussion of the issue by John Hurd in *The Origin of 1 Corinthians*, 43–47, and Helmut Merklein, "Die Einheitlichkeit des ersten Korintherbriefes," *ZNW* 75 (1984): 153–82. With regard to the partition of 2 Corinthians, see also Hans Dieter Betz, "Corinthians, Second Epistle to the," *ABD*, vol. 1, 1148–54.

9. See 1 Cor 7:1.

10. See 4:9; 1 Cor 7:1, 25; 8:1; 12:1; 16:1, 12. Comp. Mark 12:26; 13:32; John 16:11; Acts 21:25.

11. See especially Chalmer E. Faw, "On the Writing of First Thessalonians," and Malherbe, "Did the Thessalonians Write?" 250–51. Faw was inspired by Harris's suggestion that 1 Thessalonians might be a response to a letter that Paul had received. See J. Rendel Harris, "A Study in Letter-Writing."

12. On the use of the formula by Paul, see especially Ernst Baasland, "Die peri-Formel und die Argumentation(ssituation) des Paulus." See also the discussions in White, *Light from Ancient Letters*, 207–8, and Malherbe, "Did the Thessalonians Write?" 251.

13. See Malherbe, "Did the Thessalonians Write?"

14. See *Studies*, 179.

15. See Malherbe, "Did the Thessalonians Write?" 250, 255.

16. See Malherbe, "Did the Thessalonians Write?" 255. See also Best, *Thessalonians,* 14–16, 180.

17. See Malherbe, *Paul and the Thessalonians,* 2.

18. In *Light from Ancient Letters,* John L. White has published 117 letters, from Hellenistic papyri, in Greek and in English translation, along with specific commentary on each letter and a general reflection on letter writing in the Hellenistic world. The letters date from the third century B.C.E. to the third century C.E., but seven of them (letters 87–93) are contemporary with Paul's letter-writing activity in the mid-first century C.E.

19. See Malherbe, *Ancient Epistolary Theorists.*

20. In the words of the Pseudo Demetrius, "The length of a letter, no less than its style, must be kept within due bounds. Those that are too long, and further are stilted in expression, are not in sober truth real letters, but treatises with the heading 'My dear So-and-So.' This is true of many of Plato's, and of that of Thucydides" ("On Style," IV, 228). Cf. Demetrius Phalereus, "On Style," in *Aristotle in Twenty-three Volumes,* vol. 23, LCL, 199 (London: Heinemann, 1932), 440–43.

21. One of the shortest letters cited in White's collection contains but ten Greek words, "Apollonios to Zenon greeting. You did right in having sent the chickpeas to Memphis. Good-bye." To this short note is appended the date (October 3, 256 B.C.E.).

22. See White, *Light from Ancient Letters,* 104. Cf. 1 Macc 12:6, 19; Acts 15:23. The examples found in Maccabees and Acts are reports of letters and are probably composed by the authors of these books. Nonetheless, they do bear witness to the form of the Hellenistic letter then in vogue.

23. On Paul's use of the three-part greeting, the prescript or protocol, see Franz Schnider and Werner Stenger, *Studien zum neutestamentlichen Briefformular,* 3–41.

24. See, among the letters in White's collection of letters contemporary with Paul, letters nos. 90, 92, 93 (141, 144, 145). Among New Testament letters, 3 John 2 is the only expression of a health wish. See White, *Light from Ancient Letters,* 200–202.

25. See letter no. 103 in White, *Light from Ancient Letters,* 159. Other letters in the collection containing formulas of thanksgiving are nos. 16 (p. 39); 34 (p. 65); 35 (p. 66); 39 (p. 72); [52 (p. 88)]; 102 (p. 158); 103 (pp. 159 and 160); 104 (pp. 162 and 164); 109 (p. 173), and 110 (p. 174).

26. See Koskenniemi, *Studien zur Idee,* 104–14. The supplications frequently employ a *proskynema* formula and are a significant feature in the type of letters that Koskenniemi classifies as "family letters." Those who have studied the form of Paul's letters are in general agreement that Paul's expression of thanksgiving is analogous to the formula of supplication. See, for example, White, *The Form and Function of the Body of the Greek Letter: A Study of the Letter-Body in the Non-literary Papyri and in Paul the Apostle,* 69–70; "Saint Paul and the Apostolic Letter Tradition," 438; "New Testament Epistolary Literature in the Framework of Ancient Epistolography," 1741.

27. Letter no. 104 in White, *Light from Ancient Letters,* 161–62. In Sympronius's letter to his brother Maximus (second century), we read, "Before

all else I pray that you are well" (*pro tōn holōn erōsthe se euchomai;* letter 113, 180). A. B. du Toit identifies this as a *formula valetudinis,* comparable to the Pauline thanksgiving. See A. B. du Toit, "Oriënterende opmerkings oor die Pauliniese briefliteratuur," 8.

28. See White, *Light from Ancient Letters,* letters nos. 103a and 103b (159, 160).

29. See Paul Schubert, *Form and Function of the Pauline Thanksgivings,* 173.

30. The first of the *kai*'s is omitted in some manuscripts, notably D, F, G, H, and the majority of the medieval texts.

31. See the analysis by Jan Lambrecht in "Thanksgivings in 1 Thessalonians 1–3," 184–94.

32. See Lambrecht, "Thanksgivings," 200.

33. See Schmithals, *Paul and the Gnostics,* 176–81, 213 (esp. 180) and Rudolf Pesch, *Die Entdeckung des ältesten Paulus-Briefes: Paulus – neu gesehen,* 42–44, 74–76. Schmithals identifies the "joyful epistle" of 2:13–4:1 as the last extant bit of Paul's correspondence with the Thessalonians. The fact that there are similarly two thanksgiving periods in the extant 2 Thessalonians is a major reason for the claim that 2 Thessalonians is slavishly dependent on 1 Thessalonians and, therefore, probably inauthentic. See my *Letters That Paul Did Not Write,* 219.

34. See Schubert, *Pauline Thanksgivings,* 7, 21–27.

35. Schubert, *Pauline Thanksgivings,* 21.

36. See, for example, letter no. 91 in White's collection (143). There the formula occurs toward the end of a very short letter. Cf. Ernst von Dobschutz, *Die Thessalonicher-Briefe,* 155; R. Bultmann, *Der Stil der paulinischen Predigt und die kynisch-stoische Diatribe,* FRLANT, 13 (Göttingen: Vandenhoeck and Ruprecht, 1910), 101; Schnider and Stenger, *Neutestamentlichen Briefformular,* 76; and Schmithals, *Paul and the Gnostics* (132–33, 193), who writes that, with Paul, the formula "is used exclusively to introduce the concluding paraenesis" (193).

37. The most articulate proponent of the notion that Paul's letter to the Thessalonians is to be properly classified as a paraenetic letter is Abraham Malherbe, whose long awaited "Hellenistic Moralists and the New Testament" is to appear in the *ANRW,* II, 26, 267–333. I am grateful to Professor Malherbe for providing me with a galley-proof copy of this study. See also Malherbe's "Exhortation."

38. See Klaus Berger, "Apostelbrief und apostolische Rede/ Zum Formular frühchristlicher Briefe," 224.

39. See Schubert, *Pauline Thanksgivings,* 26; Doty, *Letters,* 43; and Schnider-Stenger, *Neutestamentlichen Briefformular,* 76–107, who consider the final paraenesis as a typical feature of Pauline letters, especially of those that are authentically Pauline (see 77).

40. See Koskenniemi, *Studien zur Idee,* 91–95.

41. See White, *The Body of the Greek Letter,* 64, 115–20, 125–27, 142–43. Cf. du Toit, "Oriënterende Opmerkings," 8–9.

42. Jack T. Sanders, "The Transition from Opening Epistolary Thanksgiving to Body in the Letters of the Pauline Corpus."

43. See White, "Introductory Formulae in the Body of the Pauline Letter."

44. See J. H. Roberts, "Transitional Techniques to the Letter Body in the *Corpus Paulinum*, 192–94, 196. Roberts distinguishes three kinds of personal expression: (1) desire dealing with knowledge of which an example is to be found in 2:1–12; (2) feeling or statement regarding Paul's situation (e.g., 1:4–10); and (3) an expressed desire to visit the recipients (which he identifies only at Rom 1:11, 12). Although he identifies Paul's citation of credal formulae as occasionally serving a transitional function, he does not indicate that any of the credal statements of 1 Thessalonians (1:10; 4:14; 5:10; see my *Studies*, 253–66) have this role.

45. See White, *Light from Ancient Letters*, 190.

46. See Roberts, "Transitional Techniques," 192. For a discussion of the letter body itself, see White, *Light from Ancient Letters*, 202–11.

47. See Johanson, *To All the Brethren*, 61–67.

48. See the discussion of this issue in my *Letters That Paul Did Not Write*.

49. See A. J. M. Wedderburn, "Keeping Up with Recent Studies, 8: Some Recent Pauline Chronologies," as well as the two major works that he summarizes, namely, Gerd Lüdemann, *Paul, Apostle to the Gentiles: Studies in Chronology*, and Jewett, *Chronology*. Karl Donfried, pleading for a revision of the standard (50–51 C.E.) dating of 1 Thessalonians, holds that this first of Paul's letters was written about 43 C.E. See Donfried, "The Early Paul," 4–8.

50. The principle is, of course, not absolute. The later letters of Paul can shed, retrospectively, some light on his earlier letters. Analogously, letters that were not written by Paul, but that were written soon after he wrote and with the obvious intention of imitating his style and thought, have some contribution to make to the understanding of what the real Paul wrote in his authentic letters.

51. See 2:3 and my previous comments in this regard.

52. See Johanson, *To All the Brethren*, 188.

53. See Lambrecht, "Thanksgivings," 192.

54. Similarly, Lambrecht speaks of Paul's "epistolary liberty" ("Thanksgivings," 193).

55. See Pseudo Demetrius, "On Style," 229, who writes: "There should be a certain degree of freedom in the structure of a letter. It is absurd to build up periods, as if you were writing not a letter but a speech for the law courts. And such labored letter writing is not merely absurd; it does not even obey the laws of friendship, which demand that we should 'call a spade a spade,' as the proverb has it."

56. See Acts 15:29.

57. See White, *Light from Ancient Letters*, 195–96.

58. See above, 87–88.

59. See among Paul's later letters, Rom 16:22; 1 Cor 5:9; 16:3; 2 Cor 3:1, 2, 3; 7:8 (twice); 10:9, 10, 11; among the deutero-Paulines, Col 4:16; 2 Thess

2:2, 15; 3:14, 17; elsewhere, 2 Pet 3:1, 16, and Acts 9:2; 15:30; 22:5; 23:25, 33.

60. See White, *Light from Ancient Letters*, 215–16, and my *Letters That Paul Did Not Write*, 57–87.

61. See, for example, Apollinarios's letter to his mother, letter no. 104a in White, *Light from Ancient Letters*, 161.

62. See the discussion of the full range of issues involved in E. Randolph Richards, *The Secretary in the Letters of Paul*, WUNT, 2/42. This book is based on Richards's earlier work, "The Role of the Secretary in Greco-Roman Antiquity and Its Implications for the Letters of Paul" (Southwestern Baptist Theological Seminary Ph.D. thesis, Fort Worth, Tex., 1988).

63. See the discussion in Hans Dieter Betz, *Galatians: A Commentary on Paul's Letter to the Churches in Galatia*, Hermeneia (Philadelphia: Fortress, 1979), 313–14.

64. See, however, 5:28, which Richards (*The Secretary*, 179) incorrectly identifies as 5:26.

65. One who has recently pleaded the case of Silvanus is Hermann Binder, "Paulus und die Thessalonicherbriefe," in *Thessalonian Correspondence*, edited by R. F. Collins, 87–93.

66. Richards is of the opinion that the mention of Silvanus and Timothy in the epistolary greetings does not indicate anything *less* than an *active* role in the composition of the letter (his emphasis). See Richards, *The Secretary*, 154.

67. See Richards, *The Secretary*, 189. Gordon J. Bahr considers that 1:1–3:13 is the work of a secretary, that is, approximately 60 percent of the letter was not actually "written" by Paul. See Bahr, "The Subscriptions in the Pauline Letters."

68. See White, *Light from Ancient Letters*, 214–16.

69. See letters nos. 104a and 104b in White, *Light from Ancient Letters*, 162, 164.

70. Cf. Phil 4:18.

71. On the authenticity of the pastorals and the literary portrayal of Paul conveyed therein see my *Letters That Paul Did Not Write*, 88–106, 124–29.

72. See Pseudo Demetrius, "On Style," 223–27.

73. These are the friendly (*philikos*), commendatory (*systatikos*), blaming (*memptikos*), reproachful (*oneidistikos*), consoling (*parmamythē-tikos*), censorious (*epitimētikos*), admonishing (*nouthetētikos*), threatening (*apeilētikos*), vituperative (*psektikos*), praising (*epainetikos*), advisory (*symbouleutikos*), supplicatory (*axiōmatikos*), inquiring (*erōtēmatikos*), responding (*apophantikos*), allegorical (*allēgorikos*), accounting (*aiti-ologikos*), accusing (*katēgorikos*), apologetic (*apologētikos*), congratulatory (*sygcharētikos*), ironic (*eirōnikos*), and thankful (*apeucharistikos*). The text and an English-language translation of Pseudo Demetrius's *Epistolary Types* (*Typoi epistolikoi*) has been published by Malherbe in *Ancient Epistolary Theorists*, 30–41. See White, *Light from Ancient Letters*, 203.

74. Note, too, that in the autobiographical confession of 2:1–12, Paul's

rhetoric was artfully described as that of a "true friend." See Betz, "Rhetoric and Theology," 23.

75. See 1 Thess 1:4; 2:1, 9, 14, 17; 3:7; 4:1, 10, 13; 5:1, 4, 12, 14, 25.

76. A first-person singular is implicit in the declension of the verb *"enorkizō* – I solemnly command you" in 5:27, but this verse does not make use of the emphatic *"egō* – I," as do 2:18 and 3:5.

77. See 1:4, "beloved by God."

78. The distributive *hekastos* of 2:11 is not insignificant in this regard. A father is expected to love his family as a unit; he should also love each and every member of that family individually.

79. Apropos epistolary self-commendation in the authentic and pseudepigraphic Pauline letters, see Schnider and Stenger, *Neutestamentlichen Briefformular,* 50-68.

80. See *Studies,* 178-80.

81. The NRSV's "certainly I…wanted to" renders the sense of Paul's own Greek, which consists only of the pronoun and a particle (*egō men*).

82. In Paul's Greek the three singular forms appear in a tightly knit sequence of four words, *kagō mēketi stegōn epempsa.*

83. Note the use of *monoi,* "all alone," in 3:1.

84. See Rom 16:16b, 21-23; 1 Cor 16:19-20a; 2 Cor 13:13; Phil 4:21a-22; Phlmn 23-24.

85. Occasionally discussions are entertained with regard to how many letters Paul actually wrote. While contemporary biblical scholarship commonly affirms that Paul wrote Romans, 1-2 Corinthians, Galatians, Philippians, 1 Thessalonians, and Philemon, some critics have been loathe to attribute even this many letters to the apostle. Pushing this type of criticism to the extreme, one might ask whether Paul himself wrote any of the letters.

In response one must take note of the early tradition that Paul was a letter writer. 2 Pet 3:15-16 attests to this tradition as do the New Testament pseudepigrapha that bear Paul's name (Ephesians, Colossians, 2 Thessalonians, 1-2 Timothy, Titus). Especially interesting in this regard is 2 Thessalonians, whose portrayal of Paul focuses on Paul, the epistolographer (see my *Letters That Paul Did Not Write,* 237, 239-40).

1 Thessalonians appears to be the oldest of the extant letters. Its epistolary style, with its strong philophronetic features and its extremely personal character, as well as its primitive theology (the expectation of an imminent parousia, the undeveloped state of its credal formulae, the undifferentiated state of its notion of ministry, etc.), bear witness to its relative antiquity. Paul's name appears in the body of the letter (2:18; cf. 1 Cor 1:12, 13; 3:4, 5, 22; 16:21; 2 Cor 10:1; Gal 5:2; Phlmn 9, 19) and it is the first name cited in the protocol. Hence one must infer that Paul is the one who actually wrote the letter to the Thessalonians.

There are, moreover, stylistic features in the other authentic letters comparable to those that can be identified in 1 Thessalonians. These features suggest that a single author is responsible for the composition of all seven letters. Paul's name is the only name that appears in the protocol of all seven letters (Paul alone in Romans and Galatians; Paul and Sosthenes in 1 Corinthians; Paul and Timothy in 2 Corinthians, Philippians, and Philemon). Apart from adopting a position of total skepticism, one must conclude that it is Paul himself who wrote 1 Thessalonians.

86. See Pseudo Demetrius, "On Style," 227: "It may be said that every-body reveals his own soul in his letters [*eikona hekastos tēs heautou psychēs graphei tēn epistolēn*]." In every other form of composition it is possible to discern the writer's character (*ēthos*), but in none so clearly as the epistolary."

87. See 2:7 and 2:18.

88. See Davis, "Remembering and Acting," esp. 60–72, 75–80.

89. See 3:10 and 4:12.

90. For an overview of some of the formulae that were typical of the Hellenistic letter, see White, *Light from Ancient Letters*, 203–13.

91. See "I Thessalonians: A Document of Roman Hellenism," an unpublished paper presented to the SBL Seminar on the Thessalonian Correspondence in 1979 by Edgar Krentz.

92. See Bjerkelund, *Parakalō*.

93. See *Studies*, 182–85.

94. On the subject of the theorists' understanding of the letter of consolation, see Paolo Cugusi, *Evoluzione e forme dell'epistolografia latina nella tarda repubblica e nei primi due secoli dell'imperio con cenni sull'epistolografia preciceroniana*, esp. 39–40, 108–9.

95. The exhortation to grieve not in 4:13; the use of sleep as a metaphor for death in 4:15; and the expression of hope in 4:17.

96. See Chapa, "Consolatory Patterns," 226. Cf. Adolf Deissmann, *Light from the Ancient East*, 164–67.

97. He has read papers on the topic to the 1972 SBL Seminar on Paul in Los Angeles and to the 1981 SBL Seminar on the Thessalonian Correspondence in San Francisco. Much of the material contained in the latter presentation has been published in an article entitled "Exhortation in First Thessalonians" and has been incorporated into "Hellenistic Moralists and the New Testament."

98. See Benjamin Fiore, *The Function of Personal Example in the Socratic and Pastoral Epistles*.

99. See 1:7; 2:14.

100. In this regard, Malherbe is generally supported by Chapa, "Consolatory Patterns," 220, and Thomas H. Olbricht, "An Aristotelian Rhetorical Analysis of 1 Thessalonians," 227.

101. See "Exhortation," 254.

102. See "Exhortation," 238.

103. See 1 Thess 2:12, 13; 3:2; 4:1, 10; 5:11, 14.

104. See Donfried, "Theology," 260.

105. See Olbricht, "Aristotelian Rhetorical Analysis," 227.

106. See Kennedy, *New Testament Interpretation through Rhetorical Criticism*, 142. While carefully avoiding simplistic generalizations, Bruce Johanson admits that 1 Thessalonians has a closer relation to the deliberative genre than to the other possibilities. See Johanson, *To All the Brethren*, 166.

107. See Wanamaker, *Thessalonians*, 47.

108. See Jewett, *The Thessalonian Correspondence*, 71–72, and "The Thessalonian Church as a Millenarian Movement," an unpublished paper read at the 1984 Chicago meeting of the SBL.

109. See G. Lyons, *Pauline Autobiography: Toward A New Understanding*, 219–21.

110. See W. Wuellner, "The Argumentative Structure of 1 Thessalonians as Paradoxical Encomium," esp. 126.

111. 1 Thess 4:10.

112. This is the *taxis* of classical rhetoric.

113. Wuellner takes specific issue with Michael Goulder's assertion that 1 Thessalonians "lacks any artifice or rhetorical structuring." See Goulder, "The Pauline Epistles," 480.

114. With respect to this general structure Wuellner agrees with Kennedy who, however, identifies 2:1–8 as a *refutatio* and 2:9–3:13 as a *narratio*. Somewhat similar is the structure postulated by Olbricht, in dependence on Wuellner, to wit, *exordium* (1:2–3), *argumentatio* (1:4–10), *probatio* (2:1–5:11), and the *peroratio* (5:12–28). See Kennedy, *New Testament Interpretation*, 142–43; Olbricht, "Aristotelian Rhetorical Analysis," 235.

115. See Johanson, *To All the Brethren*, 157–60. Johanson's analysis has been seconded by René Kieffer, "L'eschatologie en 1 Thessaloniciens dans une perspective rhétorique," 208–9.

116. See Hughes, "Rhetoric," 109–16. See also the summary, based on Hughes's previously unpublished paper, delivered in Uppsala, Lund, and other places, which appears in Jewett, *Thessalonian Correspondence*, 221, and Kieffer, "L'eschatologie," 207.

117. See Jewett, *The Thessalonian Correspondence*, 72–76, 221.

118. See Chapa, "Consolatory Patterns."

119. See Malherbe, "Exhortation," 254.

120. According to Chapa ("Consolatory Patterns," 226), it is only this formula that can be fitted directly into the Hellenistic background of the letter of condolence.

121. For example, Theodoret, *Ermēneia tēs A' pros Thessalonikeis epistolē*, ad 4:12 (sic), *PG* 82, 648.

122. Some authors, however, prefer to identify this pericope as a personal apologia or, in the case of Willi Marxsen, as an *apologia pro evangelio*.

123. The letter is punctuated by direct appeals to the Thessalonians. Paul's use of a formulaic *adelphoi* is an easily recognized marker of such appeals.

124. Similarly, Olbricht, "Aristotelian Rhetorical Analysis," 228–31.

125. See 2:17; 3:1, 5, 10.

126. See my *Studies*, 303–5. On the pastoral quality of Paul's paraenesis see also Malherbe, *Paul and the Thessalonians* and " 'Pastoral Care' in the Thessalonian Church." Malherbe writes of "Paul's pastoral practice" and his "pastoral concern." He describes the entire composition as "a parenetic letter that serves a pastoral purpose" (*Paul and the Thessalonians*, 94).

127. In addition, Johanson suggests that "several factors combine to strengthen an interpretation of 4:1–12 as also realizing an *ethos* appeal serving to strengthen the credibility and authority of the addressers in preparation

for dealing with the actual 'deficiencies of faith' that are located specifically in 4:13–5:11." Among these factors are the lack of any corrective function in 4:1–12 and the contrast between the old information of 4:1–12 and the new information that is imparted as of 4:13. See Johanson, *To All the Brethren,* 161.

128. Cf. 3:10, 11.

129. See Johanson, *To All the Brethren,* 101, 108.

130. See Aristotle, *Rhetoric,* 1, 2, 8.

131. See Johanson, *To All the Brethren,* 89.

132. Note the telltale *"gar – for"* in vv. 3, 5, and 9.

133. Paul also employs *"gar – for"* in 1:8, 9; 2:1, 14, 19, 20; 3:3, 4, 9; 4:2, 3, 7, 9, 10; 5:18.

134. See Olbricht, "Aristotelian Rhetorical Analysis," 231–32.

135. That is, if the *hoti* of v. 5 is a causal rather than a recitative *hoti.*

136. See the brief discussion by Olbricht, "Aristotelian Rhetorical Analysis," 221, and the reflections of Malherbe in *Social Aspects,* 54–59.

137. As has been previously noted, the NRSV, for stylistic reasons, renders the *pasin tois adelphois* of 5:27 as "all of them."

138. In Rom 16:22 the scribe Tertius adds a personal note to the effect that he has written the letter. In 1 Cor 5:9 and 2 Cor 7:8, Paul makes reference to a letter that he has written. In these instances he is obviously making reference to previous correspondence. Whether or not these two earlier communications have been assumed into the canonical 1 and 2 Corinthians remains a moot question among scholars.

139. See 1:2–10; 3:6–10.

140. As has been noted, the repeated interjection of *"adelphoi –* brothers and sisters" is an indication of Paul's direct appeal to his audience (the rhetorical device of *apostrophe*).

141. See Jewett, "The Form and Function of the Homiletic Benediction."

142. The reflections of Paul Ricoeur relative to the relationship between text and discourse are germane to this observation. Pursuing them would take us too far from the matter at hand.

143. Thus Paul's letter must be studied not only from the vantage point of the categories of classical rhetoric, but also from the standpoint of what is sometimes called the new rhetoric (and reader response criticism). In classic rhetoric, attention is drawn to the manner in which an orator/author composes the discourse. In the new rhetoric, attention is directed to the intended effect of an orator/author's discourse.

144. Johanson, as has been noted, considers "our coming to you was not in vain" to be a *propositio* that in favor of which Paul argues effectively in his letter.

145. Betz notes that Paul brings up the matter of his rhetoric in 2:1–12. The setting up of opposing character types (*synkrisis*) is well known to ancient rhetoricians. The vocabulary and figures of the pericope have a rhetorical background. See Betz, "Rhetoric and Theology," 21–23.

146. See my *Studies,* 365–70.

147. See Vanhoye, "La composition," esp. 82.

148. Paul's creativity and spontaneity are less apparent in the deutero-Pauline letters and in the Acts of the Apostles, but one could make the case that even these texts attest to a relatively spontaneous personality and a creative spirit.

149. With a footnoted reference to Vanhoye (whose oral communiqué has been published as "La composition," 86), Olbricht writes, "we shall designate this new genre 'church rhetoric' " ("Aristotelian Rhetorical Analysis," 226).

150. See Koester, "Experiment."

151. See the more Hellenistic "though absent in body, I am present in spirit" (*apōn tō sōmati parōn de tō pneumati*) in 1 Cor 5:3.

152. See Jewett, *Paul's Anthropological Terms*, 313-23.

153. Robert Funk has identified what he calls the "apostolic parousia" as an integral element of the Pauline letter. In the first of Paul's letters, it is 2:17-3:13 that merits this designation. See Funk, "The Apostolic Parousia: Form and Significance," esp. 252-53.

154. With Koester ("Experiment," 37, n. 10), one might note that in his later letters Paul typically uses *parousia* to talk about the arrival of an ordinary human being. In 1 Thessalonians *parousia* is not so used. On the other hand, in 1 Thessalonians *parousia* is used to designate the coming of the Lord Jesus (2:19; 3:13; 4:15; 5:23) – a usage that will become part of technical theological jargon. In his later letters Paul himself, however, will use *parousia* in this sense only in 1 Cor 15:23.

155. See Malbon, "No Need to Have Any One Write," 57.

156. See Koester, "Experiment," 37.

157. See 4:15, 17.

158. The case has been forcibly argued by Robert H. Gundry in "The Hellenization of Dominical Tradition and Christianization of Jewish Tradition in the Eschatology of 1-2 Thessalonians," esp. 162, 169.

159. The expression is used so frequently throughout the letter that the editors of the NRSV have used a stylistic paraphrase at 4:10; 5:4, 14, 25, 27.

160. In Paul's Greek the affirmation of his love for the Thessalonians is expressed in a simple comparative phrase that can be literally rendered "just as us for you." Grammatically and functionally the phrase cites the exemplarity of Paul and his companions. As such it is an expression of the *ethos* mode of Paul's appeal. My concern at the present time, however, is to the philophronetic character of Paul's letter as an *epistolary* composition.

161. See 2:5, 10.

162. See Jewett, *Paul's Anthropological Terms*, 316-17.

163. See above, 65.

164. The philophronetic character of the Hellenistic letter is not dissimilar to an at least implied function of the contemporary English-language letter. The standard salutation of our letters continues to suggest that those to whom we write are dear to us. Even a formal business letter typically begins "*Dear* Mr. Smith."

165. See Koester, "Experiment," 37.

166. Cf. Rom 1:1; 1 Cor 1:1; 2 Cor 1:1; Gal 1:1, the epistolary prescripts of his subsequent letters. Interestingly the two letters in the extant Pauline

corpus in which the expression of positive affection is most apparent, namely, 1 Thessalonians and Philippians, are those in which *apostolos* is not part of the epistolary prescript.

167. Koester, "Experiment." Koester does not adequately distinguish between the parousiac and the philophronetic function of Paul's letter, but the lack of this distinction does not really take away from the basic, and correct, thrust of his argument.

Koester also notes that "signs of the genre of the official letter are... absent," that is, apart from the fact that the letter serves as a substitute for the personal presence of the apostle Paul. This affirmation is too general. In his *ethos* appeal at 2:3-4 Paul seeks to establish that his authority to communicate comes from God himself. Moreover, Bjerkelund has shown that the *parakaleō* formula (4:1, 10; 5:14) as an *epistolary* formula represents diplomatic usage. Finally, in the introduction to his paraenesis in 4:1-2, Paul appeals to the authority of the Lord Jesus (v. 1), just as he had done in his oral appeal (v. 2). This latter feature is all the more weighty if 4:1 is taken to be the beginning of the body of Paul's letter or as the beginning of his *argumentatio*.

168. As always in dealing with ancient texts, there is the academic need to provide a critical edition of the text. That is not our concern here. The most important textual *cruces* (2:7; 3:2) have already been discussed. In any case, the Greek text given in N-A^{26}–GNT^3 is quite acceptable.

169. I have discussed this issue at some length in my *Studies*, 12-17, 96-135, and will not rehearse all the details. Nor will I attempt to fine-tune the discussion by studying the views of all those who have treated the issue since the appearance of my *Studies*. An overview of the early discussion has been provided by Carl Clemen in *Die Einheitlichkeit der paulinischen Briefe an Hand der bisher mit Bezug auf sie aufgestellten Interpolations- und Compilationshypothesen*, 13-17.

170. Some recent English-language exponents of this view are George Lyons and Earl Richard. See Lyons, *Pauline Autobiography*, 202-7; Richard, "Early Pauline Thought," 41.

171. This has been particularly true of the interpretation of Paul within the Lutheran tradition, which has had, in fact, a very heavy influence on Pauline scholarship. See, however, the judicious note of Edgar Krentz in "Evangelism and Spirit: 1 Thessalonians 1," 24, n. 6.

172. See Beker, *Paul the Apostle*.

173. See especially Johanson, *To All the Brethren*. Among recent authors who defend the authenticity of the passage, albeit from different points of view, are Tjitze Baarda, Ingo Broer, Georg Geiger, John Hurd, John Simpson, Jon Weatherly, and Karl Olav Sandnes. See Baarda, "Maar de toorn," 15-74; Geiger, "1 Thess 2, 13-16: Der Initiationstext des christlichen Antisemitismus?"; Hurd, "Paul Ahead of His Time: 1 Thess. 2:13-16"; Broer, "Der ganze Zorn"; Simpson, "The Future of Non-Christian Jews" and "1 Thessalonians 2:15-16"; Weatherly, "The Authenticity of 1 Thessalonians 2.13-16: Additional Evidence"; Sandnes, *Paul — One of the Prophets? A Contribution to the Apostle's Self-Understanding*, 191-94.

174. Principally Gerhard Friedrich in his commentary (1976) and an earlier article, "1. Thessalonicher 5, 1-11, der apologetische Einschub eines Späteren." The authenticity of the pericope has been defended by Joseph Plevnik in "1 Thess 5, 1-11."

175. Schmithals first published his opinion on the composite nature of 1 Thessalonians in 1960. An English-language version of his thesis has been published in *Paul and the Gnostics*, 123-218. See my *Studies*, 118-24. Schmithals's overall theory has been criticized by, among others, Gamble in "The Redaction of the Pauline Letters and the Formation of the Pauline Corpus."

176. See Pesch, *Die Entdeckung*.

177. See, for example, the writings of Earl Richard, especially *Jesus, One and Many*, 251, 282-84, "Contemporary Research on 1 (& 2) Thessalonians," 111, and "Early Pauline Thought," 41-42, 45-50. Richard is preparing the commentary on 1 Thessalonians for the Sacra Pagina series.

178. The duplicate thanksgiving is slavishly replicated in 2 Thessalonians (1:3-2:12; 2:13-17).

179. That is, with the exception of one verse, 4:2. For Richard, the earlier texts are found in 1:1-2:12 + 4:3-5:28 and 2:13-4:2.

180. Pesch holds not only that this earlier letter has been interpolated into a later letter, but also that the contents of the earlier letter have been rearranged. On his analysis, the earlier missive consisted of 2:13-16, 2:1-12, 2:17-3:5, 4:1-8, and 3:11-13.

181. Pace Reinhold Bohlen, who, after surveying the various arguments pro and contra, opines that the outcome of the discussion can go either way and suggests that making an option is preferable to a third possibility, namely, deferring one's choice until a literary-critical analysis of the entire Pauline corpus has been made. See Bohlen, "Die neue Diskussion um die Einheitlichkeit des 1. Thessalonicherbriefes: Eine Kurzinformation für die Verkündigungspraxis" ("The Unity of 1 Thessalonians").

182. That is, the words are Greek but the basic thought is not. Even today the reader of a book or article that has been translated into English has the impression that the words are quite correct, but that the thought is not clearly expressed because the translation seems to be overly literal (that is, too much a word-for-word translation). In such a case one might appropriately speak of "translation English."

183. See Rigaux, *Thessaloniciens*, 354.

184. The reader may recognize in this sentence the influence of Paul Ricoeur's notions of a text. They are germane to the present discussion. So, too, is a whole range of considerations drawn from linguists, the psychology of language, and the sociology of language, but they are far too complex to be fully treated here.

185. See Karl Plank's emphasis on the textual foreground created by Paul's language in *Paul and the Irony of Affliction*.

186. See "I Thessalonians: A Document of Roman Hellenism," a paper read by Edgar Krentz at the 1979 SBL seminar session on the Thessalonian correspondence.

5. Paul's Message

1. See 1:3.
2. See Johanson, *To All the Brethren*, 110.
3. See Olbricht, "Aristotelian Rhetorical Analysis," 232.
4. My analysis confirms Johanson's contention that "the deaths of fellow Christians before the parousia... constitutes the primary exigence to which the various persuasive strategies of the letter as a whole are directed." See Johanson, *To All the Brethren*, 58.
5. See my *Studies*, 209–29.
6. See *Studies*, 210.
7. See 1:7, where Christians throughout Macedonia and Achaia are also called "believers." These three passages (1:7; 2:10, 13) are the three passages in the letter in which Paul uses the verb *"pisteuō* – believe" in a present participial form to describe Christians. Almost by definition Christians are those who believe. The other two instances in the letter in which Paul uses this verb are 2:4, where it is used in an unusual fashion, namely in the passive voice, with the sense of "being entrusted with," and 4:14, where it appears as an introductory lemma for the credal formula.
8. 3:2, 5, 6, 7, 10; cf. 1:3, 8; 5:8.
9. Note the explanatory *"gar* – for" in v. 14. The *gar,* as has been noted, typically serves to indicate an enthymeme.
10. See my *Studies*, 253–66, and the earlier work of Ivan Havener, "Pre-Pauline Christological Credal Formulae of 1 Thessalonians" and Werner Kramer, *Christ, Lord, Son of God.*
11. The use of the *pist-* root in this introductory lemma should not be overlooked.
12. See Gal 5:6 and Phlmn 5. Cf. 1 Cor 13:13.
13. See Steele, "Jewish Scriptures," 16.
14. See Gal 5:6.
15. Both love and hope are expressions of faith. It is through love that faith works; hope is faith as confronted by the future. Although Paul prays for the growth of the Thessalonians' faith in 3:11, their love has proven to be as expansive as it is real (cf. 4:9–10). Accordingly Paul would hardly seem to have had in mind a lack of love on the part of the Thessalonians when he wrote, as he did in 4:10, about their lacking in faith.
16. Again, an explanatory *gar.*
17. See *Studies*, 215–16.
18. While Malherbe has frequently noted that Paul's letter is an expression of his pastoral care for his new converts, Elpidius Pax has thrown some useful light on the letter from the standpoint of Jewish exhortation to converts. Cf. E. Pax, "Beobachtungen zur Konvertitensprach im ersten Thessalonicherbrief" and "Konvertitenprobleme im ersten Thessalonicherbrief."
19. See Munck, "1 Thess i. 9–10" and Claus Bussmann, *Themen der paulinischen Missionspredigt auf dem Hintergrund des spätjüdisch-hellenistischen Missionsliteratur,* 38–56.
20. See my *Studies*, 263–66, 340–43.

21. See Cerfaux, *Christ,* 499; Havener, "Credal Formulae," 106.

22. See Schade, *Apokalyptische Christologie,* 120. See also Munck, who writes, "We thus have here in a new form a feature familiar from other letters by Paul... that is, the apostle in the introductory words states the essential message of the letter" ("1 Thess i.9–10," 108).

23. The salvific formula "*syn autō* – with the Lord/with him" appears in both v. 17 and v. 14.

24. See Munck, "1 Thess i. 9–10 and the Missionary Preaching of Paul: Textual Exegesis and Hermeneutic Reflexions," *NTS* 9 (1962–63): 95–110; Graydon F. Snyder, "A Summary of Faith in an Epistolary Context: 1 Thess 1, 9.10."

25. "*Peri*" also occurs in 1:2, 9; 3:9; 4:6; 5:25, and, in some manuscripts, 5:10. These are not, however, instances, of an epistolary use of "*peri* – concerning" to introduce a topic (*topos*).

26. Note the explanatory "*gar* – for" and the emphatic "*autoi* – yourselves" in 4:9b and 5:2, accompanied by phraseology that implies their knowledge: "taught by God to love" (*theodidaktoi eis to agapan*) and "you know very well" (*akribōs oidate*). Paul's phraseology implies that there is an extraordinary quality in their having been taught ("by God") and in their knowledge ("very well").

27. Is this another indication of the triadic structuring of Paul's thought?

28. This is seen in the decalogue (Exod 20:2–17; Deut 5:6–21), where the first words pertain to the relationship between the people and their God and the last words have to do with relationships among the people. An early Christian tradition summed up this dual responsibility in the twofold commandment of love (Matt 22:34–40; Mark 12:28–34; Luke 10:25–28; cf. Matt 19:19). Within the covenantal pattern, intra-popular responsibility is directed toward those who are members of the covenanted people (cf. Luke 10:29–37). In Paul's letter to the Thessalonians, faith is directed toward God (1:8), love principally toward other Christians (3:12; 4:9). On the decalogue and its appropriation by early Christian tradition see my "Commandment," *ABD,* vol. 1, 1097–99; "Matthew's *ENTOLAI:* Towards an Understanding of the Commandments in the First Gospel." In *The Four Gospels 1992: Festschrift Frans Neirynck,* vol. 2, 1325–48, BETL 100B (Louvain: University Press–Peeters, 1992).

29. See Gal 5:6.

30. See *Studies,* 154–72.

31. Whence the opinion of some interpolationists that it did not belong to Paul's original letter.

32. See 1:10; 2:16.

33. See Focant, "Les fils du Jour," 348–55.

34. See Langevin, "L'intervention de Dieu," 254–55; Jewett, "The Homiletic Benediction," 18–34; *The Thessalonian Correspondence,* 107; Wiles, *Paul's Intercessory Prayers,* 63, 65. Wiles notes that this wish prayer "gathers up" the main pastoral exhortations of the preceding paraenetic section (4:1–5:22). Langevin considers v. 24 to be part of the blessing, as does Gordon Wiles (68). It is, however, clear that the form of v. 24 is different from that of

v. 23. Wiles comments: "The statement (5:9)... is answered by the exultant declaration of God's faithfulness – the 'Amen' sentence of verse 24" (67–68). For Johanson, who makes the case that vv. 23–24 is a coherent unit, v. 23 is the wish prayer and v. 24 a "closing assurance." Cf. B. J. Johanson, *To All the Brethren*, 140–41.

35. Paul's *holoklēron hymōn to pneuma... amemptōs... tērētheiē*" might be better rendered "may your whole spirit, soul, and body be kept blameless."

36. See P. A. Van Stempvoort, "Eine stilistische Lösung einer alten Schwierigkeit in 1. Thess. V. 23."

37. See Rom 15:33; 16:20; 1 Cor 14:33; 2 Cor 13:11; Phil 4:9 (cf. Heb 13:20).

38. See 1:5, 6; 4:8; 5:19.

39. Thus, B. Mariani in "Corpo-anima-spirito."

40. Thus, José O'Callaghan, "Una nueva interpretación de 1 Thess 5, 23?"

41. See Jewett, *Paul's Anthropological Terms*, 175–82; *The Thessalonian Correspondence*, 108.

42. See Jewett, *Paul's Anthropological Terms*, 17; "Enthusiastic Radicalism and the Thessalonian Correspondence"; *The Thessalonian Correspondence*, 100–102, 107–8.

43. See Wiles, *Paul's Intercessory Prayers*, 67.

44. See Wiles, *Paul's Intercessory Prayers*, 65.

45. *Hagiōsynē*, but see also "with all the saints – *hagiōn*."

46. See Johanson, *To All the Brethren*, 109–10.

47. See Wiles, *Paul's Intercessory Prayers*, 61.

48. The wish prayer of 5:23 has a verb in the optative, but the "petition" of 3:13 is in the form of an infinitive clause of purpose, introduced by *eis*.

49. See also H. D. Betz, "Rhetoric and Theology," 23.

50. For a history of the interpretation of this passage, see Hubert Jurgensen, "Saint Paul et la parousie: I Thessaloniciens 4, 13–5, 11 dans l'exégèse moderne et contemporaine."

51. In 4:13 Paul uses the present participle in the middle or passive deponent form; in 4:14 and 15 he uses the aorist participle in the passive deponent form.

52. Sophocles used the verb in this sense, as did Paul (1 Cor 7:39; 11:30; 15:6, 18, 20, 51 in addition to 1 Thess 4:13, 14, 15) and other passages in the New Testament. See T. L. Howard, "The Meaning of 'Sleep' in 1 Thessalonians 5:10 – A Reappraisal," who correctly argues that *koimaomai* is a metaphor for death. He rightly disagrees with Edgar, who took the expression as a metaphor for "failing to watch," that is, a kind of spiritual insensitivity. See T. R. Edgar, "The Meaning of 'Sleep' in 1 Thessalonians 5:10."

53. Cf. 1 Cor 12:1–4 where the interfacing of "*ta pneumatika* – spiritual gifts" and "*ta charismata* – gifts" has a critical function.

54. From Paul's usage in 1 Corinthians 15 (vv. 6, 18, 20, 51; cf. 1 Cor 7:39; 11:30), where it is also interchangeable with "*hoi nekroi* – the dead" (1 Cor 15:12, 13, 15, 16, 20, 21, 29, 32, 35, 42, 52), one might draw the conclusion that, in the light of the resurrection, death is to be considered

otherwise than it would have been had Jesus not been raised from the dead and there be no resurrection from the dead.

55. See Joël Delobel, "The Fate of the Dead according to 1 Thes 4 and 1 Cor 15," 342–43, n. 12.

56. See 1:1; 2:14; 5:18.

57. There has been a significant discussion (by A. Schweitzer, A. Wikenhauser, etc.) in earlier decades of this century as to whether the "in Christ" formula implied some sort of a mystical union between the believer and Christ, but this need not detain us here.

58. See 1:6; 3:3, 7.

59. See 2:14–15.

60. See Hans Conzelmann, *An Outline of the Theology of the New Testament*, 200.

61. See 1:10 where Paul, nonetheless, has likewise made use of a credal formula.

62. Paul Ellingworth notes that the verb *"axei* – will bring" has the connotation of "gather" and that, in context, it implies an upward movement. See Ellingworth, "Which Way Are We Going? A Verb of Movement, especially in 1 Thess 4, 14b."

63. That is, minuscule 1739, according to the standard system of cataloguing New Testament manuscripts.

64. The story of the resurrection begins with that of Jesus. See Holtz, *Der erste Brief,* 193.

65. John Gillman has drawn attention to the parallel between 1 Thess 4:13–18 and 1 Cor 15. Both passages have a paraenetic context. Both draw attention to the common faith of believers, by means of a credal formula, and then draw out its implications. See Gillman, "Signals of Transformation in 1 Thessalonians 4:13–18" (see also the summary in Delobel, "The Fate of the Dead," 343–44, n. 14). Within their respective epistolary contexts, each of these passages has its own purpose. Hence it might be useful to apply Beker's coherence-contingency scheme to them rather than to speak of a strict parallel. See his *Paul the Apostle,* as well as his subsequent writings, esp. the succinct explanation in "Recasting Pauline Theology."

66. See 1:5; 2:5, 7; 4:1–2.

67. See the succinct summary by Frans Neirynck in "Paul and the Sayings of Jesus," 308–11.

68. Comp. Matt 24:30–31 (see N. Hyldahl, "Auferstehung Christi, Auferstehung der Toten [1 Thess 4, 13–18]," esp. 130) or John 5:25; 6:39–40; 11:25–26 (see P. Nepper-Christensen, "Das verborgene Herrenwort: Eine Untersuchung über 1 Thess 4, 13–18"; R. H. Gundry, "The Hellenization of Dominical Tradition and Christianization of Jewish Tradition in the Eschatology of 1–2 Thessalonians," 164–66). Christopher Tuckett has criticized the view that Paul was making use of such evangelical logia in "Synoptic Tradition in 1 Thessalonians?" esp. 176–82.

69. The expression *"logos theou* – word of the Lord" is used nowhere else of a saying of Jesus.

70. See *Studies,* 160–62, and Harnisch, *Eschatologische Existenz,* 44–45.

71. Cf. Nikolas Walter, "Paulus und die urchristliche Jesustradition," *NTS* 31 (1985): 498-522, 507-8. Walter notes that sometimes the discussion about the identification of the precise content of the traditional logion extends to 5:2, where the metaphor of the thief in the night is similar to that found in Matt 24:43 and Luke 12:39. Walter's article generally restricts Paul's use of the Jesus tradition to paraenetic motifs and very general usage.

72. This is the third and last time in this pericope that the verb *"koimaomai* – sleep" is used to designate the dead.

73. For example, 4 Ezra 13:13-24, "But much more woe unto them that do not survive! For they that do not survive must be sorrowful, knowing as they do what things are reserved in the last days, but not attaining unto them.... Know, therefore, that those who survive are more blessed than those who have died." Cf. R. H. Charles, *APOT,* 2, 168; Delobel, "The Fate of the Dead," 345, n. 15. Some apocalyptic texts that separate the resurrection of the dead from other eschatological events are 2 Esdr 7:25-44; 2 *Bar* 29-30. For a discussion of some of the pertinent issues, see A. F. J. Klijn, "I Thessalonians 4, 13-18 and its Background in Apocalyptic Literature," 67-73.

74. For Niels Hyldahl, the problem is that some, under the influence of a gnostic disturbance, had actually denied the resurrection from the dead. Accordingly, Paul affirms both the resurrection *and* the parousia. See Hyldahl, "Auferstehung Christi."

75. See Günter Kegel, *Auferstehung Jesus – Auferstehung der Toten: Eine traditionsgeschichtliche Untersuchung zum Neuen Testament,* 36; Jürgen Becker, *Auferstehung der Toten im Urchristentum,* 39, 46; Marxsen, *Der erste Brief;* Lüdemann, *Paul,* 219-20.

76. See Paul Hoffmann, *Die Toten in Christus: Eine religionsgeschichtliche und exegetische Untersuchung zur paulinischen Eschatologie,* 207-38; Joseph Plevnik, "The Taking Up of the Faithful and the Resurrection of the Dead in 1 Thessalonians 4:13-18," 276; Delobel, "The Fate of the Dead," 345; Best, *Thessalonians,* 181; Wanamaker, *Thessalonians,* 171-72; Morris, *Thessalonians,* 140, etc.

77. Note the *"hoti* – for" with which v. 15 begins.

78. Paul was not only familiar with Jewish apocalyptic motifs, he was thoroughly steeped in Jewish apocalypticism. See Beker, *Paul the Apostle,* esp. 135-81.

79. John J. Collins writes: "The language of the apocalypses is not descriptive, referential newspaper language, but the *expressive* language of poetry, which uses symbols and imagery to articulate a sense of feeling about the world. Their abiding value does not lie in the pseudoinformation they provide about cosmology or future history, but in their affirmation of a transcendent world." Cf. J. J. Collins, *The Apocalyptic Imagination: An Introduction to the Jewish Matrix of Christianity,* 214.

80. On the prominence of statements about God in this passage, see Jerome H. Neyrey, "Eschatology in 1 Thessalonians: The Theological Factor in 1:9-10; 2:4-5; 3:11-13; 4:6 and 4:13-18," 225-27. See also Gillman, "Signals of Transformation," 276, who draws attention to the importance of the passive *"harpagēsometha* – will be caught up" in this regard.

81. See D. S. Russell, *The Method and Message of Jewish Apocalyptic, 100 BC–AD 100,* OTL (London: SCM, 1964), 205–34.

82. See Wolfgang Weifel, "Die Hauptrichtung des Wandels im eschatologischen Denkens des Paulus," *TZ* 30 (1974): 65–81, who describes 4:13–18 as a "thoroughly apocalyptic piece" (81).

83. See Russell, *Jewish Apocalyptic,* 122–27.

84. Cf. Joseph Plevnik, "The Parousia as Implication of Christ's Resurrection (An Exegesis of 1 Thess 4, 13–18)," 233–72.

85. Cf. 4 Ezra, 2 *Bar.* The Jewish tradition was generally associated with figures like Moses, Elijah, Enoch, or the Messiah.

86. See Gerhard Lohfink, *Die Himmelfahrt Jesu: Untersuchungen zu den Himmelfahrts- und Erhöhhungstexten bei Lukas,* 32–78; Plevnik, "The Taking Up of the Faithful," 278–83.

87. Alternatively, ultimate salvation includes deliverance from the wrath to come (1:10; 5:9).

88. Cf. 5:9.

89. Note the apocalyptic motifs in Matthew's Jewish-Christian description of the resurrection of Jesus (Matt 28:1–2; cf. 27:51–53).

90. García del Moral's contention that Paul is envisioning two stages in salvation, one acorporeal, the other corporeal, is implausible. García del Moral bases his argumentation of the supposition of Paul's chiastic use of Ps 115:17–18. Cf. A. García del Moral, " 'Nosotros los vivos': Convicción personal de Pablo o reinterpretación de un salmo? (1 Tes 4, 13–5, 11."

91. See Hans C. Cavallin, "Parusi och uppstandelse. 1 Th. 4:13–18 som kombination av tva slags eskatologi," *STK* 59 (1983): 54–63. Cavallin compares Paul's use of the resurrection motif with the (Pharisaic) doctrine of the resurrection of the dead (cf. Dan 12:1–3) and Paul's exposition of the parousia event with the translation of the Son of Man (cf. Dan 7).

92. See *Studies,* 161; Gundry, "Eschatology," 165.

93. Heinz Giesen argues, strongly and somewhat curiously, that Paul had never taught the expectation of an imminent parousia. At best, he is willing to concede that some, in an eagerness that it come soon, might have misunderstood Paul's announcement of the parousia. The point of Paul's teaching in 4:13–18 is that each generation should be understood in the light of the parousia; those who are alive must live in such a manner as to be prepared for the parousia. In effect the basic thrust of 4:13–18 is similar to that of 5:1–11. See Giesen, "1 Thess 4, 13–18."

94. The classic exposition of this approach is that of Erik Peterson. See Peterson, "Die Einholung des Kyrios" and *"apantēsis," TDNT,* vol. 1, 380–81.

95. See, especially, Jacques Dupont, *SYN CHRISTOI: L'union avec le Christ suivant saint Paul* (Bruges: Abbaye de Saint-André, 1952), 64–73; Maurits Sabbe, "De Paulinische beschrijving van de parousie," *Collationes Brugenses et Gandavenses* 7 (1961): 86–114; Plevnik, "Parousia as Implication," esp. 212–24, 229–72; Holtz, *Der erste Brief,* 194–208, etc.

96. Cf. Phil Ware, "The Coming of the Lord: Eschatology and 1 Thessalonians."

97. The description is drawn from the title of Gundry's article, "The

Hellenization of Dominical Tradition and the Christianization of Jewish Tradition in the Eschatology of 1-2 Thessalonians," but he postulates a much too precise dependence of Paul on a specific dominical tradition.

98. See de Jonge, *Christology in Context.*

99. See, for example, Scott Gambrill Sinclair, who writes: "If Paul did tailor the christology of a letter to achieve specific pastoral goals, he must have expressed that christology in a way that readers would feel its impact as they went along." See Sinclair, *Jesus Christ according to Paul: The Christologies of Paul's Undisputed Epistles and the Christology of Paul,* 12.

100. For recent overviews see, in addition to the essay in my *Studies,* 252–84, and the studies there referenced, de Jonge, *Christology in Context,* 33–39; Richard, *Jesus: One and Many,* 248–52; S. G. Sinclair, "The Christology of I Thessalonians," in *Jesus Christ according to Paul,* 119–29; Otto Merk, "Zur Christologie im 1. Thessalonicherbrief," 97–110.

101. J. Paul Sampley provides a useful list of sixteen procedures that may be helpful in the determination of the coherencies in Paul's thought. The procedures have not been systematically applied in what follows. Nonetheless, their application would highlight some of the principal elements to which attention is drawn in the summary that follows. See Sampley, "From Text to Thought World: The Route to Paul's Ways." In *Pauline Theology,* vol. 1, edited by Jouette M. Bassler, 3–14, 9–14.

102. On the theology of the letter, see my *Studies,* 230–52, and *"ho theos."*

103. See Merk, "Christologie," 104–8.

104. One might note again the singularity of Paul's prayer in 3:11, a prayer addressed to God and our Lord Jesus, as if they acted in consort.

105. See Merk, "Christologie," 108–9.

106. Cf. 1 Cor 15:3-8, where each member of the twofold creed is developed by means of a proof, an indication of the hermeneutical key, and an element of explanation.

107. *"Ek tōn nekrōn —* from the dead" is in the plural number, that is, Paul and the tradition that he here echoes look upon the resurrection of Jesus not as an event in some sort of clinical isolation, but as a reality whose frame of reference is (all) those who have died.

108. Some significant manuscript evidence for a *"peri hēmōn"* reading of the formula, including the *prima manus* of the Codex Sinaiticus and the Codex Vaticanus. The weight of this evidence is such that the *peri-* reading appeared in the twenty-fifth edition of the Nestle text and has won the support of Henk de Jonge. Were the *peri-* reading to be adopted, the Greek would still be rendered "died for us," and the soteriological implications of the formula would remain manifest. See the textual discussion in de Jonge, "The CHRISTOS APETHANEN HYPER Formula," 229–30.

109. De Jonge, "The CHRISTOS APETHANEN HYPER Formula," 235. De Jonge takes issue with those like Jeremias, Lohse, Riesenfeld, and Hengel (see also Chapa, "Consolatory Patterns," 281–82), who identify the celebration of the eucharist as the most plausible *Sitz-im-Leben* for the dying formula.

110. See Otto Merk, "Nachahmung Christi: Zu ethischen Perspektiven in

der paulinischen Theologie," 193–96. Merk makes reference to much of the recent German-language literature on the imitation motif.

111. See, further, particularly with respect to 3:4, Michael Wolter, "Der Apostel und seine Gemeinden als Teilhaber am Leidensgeschick Jesu Christi: Beobachtungen zur paulinischen Leidenstheologie."

112. What follows is a modest paraphrase of the conclusion of my earlier work on the christology of 1 Thessalonians. See my *Studies*, 284.

113. See also Plevnik, "The Center of Pauline Theology," *CBQ* 51 (1989): 461–78, 477.

114. See Sinclair, *Jesus Christ according to Paul*, 122–23.

115. Sampley cites the importance of prayer, albeit the thanksgiving, as worthy of scrutiny in the effort to determine the consistencies of Paul's thought world. See Sampley, "From Text to Thought World," 12.

116. See 1:3; 2:19; 3:13; 4:15 (twice), 16, 17 (twice); 5:9, 23, 28.

117. See my *Studies*, 269–71.

118. See 4:15.

119. See Udo Schnelle, "Der erste Thessalonicherbrief und die Entstehung der paulinischen Anthropologie," 209; Lambrecht, "Evangelisation," 328. Siegfried Schulz offers an overview of the various grounds and motivational factors of early Pauline paraenesis in *Neutestamentliche Ethik*, 310–19.

120. See Geiger, "Der Initiationstext des christlichen Antisemitismus?"

121. See Johanson, *To All the Brethren*, 84–85.

122. Cf. Rom 1:24–27. There is, moreover, the possibility that Paul was putting the Thessalonians on guard against the cult of Aphrodite itself or the intrusion of some of its elements into the Christian experience. See Ulonska, "Christen und Heiden."

123. See *Studies*, 299–335. My understanding of Paul's text is such that the translation of the RSV is preferable to that of the NRSV in this instance. See also O. Larry Yarbrough, *Not Like the Gentiles: Marriage Rules in the Letters of Paul*, 65–87, who has examined the passage, in depth, in the light of Jewish and Greco-Roman moral traditions. Our positions have been criticized, inadequately, by Michael McGehee, "A Rejoinder to Two Recent Studies Dealing with 1 Thess 4:4," *CBQ* 51 (1989): 82–89. See also Norbert Baumert, "Brautwerbung – das einheitliche Thema von 1 Thess 4, 3–8," 318–29, for whom "acquiring a woman" essentially means being in love with her with marriage intended.

124. Attentive to the social situation of the Thessalonian community, existing in a Greco-Roman society in which slavery was an institution, Scott Bartchy has suggested to me the possibility that the reflexive pronoun "*heautou* – his own," whose presence in the metaphorical expression is one reason for my conviction that the referent of "*skeuos* – vessel" cannot be the man's own body, may be an indication that Paul intended the Thessalonian males to marry and have sexual intercourse with their own wives rather than with their slaves.

125. See my *Studies*, 326–35. Cf. Baumert, "Brautwerbung," esp. 329–35.

126. See Jer 2:26; 9:9; Job 24:14, etc.

127. See Matt 24:43-44; Luke 12:39-40; 2 Pet 3:10; Rev 3:3; 16:15; cf. *Gos. Thom.*, 21.

128. *Iliad*, 11, 268 ff.

129. See Ps 48:7; Isa 21:3; 26:17; Jer 4:31; 6:24; 13:21; 22:23; 50: 47; Mic 4:9; *Hen* 62:4; 1QH 3:7-12; 4 Ezra 4:40-42.

130. See Jer 51:39; 1 Pet 4:8.

131. See Wis 5:15 and several passages in the Qumran texts.

132. See 1QM 1:9, 10, 11, 12.

133. On the Thessalonians' perception of time (and space), see Georgia Masters Keightley, "The Church's Memory of Jesus: A Social Science Analysis of 1 Thessalonians," 153-55, and my "God in the First Letter," 148-53.

134. See particularly Harnisch, *Eschatologische Existenz*.

135. See Jer 6:14; 8:11; Ezek 13:10; Mic 3:5.

136. See Victor Hasler, *"eirēnē," EDNT*, vol. 1, 394-97, 396.

137. See Rigaux, "Tradition et rédaction dans 1 Th. v. 1-10," 325.

138. See Focant, "Les fils du Jour," 354.

139. There are no explicit citations or scriptural argumentation in 1 Thessalonians. The lack of scriptural argumentation is to be expected in a letter written to persons who had formerly been Gentiles. Since they were relatively new converts, it is quite unlikely that they would have been familiar with the Jewish scriptures.

140. The imbalance between *"eis orgēn –* for wrath" and *"eis peripoēsin sōterias –* for obtaining salvation" and the complex nature of the latter expression, literally, "for the acquisition of salvation," need not detain us. The antithesis is clearly expressed by Paul's *"ouk... alla –* not ... but."

141. Cf. Acts 22:3.

142. One's choice of words must necessarily be nuanced. Paul had a dichotomous view of the world. People were neatly separated into those who knew God and those who did not. It is clear that the Thessalonians to whom Paul was writing had been among those who did not know God. At the time that Paul wrote to them, however, they did know God (1:9). They had become God-knowers, Jews, in effect. The language of election in 1:1, 4 and the language of sanctification in 4:3-8 show that Paul considers those to whom he wrote to have been coopted into the chosen people, God's own people.

143. See 5:18, especially as compared with 4:3, in its epistolary context.

144. *"Parelabete –* learned" corresponds to the Hebrew *qibbel*, the term used of the transmission of traditional material in rabbinism. *"Peripatein,"* literally, "to walk," used twice in 4:1 ("to live"; "you are doing"), reflects the Hebrew *halak*, from which is derived halakah, the collection of norms for living derived from the scriptures. "The will of God" was a major motif in late Judaism. See my *Studies*, 304, 327-34.

145. See Denis, "L'apôtre Paul"; my *Studies*, 189-91; K. O. Sandnes, *Paul*. The final words of Sandnes's study contain a judicious and accurate reflection, to wit, " ... there are two, relatively different, kinds of prophet in the NT: The apostle-prophet and the early Christian prophets. The apostle-prophet we consider in many ways a successor to the OT canonical prophets, while the early Christian prophets stand within the wider stream of prophecy in OT

Judaism and the Greco-Roman World" (245–46). Paul and his companions were prophets of the first sort.

146. The verb "*paralambanō* – deliver" does, however, appear. See 2:13; 4:1.

147. My rather minimalistic expression is simply an attempt to obviate the necessarily lengthy discussion of the nature and formulation of early Christian christology.

148. See the *Marana tha* formulation in 1 Cor 16:23.

149. In my *Studies* I have studied the possible influences of early Christian liturgical tradition on 1 Thessalonians at some length (136–53).

150. With regard to 1:10 the point has been especially developed by Langevin. I would, however, take issue with his contention that Paul's use of the "*Huios* – Son" title per se derives from the Son of Man tradition. See Langevin, "Le Seigneur Jésus" and *Jésus Seigneur*.

151. See Harnisch, *Eschatologische Existenz*, 44–45; my *Studies*, 160–61.

152. See Ulrich Luz, *Das Geschichtsverständnis des Paulus*, 327–28; my *Studies*, 159, etc. The point is, as has been noted, a moot issue. Some scholars continue to hold that the saying derives from the historical Jesus or that it results from a revelation to Paul.

153. See Paul-Emile Langevin, *Jésus Seigneur*, 304–10.

154. Especially *Paul and the Thessalonians* and the essays contained in *The Popular Philosophers*.

155. The contemporary interpreter of Paul's letter must take the phenomenon of intertextuality into account in understanding how Paul's letter has been understood throughout its almost two millennia of existence. Due attention must also be paid to intertextuality as an operative factor in the composition of the letter.

156. See Exod 4:31 (3:9).

157. See Ps 9:9; 31:7; 33:6, 17; 36:39–40; Hab 3:16; Zeph 1:15; Dan 12:1; etc.

6. The Birth of the New Testament

1. Literally "*hoi...pantes adelphoi* – all the brothers."

2. See, however, 1 Thess 2:7, where all three are simply called "apostles of Christ." Paul's manner of speaking in this passage suggests that being an apostle of Christ so constitutes a person that he or she might legitimately make claims upon those to whom they have been sent.

3. See also Acts 16:14. On the women at Philippi, see, among other works, Malinowski, "Brave Women," and Florence Morgan Gillman, *Women Who Knew Paul*, 43–49.

4. This letter is probably to be dated around 56–57 c.e., but there are some scholars who hold that it was written during Paul's Roman imprisonment. In the latter case, it would have been composed shortly after 60 c.e. and would be the latest of Paul's extant letters.

5. See S. Scott Bartchy, "Philemon, Epistle to," 307.

6. Note the "your" (*sou*, in the singular) modifying "house" in v. 2.

7. The RSV's and REB's translation of *presbytēs* as "ambassador" deprives the term of its proper rhetorical force.

8. That is, he is brother not only to Paul but also to Philemon and all those gathered in his house. Specifically one should note the correlation between "Timothy our brother" as the co-sender of the letter and "Apphia our sister" as one of its named and identified recipients.

9. See Joseph Fitzmyer, "Paul," *NJBC,* 1336; Hans Dieter Betz, "Corinthians, Second Epistle to the."

10. See, for example, the *NJBC,* where both Fitzmyer ("Paul," 1336) and Raymond Brown (in R. E. Brown and R. F. Collins, "Canonicity," 1034–54, 1045) date the Corinthian correspondence to the year 57.

11. I have dealt, if somewhat cursorily, with the ecclesiastical implications of the various Pauline epistolary addresses to the churches in "Glimpses into Some Local Churches."

12. The expression is taken from the title of an article by Günther Bornkamm, "The Letter to the Romans as Paul's Last Will and Testament." Paul's letter to the Romans was probably written in the year 58 C.E., not yet a decade after he wrote 1 Thessalonians, the first of his letters.

13. As to its specific literary genre, see, among others, Martin Luther Stirewalt, Jr., "The Form and Function of the Greek Letter-Essay," and David E. Aune, "Romans as a *Logos Protreptikos.*"

14. See Harry Gamble, *The Textual History of the Letter to the Romans: A Study in Textual and Literary Criticism,* and Donfried, "A Short Note on Romans 16."

15. See the discussions in Fitzmyer, "The Letter to the Romans," 831–32, and Charles D. Myers, Jr., "Romans, Epistle to the," 818–20.

16. In this overview I have followed the general consensus as to the relative chronology of the seven letters whose Pauline authorship is undisputed. See in addition to Brown, "Canonicity," 1045, and Fitzmyer, "Paul," 1336, Wedderburn, "Recent Pauline Chronologies." Among the important participants in the discussion have been Jewett, *Chronology,* and Lüdemann, *Paul.*

17. On the non-Pauline character and significance of these texts see my *Letters That Paul Did Not Write.*

18. Victor Paul Furnish holds, nonetheless, that it is impossible to date Colossians more closely than to assign it to the 65–90 C.E. period. See Furnish, "Colossians, Epistle to the," 1095.

19. It has been established that the epistle to the Colossians is literarily dependent upon Romans, Corinthians (1 and 2), Galatians, and Thessalonians. See, in this regard, E. P. Sanders, "Literary Dependence in Colossians."

20. As one might expect, the manuscript tradition gives ample evidence of scribes expanding the greeting of Col 1:2 so that it is more fully conformed to the Pauline model.

21. On the significance of this verse, see my *Studies,* 365–70, and *Letters That Paul Did Not Write,* 189.

22. And a characteristic "church in her house" in 4:15.

23. In addition to my brief observations in *Letters That Paul Did Not Write*, 143-44, see the summary of the discussion in Furnish, "Ephesians, Epistle to the." Furnish (541) opines that the epistle can be dated broadly to the 70-95 C.E. period.

24. See the discussion in Metzger, *Textual Commentary*, 601, and my *Letters That Paul Did Not Write*, 139-41.

25. My presumption is that the canonical deutero-Pauline letters were written by males. My judgment is that women had positions of leadership in the early Pauline communities, as the letters of Paul so clearly attest (Rom 16:1-2, 3-5a, 6, 7, 12, 15; 1 Cor 16:19; Phil 4:2-3; Phlmn 2, not to mention the references in Acts and the deutero-Paulines). However, there was a later movement toward patriarchal structures, even in the Pauline communities. In the light of this phenomenon (cf. Eph 5:22-24), it cannot be presumed that women read letters in the Christian assembly in the time or place that Ephesians was written.

26. The intended exchange of letters may, however, have been prompted by the pseudepigraphal character of Colossians. It may have been a clever way of insuring that the epistle to the Colossians was read to the Colossians. See my *Letters That Paul Did Not Write*, 189, and Charles P. Anderson, "Laodiceans, Epistle to the." In this case there would not have existed any first-century letter to the Laodiceans, whose existence is problematic on any reading of the text. There is no extant letter to the Laodiceans, except if, as Marcion believed, the extant epistle to the Ephesians was intended for the Laodiceans, or, as John Knox held, the author of Col 4:16 had the letter to Philemon in mind. An apocryphal letter to the Laodiceans appeared in the East during the fourth century.

27. See Metzger, *The Canon of the New Testament: Its Origin, Development, and Significance*, 265. Without the use of the descriptive epithet, Richard Bauckham similarly explains the omission of a geographical destination from the prescript of the epistle of Jude. See Bauckham, "Jude, Epistle of," 1102.

28. Michael Prior, who argues for the authenticity of 2 Timothy, holds that the thanksgiving of 2 Tim 1:3-5 functions in much the same way as do the other Pauline thanksgivings. See Prior, *Paul the Letter-Writer and the Second Letter to Timothy*, 62.

29. Jerome Murphy-O'Connor has noted the difference between the address of the second letter to Timothy and the addresses of the other two pastoral epistles. From the cumulative results of his study, which is attentive to other points as well, Murphy-O'Connor calls into question the hypothesis of the literary unity of the pastorals. See Murphy-O'Connor, "2 Timothy Contrasted with 1 Timothy and Titus."

30. It would therefore be appropriate to speak about these texts as being doubly pseudonymous: not only was the apostle Paul not their real author, but also Timothy and Titus were not the names of the historical persons for whom they were destined.

31. See my *Letters That Paul Did Not Write*, 214, 217, 236.

32. Scholars generally agree that some interest in gathering Paul's correspondence had been generated by the end of the first century. See Gamble, "The Pauline Corpus and the Early Christian Book," 271; *The New Testament Canon: Its Making and Meaning*, 36-41; and Quinn, "Timothy and Titus, Epistles to," 568.

33. For a brief overview and critical reflection, see my *Letters That Paul Did Not Write*, 134-35, and Furnish, "Ephesians," 541.

In a study of the Pauline collection David Trobisch has argued for a major role to have been played in a rather complex history by the church at Ephesus. There, he holds, was an initial collection (Romans, 1-2 Corinthians, Galatians), later expanded with other congregational letters (Ephesians, Philippians, Colossians, Thessalonians), and supplemented by a collection of letters to individuals with Philemon as the focus. See Trobisch, *Die Entstehung der Paulusbriefsammlung: Studien zu den Anfängen christlicher Publizistik*.

34. See Jerome Carcopino, *Cicero: The Secrets of His Correspondence*, vol. 1 (reprint of 1951 ed.; New York: Greenwood, 1969), 4-37.

35. The idea of a collection of letters to churches is also evident in the Muratorian Canon: "For the blessed Apostle Paul himself, following the rule of his predecessor John, writes only by name to seven churches in the following order – to the Corinthians a first, to the Ephesians a second, to the Philippians a third, to the Colossians a fourth, to the Galatians a fifth, to the Thessalonians a sixth, to the Romans a seventh; although for the sake of admonition there is a second to the Corinthians and to the Thessalonians, yet one Church is recognized as being spread over the entire world."

Many historians believe that the fragmentary manuscript, from which this citation has been taken, represents a second-century Roman text. There are, however, reasons to believe that it is a fourth-century Eastern document. See my *Introduction*, 32-35, which reflects the pioneering revisionist work of A. C. Sundberg, and, further, Geoffrey Mark Hahneman, *Muratorian Fragment and the Development of the Canon*.

36. Marcion's inscription identified the canonical epistle to the Ephesians as *"ad Laodicenses."* That he does so is an indication that the text of Ephesians available to him was one in which the geographical designation was absent from verse 1.

37. Tertullian, *Adversus Marcionem*, V, 21; *PL* 2, 524. The letter is, as has been noted above, actually addressed to Philemon... and the church in your house" (Phlmn 1-2).

38. Thus Jerome Quinn in *The Letter to Titus*, AB, 35 (New York: Doubleday, 1990), 7, and "Timothy and Titus" (the text is to a large extent the same as the introduction to his commentary), 564, "The Last Volume of Luke; The Relation of Luke-Acts and the PE," 63-64, 72. Quinn believes that the long and rather out of character epistolary prescript to Titus indicates that it headed the collection.

39. See C. Bradford Welles, "The Yale Genesis Fragment," *Yale University Library Gazette* 39 (July 1964): 1-8; C. H. Roberts, "P. Yale I and the Early Christian Book," *Essays in Honor of C. G. Bradford Welles: American Stud-*

ies in Papyrology, 1 (New Haven, Conn.: American Society of Papyrologists, 1966), 25–28. For these references, see Quinn, "P⁴⁶," 383, n. 30.

40. See Donfried, "Paul as *Scēnopoios.*"

41. See C. P. Anderson, "Laodiceans."

42. See Dana Andrew Thomaso, "Corinthians, Third Epistle to the," *ABD,* vol. 1, 1154; Metzger, *Canon,* 118, 219, 223

43. Eight letters are attributed to Seneca. It is apparently on the basis of this pseudepigraphal correspondence that Jerome, the biblicist, considered Seneca as a Christian saint. A critical edition of the correspondence has been published by Robert Weber in *Biblia Sacra iuxta Vulgatam Versionem,* 2 (2d ed.; Stuttgart: Wurttenbergische Bibelanstalt, 1975).

44. See 2 Tim 3:14–17.

45. See Phlmn 24 and Acts 15: 36–41; Col 4:10; 2 Tim 4:11.

46. *Ecclesiastical History,* III, 39, 15–16.

47. The detail that Mark had been Peter's interpreter may well be legendary. By the time of Eusebius the tradition of the apostolic foundation of the church and the apostolic origin of the foundational texts had been rather well established.

48. See J. Andrew Overman, *Matthew's Gospel and Formative Judaism: The Social World of the Matthean Community* (Minneapolis: Fortress, 1990).

49. See Raymond E. Brown, *The Community of the Beloved Disciple: The Life, Love and Hates of an Individual Church in New Testament Times.*

50. See my "The Twelve: Another Perspective," in *These Things Have Been Written,* 68–86.

51. See my *John and His Witness,* 68–78.

52. The papers read during the 39th session of the Louvain Biblical Colloquium (August 7–9, 1990) represent a departure from the consensus in that they generally postulate the dependence of the fourth gospel on the Synoptics. See Adelbert Denaux, *John and the Synoptics,* especially the contribution of Frans Neirynck, who chronicles the recent history of the discussion of the issue in "John and Synoptics: 1975–1990," 3–62.

53. See J. Louis Martyn, *History and Theology in the Fourth Gospel,* and the many authors who have since followed his insights.

54. See C. K. Barrett, "The Place of John and the Synoptics within the Early History of Christian Thought," 74. In this regard it may be interesting to note that Rudolf Schnackenburg's attempts to characterize the heresy addressed by 1 John, whose links with the Johannine gospel are manifest, notes: "The gnostic movement is in the ascendant. The imagery and terms of this movement have won out against the Pauline tradition and are creating a powerful impression." See Rudolf Schnackenburg, *The Johannine Epistles: Introduction and Commentary,* 17.

55. See Raymond E. Brown, *The Epistles of John,* AB, 30 (Garden City, N.Y.: Doubleday, 1982), 3–146. Brown writes: "Most probably I John was written not only after GJohn but after an interval long enough for a debate to have arisen about the implications of GJohn and for a schism to have taken place" (101). Although most scholars today agree about the priority of the gospel, a

number caution that the issue is moot and that, in any case, one must allow for the possibility that the epistle was composed before the final redaction of the gospel. See, for example, Philippe H. Menoud, *L'Evangile de Jean d'après les recherches récentes,* 71–72, and Martin Hengel, *The Johannine Question,* 52.

56. See Barrett, "The Place of John and the Synoptics," 74.

57. See R. E. Brown, *Epistles of John,* ix, 86–92.

58. See R. E. Brown, *Epistles of John,* ix; R. Schnackenburg, *The Johannine Epistles,* 267.

59. See *These Things Have Been Written,* 228–32.

60. See Brown, *Community,* 6.

61. See Sophie Laws, "James, Epistle of," 625.

62. The Greek text does not contain the word *epistolē.*

63. See John H. Elliott, "Peter, First Epistle of," 270–71.

64. Elliott (271) offers the following synopsis: 1 Pet 1:14–16 (Rom 12:2); 1:21 (Rom 4:24); 1:22, 3:8–9 (Rom 12:9–19); 2:4–10 (Rom 9:25, 32–33); 2:5 (Rom 12:1); 2:13–17 (Rom 13:1–7); 2:21 (Rom 4:12); 3:22 (Rom 8:34); 4:1 (Rom 6:7); 4:7–11, 14–16 (Rom 12:3–8, 13:8–10); 4:12–13, 5:1 (Rom 8:17); but the Paulinisms of 1 Peter are not to be restricted to these passages alone.

65. Since no authentic writings of Peter are in existence, Barrett notes that "we should speak of a deuteropetrine literature without being able to point to anything that can properly be called petropetrine." See Barrett, "The Place of John and the Synoptics," 74.

66. Cf. Gal 1:10; Tit 1:1; Jas 1:1; Jude 1.

67. Elliott dates it to "sometime in the first quarter of the 2d century." Other scholars opine that it was written as late as 135 C.E. See J. H. Elliott, "Peter, Second Epistle of," 287.

68. See Andreas Lindemann, "Paul in the Writings of the Apostolic Fathers."

69. See Gamble, "The Pauline Corpus," 271–75.

70. See also the curious remark in Col 4:16 as well as the ninth-century Codex Boernerianus (G) which, along with a few other ancient Greek manuscripts, omits "in Rome" from Rom 1:7.

71. Gamble offers the hypothesis that it was the collection of Paul's letters into a codex that provided the impetus for early Christians to use the codex as the preferred form of publication for their own Christian scriptures. See Gamble, "The Pauline Corpus," 275–78.

72. The precise relationship between Marcion's efforts and the development of the canon remains a moot issue among scholars. See Metzger, *Canon,* 97–99.

73. The Canon of Muratori also includes some critical remarks apropos the Marcionites.

74. Note that Paul writes about "my gospel" (Rom 2:16; 16:25; cf. 2 Tim 2:8) or "our gospel" (2 Cor 4:3; 1 Thess 1:5; cf. 2 Thess 2:14).

75. Marcion's version of Luke is, nonetheless, heavily edited in keeping with his own theological vision.

76. See Phlmn 24; cf. 2 Tim 4:11.

77. See Col 4:16.

78. See Metzger, *Canon*, 99.

79. Among the early papyri only P[64],[67] (Matt and Luke) seems to have contained more than one gospel. See Gamble, "The Pauline Corpus," 279, 398, n. 55.

80. The Muratorian fragment expresses a similar conviction: "Therefore, though various ideas are taught in the several books of the Gospels, yet it makes no difference to the faith of believers, since by one sovereign Spirit all things are declared in all of them concerning the Nativity, the Passion, the Resurrection, the conversation with his disciples and his two comings, the first in lowliness and contempt, which has come to pass, the second glorious with royal power, which is to come."

81. *Adversus Haereses*, III, 11, 7; *PL* 7, 1884.

82. *Adversus Haereses*, III, 11, 7; *PL* 8, 1885.

83. See F. G. Kenyon, *The Chester Beatty Biblical Papyri: Descriptions and Texts of Twelve Manuscripts on Papyrus of the Greek Bible*, vol. 2: *The Gospels and Acts. Text* (London: Emery Walker, 1933); *Plates* (1934).

84. See Gamble, "The Pauline Corpus," 279.

85. In the paragraphs that follow our concentration will be on the apocrypha with apostolic patronyms. A summary overview of the situation is provided by Stephen J. Patterson, in "New Testament Apocrypha," *ABD*, vol. 1, 294–96. See also my *Introduction*, 26–31. English language translations of many of the texts can be found in Edgar Hennecke and Wilhelm Schneemelcher, *New Testament Apocrypha*, 2 vols. (London: Lutterworth, 1965–73), and James M. Robinson, ed., *The Nag Hammadi Library* (3d completely rev. ed.; Leiden: Brill, 1988).

86. See Metzger, *Canon*, 181–83. The date and place of origin of this epistle, whose existence was not known until 1895, continues to be the subject of much debate.

87. On the Pauline apocalypses and Pauline Acts, see MacDonald, "Apocryphal and Canonical Narratives," 55–63.

88. In this regard, Origen wrote: "... the thoughts are those of the Apostle, but the phraseology and the composition are those of someone who recalled to mind the teaching of the Apostle and who, as it were, had made notes on what was said by the teacher. If any church, then, holds this epistle to be Paul's let it be commended for this, for not without reason have the men of old handed it down as Paul's" (from a fragment of Origen's *Homilies on Hebrews*, known only insofar as it is quoted by Eusebius, *Ecclesiastical History*, 6, 25; *PG* 20, 584). One should also note that the oldest manuscript of Hebrews, P[46], places it between Paul's letter to the Romans and his first letter to the Corinthians, thereby insinuating its Pauline authorship. On the issue of the authorship of Hebrews, see my *Letters That Paul Did Not Write*, 47–55.

89. *PG* 26, 1177.

90. DS 180.

91. White opines that the Pauline letter is "foundational," that is, that all,

or most, of the other NT letters were influenced specifically by his practice. See White, "The Apostolic Letter Tradition," 442.

92. As has been noted, the formation of "the canon" was the church's response to the formation of the canon by Marcion. To say that the late fourth-century canon was a direct response to Marcion's mid-second-century formation of the *Apotolikon* is far too simplistic and far from true.

93. This overview is necessarily superficial, but it is written in order to highlight some of the analogies between Paul's composition of a letter and the church's composition of the canon of the New Testament. It is superficial because, on the one hand, it has not addressed itself to the church's parallel recognition of the "Old Testament," the Jewish scriptures in a Greek version, as part of its authoritative heritage. It is superficial, on the other hand, because the process of "canonization" is not as simple as it is here described. Neither Alexandria nor Rome, neither Athanasius nor Damasus, promulgated the canon for the universal church. What transpired was an early fifth-century kind of consensus as to the "canon," a consensus to which the authority of the aforementioned bishops and the status of their churches made no small contribution. To speak of an official proclamation of a New Testament canon for the universal church, one would have to look – at least within the tradition of Roman Catholicism – to the fourth session of the Council of Trent (February 4, 1546; DS 1503). By that time, however, the unity of the church was but a memory and a hope. One should not forget, however, that the Tridentine decree on the canon was an expression of concern to maintain the apostolic witness in the midst of crisis.

94. See Brevard Childs, *The New Testament as Canon* (Philadelphia: Fortress, 1984).

Bibliography

Adinolfi, Marco. *La prima lettera ai Tessalonicesi nel mondo greco-romano*. Bibliotheca Pontificii Anthenaei Antoniani, 31. Rome: Pontificium Athenaeum Antonianum, 1990.

Adinolfi, Marco. "La santità del matrimonio in 1 Tess. 4, 1-8," *RivB* 24 (1976): 165-84.

Aland, Kurt. *Text und Textwert der griechischen Handschriften des neuen Testaments*, II, 4: *Die paulinischen Briefe: Kolosserbrief bis Hebräerbrief*, 199-361. ANTF, 19. Berlin-New York: de Gruyter, 1991.

Anderson, Charles "Laodiceans, Epistle to the," *ABD*, vol. 4, 231-33.

Aune, David E. "Romans as a *Logos Protreptikos*." In *The Romans Debate*, edited by K. P. Donfried, 278-96.

Baarda, Tjitze. "1 Thess. 2:14-16: Rodrigues in 'Nestle-Aland,'" *NedTTs* 39 (1985): 186-93.

Baarda, Tjitze. "'Maar de toorn is over hen gekomen' (1 Thess 2:16c)." In *Paulus en de andere joden: Exegetische Bijdragen en Discussie*, edited by Hans Jansen, S. J. Noorda, and J. S. Vos, 15-74.

Baasland, Ernst. "Die peri-Formel und die Argumentation(ssituation) des Paulus," *ST* 42 (1988): 69-87.

Babcock, William S., ed. *Paul and the Legacies of Paul*. Dallas: Southern Methodist University Press, 1990.

Bahr, Gordon J. "The Subscriptions in the Pauline Letters," *JBL* 87 (1968): 27-41.

Balch, David L., Everett Ferguson, and Wayne A. Meeks, eds., *Greeks, Romans, and Christians: Essays in Honor of Abraham J. Malherbe*. Minneapolis: Fortress, 1990.

Barbaglio, Giuseppe. "Analisi formale e letteraria di I Tess. 1-3." In *Testimonium Christi: Scritti in onore di Jacques Dupont*, 35-56. Brescia: Paideia, 1985.

Barclay, John M. G. "Thessalonica and Corinth: Social Contrasts in Pauline Christianity," *JSNT* 47 (1992): 49-74.

Barrett, C. K. *The Signs of an Apostle*. London: Epworth, 1970.

Barrett, C. K. "The Place of John and the Synoptics within the Early History of Christian Thought." In *John and the Synoptics,* edited by A. Denaux, 63–79.

Bartchy, S. Scott. "Philemon, Epistle to," *ABD,* vol. 5, 305–10.

Bassin, François. *Les épîtres de Paul aux Thessaloniciens.* Vaux-sur-Seine: Edifac, 1991.

Bassler, Jouette M., ed. *Pauline Theology,* vol. 1: *Thessalonians, Philippians, Galatians, Philemon.* Minneapolis: Fortress, 1991.

Bassler, Jouette M. "Peace in All Ways. Theology in the Thessalonian Letters: A Response to R. Jewett, E. Krentz, and E. Richard," in *Pauline Theology,* vol. 1, 71–85.

Bauckham, Richard. "Jude, Epistle of," *ABD,* vol. 3, 1098–1103.

Baumert, Norbert. "Brautwerbung – das einheitliche Thema von 1 Thess 4, 3–8." In *The Thessalonian Correspondence,* edited by R. F. Collins, 316–39.

Baumert, Norbert. "Brüche im paulinischen Satzbau," *FilolNT* 4 (1991): 3–20.

Baumert, Norbert. "*Omeiromenoi* in 1 Thess 2, 8," *Bib* 68 (1987): 552–63.

Baumert, Norbert. " 'Wir lassen uns nicht beirren.' Semantische Fragen in 1 Thess 3, 2f," *FilolNT* 5 (1992): 45–60.

Becker, Jürgen. *Auferstehung der Toten im Urchristentum.* SBS, 82. Stuttgart: Katholisches Bibelwerk, 1976.

Becker, Jürgen. "Die Erwählung der Völker durch das Evangelium: Theologiegeschichtliche Erwägungen zum 1. Thessalonicherbrief." In *Studien zum Text und zur Ethik des Neuen Testaments: Festschrift zum 80. Geburtstag von Heinrich Greeven,* edited by W. Schrage, 82–101.

Becker, Jürgen. *Paulus. Der Apostel der Völker.* Tübingen: Mohr, 1989.

Beker, J. Christiaan. *Paul the Apostle: The Triumph of God in Life and Thought.* Philadelphia: Fortress, 1980.

Beker, J. Christiaan. "Recasting Pauline Theology: The Coherence-Contingency Scheme as Interpretive Model." In *Pauline Theology,* edited by J. M. Bassler, vol. 1, 15–24.

Berger, Klaus. "Apostelbrief und apostolische Rede: Zum Formular frühchristlicher Briefe," *ZNW* 65 (1974): 190–231.

Best, Ernest. *A Commentary on the First and Second Epistles to the Thessalonians.* BNTC. London: A. & C. Black, 1972.

Betz, Hans Dieter. "Corinthians, Second Epistle to the," *ABD,* vol. 1, 1148–54.

Betz, Hans Dieter. "The Problem of Rhetoric and Theology according to the Apostle Paul." In *L'apôtre Paul: Personnalité, style et conception du ministère,* edited by Albert Vanhoye, 16–48.

Bicknell, E. J. *The First and Second Epistles to the Thessalonians.* London: Methuen, 1932.

Bjerkelund, Carl J. *Parakalō: Form, Funktion und Sinn der parakalō-Sätze in den paulinischen Briefen.* Bibliotheca Theologica Norvegica, 1. Oslo, Bergen, Tromso: Universitetsforlaget, n.d. (1967).

Black, David Alan. *Paul, Apostle of Weakness: Astheneia and Its Cognates in the Pauline Literature.* American University Studies. Series VII: Theology and Religion, 3. New York, Berne, Frankfurt, Nancy: Peter Lang, 1984.

Black, David Alan. "The Weak in Thessalonica: A Study in Pauline Lexicography," *JETS* 25 (1982): 307-21.

Boers, Hendrikus. "The Form-Critical Study of Paul's Letters: 1 Thessalonians as a Test Case," *NTS* 22 (1975-76): 140-58.

Bohlen, Reinhold. "Die neue Diskussion um die Einheitlichkeit des 1. Thessalonicherbriefes: Eine Kurzinformation für die Verkündigungspraxis," *TTZ* 96 (1987): 313-17; summarized in "The Unity of 1 Thessalonians," *TD* 36 (1989): 132-34.

Bornkamm, Günther. "The Letter to the Romans as Paul's Last Will and Testament," *ABR* 11 (1963): 2-14. Reprinted in *The Romans Debate,* edited by K. Donfried, 16-28.

Bosch, Jorge Sanchez. *"Gloriarse" según San Pablo: Sentido y teología de chachaomai.* AnBib, 40. Rome: Pontifical Biblical Institute, 1970.

Bosch, Jorge Sanchez. "La chronologie de la première aux Thessaloniciens et les relations de Paul avec d'autres églises," *NTS* 37 (1991): 336-47.

Branick, Vincent. *The House Church in the Writings of Paul.* Zacchaeus Studies: New Testament. Wilmington, Del.: Glazier, 1989.

Broer, Ingo. " 'Der ganze Zorn ist schon über sie gekommen': Bemerkungen zur Interpolationshypothese und zur Interpretation von 1 Thess 2, 14-16." In *Thessalonian Correspondence,* edited by R. F. Collins, 137-59.

Brown, Raymond E. *The Community of the Beloved Disciple: The Life, Love and Hates of an Individual Church in New Testament Times.* New York: Paulist, 1979.

Brown, Raymond E. *The Epistles of John.* AB, 30. Garden City, N.Y.: Doubleday, 1982.

Brown, Raymond E., and Raymond F. Collins. "Canonicity," *NJBC,* 1034-54.

Bruce, F. F. *1 and 2 Thessalonians.* WBC, 45. Waco, Tex.: Word, 1982.

Bruce, F. F. *Commentary on the Book of the Acts.* NICNT. Grand Rapids, Mich.: Eerdmans, 1954.

Bruce, F. F. *Paul: Apostle of the Heart Set Free.* Grand Rapids, Mich.: Eerdmans, 1977.

Bultmann, Rudolf. *Theology of the New Testament,* vol. 1. London: SCM, 1952.

Bussmann, Claus. *Themen der paulinischen Missionspredigt auf dem Hintergrund der spätjüdisch-hellenistischen Missionsliteratur.* Europäische Hochschulschriften, XIII, 3. 2d ed. Bern: Lang, 1975.

Buzy, Denis. "Epîtres aux Thessaloniciens." In *La sainte Bible,* edited by Louis Pirot and Albert Clamer, vol. 12, 127-70. 3d rev. ed. Paris: Letouzey, 1951.

Carcopino, Jerome. *Cicero: The Secrets of His Correspondence,* 1. Reprint of 1951 ed. New York: Greenwood, 1969.

Cavallin, Hans C. "Parusi och uppstandelse: 1 Th. 4:13-18 som kombination av tva slags eskatologi," *STK* 59 (1983): 54-63.

Cerfaux, Lucien. *Christ in the Theology of St. Paul.* New York: Herder, 1959.

Chapa, Juan. "Consolatory Patterns? 1 Thes 4, 13.18; 5, 11." In *The Thessalonian Correspondence,* edited by R. F. Collins, 220-28.

Chattuvakulam, Mathaeus. "The Efficacy of the Word of God according to St. Paul." Gregorian University S.T.D. Thesis, Freiburg, 1974.

Chevallier, Max-Alain. *Esprit de Dieu, paroles d'hommes: le rôle de l'esprit dans les ministères de la parole selon l'apôtre Paul.* Bibliothèque théologique. Neuchatel: Delachaux et Niestlé, 1966.

Chevallier, Max-Alain. *Souffle de Dieu: le Saint-Esprit dans le Nouveau Testament.* Le point théologique, 26. Paris: Beauchesne, 1978.

Clemen, Carl. *Die Einheitlichkeit der paulinischen Briefe an Hand der bisher mit Bezug auf die aufgestellten Interpolations- und Compilationshypothesen.* Göttingen: Vandenhoeck and Ruprecht, 1894.

Collins, John J. *The Apocalyptic Imagination: An Introduction to the Jewish Matrix of Christianity.* New York: Crossroad, 1984.

Collins, Raymond F. "The First Letter to the Thessalonians," *NJBC,* 772-79.

Collins, Raymond F. "Glimpses into Some Local Churches of New Testament Times," *LTP* 42 (1986): 291-316.

Collins, Raymond F. "God in the First Letter to the Thessalonians: Paul's Earliest Written Appreciation of *ho theos,*" *LS* 16 (1991): 137-54.

Collins, Raymond F. "Gospel." In *The Encyclopedia of Religion,* edited by Mircea Eliade, vol. 6, 79-82. New York: Macmillan - Free Press, 1987.

Collins, Raymond F. " 'The Gospel of Our Lord Jesus' (2 Thes 1, 8): A Symbolic Shift of Paradigm." In *The Thessalonian Correspondence,* edited by R. F. Collins, 426-40.

Collins, Raymond F. "The Image of Paul in the Pastorals," *LTP* 31 (1975): 147-73.

Collins, Raymond F. *Introduction to the New Testament.* Garden City, N.Y.: Doubleday; London: SCM, 1983.

Collins, Raymond F. *John and His Witness.* Zacchaeus Studies: New Testament. Collegeville, Minn.: Liturgical, 1991.

Collins, Raymond F. *Letters That Paul Did Not Write: The Epistle to the Hebrews and the Pauline Pseudepigrapha.* GNS, 28. Wilmington, Del.: Glazier, 1988.

Collins, Raymond F. "The Lord Jesus Christ," *BibT* 26 (1988): 338-43.

Collins, Raymond F. "Paul's Damascus Experience: Reflections on the Lukan Account," *LS* 11 (1986): 99-118.

Collins, Raymond F., ed. *The Thessalonian Correspondence,* BETL, 87. Louvain: University Press, 1990.

Collins, Raymond F. *Studies on the First Letter to the Thessalonians.* BETL, 66. Louvain: University Press, 1984.

Collins, Raymond F. *These Things Have Been Written: Studies on the Fourth Gospel.* LTPM, 2. Louvain: Peeters, 1990; Grand Rapids, Mich.: Eerdmans, 1991.

Comfort, Philip W. *Early Manuscripts and Modern Translations.* Wheaton, Ill.: Tyndale, 1990.

Conzelmann, Hans. *Acts of the Apostles.* Hermeneia. Philadelphia: Fortress, 1987.

Conzelmann, Hans. *An Outline of the Theology of the New Testament.* NTL. London: SCM, 1969.

Coppens, Josef, Albert Descamps, and Edouard Massaux, eds., *Sacra Pagina: Miscellanea biblica Congressus internationalis catholici de re biblica,* vol. 2. BETL, 13. Paris: Gabalda; Gembloux: Duculot, 1959.

Crawford, Charles. "The 'Tiny' Problem of 1 Thessalonians 2, 7," *Bib* 54 (1973): 69-72.

Cugusi, Paolo. *Evoluzione e forme dell'epistolografia latina nella tarda repubblica e nei primi due secoli dell'imperio con cenni sull'epistolografia preciceroniana.* Rome: Herder, 1983.

Cuming, C. J. "Service-Endings in the Epistles," *NTS* 22 (1975-76): 110-13.

Dahl, Nils A. "The Origin of the Earliest Prologues to the Pauline Letters," *Semeia* 12 (1978): 233-37.

Davis, Richard Howard. "Remembering and Acting: A Study of the Moral Life in Light of I Thessalonians." Ph.D. dissertation, Yale University, 1971.

de Jonge, Henk J. "The Original Setting of the CHRISTOS APETHANEN HYPER Formula." In *The Thessalonian Correspondence,* edited by R. F. Collins, 229-35.

de Jonge, Marinus. *Christology in Context: The Earliest Christian Response to Jesus.* Philadelphia: Fortress, 1988.

Deissmann, Adolf. *A Light From the East: The New Testament Illustrated by Recently Discovered Texts of the Graeco-Roman World.* London: Hodder and Stoughton, 1910.

Delebecque, Edouard. "Paul à Thessalonique et à Berée selon le texte occidental des Actes (XVII, 4-15)," *RevThom* 82 (1982): 605-15.

Delobel, Joël. "The Fate of the Dead according to 1 Thes 4 and 1 Cor 15." In *The Thessalonian Correspondence*, edited by R. F. Collins, 340–47.

Denaux, Adelbert, ed. *John and the Synoptics*. BETL, 101. Louvain: University Press, 1992.

Denis, Albert-Marie. "L'apôtre Paul, prophète 'messianique' des gentils: Etude thématique de 1. Thess., II, 1–6," *ETL* 33 (1959): 245–318.

Dewailly, L.-M. *La jeune église de Thessalonique: Les deux premières épîtres de saint Paul*. LD, 37. Paris: Cerf, 1963.

Dibelius, Martin. *An die Thessalonicher I–II: An die Philipper*. HNT, 11. 3d ed. Tübingen: Mohr, 1937.

Donfried, Karl. "1 Thessalonians, Acts and the Early Paul." In *The Thessalonian Correspondence*, edited by R. F. Collins, 3–26.

Donfried, Karl. "The Cults of Thessalonica and the Thessalonian Correspondence," *NTS* 31 (1985): 336–56.

Donfried, Karl. "Paul and Judaism: I Thessalonians 2:13–16 as a Test Case," *Int* 38 (1984): 242–53.

Donfried, Karl Paul. "Paul as *Scēnopoios* and the Use of the Codex in Early Christianity." In *Christus bezeugen*, edited by K. Kertelge, T. Holtz, and C.-P. März, vol. 1, 249–56.

Donfried, Karl P., ed. *The Romans Debate: Revised and Expanded Edition*. Peabody, Mass.: Hendrickson, 1991.

Donfried, Karl. "A Short Note on Romans 16," *JBL* 89 (1970): 441–49; reprinted in *The Romans Debate*, 44–52.

Donfried, Karl. "The Theology of 1 Thessalonians as a Reflection of Its Purpose." In *To Touch the Text*, edited by M. Horgan and J. Kobelski, 243–60.

Doty, William G. *Letters in Primitive Christianity*. GBS. Philadelphia: Fortress, 1973.

du Toit, Andrie B. "Oriënterende opmerkings oor die Pauliniese briefliteratuur." In *Handleiding by die Nuwe Testament*, edited by A. B. du Toit, vol. 5, 1–22. Pretoria: Kerkboekhandel, 1984.

Edgar, T. R. "The Meaning of 'Sleep' in 1 Thessalonians 5:10," *JETS* 22 (1979): 345–49.

Edson, Charles, "Macedonia: State Cults of Thessaloniki," *Harvard Studies in Classical Philology* 51 (1940): 125–36.

Egelkraut, Helmuth. "Die Bedeutung von 1 Thess 4, 13ff für eine Umschreibung christlicher Zukunftserwartung." In *Zukunftserwartung in biblischer Sicht*, edited by Gerhard Maier, 86–97.

Elliger, Winfried. *Paulus in Griechenland: Philippi, Thessaloniki, Athen, Korinth*. SBS 92/93. Stuttgart: Katholisches Bibelwerk, 1978.

Ellingworth, Paul, and Eugene Nida. *A Translator's Handbook on Paul's Letters to the Thessalonians*. Helps for Translators. Stuttgart: United Bible Societies, 1976.

Elliott, John H. "Peter, First Epistle of," *ABD*, vol. 5, 269-79.

Elliott, John H. "Peter, Second Epistle of," *ABD*, vol. 5, 282-87.

Evans, Robert Maxwell. "Eschatology and Ethics: A Study of Thessalonica and Paul's Letters to the Thessalonians." D.Th. dissertation, University of Basel, 1967. Princeton, N.J.: McMahon, 1968.

Fabris, Rinaldo. "Il Lavoro nel metodo missionario e pastorale di Paolo." In *Testimonium Christi: Scritti in onore di Jacques Dupont*, 177-91. Brescia: Paideia, 1985.

Faw, Chalmer E. "On the Writing of First Thessalonians," *JBL* 71 (1952): 217-25.

Fiore, Benjamin. *The Function of Personal Example in the Socratic and Pastoral Epistles.* AnBib, 105. Rome: Pontifical Biblical Institute, 1986.

Fitzmyer, Joseph A. "The Letter to the Romans," *NJBC*, 830-68, 831-32.

Fitzmyer, Joseph A. "Paul," *NJBC*, 1329-37.

Focant, Camille. "Les fils du Jour (1 Thes 5, 5)," in *The Thessalonian Correspondence*, edited by R. F. Collins, 348-55.

Forestell, J. Terence. "The Letters to the Thessalonians," *JBC*, 2, 227-35.

Fortna, Robert T., and Beverly R. Gaventa, eds. *The Conversation Continues: Studies in Paul and John. In Honor of J. Louis Martyn.* Nashville: Abingdon, 1990.

Fowl, Stephen. "A Metaphor in Distress: A Reading of *NĒPIOI* in 1 Thessalonians 2.7," *NTS* 36 (1990): 469-73.

Friedrich, Gerhard. "1. Thessalonicher 5, 1-11, der apologetische Einschub eines Späteren," *ZTK* 70 (1973): 288-315, reprinted in *Auf das Wort kommt es an*, 251-78. Göttingen: Vandenhoeck and Ruprecht, 1978.

Friedrich, Gerhard. "Der erste Brief an die Thessalonicher," in Jürgen Becker, Hans Conzelmann, and Gerhard Friedrich, *Die Briefe an die Galater, Epheser, Philipper, Kolosser, Thessalonicher und Philemon*, 202-51. NTD, 8. Göttingen: Vandenhoeck and Ruprecht, 1976.

Friedrich, Gerhard. "Ein Tauflied hellenistischer Judenchristen," *TZ* 21 (1965): 502-16.

Funk, Robert W. "The Apostolic Parousia: Form and Significance." In *Christian History and Interpretation: Studies Presented to John Knox*, edited by W. R. Farmer, C. F. D. Moule, and R. R. Niebuhr, 249-68. Cambridge: University Press, 1967.

Furnish, Victor. "Colossians, Epistle to the," *ABD*, vol. 1, 1090-96.

Furnish, Victor. "Ephesians, Epistle to the," *ABD*, vol. 2, 535-42.

Gamble, Harry Y. "The Pauline Corpus and the Early Christian Book." In *Paul and the Legacies of Paul*, edited by W. S. Babcock, 265-80.

Gamble, Harry Y. "The Redaction of the Pauline Letters and the Formation of the Pauline Corpus," *JBL* 94 (1975): 403-18.

Gamble, Harry Y. *The New Testament Canon: Its Making and Meaning.* Philadelphia: Fortress, 1985.

Gamble, Harry Y. *The Textual History of the Letter to the Romans: A Study in Textual and Literary Criticism.* SD, 42. Grand Rapids, Mich.: Eerdmans, 1977.

García del Moral, Antonio. "'Nosotros los vivos': Convicción personal de Pablo o reinterpretación de un salmo? (I Tes 4, 13-5, 11)," *Communio* 20 (1987): 3-56.

Gaventa, Beverly R. "Apostles as Babes and Nurses in 1 Thessalonians 2:7." In *Faith and History: Essays in Honor of Paul W. Meyer,* edited by John T. Carroll, Charles H. Cosgrove, and E. Elizabeth Johnson, 193-207. Atlanta: Scholars, 1990.

Geiger, Georg. "1 Thess 2, 13-16: Der Initiationstext des christlichen Antisemitismus?" *BLit* 59 (1986): 154-60.

Getty, Mary Ann. "The Imitation of Paul in the Letters to the Thessalonians." In *The Thessalonian Correspondence,* edited by R. F. Collins, 277-83.

Gibbs, James M. "Canon Cuming's 'Service-Endings in the Epistles': A Rejoinder," *NTS* 24 (1977-78): 545-47.

Giesen, Heinz. "Naherwartung des Paulus in 1 Thess 4, 13-18?," *SUNT* 10 (1985): 123-50.

Gillman, Florence Morgan. "Jason of Thessalonica." In *The Thessalonian Correspondence,* edited by R. F. Collins, 39-49.

Gillman, Florence Morgan. *Women Who Knew Paul.* Zacchaeus Studies: New Testament. Collegeville, Minn.: Liturgical, 1992.

Gillman, John. "Signals of Transformation in 1 Thessalonians 4:13-18," *CBQ* 47 (1985): 263-81.

Goulder, Michael. "The Pauline Epistles." In *The Literary Guide to the Bible,* edited by Robert Alter and Frank Kermode, 479-502. Cambridge, Mass.: Harvard University Press, 1987.

Goulder, M. D. "Did Luke Know Any of the Pauline Letters?" *Perspectives in Religious Studies* 13 (1986): 97-112.

Gribomont, Jean. "Facti sumus parvuli: La charge apostolique (1 Th 2, 1-12)." In *Paul de Tarse: apôtre de notre temps,* edited by Lorenzo De Lorenzi, 311-38. Série monographique de "Benedictina." Section paulinienne, 1. Rome: Abbaye de S. Paul, 1979.

Groh, Dennis E., and Robert Jewett, eds. *The Living Text: Essays in Honor of Ernest W. Saunders.* Lanham, Md.: University Press of America, 1985.

Gundry, Robert H. "The Hellenization of Dominical Tradition and Christianization of Jewish Tradition in the Eschatology of 1-2 Thessalonians," *NTS* 33 (1987): 161-78.

Gutierrez, Pedro. *La paternité spirituelle selon Saint Paul.* Ebib. Paris: Gabalda, 1968.

Haenchen, Ernst. *The Acts of the Apostles: A Commentary.* Oxford: Blackwell, 1971.

Hahneman, Geoffrey Mark. *Muratorian Fragment and the Development of the Canon.* Oxford Theological Monographs. Oxford: Clarendon, 1992.

Hainz, Josef. *Ekklesia: Strukturen paulinischer Gemeinde-Theologie und Gemeinde-Ordnung.* BU, 9. Regensburg: Pustet, 1972.

Harnisch, Wolfgang. *Eschatologische Existenz: Ein exegetischer Beitrag zum Sachanliegen von 1 Thessalonicher 4, 13-5, 11.* FRLANT, 110. Göttingen: Vandenhoeck and Ruprecht, 1973.

Harris, J. Rendel. "A Study in Letter-Writing," *The Expositor* 5th ser., 8 (1898): 161-80.

Havener, Ivan. "Pre-Pauline Christological Credal Formulae of 1 Thessalonians." In *Society of Biblical Literature 1981 Seminar Papers,* edited by Kent Harold Richards, 105-28. Chico, Calif.: Scholars, 1981.

Hellholm, David, ed. *Apocalypticism in the Mediterranean World and the Near East: Proceedings of the International Colloquium on Apocalypticism. Uppsala, August 12-17, 1979.* Tübingen: Mohr, 1983.

Hemer, Colin J. *The Book of Acts in the Setting of Hellenistic History.* WUNT, 49. Tübingen: Mohr, 1989.

Hendrix, Holland Lee. "Archaeology and Eschatology at Thessalonica." In *The Future of Early Christianity,* edited by Birger A. Pearson, 107-18.

Hendrix, Holland Lee. "Thessalonicans Honor Romans." Th.D. thesis, Harvard University, 1984.

Hengel, Martin. *La crucifixion dans l'antiquité et la folie du message de la croix.* LD, 105. Paris: Cerf, 1981.

Hengel, Martin. *The Johannine Question.* Philadelphia: Trinity Press International, 1989.

Henneken, Bartholomäus. *Verkündigung und Prophetie im 1. Thessalonicherbrief: Ein Beitrag zur Theologie des Wortes Gottes.* SBS, 29. Stuttgart: Katholisches Bibelwerk, 1969.

Hock, Ronald F. "Paul's Tentmaking and the Problem of his Social Class," *JBL* 97 (1978): 555-64.

Hock, Ronald F. *The Social Context of Paul's Ministry: Tentmaking and Apostleship.* Philadelphia: Fortress, 1980.

Hock, Ronald F. "The Workshop as a Social Setting for Paul's Missionary Activity," *CBQ* 41 (1979): 438-50.

Hoffmann, Paul. *Die Toten in Christus: Eine religionsgeschichtliche und exegetische Untersuchung zur paulinischen Eschatologie.* NTAbh, New Series, 2. Münster: Aschendorff, 1966.

Holtz, Traugott. "Der Apostel des Christus: Die paulinische 'Apologie' 1 Thess. 2, 1-12." In *Als Boten des gekreuzigten Herrn* (Fs. W. Krusche), edited by H. Falcke, M. Onnasch, and H. Schultze, 101–16. Berlin: Evangelische Verlagsanstalt, 1982.

Holtz, Traugott. *Der erste Brief an die Thessalonicher.* EKKNT, 13. Zurich: Benziger; Neukirchen: Neukirchener, 1986.

Holtz, Traugott. "The Judgment on the Jews and the Salvation of All Israel: 1 Thes 2, 15–16 and Rom 11, 25–26." In *The Thessalonian Correspondence,* edited by R. F. Collins, 284–94.

Holtz, Traugott. "Traditionen im 1. Thessalonicherbrief." In *Die Mitte des Neuen Testaments: Einheit und Vielfalt neutestamentlicher Theologie,* edited by U. Luz and H. Weder, 55–78.

Horgan, Maurya, and Paul J. Kobelski, eds. *To Touch the Text: Biblical and Related Studies in Honor of Joseph A. Fitzmyer, S.J.* New York: Crossroad, 1989.

Horsley, G. H. R. *New Documents Illustrating Early Christianity: A Review of the Greek Inscriptions and Papyri Published in 1977.* North Ryde, N.S.W.: Macquarie University, 1982.

Horsley, G. H. R. "Politarchs," *ABD,* vol. 5, 384–89.

Howard, T. L. "The Meaning of 'Sleep' in 1 Thessalonians 5:10 – A Reappraisal," *GTJ* 6 (1985): 337–48.

Hughes, Frank Witt. "The Rhetoric of 1 Thessalonians." In *The Thessalonian Correspondence,* edited by R. F. Collins, 94–116.

Hurd, John. *The Origin of 1 Corinthians.* 2d ed. Macon, Ga.: Mercer, 1983.

Hurd, John C. "Paul Ahead of His Time: 1 Thess. 2:13–16." In *Anti-Judaism in Early Christianity,* 1: *Paul and the Gospels,* edited by Peter Richardson, 21–36. Studies in Christianity and Judaism, 2. Waterloo, Ontario: Wilfrid Laurier University, 1986.

Hyldahl, Niels. "Auferstehung Christi, Auferstehung der Toten (1 Thess 4, 13–18)." In *Die Paulinische Literatur und Theologie: The Pauline Literature and Theology,* edited by S. Pedersen, 119–35. Skandinavische Beiträge, 7. Aarhus: Aros, 1980.

Jansen, Hans, S. J. Noorda and J. S. Vos, eds, *Paulus en de andere joden.* Delft: Meinema, 1984.

Jewett, Robert. *A Chronology of Paul's Life.* Philadelphia: Fortress, 1979.

Jewett, Robert. "Enthusiastic Radicalism and the Thessalonian Correspondence." In *Society of Biblical Literature 1972 Proceedings,* edited by L. C. McGaughy, vol. 1, 181–45.

Jewett, Robert. "The Form and Function of the Homiletic Benediction," *ATR* 51 (1969): 18–34.

Jewett, Robert. *Paul's Anthropological Terms: A Study of their Use in Conflict Settings.* AGJU, 10. Leiden: Brill, 1971.

Jewett, Robert. *The Thessalonian Correspondence: Pauline Rhetoric and Millenarian Piety.* Foundations and Facets. Philadelphia: Fortress, 1986.

Johanson, Bruce C. *To All the Brethren: A Text-Linguistic and Rhetorical Approach to I Thessalonians.* ConNT, 16. Stockholm: Almqvist & Wiksell, 1987.

Johnson, Sherman E. *Paul the Apostle and His Cities.* GNS, 21. Wilmington, Del.: Glazier, 1987.

Judge, Edwin A. "The Decrees of Caesar at Thessalonica," *The Reformed Theological Review* 30 (1971): 1-7.

Jurgensen, Hubert. "Saint Paul et la parousie: I Thessaloniciens 4, 13-5, 11 dans l'exégèse moderne et contemporaine." Strasbourg Th.D. thesis, 1992.

Kampling, Rainer. "Freude bei Paulus," *TTZ* 101 (1992): 69-79.

Kegel, Günter. *Auferstehung Jesu – Auferstehung der Toten: Eine traditionsgeschichtliche Untersuchung zum Neuen Testament.* Gütersloh: Mohn, 1970.

Keightley, Georgia Masters. "The Church's Memory of Jesus: A Social Science Analysis of 1 Thessalonians," *BTB* 17 (1987): 149-56.

Kemmler, Dieter Werner. *Faith and Human Reason: A Study of Paul's Method of Preaching as Illustrated by 1-2 Thessalonians and Acts 17, 2-4.* NovTSup, 40. Leiden: Brill, 1975.

Kennedy, George A. *New Testament Interpretation through Rhetorical Criticism.* Chapel Hill, London: University of North Carolina Press, 1984.

Kenyon, Frederic G. *The Chester Beatty Biblical Papyri: Descriptions and Texts of Twelve Manuscripts on Papyrus of the Greek Bible,* vol. 2: *The Gospels and Acts. Text* (London: Emery Walker, 1933); *Plates* (1934); vol. 3: *Pauline Epistles and Revelation. Text* (1934); *Supplement: Pauline Epistles. Text* (1936); *Plates* (1937).

Kertelge, Karl, Traugott Holtz, and Claus-Peter März, eds. *Christus bezeugen: Festschrift für Wolfgang Trilling zum 65. Geburtstag.* ETS, 59. Leipzig: St. Benno, 1989

Kieffer, René. "L'eschatologie en 1 Thessaloniciens dans une perspective rhétorique." In *The Thessalonian Correspondence,* edited by R. F. Collins, 206-19.

Kim, Young Kyu. "Paleographical Dating of P[46] to the Later First Century," *Bib* 69 (1988): 248-57.

Klauck, Hans-Josef. "Die Hausgemeinde als Lebensform im Urchristentum," *MTZ* 31 (1981): 1-15, digested as "The House Church as a Way of Life," *TD* 30 (1982): 153-57.

Klauck, Hans-Josef. *Hausgemeinde und Hauskirche im frühen Christentum.* SBS, 103. Stuttgart: Katholisches Bibelwerk, 1981.

Klijn, A. F. J. "I Thessalonians 4, 13-18 and Its Background in Apocalyptic Literature." In *Paul and Paulinism: Essays in Honour of C. K. Barrett,* edited by M. D. Hooker and S. G. Wilson, 67-73. London: SPCK, 1982.

Koester, Helmut. "I Thessalonians – Experiment in Christian Writing." In *Continuity and Discontinuity in Church History: Essays Presented to George Hunston Williams*, 34-44. Studies in the History of Christian Thought, 19. Leiden: Brill, 1979.

Koester, Helmut. "Apostel und Gemeinde in den Briefen an die Thessalonicher." In *Kirche: Festschrift für Günther Bornkamm zum 75. Geburtstag*, edited by Dieter Lührmann and Georg Strecker, 287-98. Tübingen: Mohr, 1980.

Koester, Helmut. "From Paul's Eschatology to the Apocalyptic Schemata of 2 Thessalonians." In *The Thessalonian Correspondence*, edited by R. F. Collins, 441-58.

Koester, Helmut. "The Text of 1 Thessalonians," in *The Living Text*, edited by Dennis E. Groh and Robert Jewett, 219-27.

Koskenniemi, Heikki. *Studien zur Idee und Phraseologie des griechischen Briefes bis 400 n. Chr.* Annales Academiae scientiarum Fennicae, B, 102, 2. Helsinki: Akateeminen Kirjakaupaa, 1956.

Kramer, Werner. *Christ, Lord, Son of God.* SBT, 50. London: SCM, 1966.

Krentz, Edgar. "1 Thessalonians," *ABD*, vol. 6, 515-17.

Krentz, Edgar. "Evangelism and Spirit: 1 Thessalonians 1," *CurTM* 14 (1987): 22-30.

Kurz, William S. "Hellenistic Rhetoric in the Christological Proof of Luke-Acts," *CBQ* 42 (1980): 171-95.

Kuss, Otto. *Die Thessalonicherbriefe.* RNT, 7. 3d ed. Regensburg: Pustet, 1959.

Lambrecht, Jan. "De apostolische Inzet van de eerste Christenen: Een actualiserende Lezing van 1 Tessalonicenzen," *Collationes* 18 (1988): 403-17; revised, translated and with notes added: "A Call to Witness by All: Evangelisation in 1 Thessalonians." In *Teologie in Konteks* (Fs. Andrie B. du Toit), edited by J. H. Roberts, W. S. Vorster, J. N. Vorster, and J. G. van der Watt, 321-43. Pretoria: Orion, 1991.

Lambrecht, Jan. "Thanksgivings in 1 Thessalonians 1-3." In *The Thessalonian Correspondence*, edited by R. F. Collins, 183-205.

Langevin, Paul-Emile. "Conseils et prière," *Assemblées du Seigneur* 7 (1969): 34-39.

Langevin, Paul-Emile. "L'intervention de Dieu selon I Thes 5, 23-24." In *The Thessalonian Correspondence*, edited by R. F. Collins, 236-56.

Langevin, Paul-Emile. *Jésus Seigneur et l'eschatologie: Exégèse de textes prépauliniens.* Studia, 21. Bruges-Paris: Desclée de Brouwer, 1967.

Langevin, Paul-Emile. "Le Seigneur Jésus selon un texte prépaulinien, 1 Thess, 1, 9-10," *ScEccl* 17 (1965): 263-82, 473-512.

Laub, Franz. *1. und 2. Thessalonicherbrief.* Die Neue Echter-BibelNT, 13. Würzburg: Echter, 1985.

Laub, Franz. *Eschatologische Verkündigung und Lebensgestaltung nach Paulus.* BU, 10. Regensburg: Pustet, 1973.

Laws, Sophie. "James, Epistle of," *ABD*, vol. 3, 621–28.

Lifschitz, B., and J. Schiby. "Une synagogue samaritaine à Thessalonique," *RB* 75 (1968): 368–78.

Lindemann, Andreas. "Paul in the Writings of the Apostolic Fathers." In *Paul and the Legacies of Paul*, edited by W. S. Babcock, 25–45.

Lohfink, Gerhard. *Die Himmelfahrt Jesu: Untersuchungen zu den Himmelfahrts- und Erhöhungstexten bei Lukas.* SANT, 26. Munich: Kösel, 1971.

Longenecker, R. N. "The Nature of Paul's Early Eschatology," *NTS* 31 (1985): 85–95.

Louw, Johannes, and Eugene A. Nida, eds. *Greek-English Lexicon of the New Testament Based on Semantic Domains*, vol. 1. 2d ed. New York: United Bible Societies, 1989.

Luz, Ulrich. *Das Geschichtsverständnis des Paulus.* BEvT, 49. Munich: Kaiser, 1968.

Lüdemann, Gerd. *Paul, Apostle to the Gentiles: Studies in Chronology.* Philadelphia: Fortress, 1984.

Lüdemann, Gerd. *Paulus und das Judentum.* Theologische Existenz heute, 215. Munich: Chr. Kaiser, 1983.

Lührmann, Dieter. "The Beginnings of the Church at Thessalonica." In *Greeks, Romans, and Christians*, edited by D. L. Balch, E. Ferguson, and W. A. Meeks, 237–49.

Luz, Ulrich, and Hans Weder, eds., *Die Mitte des Neuen Testaments: Einheit und Vielfalt neutestamentlicher Theologie: Festschrift für Eduard Schweizer zum 70. Geburtstag.* Göttingen: Vandenhoeck and Ruprecht, 1983.

Lyons, George. *Pauline Autobiography: Toward a New Understanding.* SBLDS, 73. Atlanta: Scholars, 1985.

MacDonald, Dennis R. "Apocryphal and Canonical Narratives about Paul." In *Paul and the Legacies of Paul*, edited by W. S. Babcock, 55–70.

Maier, G., ed. *Zukunftserwartung in biblischer Sicht.* Wuppertal: Brockhaus, 1984.

Malbon, Elizabeth Struthers. " 'No Need to Have Any One Write'?: A Structural Exegesis of 1 Thessalonians." In *1980 SBL Seminar Papers*, edited by Paul J. Achtemeier, 301–35. Chico, Calif.: Scholars, 1980. Revised, in *Semeia* 26 (1983): 57–83.

Malherbe, Abraham J. "Ancient Epistolary Theorists," *Ohio Journal of Religious Studies* 5, 2 (1977): 3–77. Republished, with minor revisions, as *Ancient Epistolary Theorists.* SBLSBS, 19. Atlanta: Scholars, 1988.

Malherbe, Abraham J. "Did the Thessalonians Write to Paul?" In *The Conversation Continues*, edited by R. T. Fortna and B. R. Gaventa, 246–57.

Malherbe, Abraham J. "Exhortation in First Thessalonians," *NovT* 25 (1983): 238–56.

Malherbe, Abraham J. " 'Gentle as a Nurse': The Cynic Background to 1 Thess 2," *NovT* (1970): 203-17. Reprinted in *Paul and the Popular Philosophers,* 35-48.

Malherbe, Abraham J. "Hellenistic Moralists and the New Testament," *ANRW,* II, 26, 267-333.

Malherbe, Abraham J. " 'Pastoral Care' in the Thessalonian Church," *NTS* 36 (1990): 375-91.

Malherbe, Abraham J. *Paul and the Popular Philosophers.* Minneapolis: Fortress, 1989.

Malherbe, Abraham J. *Paul and the Thessalonians: The Philosophic Tradition of Pastoral Care.* Philadelphia: Fortress, 1987.

Malherbe, Abraham J. *Social Aspects of Early Christianity.* 2d ed. Philadelphia: Fortress, 1983.

Malinowski, Francis X. "The Brave Women of Philippi," *BTB* 15 (1985): 60-64.

Manus, Chris Ukachukwu. "Luke's Account of Paul in Thessalonica (Acts 17, 1-9)." In *The Thessalonian Correspondence,* edited by R. F. Collins, 27-38.

Mariani, Bonaventura. "Corpo-anima-spirito," *Euntes docete* 14 (1961): 308-18.

Marrow, Stanley B. "*Parrhesia* and the New Testament," CBQ 44 (1982): 431-46.

Marrow, Stanley B. *Speaking the Word Fearlessly: Boldness in the New Testament.* New York, Ramsey, N.J.: Paulist, 1980.

Marshall, I. Howard. "Election and Calling to Salvation in 1 and 2 Thessalonians." In *The Thessalonian Correspondence,* edited by R. F. Collins, 259-76.

Martyn, J. Louis. *History and Theology in the Fourth Gospel.* Rev. ed. Nashville: Abingdon, 1979.

Marxsen, Willi. "Auslegung von 1 Thess 4, 13-18," *ZTK* 66 (1969): 22-37.

Marxsen, Willi. *Der erste Brief an die Thessalonicher.* Zürcher Bibelkommentare, Neues Testament 11/1. Zurich: Theologischer Verlag, 1979.

Masson, Charles. *Les deux épîtres de saint Paul aux Thessaloniciens.* CNT, 11a. Neuchatel, Paris: Delachaux & Niestlé, 1967.

Meeks, Wayne A. *The First Urban Christians: The Social World of the Apostle Paul.* New Haven, Conn.: Yale University Press, 1983.

Meeks, Wayne A. "Social Functions of Apocalyptic Language in Pauline Christianity." In *Apocalypticism in the Mediterranean World and the Near East: Proceedings of the International Colloquium on Apocalypticism. Uppsala, August 12-17, 1979,* edited by David Hellholm, 687-705.

Menoud, Philippe H. *L'Evangile de Jean d'après les recherches récentes.* Cahiers théologique de l'actualité protestante, 3. 2d ed. Neuchatel: Delachaux et Niestlé, 1947.

Merk, Otto. "Nachahmung Christi: Zu ethischen Perspektiven in der paulinischen Theologie." In *Neues Testament und Ethik: Für Rudolf Schnackenburg,* edited by Helmut Merklein, 172-206. Freiburg, Basel, Vienna: Herder, 1989.

Merk, Otto. "Zur Christologie im 1. Thessalonicherbrief." In *Anfänge der Christologie: Festschrift für Ferdinand Hahn zum 65. Geburtstag,* edited by Cilliers Breytenbach and Henning Paulsen, 97-110. Göttingen: Vandenhoeck and Ruprecht, 1991.

Metzger, Bruce M. *The Canon of the New Testament: Its Origin, Development, and Significance.* Oxford: Clarendon, 1987.

Metzger, Bruce M. *A Textual Commentary on the Greek New Testament: A Companion Volume to the United Bible Societies' Greek New Testament.* London, New York: United Bible Societies, 1971.

Michel, Otto. "Fragen zu 1 Thessalonicher 2, 14-16: Anti-jüdische Polemik bei Paulus." Reprinted in *Dienst am Wort,* edited by K. Haacker, 202-10. Neukirchen-Vluyn: Neukirchener, 1986.

Míguez, O. Nestor. "La Composición social de la iglesia en Tesalónica," *RevistB* 51 (1989): 65-89.

Morris, Leon. "*Kai hapax kai dis,*" *NovT* 1 (1956): 205-8.

Morris, Leon. *The First and Second Epistles to the Thessalonians.* NICNT. Rev. ed. Grand Rapids, Mich.: Eerdmans, 1991.

Munck, Johannes. "1 Thess i. 9-10 and the Missionary Preaching of Paul: Textual Exegesis and Hermeneutic Reflexions," *NTS* 9 (1962-63): 95-110.

Murphy-O'Connor, Jerome. "2 Timothy Contrasted with 1 Timothy and Titus," *RB* 98 (1991): 403-18.

Myers, Charles D., Jr. "Romans, Epistle to the," *ABD,* vol. 5, 816-30.

Neirynck, Frans. "John and Synoptics: 1975-1990." In *John and the Synoptics,* edited by A. Denaux, 3-62.

Neirynck, Frans. "Paul and the Sayings of Jesus." In *L'apôtre Paul: Personnalité, style et conception du ministère,* edited by Albert Vanhoye, 265-321.

Nepper-Christensen, Paol. "Das verborgene Herrenwort: Eine Untersuchung über 1 Thess 4, 13-18," *ST* 19 (1965): 136-54.

Neyrey, Jerome H. "Eschatology in 1 Thessalonians: The Theological Factor in 1:9-10; 2:4-5; 3:11-13; 4:6 and 4:13-18." *Society of Biblical Literature 1980 Seminar Papers,* edited by Paul J. Achtemeier, 219-31. Missoula, Mont.: Scholars, 1980.

Olbricht, Thomas H. "An Aristotelian Rhetorical Analysis of 1 Thessalonians." In *Greeks, Romans and Christians,* edited by D. L. Balch, E. Ferguson, and W. A. Meeks, 216-36.

Palliparambil, Jacob. "The Will of God in Paul: A Commitment to Man: An Exegetico-Theological Study of 'theo-thelema' Vocabulary in the Writings of Paul." Gregorian University STD dissertation, Rome, 1986.

Palmer, D. W. "Thanksgiving, Self-Defence, and Exhortation in 1 Thessalonians 1-3," *Colloquium* 14 (1981): 23-31.

Pax, Elpidius. "Beobachtungen zur Konvertitensprache im ersten Thessalonicherbrief," *SBFA* 21 (1971): 220-61.

Pax, Elpidius. "Konvertitenprobleme im ersten Thessalonicherbrief," *BibLeb* 13 (1972): 24-37.

Pearson, Birger A. "1 Thessalonians 2, 13-16: A Deutero-Pauline Interpolation," *HTR* 64 (1971): 79-94.

Pearson, Birger A., ed. *The Future of Early Christianity: Essays in Honor of Helmut Koester.* Minneapolis: Fortress, 1991.

Perkins, Pheme. "1 Thessalonians and Hellenistic Religious Practices." In *To Touch the Text,* edited by M. Horgan and P. J. Kobelski, 325-34.

Pervo, Richard I. *Profit with Delight: The Literary Genre of the Acts of the Apostles.* Philadelphia: Fortress, 1987.

Pesch, Rudolf. *Die Entdeckung des ältesten Paulus-Briefes: Paulus – neu gesehen. Die Briefe and die Gemeinde der Thessalonicher.* Herderbücherei, 1167. Herder: Freiburg, 1984.

Petersen, Norman R. *Rediscovering Paul: Philemon and the Sociology of Paul's Narrative World.* Philadelphia: Fortress, 1985.

Peterson, Erik. *"Apantēsis," TDNT,* vol. 1, 380-81.

Peterson, Erik. "Die Einholung des Kyrios," *ZST* 7 (1930): 682-702.

Petzer, J. H., and Patrick J. Hartin, eds., *A South African Perspective on the New Testament: Essays by South African New Testament Scholars Presented to Bruce Manning Metzger during His Visit to South Africa in 1985.* Leiden: Brill, 1986.

Pfitzner, Victor C. *Paul and the Agon Motif: Traditional Athletic Imagery in the Pauline Literature.* NovTSup, 16. Leiden: Brill, 1967.

Plank, Karl A. *Paul and the Irony of Affliction.* SBLSS. Atlanta: Scholars, 1987.

Plevnik, Joseph. "1 Thess 5, 1-11: Its Authenticity, Intention and Message," *Bib* 60 (1979): 71-90.

Plevnik, Joseph. "The Parousia as Implication of Christ's Resurrection (An Exegesis of 1 Thess 4, 13-18)." In *Word and Spirit: Essays in Honor of David Michael Stanley on his 60th Birthday,* edited by J. Plevnik, 199-277. Toronto: Regis College, 1975.

Plevnik, Joseph. "Pauline Presuppositions." In *The Thessalonian Correspondence,* edited by R. F. Collins, 50-61.

Plevnik, Joseph. "The Taking Up of the Faithful and the Resurrection of the Dead in 1 Thessalonians 4:13-18," *CBQ* 46 (1984): 274-83.

Pobee, John S. *Persecution and Martyrdom in the Theology of Paul.* JSNTSup, 6. Sheffield: JSOT, 1985.

Prior, Michael. *Paul the Letter-Writer and the Second Letter to Timothy.* JSNTSup, 23. Sheffield: JSOT, 1989.

Purvis, James D. "The Paleography of the Samaritan Inscription from Thessalonica," *BASOR* 221 (1976): 121-23.

Puthiyidom, Mani. "Confessions of Faith in Pauline Writings." Gregorian University STD dissertation, Rome, 1986.

Quinn, Jerome D. "The Last Volume of Luke; The Relation of Luke-Acts and the PE." In *Perspectives on Luke-Acts,* edited by C. H. Talbert, 62-75.

Quinn, Jerome D. *The Letter to Titus.* AB, 35. New York: Doubleday, 1990.

Quinn, Jerome D. "P^{46} – The Pauline Canon?" *CBQ* 36 (1974): 379-85.

Quinn, Jerome D. "Timothy and Titus, Epistles to," *ABD,* vol. 6, 560-71.

Reumann, John. "The Theologies of 1 Thessalonians and Philippians: Contents, Comparison, and Composite." In *Society of Biblical Literature 1987 Seminar Papers,* edited by K. H. Richards, 521-36. Atlanta: Scholars Press, 1987.

Richard, Earl. "Contemporary Research on 1 (& 2) Thessalonians," *BTB* 20 (1990): 107-15.

Richard, Earl. "Early Pauline Thought: An Analysis of 1 Thessalonians." In *Pauline Theology,* vol. 1, edited by J. M. Bassler, 39-51. Minneapolis: Fortress, 1991.

Richard, Earl. *Jesus, One and Many: The Christological Concept of New Testament Authors.* Wilmington, Del.: Glazier, 1988.

Richards, E. Randolph. *The Secretary in the Letters of Paul.* WUNT, 2/42. Tübingen: Mohr, 1991.

Rigaux, Béda. "Evangelium im ersten Thessalonicherbrief," *Wissenschaft und Weisheit* 35 (1972): 1-12.

Rigaux, Béda. *Saint Paul: Les épîtres aux Thessaloniciens.* Ebib. Paris: Gabalda; Gembloux: Duculot, 1956.

Rigaux, Béda. "Tradition et rédaction dans 1 Th. v. 1-10," *NTS* 21 (1974-75): 318-40.

Rigaux, Béda. "Vocabulaire chrétien antérieur à la première épître aux Thessaloniciens." In *Sacra Pagina: Miscellanea biblica Congressus internationalis catholici de re biblica,* edited by J. Coppens, A. Descamps, and E. Massaux, vol. 2, 380-89,

Rinaldi, Giovanni. "Il Targum palestinese del Pentateucho," *BeO* 17 (1975): 75-77.

Rivera, L. F. "Cristianismo existencial y expresión eucarística de la religión: 1 y 2 Tesalonicenses," *RevistB* 41 (1979): 75-89.

Roberts, J. H. "Transitional Techniques to the Letter Body in the *Corpus Paulinum.*" In *A South African Perspective on the New Testament,* edited by J. H. Petzer and J. Hartin, 187-201.

Roetzel, Calvin J. "I Thess. 5:12-28: A Case Study." In *Society of Biblical Literature 1972 Proceedings*, vol. 2, edited by Lane C. McGaughy, 367-83.

Roetzel, Calvin J. *"Theodidaktoi"* and Handwork in Philo and I Thessalonians." In *L'Apôtre Paul: Personnalité, style et conception du ministère*, edited by Albert Vanhoye, 324-31.

Rossano, Piero. "Preliminari all'esegesi di 1 Tess 2, 1-12," *BeO* 7 (1965): 117-21.

Sanchez Bosch, Jorge. "La chronologie de la première aux Thessaloniciens et les relations de Paul avec d'autres églises," *NTS* 37 (1991): 336-47.

Sanders, E. P. "Literary Dependence in Colossians," *JBL* 85 (1966): 28-45.

Sanders, Jack T. *The Jews in Luke-Acts*. London: SCM, 1987.

Sanders, Jack T. "The Transition from Opening Epistolary Thanksgiving to Body in the Letters of the Pauline Corpus," *JBL* 90 (1971): 91-97.

Sandnes, Karl Olav. *Paul — One of the Prophets? A Contribution to the Apostle's Self-Understanding*. WUNT, 2/43. Tübingen: Mohr, 1991.

Schade, Hans-Heinrich. *Apokalyptische Christologie bei Paulus: Studien zum Zusammenhang von Christologie und Eschatologie in den Paulusbriefen*. GTA, 18. Göttingen: Vandenhoeck and Ruprecht, 1981.

Schäfer, Klaus. *Gemeinde als "Bruderschaft": Ein Beitrag zum Kirchenverständnis des Paulus*. Europäische Hochschulschriften, Reihe 23: Theologie, 333. Berlin: Lang, 1989.

Schmidt, Daryl D. "1 Thess 2, 13-16: Linguistic Evidence for an Interpolation," *JBL* 102 (1983): 269-79.

Schmithals, Walther. "1. Thessalonicher 4, 13-14," *Göttinger Predigtmeditationen* 77 (1988): 194-98.

Schmithals, Walter. *Gnosticism in Corinth*. Nashville: Abingdon, 1971.

Schmithals, Walter. *Paul and the Gnostics*. Nashville, New York: Abingdon, 1972.

Schnackenburg, Rudolf. *The Johannine Epistles: Introduction and Commentary*. New York: Crossroad, 1992.

Schnelle, Udo. "Der erste Thessalonicherbrief und die Entstehung der paulinischen Anthropologie," *NTS* 32 (1986): 207-24.

Schnelle, Udo. "Die Ethik des 1. Thessalonicherbriefes." In *The Thessalonian Correspondence*, edited by R. F. Collins, 293-305.

Schnider, Franz, and Werner Stenger. *Studien zum neutestamentlichen Briefformular*. NTTS, 11. Leiden: Brill, 1987.

Schoon-Janssen, Johannes. *Umstrittene "Apologien" in den Paulusbriefen: Studien zur rhetorischen Situation des 1. Thessalonicherbriefes, des Galaterbriefes und des Philipperbriefes*. GTA, 45. Göttingen: Vandenhoeck and Ruprecht, 1991.

Schrage, Wolfgang, ed. *Studien zum Text und zur Ethik des Neuen Testaments: Festschrift zum 80. Geburtstag von Heinrich Greeven.* BZNW, 47. Berlin: DeGruyter, 1986.

Schubert, Paul. *Form and Function of the Pauline Thanksgivings.* BZNW, 20. Berlin: Töpelmann, 1939.

Schuler, C. "The Macedonian Politarchs," *CP* 57 (1960): 90-100.

Schulz, Siegfried. *Neutestamentliche Ethik.* Zürcher Grundrisse zur Bibel. Zurich: Theologischer Verlag, 1987.

Simpson, John W., Jr. "The Future of Non-Christian Jews: 1 Thessalonians 2:15-16 and Romans 9-11." Fuller Theological Seminary Ph.D. dissertation, 1988.

Simpson, John W., Jr. "The Problems Posed by 1 Thessalonians 2:15-16 and a Solution," *HBT* 12 (1990): 42-72.

Sinclair, Scott Gambrill. *The Christologies of Paul's Undisputed Epistles and the Christology of Paul.* Bibal Monograph Series, 1. Berkeley, Calif.: BIBAL, 1988.

Smith, Abraham. "The Social and Ethical Implications of the Pauline Rhetoric in I Thessalonians." Vanderbilt Ph.D. thesis, 1989.

Snyder, Graydon F. "A Summary of Faith in an Epistolary Context: 1 Thess 1, 9.10." In *Society of Biblical Literature 1972 Proceedings,* edited by L. C. McGaughy, vol. 2, 355-65. N.p., 1962.

Söding, Thomas. "Der erste Thessalonicherbrief und die frühe paulinische Evangeliumsverkündigung: Zur Frage einer Entwicklung der paulinischen Theologie," *BZ* 35 (1991): 180-203.

Söding, Thomas. "Widerspruch und Leidensnachfolge: Neutestamentliche Gemeinden im Konflikt mit der paganen Gesellschaft," *MTZ* 40 (1989): 137-55.

Sordet, J.-M. "La venue du Seigneur: Deux discours d'espérance à la lumière de deux hypothèses: 1 Thessaloniciens 4, 13-18 et 2 Thessaloniciens 2, 1-12," *Hokhma* 35 (1987): 35-37.

Spicq, Ceslas. *Agape in the New Testament,* vol. 2: *Agape in the Epistles of St. Paul.* St. Louis: Herder, 1965.

Spicq, Ceslas. *Notes de lexicographie néo-testamentaire.* 2 vols. Vol. 3: *Supplément.* OBO, 22/1-3. Fribourg: Editions universitaires; Göttingen: Vandenhoeck and Ruprecht, 1978-82.

Spicq, Ceslas. "Les Thessaloniciens 'inquiets' étaient-ils des paresseux?," *ST* 10 (1956): 1-13.

Stanley, David M. " 'Become Imitators of Me.' The Pauline Conception of Apostolic Tradition." In *The Apostolic Church in the New Testament,* 371-89, 376-77. Westminster, Md.: Newman, 1967.

Steele, E. Springs. "The Use of Jewish Scriptures in 1 Thessalonians," *BTB* 14 (1984): 12-17.

Stegemann, Wolfgang. "Anlass und Hintergrund der Abfassung von 1 Th 2, 1-12." In *Theologische Brosamen für Lothar Steiger,* edited by Gerhard Freund and Ekkehard Stegemann, 397–416. Diehlheimer Blätter zum Alten Testament und seiner Rezeption in der Alten Kirche, 5. Heidelberg: Esprint, 1985.

Stirewalt, Martin Luther, Jr. "The Form and Function of the Greek Letter-Essay." In *The Romans Debate*, edited by K. Donfried, 147–71.

Stuhlmacher, Peter. *Das paulinische Evangelium*. FRLANT, 95. Göttingen: Vandenhoeck and Ruprecht, 1968.

Talbert, Charles H., ed. *Perspectives on Luke-Acts*. Macon, Ga.: Mercer, 1978.

Tambyah, T. Isaac. "*Theodidaktoi:* A Suggestion of an Implication of the Deity of Christ," *ExpTim* 44 (1932-33): 527–28.

Tarazi, Paul Nadim. *1 Thessalonians: A Commentary*. Orthodox Biblical Studies. Crestwood, N.Y.: St. Vladimir's Seminary, 1982.

Theissen, Gerd. *The Social Setting of Pauline Christianity: Essays on Corinth*. Philadelphia: Fortress, 1982.

Theobald, Michael. " 'Prophetenworte verachtet nicht!' (1 Thess 5, 20): Paulinische Perspektiven gegen eine institutionelle Versuchung," *TQ* 171 (1991): 30–47.

Thomaso, Dana Andrew. "Corinthians, Third Epistle to the," *ABD*, vol. 1, 1154.

Thraede, Klaus. *Grundzüge griechisch-römischer Brieftopik*. Zetemata: Monographien zur klassischen Altertumswissenschaft, 4. Munich: Beck, 1970.

Tov, Emmanuel. "Une inscription grecque d'origine samaritaine à Thessalonique," *RB* 81 (1974): 394–99.

Trevijano Etcheverria, Ramón. "La misión en Tesalónica (1 Tes 1, 1–2, 16)," *Salmanticensis* 32 (1985): 263–91.

Trilling, Wolfgang. "Die beiden Briefe des Apostels Paulus an die Thessalonicher: Eine Forschungsübersicht," in Wolfgang Haase, ed., *ANRW* II, 25, 4, 3365-3403. Berlin: De Gruyter, 1987.

Trobisch, David. *Die Entstehung der Paulusbriefsammlung: Studien zu den Anfängen christlicher Publizistik*. NTOA, 10. Göttingen: Vandenhoeck and Ruprecht, 1989.

Tuckett, Christopher. "Synoptic Tradition in 1 Thessalonians?" In *The Thessalonian Correspondence*, edited by R. F. Collins, 160–82.

Ulonska, Herbert. "Christen und Heiden: Die paulinische Paränese in I Thess 4, 3–8," *TZ* 43 (1987): 210–18.

Vander Stichele, Caroline. "The Concept of Tradition and 1 and 2 Thessalonians." In *The Thessalonian Correspondence*, edited by R. F. Collins, 499–504.

Vanhoye, Albert, ed. *L'Apôtre Paul: Personnalité, style et conception du ministère*. BETL, 73. Louvain: University Press, 1986.

Vanhoye, Albert. "La composition de 1 Thessaloniciens." In *The Thessalonian Correspondence*, edited by R. F. Collins, 73–86.

van Rensburg, Janse J. "An argument for reading NEPIOI in 1 Ts 2:7." In *A South African Perspective on the New Testament,* edited by J. H. Petzer and J. Hartin, 252-59.

Van Stempvoort, A. "Eine stilistische Lösung einer alten Schwierigkeit in 1. Thess. V. 23," *NTS* 7 (1960-61): 262-65.

van Unnik, W. C. "The Christian's Freedom of Speech in the New Testament." In *Sparsa Collecta,* vol. 2, 269-89. NovT Sup, 30. Leiden: Brill, 1980.

van Unnik, W. C. " 'Den Geist löschet nicht aus' (I Thessalonicher V, 19)" *NovT* 10 (1968): 255-69.

van Unnik, W. C. "The Semitic Background of *parrēsia* in the New Testament." In *Sparsa Collecta,* vol. 2, 290-306.

Viard, André. "L'Evangile de Jesus Christ dans la première Epître aux Thessaloniciens," *Ang* 56 (1979): 413-27.

von Dobschutz, Ernst. *Die Thessalonicher-Briefe.* KEK, 10. 7th ed. Göttingen: Vandenhoeck and Ruprecht, 1909.

Wallace, Daniel B. "A Textual Problem in 1 Thessalonians 1:10: *Ek tēs Orgēs* vs. *Apo tēs Orgēs.*" *BSac* 147 (1990): 470-77.

Walter, Nikolaus. "Paulus und die urchristliche Jesustradition," *NTS* 31 (1985): 498-522.

Wanamaker, Charles. *The Epistles to the Thessalonians: A Commentary on the Greek Text.* NIGTC. Grand Rapids, Mich.: Eerdmans, 1990.

Ware, James. "The Thessalonians as a Missionary Congregation: 1 Thessalonians 1, 5-8," *ZNW* 83 (1992): 126-31.

Ware, Phil. "The Coming of the Lord: Eschatology and 1 Thessalonians," *ResQ* 22 (1979): 109-20.

Weatherly, Jon A. "The Authenticity of 1 Thessalonians 2.13-16: Additional Evidence," *JSNT* 42 (1991): 79-98.

Weber, Robert. *Biblia Sacra iuxta Vulgatam Versionem,* 2. 2d ed. Stuttgart: Wurttenbergische Bibelanstalt, 1975.

Wedderburn, A. J. M. "Keeping Up with Recent Studies, 8: Some Recent Pauline Chronologies," *ExpTim* 92 (1980): 103-8.

White, John L. *Light from Ancient Letters.* Foundations and Facets. Philadelphia: Fortress, 1986.

White, John Lee. *The Form and Function of the Body of the Greek Letter: A Study of the Letter-Body in the Non-literary Papyri and in Paul the Apostle.* SBLDS, 2. Missoula, MT: SBL, 1972.

White, John Lee. "Introductory Formulae in the Body of the Pauline Letter," *JBL* 90 (1971): 91-97.

White, John Lee. "New Testament Epistolary Literature in the Framework of Ancient Epistolography," *ANRW,* II, 25, 2, 1730-56.

White, John Lee. "Saint Paul and the Apostolic Letter Tradition," *CBQ* 45 (1983): 433-44.

Whiteley, D. E. H. *Thessalonians in the Revised Standard Version.* New Clarendon Bible. London: Oxford, 1969.

Wiederkehr, Dietrich. *Die Theologie der Berufung in den Paulusbriefen.* Studia Friburgensia, Neue Folge, 36. Freiburg: Universitätsverlag, 1963.

Wiles, Gordon. *Paul's Intercessory Prayers: The Significance of the Intercessory Prayer Passages in the Letters of St. Paul.* SNTSMS, 24. Cambridge: University Press, 1974.

Wolter, Michael. "Der Apostel und seine Gemeinden als Teilhaber am Leidensgeschick Jesu Christi: Beobachtungen zur paulinischen Leidenstheologie," *NTS* 36 (1990): 535–57.

Wuellner, Wilhelm. "The Argumentative Structure of 1 Thessalonians as Paradoxal Encomium." In *The Thessalonian Correspondence,* edited by R. F. Collins, 117–36.

Yarbrough, O. Larry. *Not Like the Gentiles: Marriage Rules in the Letters of Paul.* SBLDS, 80. Atlanta: Scholars, 1985.

Index of Names

Achaicus, 125
Adinolfi, M., 236, 237, 238, 244, 258, 259
Aland, K., 225, 241
Alexander, 5
Almgvist, H., 259
Ambrosiaster, 241
Amiot, F., 234
Amos, 175
Anderson, C. P., 288, 290
Andrew, 207
Andriscus, 6
Antipater, 8, 53, 243
Antisthenes, 14
Antony, 7, 8
Apion, 117
Apollinarios, 117, 124, 125
Apollonios, 266
Apollonius Dyskolos, 116
Apollos, 187
Apphia, 186, 287
Appian, 6, 216
Aquila, 15, 193
Archippus, 186
Aristarchus, 230
Aristo, 236
Aristophanes, 236
Aristotle, 125, 132, 236, 266, 273
Artemas, 125
Artemon, 125
Asclepiades of Phlonta, 220
Asklas, 116
Asklepiodoros, 7

Athanasius of Alexandria, 208, 293
Athenogenes, 7
Augustine of Hippo, 237
Aune, D. E., 287

Baarda, T., 247, 275
Baasland, E., 265
Bahr, G. J., 269
Balz, H., 60, 244
Barbaglio, G., 221
Barclay, J. M. G., 244, 252, 253, 264
Barnabas, 32, 208
Barrett, C. K., 200, 224, 234, 255, 290, 291
Bartchy, S. S., 284, 286
Bartoletti, V., 215
Bassin, F., 255
Bassler, J. M., 236, 283
Bauckham, R., 288
Bauer, J. B., 246
Baumert, N., 19, 221, 222, 247, 284
Bawley, R. L., 229
Beatty, A. C., 1, 3, 196, 206, 215
Becker, J., 261
Behm, J., 256
Beker, J. C., 223, 233, 244, 248, 251, 275, 280, 281
Berger, K., 267
Bertman, G., 225
Best, E., 235, 237, 247, 266, 281
Betz, O., 225

317